The Music Has Gone Out of the Movement

DAVID C. CARTER

The Music Has Gone Out of the Movement

Civil Rights and the Johnson Administration, 1965–1968

THE UNIVERSITY OF NORTH CAROLINA PRESS

CHAPEL HILL

Designed by Michelle Coppedge
Set in Electra with Grotesque display by Rebecca Evans
Manufactured in the United States of America

The paper in this book meets the guidelines for permanence
and durability of the Committee on Production Guidelines for
Book Longevity of the Council on Library Resources.

The University of North Carolina Press has been a member
of the Green Press Initiative since 2003.

Library of Congress Cataloging-in-Publication Data
Carter, David C. (David Charles), 1970–
The music has gone out of the movement : civil rights and the
Johnson administration, 1965–1968 / David C. Carter. — 1st ed.
p. cm.
Includes bibliographical references and index.
ISBN 978-0-8078-3280-6 (cloth : alk. paper)
ISBN 978-1-4696-2200-2 (pbk. : alk. paper)
ISBN 978-1-4696-0657-6 (ebook : alk. paper)
1. African Americans—Civil rights—History—20th century.
2. Civil rights movements—United States—History—20th century.
3. United States—Politics and government—1963–1969. I. Title.
E185.615.C3517 2009
323.1196'07309046—dc22
2009004945

FOR LESLIE,
sweet descant to
my emancipated
dissonance

FOR MY PARENTS,
in the mountains,
from whence cometh
my help

Contents

Illustrations

Preface

On March 15, 1965, Lyndon Baines Johnson addressed a Joint Session of Congress to call for federally enforced voting rights legislation. He spoke just eight days after "Bloody Sunday," when Alabama state troopers, local law enforcement officials, and deputized white supremacists had brutally attacked African Americans on Selma's Edmund Pettus Bridge as they peacefully marched for voting rights. "There is no Negro problem," the president insisted in the nationally televised speech. "There is no Southern problem. There is no Northern problem. There is only an American problem."[1] In evoking Gunnar Myrdal's 1944 characterization of race as an "American dilemma," Johnson sought to forge a national consensus on the need to eliminate discrimination at the ballot box.

Three months later, in a June 4, 1965, address at historically black Howard University, the president challenged the nation to confront the interwoven problems of poverty and discrimination that still hobbled black America — "another nation." Lyndon Johnson's rhetoric committed his administration to an expanded definition of equality that promised equal results rather than simply equal opportunity. In the aftermath of the Selma beatings, Johnson's insistence that race was a national issue had seemed designed to soften the sense of regional persecution felt by many white southerners who were well aware that their region would be disproportionately affected by his call for voting rights legislation. If black Americans shared Johnson's view that racism was a national issue, however, most white Americans living north of the Mason-Dixon Line in the spring of 1965 still saw the dilemma of race as a "southern problem."

Delivered during the months that are often seen as the high-water mark of the civil rights movement — and of the Johnson administration — the speech at Howard read differently in the aftermath of the Watts riots in August 1965 and during subsequent outbreaks of urban unrest. Despite several riots the previous summer in depressed inner-city neighborhoods, not until the urban explosion in the Watts area of Los Angeles did most whites appear ready to accept the president's argument that race was fundamentally an "American problem."[2]

It is not clear whether Johnson initially grasped the most far-reaching implications of the Howard speech's lofty rhetoric. Nor could he have foreseen the ways in which the nation's growing military involvement in Southeast Asia would complicate the domestic political landscape and jeopardize once-close relationships with increasingly impatient blacks—and with erstwhile progressive white allies as well. As controversies surrounding the president's War on Poverty grew and the political fallout increased in the North as well as in the South, a beleaguered president had to face a grim succession of riots in some of the nation's largest cities. Publicly he reacted with moderation. Privately he complained that the "ingratitude" of rioters threatened to unravel the liberal consensus so essential to his ambitious domestic programs, and he could not fully shake his suspicions that the incendiary rhetoric of emerging black radical voices was evidence of a sinister conspiracy.

Despite such tensions and frustrations, the administration did not completely disengage from its civil rights agenda after 1965. In his Howard University speech, the president had sought to "leapfrog" the black freedom struggle and call the tune of racial reform by outlining an ambitious program of civil rights and antipoverty measures. The powerful Texan's vision of mastery and control was always an illusion, however, for local people continued to make their own history. As grassroots movements and their antagonists forced the Johnson administration to respond to events rather than dictate policy, new, if sometimes fractious, relationships and pressures shaped the history of the period in unpredictable ways.

This book builds on the work of those committed to understanding African Americans' struggles for equality as part of a "long civil rights movement," which began well before the Supreme Court's 1954 *Brown v. Board of Education* landmark school desegregation ruling and which continued even through the years of white backlash and ascendant national conservatism.[3] In that long struggle for racial equality, particularly from the New Deal to the passage of the Voting Rights Act in 1965, assistance and intervention *from above* in the form of court decisions, legislation, or executive action only emerged after sustained pressure *from below* by those at the grassroots level championing fundamental social reform. Steven F. Lawson has noted the importance of "bringing the state back home," demonstrating how mapping "civil rights crossroads" can transform our understandings of social change, political reform, and reaction.[4]

In contrast to the rich outpouring of studies of the civil rights movement from its earliest origins to its high tide in the first half of the 1960s, the years after 1965 have attracted far less scrutiny. I have tried to tell what I believe is a neglected story of the interactions between the local and the national during the last three years of the Johnson presidency, tracing the trajectory of executive- and bureaucratic-level action—and inaction—while also emphasizing the importance of the grass roots.

Mississippi offers a compelling example of these interactions, demonstrating how grassroots politics shaped competing outlooks on civil rights at the local, state, and national levels. That state's central role in shaping White House understandings of voting rights between 1961 and 1965 has too often been overshadowed by the drama in neighboring Alabama, with its climax in Selma in the spring of 1965. Keeping the focus on Mississippi, I argue that the federal government's shifting responses to the controversial Child Development Group of Mississippi (CDGM) and other antipoverty programs perceived to be "left of center" in and after 1965 illuminate the links between Johnson's civil rights and economic justice policies.[5]

More visible on the national stage, the Watts riots and the release of the Moynihan Report each played an important role in souring relations between the Johnson administration and key black civil rights constituencies. Such flash points regularly disrupted civil rights and War on Poverty policy formulation in the White House. The rapid rise of Black Power as a concept also complicated the interactions between Washington and the grass roots, redefining the relationships between the Johnson administration and various constituencies, both those within the broadening spectrum of civil rights movements and those arrayed against any expansion of the reform agenda.

In my last chapters, I focus on the growing importance of the Vietnam War and on the Johnson administration's attempts to understand, forestall, and, ultimately, contain urban unrest. Riots in the nation's inner cities—often presented to horrified Americans via television and print media with a heavy dose of sensationalism—undercut the impulse for reform even as they seemed to necessitate and reinforce the need for dramatic action. Media coverage and the desire to manage public opinion shaped and in some cases even dictated the policy responses of the Johnson administration to the riots and to the issue of civil rights in general.

The closing months of the Johnson administration saw a policy drift that served to widen the gap between the White House and grassroots civil rights activists. The lack of a coherent policy approach was heightened by miscommunication and a climate of distrust between policymakers and civil rights leaders. The extent of the breakdown in communication between the White House and an increasingly diverse pool of black leaders and their communities was nowhere more apparent than in the president's reaction to the findings of the Kerner Commission.

Early in 1968, the Report of the National Advisory Commission on Civil

Disorders arrived on Johnson's desk. The findings of the commission (headed by Illinois governor Otto Kerner) mirrored the concerns—and explicitly echoed the language—of Johnson's Howard University address delivered two and a half years earlier. That speech and the Kerner Commission Report serve as both chronological and rhetorical bookends to this study. Seeking to explain the "long, hot summers" of convulsive urban riots, in particular the explosions in Newark and Detroit that had just taken place in the summer of 1967, the Kerner Commission Report's authors indicted "white racism" in their diagnosis of the root causes of African American rioters' self-evident despair and anger. At Howard University in June 1965, the president had called attention to the plight of many blacks who he suggested made up "another nation," one falling behind economically. The Kerner Commission built on the same metaphor of an American house divided with its bleak warning: "Our Nation is moving toward two societies, one black, one white—separate and unequal."[6] To reverse this trend, the Kerner Commission called for a massive commitment of the nation's resources to narrow the persistent economic gap between whites and blacks.

Whether it was the parallelism between 1965's "another nation" and 1968's "two nations" or the focus on race and economics with sweepingly ambitious proposed remedies to close the gap, there was a striking degree of harmony between the underlying assumptions of the Howard speech and the Kerner Commission Report. Yet the official White House response to the report—its members had all been handpicked by LBJ—was stony silence. Behind closed doors, the president angrily dismissed the report as a personal insult, a bitter response that illustrated just how much the Johnson administration's aspirations had fallen by the wayside.

By the time Lyndon Johnson announced his decision not to seek reelection later in the spring of 1968, his administration had alienated many civil rights activists, grassroots foot soldiers and national leaders alike. It had also failed to moderate white backlash, for however muddled White House efforts may appear in retrospect, by continuing the earlier search for a national consensus on how to address the perceived "problem" of race the president managed to alienate both black Americans and white Americans.

But none of this was foreordained, and none of it happened overnight.

Many who have chronicled the 1960s have found it tempting to describe events in the second half of that decade as interconnected scenes in an overarching tragic narrative. As powerful as many of these accounts have been, I have found this approach to be more poetic than persuasive. History is a jumble of improvisations, non sequiturs, and equations that refuse to balance.

As dramatists go, Samuel Beckett is arguably a more reliable guide than Shakespeare. Chaos theory is more instructive than calculus. If we discern patterns, we must always be on our guard against the risks of imposing understandings on the past that undercut the historical agency of our subjects—their ability to shape and influence the past even as they experience and are shaped by it. This may be even more essential when we insist that unbilled actors, those most marginalized in traditional historical accounts, move from the wings to claim a place on stage every bit as commanding as that held by the leads.

We owe it to unbilled actors and leading players alike to relate their history without allowing an artificial narrative of declension to highjack the messy realities of the past. As early as 1966, journalist Mary McGrory argued that "the music has gone out of the [civil rights] movement." As far as most reporters were concerned, dissension and pessimism had replaced the harmony and optimism that seemed to grace the movement at its zenith. But the long effort to achieve full equality for the descendants of slaves had always been marked by tension as well as unity. To acknowledge that unruly improvisation lay at the heart of the civil rights movement should not in any way dim our admiration for the brilliant organizational efforts and ideological, strategic, and tactical innovations pioneered by generations of freedom's children. In the aftermath of the passage of landmark civil rights legislation in the 1960s there would be new ways of continuing that struggle. To change, however, is not to disappear. While I find McGrory's musical epitaph simplistic and premature, I hear echoes of her judgment even today. Despite impressive gains, both concrete and symbolic, we as a nation have still failed to grapple with the full legacy of a civil rights movement whose revolutionary promise remains unrealized.

Text Abbreviations

CAP   Community Action Program

CDGM   Child Development Group of Mississippi

CIA   Central Intelligence Agency

COFO   Council of Federated Organizations

CORE   Congress of Racial Equality

CRS   Community Relations Service

FBI   Federal Bureau of Investigation

MAP   Mississippi Action for Progress

MFDP   Mississippi Freedom Democratic Party

NAACP   National Association for the Advancement of Colored People

OEO   Office of Economic Opportunity

PCEEO   President's Committee on Equal Employment Opportunity

PCEO   President's Council on Equal Opportunity

SCLC   Southern Christian Leadership Conference

SNCC   Student Nonviolent Coordinating Committee

The Music Has Gone Out of the Movement

CHAPTER ONE

Leapfrogging the Movement

The Howard University Speech
and the Tragic Narrative

S een from beyond the reach of earth's atmosphere, Vietnam's verdant sliver blurred into the South China Sea, the divided country's "Demilitarized Zone" and borders with Laos and Cambodia as fluid from this perspective as they were to become to the thousands of men and women fighting and dying over them on the ground. In the gathering twilight, the faintly outlined island geographies of Cuba, Haiti, and the Dominican Republic hopscotched across the Caribbean. Los Angeles, Cleveland, Washington, and New York materialized as flecks of light, absorbing, enveloping, then reflecting into the now dark sky the faltering streetlights and glowing signs of Watts, Hough, Congress Heights, and Harlem. Unpaved rural roads of Louisiana and Mississippi did not register from above.

American astronauts James A. McDivitt and Edward H. White II commanded an unparalleled view through the small porthole of the Gemini 4 as they orbited the planet in the first days of June 1965, defying the logic of morning's and evening's sway. Newspapers around the world chronicled each moment in their four-day spaceflight. Americans reveled in Gemini's successful sixty-two orbits of earth and argued passionately over whether to condemn or applaud White's "insubordination" (so euphoric was the astronaut in the early moments of his tethered spacewalk—an American first—that he jovially refused Mission Control's order to reenter the module, remaining outside for several minutes longer than was necessary to best a Soviet cosmonaut's recent record).

The national exultation about the United States' improving fortunes vis-à-vis the Soviets in the "space race" meant that two other news stories went largely unnoticed. On the eve of the Gemini 4 liftoff, Captain Edward J. Dwight Jr., one of a handful of black air force test pilots, leveled scathing criticisms against that branch of the military. When his confidential letter of complaint about discrimination brought no response from the military chain of command, Dwight elected to go public. In an interview in *Ebony*, he claimed to have endured systematic racial bias while serving as the first black in a training program for potential astronauts at Edwards Air Force Base in the Mojave Desert. One of Dwight's commanding officers at Edwards allegedly asked the black pilot: "Who got you into this school? Was it the N.A.A.C.P., or are you some kind of Black Muslim out here to make trouble? . . . Why in hell would a colored guy want to go into space anyway? As far as I'm concerned, there'll never be one to do it. And if it was left to me, you guys wouldn't even get a chance to wear an Air Force uniform." NASA officials later passed over Dwight when they selected pilots for additional astronaut training, and the air force reacted stonily to the accounts of Dwight's mistreatment. Citing the military's nondiscrimination policies, a spokesperson cryptically noted that Dwight had since "received another assignment."[1]

On Wednesday, June 2, in a second story that received little scrutiny, three whites in a pickup truck cruising along a rural road a few miles outside of Bogalusa, Louisiana, had opened fire on two unsuspecting and newly appointed sheriff's deputies. The fusillade struck Creed Rogers in the shoulder and O'Neal Moore in the head. Rogers survived, but Moore died where he fell. Both victims were African Americans.[2]

With *Time* and *Newsweek* cover stories and all the leading newspapers featuring every detail of the Gemini mission from liftoff to splashdown, the space race threatened to overshadow two major presidential addresses. June, the peak of commencement season, presented prime opportunities for presidential speeches geared to a national audience. And Lyndon Johnson, like the Gemini 4 astronauts, appeared to have his sights set on the larger world. Media-driven rumors about peace "feelers" to the Soviets and North Vietnamese circulated widely following his speech to Democratic Party loyalists in Chicago on June 3. Two days later, at Catholic University, the president called for greater dialogue with the Russian people. When he spoke of East and West joining to "walk together toward peace," news commentators speculated that Johnson was also making an indirect overture for the North Vietnamese to come to the peace table.[3]

Five weeks earlier, the president had unilaterally deployed American Marines to the Dominican Republic, citing the need to protect American lives but equally concerned with foiling an allegedly communist-controlled countercoup against a ruling military junta. The simmering crisis in the Caribbean appeared to be stabilizing on terms favorable to White House interests in containing the Cuban "virus."[4]

Friday, June 4, brought LBJ to Howard University, the flagship of the nation's historically black colleges, for a midday commencement speech. Beset by foreign policy crises (the last civilian government in South Vietnam was unraveling and only a week away from a coup by its own military junta), he had refused to commit himself to the speech until twenty-four hours before graduation day. And he warned Howard president James Nabrit that any advance leak would likely lead to the cancellation of his speech.[5]

With the nation riveted by the reports of the Gemini craft as it revolved around the globe, Johnson began: "Our earth is the home of revolution. . . . Men charged with hope . . . reach for the newest of weapons to realize the oldest of dreams." With no advance information about the content of the address, the opening must have sounded like yet another foreign policy statement to the nearly one thousand graduates and the many times larger number of predominantly African American well-wishers in the audience.[6] But having linked the fortunes of American democracy with the process of revolutionary ferment abroad, he abruptly turned to the domestic front: "Nothing in any country touches us more profoundly, nothing is more freighted with meaning for our own destiny, than the revolution of the Negro American. . . . In far too many ways American Negroes have been another nation: deprived of freedom, crippled by hatred, the doors of opportunity closed to hope."[7]

The president paid tribute to the catalytic effect of black-led civil rights protests: "The American Negro, acting with impressive restraint, has peacefully protested and marched . . . demanding a justice that has long been denied. The voice of the Negro was the call to action," he conceded, but the federal courts and Congress deserved praise for having heeded this moral summons. On the drive over to the university, Johnson told his aides that "people need a hero, a strong leader who they can believe in."[8] Clearly he saw himself as that leader, but in his speech he was far more modest, briefly acknowledging his own involvement in securing civil rights legislation, first as Senate majority leader and then more notably as president.

Johnson applauded the impact of the newly enacted Civil Rights Act of 1964 and drew attention to the anticipated passage of the Voting Rights Act still pending before Congress. Those victories were essential, but, in the words of Winston Churchill, they were "not the end . . . not even the beginning of the end. But . . . perhaps, the end of the beginning." "That beginning," he intoned, "is freedom . . . the right to be treated in every part of our national life as a person equal in dignity and promise to all others." He paused: "But freedom is not enough." In the oft-quoted crux of the address, drafted by gifted speechwriter and Kennedy holdover Richard Goodwin, the president sought to illuminate shifting terrain in the ongoing struggle for black equality:

> You do not wipe away the scars of centuries by saying: Now you are free to go where you want and do as you desire and choose the leaders you please. You do not take a person who, for years, has been hobbled by chains and liberate him, bring him to the starting line of a race, and then say you are free to compete with all the others, and still . . . believe that you have been completely fair. Thus it is not enough just to open the gates of opportunity. All our citizens must have the ability to walk through those gates. This is the next and the more profound stage of the battle for civil rights. We seek not just freedom but opportunity. We seek not just legal equity but human ability, not just equality as a right and a theory but equality as a fact and equality as a result.

The starting line metaphor was a powerful one. In private conversations with his aides, Johnson had often discussed the handicaps placed upon different participants in the race, comparing the challenge of aiding African Americans to "converting a crippled person into a four minute miler."[9] Allowing his audience little more than a breath to digest the crucial language about the inherent limitations in the concept of equal opportunity, he plunged ahead. He lauded the graduating seniors in his predominantly middle-class black audience, their achievements "witness to the indomitable determination of the Negro American to win his way in American life." But the Howard students' success was "only [part of] the story," Johnson said. The speech proceeded quickly to a litany of grim statistics, a "seamless web" of adverse circumstances affecting the lives of "the great majority of Negro Americans—the poor, the unemployed, the uprooted and the dispossessed. . . . They still are another nation. . . . For them the walls are rising and the gulf is widening."

In outlining the extent of black poverty, LBJ relied on—but never identified—an urgent report confidentially circulating in the upper echelons of the Department of Labor and in the White House itself. Authored by Assistant Secretary of Labor Daniel Patrick Moynihan, it was entitled "The Negro Family: A Case for National Action."[10] Despite gains in other areas of civil rights, patterns of residential segregation appeared to be deepening, particularly in the deteriorating urban centers where African Americans found themselves trapped by "inherited, gateless poverty." Confined in the nation's slums, Johnson declaimed, they made up a "city within a city."

President Lyndon Johnson argues that "freedom is not enough" as he delivers the commencement address at Howard University on June 4, 1965. Courtesy of the LBJ Library.

The unseen hand of Moynihan again loomed large as the president spoke at length about the unique nature of black poverty. A long heritage of racial prejudice, stretching from the "ancient brutality" of bondage through the indignities of Jim Crow to the present ferment, differentiated African Americans' experiences from those of other immigrant minorities. The speech, simplifying Moynihan's complex arguments, undoubtedly glossed over the realities of long-standing prejudices and unique hardships faced by other immigrant groups whose efforts at assimilation and progress the president deemed "largely successful." Johnson did, however, eloquently state the case that whites' obsession with blackness represented a "feeling whose dark intensity is matched by no other prejudice in our society." The psychic scars inflicted by white racism could be "overcome," he asserted, subtly alluding to the refrain of the popular civil rights anthem, "but for many, the wounds are always open."

"Much of the Negro community is buried under a blanket of history and circumstance," Johnson explained, relating a metaphor that White House insiders remembered him using repeatedly that spring and summer to anyone who would listen.[11] Given the Texan's propensities for subjecting hapless bystanders to the now proverbial "Johnson treatment," the blanket metaphor was guaranteed wide currency. "It was like you couldn't pick up the blanket off a Negro at one corner, you had to pick it all up," an aide reminisced. "It had to be housing and it had to be jobs and . . . everything you could think of." The problems facing African Americans—and broadly implicating whites—were far too complicated. The president identified the "breakdown of the Negro family structure" as a crisis demanding immediate action. It was of paramount concern for those committed to economic justice to shore up the family, the "cornerstone of our society." Without redress, it would be impossible "to cut completely the circle of despair and deprivation."

These and other problems defied a "single, easy answer," Johnson asserted, his tone reflecting what one reporter described as "a hint of bafflement and frustration" as he neared the end of his wide-ranging thirty-minute address. Full implementation and enforcement of existing and pending civil rights legislation would help, as would a broadening of the agenda to secure the Great Society. The battle to eradicate poverty, already declared by Johnson in 1964 as an "unconditional war," would require further escalation. The president announced that he would convene a special White House conference in the fall of 1965 to attempt to come to grips with the full extent of the challenges facing African Americans in this "next and . . . more profound stage of the battle for civil rights" and to set an agenda for continued progress. The gathering would have as its theme "To Fulfill These Rights," implicitly harking back to the landmark Truman era report entitled "To Secure These Rights" and its rhetorical antecedents in the Declaration of Independence. Having been interrupted a dozen times by applause—both the media and trusted aides familiar with the Texan's prodigious ego kept meticulous count—Johnson briefly drew a burst of stifled laughter when in his evident excitement he elided his text and boasted that the proposed conference would be attended by "scholars, and experts, and outstanding Negro leaders of both races."[12]

Johnson, at once deeply suspicious and desperately anxious to secure the approval of those with whom his predecessor, John Kennedy, had shared such an easy rapport, would of course enlist experts and scholars for this conference. Black and white "leaders" both in and out of government, from battle-hardened civil rights workers to lower-echelon bureaucrats, would also presumably have a crucial role to play. But the president concluded his address with an appeal

As the audience at Howard University listens, Johnson calls for a White House Conference with the theme "To Fulfill These Rights." Courtesy of the LBJ Library.

to a much broader constituency when he called on all Americans to lead in "dissolv[ing] . . . the antique enmities of the heart which diminish the holder, divide the great democracy, and do wrong—great wrong—to the children of God." The peroration hammered home a theme of "two nations" and the prejudice that kept them apart. The religious inflection, and the emphasis on redemptive possibilities, might have been that of Martin Luther King Jr.[13]

White House aide Richard Goodwin had grappled with the semantic shades of the concepts of freedom and equality in the Howard address's introduction. The speech's conclusion was a rhapsodic meditation on American justice, its stylistic lurch toward homiletics perhaps the excusable toll of the hours the time-pressed speechwriter had spent drafting and redrafting, his efforts unbroken by sleep. But then, in the final lines of text, came short, elegant phrases laden with meaning: "We have pursued [justice] faithfully to the edge of our imperfections. And we have failed to find it for the American Negro." Taking a page from the Kennedy manual, Goodwin's draft had Johnson close the How-ard speech with one of the central metaphors of the New Testament. (The slain president had couched civil rights as a dilemma "as old as the Scriptures" on the night of Alabama governor George Wallace's "stand in the schoolhouse door," not coincidentally the night of Medgar Evers's assassination in Jackson, Mississippi.)[14] Drawing on the opening verses of the Gospel according to John, President Johnson called on both blacks and whites "to light a candle of under-standing in the heart of all America. And, once lit, it will never again go out."[15]

For LBJ to proclaim the need to expand the civil rights agenda to include basic economic rights seemed a logical outgrowth of the administration's Great Society and antipoverty rhetoric. The Howard speech's premise that "equal opportunity is essential, but not enough" reflected growing concerns within the civil rights communities and academia and in some elements of the federal government about the persistence of racial inequality and links between racism and poverty. Still, the president's professed commitment to equality of "results," expressed as clearly as it was, struck at least some in his im-mediate and wider national audience as a stunning deviation from a far more widely accepted definition of equality in terms of individual opportunity.[16]

A central question, then, is whether the Howard University speech repre-sented a fundamental reconceptualization of civil rights within the Johnson White House from a narrow definition guaranteeing equality of opportunity to a broader vision promising equality of results. Or was the speech little more than a rhetorical watershed, an eloquently expressed vision of grander expecta-tions designed to sway "hearts and minds" as much as swing votes for substan-tive departures in policy? How grounded in political reality was the oratorical flight taken by the president in June of 1965?

Academics and other students of the 1960s, as well as veterans of civil rights movements and even the Johnson administration, are nearly unanimous in their judgment that the White House largely failed to translate the Howard speech's rhetorical commitment to equal results into new policy initiatives for which Lyndon Johnson was willing to risk dwindling political capital in the period following the summer of 1965.[17] Historians—and, even more notably, historical participants—have been too quick to view the events of the post-1965 period through the filter of hindsight. And they have been far too eager to force a tragic narrative onto what was a vastly more complicated drama. No set piece, it was an exercise in constant improvisation, a dizzyingly large cast of characters interacting on a crowded national stage, without the predictability of a director's stage-blocking and tightly crafted script.

The increased attention that the Howard address paid to the glaring and persistent economic inequalities faced by the majority of African Americans served as the harbinger of passionate and often angry debates over what historian Hugh Davis Graham has labeled "compensatory justice" (more commonly discussed as "affirmative action," or, more negatively, as "group preferment," or even "reverse discrimination" and "reverse racism," depending on the debater's political, ideological, and racial bearings).[18] But, in June 1965, these later debates did not dominate—and had not yet polarized—the political landscape.

The Johnson administration appeared at high tide that year. Daniel Patrick Moynihan has suggested that many Americans—especially white Americans—were in a smugly self-congratulatory mood on the issue of race.[19] Although an increasing number of voices in the media and policy experts criticized Johnson's conduct of foreign policy as maladroit at best—or worse, sinister—most Americans still gave him high marks for his handling of domestic affairs. The president's legislative accomplishments in his first eighteen months in the White House dwarfed those of the legislation-impoverished Kennedy era. Johnson's consummate skills on Capitol Hill garnered a popular tax cut, the Economic Opportunity Act, the landmark Civil Rights Act, federal assistance to all levels of education on an unprecedented scale, and Medicare. The pace of legislative activity approached that of the remarkable first "one hundred days" of Franklin D. Roosevelt, whom the ambitious Texan viewed simultaneously as political mentor, father figure, and competitor for the favor of history. Historian Gareth Davies described the setting following the legislative successes of 1964 as a "transcendent mood of liberal optimism: even where problems were acknowledged, they were frequently converted into welcome challenges."[20]

The ebullient Johnson still held abundant stores of political capital in mid-1965, even if, as a recent biographer has pointed out, his prediction that the popular margin earned in his landslide 1964 electoral victory would erode "now that Barry Goldwater wasn't around to scare the hell out of people" had been partially borne out.[21] Unquestionably, the pattern of legislative success helped to give the president the confidence to push his sweeping agenda even further when he ultimately introduced voting rights legislation and when he promised a broadened commitment to the economic agenda at Howard. That address's message seemed calculated to puncture dramatically the nation's inflated sense of accomplishment and mood of complacency; in doing so, however, it reset the bar of political and social expectations at a daunting new height.

But success alone did not determine the administration's timetable for reform. Although early debates about implementation of the newly enacted Civil Rights Act and the anticipated voting rights bill were important, the logic behind Johnson's speech at Howard also emerged in tandem with the escalating "War on Poverty," funded largely through the Office of Economic Opportunity (OEO). That logic represented a potential revolution in the abstract conception of what constituted equality, a decisive shift from classical liberalism's single-minded focus on individual opportunity to a growing recognition that the unequal "life chances" of millions of Americans rendered the promise of equal opportunity largely meaningless. Heavily influenced by the disturbing findings of Moynihan and elegantly written by Richard Goodwin at Johnson's behest, many of the speech's themes were simply refined arguments of a debate that African Americans had long conducted within their own communities and, on occasion, with both political allies and political enemies.

That stream of debate had ebbed and flowed over time, shifting channels to cut new ones, at times slowing to a trickle, but never running dry. From the Civil War demands of black Union soldiers for equal pay and the Port Royal "experiment," to the shattered Reconstruction promise of "Forty Acres and a Mule." Through the bitter "Nadir" period when an epidemic of lynchings and the brutal repression of African Americans punctuated the dawning of the new century, to Garveyism and the thwarted promise of the Black Star Steamship Line. In recurrent waves of migration from rural hinterlands to southern cities and an ambivalent reception in the urban "Promised Land" of the North, through the high hopes and shortcomings of the New Deal era and the racially egalitarian promise of communism for black sharecroppers and urban laborers in and beyond Depression-devastated Alabama. Forward to the strategic pressure of plans for a black March on Washington on the eve of American entry into the Second World War, the marginal success of the resultant Fair Employment Practices Commission, and the rhetoric of twin victories over fascism abroad and racism at home.

Stretching across the years, the stream sprang from what some have labeled the "dual agenda" of racial and economic equality, and those debates took place alongside equally profound efforts on the part of blacks to realize the full measure of American citizenship and advance the broad interests of African Americans, with those more fortunate "lifting [others] as we climb."[22] World War II's "Double V" campaign crystallized African Americans' long-standing concerns over both the deprivation of human rights (at home and abroad) and economic inequalities maintained by structural forces and the active discrimination of whites. Most traditional treatments of the black struggle for equality, however, have failed to appreciate adequately that a persistent critique rooted in economics accompanied the centuries-long struggle for freedom and civil rights.

When African Americans A. Philip Randolph—the doyen of black labor movements and father of the 1941 March on Washington Movement—and Bayard Rustin conceived of the much-heralded August 1963 gathering of civil rights supporters on the Washington, D.C., Mall, they summoned blacks and their liberal white allies to a "March for Jobs." Under pressure from more moderate participants, however, the campaign became a "March for Jobs and Freedom," its climax the vehicle for Martin Luther King Jr.'s unforgettable "I Have a Dream" sermon. And there were still those among the march's planners who privately resented the way in which King's moving reverie on a racial utopia monopolized the public's imagination, distracting attention from the issue of economic discrimination that the majority of other speakers on the platform addressed and making the call for "Jobs" appear to be a tacked-on afterthought. In part, the media subtly shaped the public's response by giving little attention to the economic demands of the marchers, focusing instead upon issues of race and justice.[23] Oddly enough, the Howard speech, with its recognition of the crippling impact of racial bias in denying economic benefits to blacks, would have offered a better fit for the thematic bill of the 1963 "March for Jobs" as Randolph and Rustin originally envisioned it—even though Johnson's eloquence would have paled beside the electrifying baritone cadences of King's "I Have a Dream." But the Howard speech was the result of the unique trajectory of struggle between 1963 and 1965. In the intervening months, civil rights forces launched a revolution in political possibility.

In the years 1954 to 1965, the traditional periodization of the civil rights movement, the abuses of Jim Crow's de jure segregation and voting discrimination were so glaring—and so pervasive—that they presented African Americans with the most obvious target for an at first tactically cautious challenge and ultimately a full-scale frontal assault in the massive direct action campaigns of the early 1960s. Still, even when the dominant discourse in the black struggle for equality had in fact been skewed toward a "politics of rights," the "politics of resources" that was emphasized in the dual agenda always percolated just below the surface. As longtime civil rights organizer Ella Baker insisted when she addressed the founders of the Student Nonviolent Coordinating Committee (SNCC) in April 1960, the civil rights revolution was about "more than a hamburger." She exhorted the young students to move from integrating lunch counters to tackling broader social and economic concerns.[24] As America approached the midpoint of the decade, this underlying demand for economic justice began to bubble up with greater frequency. Thus, although many in the mainstream media found Johnson's thrust at Howard new, Bayard Rustin had significantly broadened the parameters of debate four months earlier in the February 1965 issue of *Commentary*.

Rustin, a veteran civil rights organizer and intellectual whose activist roots dated back to the 1930s, argued that the "classical . . . phase of the civil rights movement" had ultimately prevailed by attacking "Jim Crow precisely where it was most anachronistic, dispensable, and vulnerable."[25] That stage of the civil rights campaign, he optimistically predicted, now essentially amounted to a mopping-up operation. Rustin was quick to acknowledge the sacrifices of veterans of direct action, but the battlegrounds of both Birmingham and rural Mississippi were now serving as the testing areas for new protest weapons, new tactics, and even new foot soldiers. In the highly industrialized Alabama city, local citizens and Southern Christian Leadership Conference (SCLC) organizers, led by Martin Luther King Jr., Fred Shuttlesworth, and others, had tied their concerns over employment and housing discrimination to their demands for the desegregation of public facilities. Birmingham, Rustin predicted, would be the model for expanding protests in the North.

Murder and white-authored violence in Mississippi, meanwhile, had led African Americans in and beyond the Magnolia State to move toward challenging the system through explicitly political means, making "a conscious bid for political power." Blacks' struggle for true equality was "essentially revolutionary. . . . Their quest cannot *objectively* be satisfied within the framework of existing political and economic relations." Only through political power could African Americans hope to alter a status quo that would remain fundamentally unjust even in the aftermath of early civil rights reforms. Rustin was suggesting a crucial shift: "The civil rights movement is evolving from a protest movement into a full-fledged *social movement*—an evolution calling its very name into question. It is now concerned not merely with removing the barriers to full *opportunity* but with achieving the fact of *equality*.[26]

Militancy and shock tactics were a no-win option. Blacks would need to build a political movement, and effecting a transformation of society would need allies. Indeed, that movement would fail without intensive cultivation of ties with organized labor, religious groups, and white liberals generally, the kind of progressive coalition that had helped secure Johnson's landslide 1964 victory and that had its roots in the enduring Roosevelt coalition. Should such an alliance fail, Rustin warned, or should blacks themselves opt out of the coalition, the results could be dire. In America, "class and color definitions [were] converging disastrously," and civil unrest was the logical, if regrettable, result: "Last summer's riots were not race riots; they were outbursts of class aggression."

Urban disturbances during the summer of 1964 in Harlem, Rochester, and several other northeastern cities disturbed Daniel Patrick Moynihan as well as he compiled evidence for the "Report on the Negro Family" the following spring. The assistant in the Department of Labor stated his 1965 case for national action most starkly when he wrote: "The principal challenge of the next phase of the Negro revolution is to make certain that equality of results will now follow. If we do not, there will be no social peace in the United States for generations."[27]

The maintenance of social peace had been the cardinal principle guiding the Johnson administration's civil rights policies—and those of its predecessors—up through 1965 as it struggled to respond to civil rights brushfires in previously unheard-of local communities, to full-scale crises like Selma, Alabama, and to urban unrest in the North. Black civil rights struggles consistently pressured the hand of the White House. Little Rock, Arkansas, Oxford, Mississippi, and Tuscaloosa, Alabama, were for both the Eisenhower and Kennedy administrations uncomfortable departures from a narrow construction of the theory of federalism and an ethos that stressed negotiation and conciliation over confrontation and contestation.

African Americans had sought entry to segregated institutions, but white political brinkmanship ultimately led to showdowns with the federal government. That white segregationists also forced the administration's timetable for racial reform was a noteworthy irony. Even after federal interventions in Oxford in 1962 and Tuscaloosa in 1963, Burke Marshall of the Justice Department's Civil Rights Division still clung to a strict construction of the theory of federalism. Privately, Marshall and Robert Kennedy compared the harrowing experience at Ole Miss to "losing one's virginity." After the first time, the metaphor implied, it was far easier to repeat the experience.[28]

The SNCC and SCLC strategy of putting bodies on the line paid a brutal dividend in confrontations with Birmingham Public Safety Commissioner Bull Connor's infamous fire hoses and police dogs and the national crisis it precipitated. During Mississippi's Freedom Summer of 1964, civil rights organizations agonized over a calculus of what constituted acceptable risk in the face of anticipated racial violence. As SNCC and other organizations involved in grassroots organizing quickly proved, attempting to register to vote in many areas of the rural Deep South without a doubt constituted "direct action." White racists fulfilled activists' worst fears when they killed three civil rights organizers, one black and two whites, near the small town of Philadelphia, Mississippi. Some extremist whites offered the rationalization that the three victims, especially whites Andrew Goodman and Michael Schwerner, were essentially part of an invasion force; as such they became justifiable casualties of war rather than victims of murder. But white terrorists had irreparably damaged their cause the previous year when the bombing of Birmingham's Sixteenth Street Baptist Church claimed the lives of four black girls waiting for their Sunday school class to begin.

Whether strategically provoked by African Americans or expressed in the form of random terror, white-on-black violence served both to prick the national conscience and to restrict the maneuvering room of successive presidential administrations. (As blacks often noted pointedly, when white racists killed or brutalized *white* civil rights activists it touched an even deeper nerve with white national audiences.) But even for those not privy to the heated internal tactical debates of the civil rights organizations, it was hard to fail to appreciate this consistent dynamic of grassroots stimulus and federal response, civil rights action and White House reaction.

This model of interaction may have reached its climax on March 7, 1965, "Bloody Sunday." Mounted Alabama state troopers and Sheriff Jim Clark's vicious posse of irregularly deputized whites savagely beat and gassed nonviolent demonstrators marching for voting rights as they attempted to cross the Edmund Pettus Bridge outside of Selma. Despite his best efforts, events outpaced Lyndon Johnson's ability to wait out the crisis. On March 15, the president appeared before a Joint Session of Congress and a national television audience to demand strong voting rights legislation. That speech, also written by Richard Goodwin but with far greater direct participation from LBJ, in some ways read like a first draft of the Howard address:

> Even if we pass this bill, the battle will not be over. What happened in Selma is part of a far larger movement which reaches into every section and State of America. It is the effort of American Negroes to secure for themselves the blessings of American life.
>
> Their cause must be our cause too. Because it is not just Negroes, but really it is all of us, who must overcome the crippling legacy of bigotry and injustice.
>
> And we shall overcome.[29]

A few commentators suggest that the president's use of the phrase "we shall overcome" was an act of "co-optation"—the White House was stealing the populist thunder of the movement.[30] Most historians and contemporaries, however, have seen Johnson's adoption of the anthem of the freedom struggle as the zenith of presidential involvement in civil rights, the stunning addition of the strong voice of the federal government to the popular chorus of protest. In his memoir, Goodwin tried to convey the impact of the moment both in the House chambers and around the nation when Johnson spoke those last four words:

> There was an instant of silence, the gradually apprehended realization that the president had proclaimed, adopted as his own rallying cry, the anthem of black protest, the hymn of a hundred embattled black marches. . . . Grouped around thousands of television sets in university halls and private homes, millions of people, especially the young, felt a closeness—an almost personal union—with their government and with their country, which exposed the masquerade of fashionable cynicism, unveiled the hunger for love of country, not as an abstraction, but as the binding force of a community whose largeness magnified each of its members.[31]

Johnson's self-identification with the fortunes of the civil rights movement seemed to inaugurate a new era of government interaction with the movement, one based more on close cooperation and ideological resonance than on the dialectic of pressure from below yielding grudging intervention from above. The speech at Howard University, less than three months later, held out the possibility of cementing that union.[32]

The president had passed over Howard University when selecting planned commencement speaking opportunities from a list of May and June engagements proffered by his aides in mid-March of 1965, politely rejecting an invitation from Howard president Dr. James M. Nabrit Jr. Perhaps the fact that he had spoken at Howard's commencement as vice president four years earlier factored into his initial decision. In that speech, in June 1961, he had admonished the graduating class: "You are not graduating into a nation of perfection . . . [but into] a nation that is striving for perfection and in which the national conscience is on the side of morality, justice, and right."[33]

In the aftermath of the Selma crisis and the "We Shall Overcome" speech, however, Johnson reevaluated his decision and by late April had upgraded the Howard commencement to the status of possible. But in the weeks preceding the speech date, Johnson was deeply embroiled in international affairs, especially the Dominican crisis; his night reading reveals no sign of plans for a major civil rights departure.[34]

Late in May, Johnson called Richard Goodwin to his office and congratulated him on his work drafting the voting rights message of ten weeks earlier.

According to Goodwin, the president then—in his inimitable rapid-fire stream-of-consciousness mixture of barnyard metaphors with high policy statements—talked out a speech whose basic premise ran: "Voting rights are important. But it's only the tail on the pig, when we ought to be going for the whole hog. During the depression I ran an NYA [National Youth Administration] project in Texas. All the boys, white and Negroes, were poor. But the poor Negroes were kept separate over in Prairie View, and always got the short end."

Johnson often refracted contemporary issues through his oversized Texan past, harking back to the period of the Great Depression and New Deal. He seldom concluded a speech or conversation dealing with civil rights without at least one reference to the effects of bigotry he had seen firsthand either in the National Youth Administration or as a young schoolteacher in Cotulla, Texas, "either to make a point or to prove his humanitarian instincts." (Indeed, the only time the president interrupted Goodwin during the frantic last-minute drafting of the Howard speech was to telephone with a quick suggestion that the address make reference to the "uncomprehending pain in the eyes of the little Mexican-American schoolchildren that I taught many years ago" whenever they encountered prejudice.)[35]

Johnson continued:

> Now the whole country's like one big Prairie View. Not everywhere, but most places. The problem's not just civil rights. Hell, what good are rights if you don't have a decent home or someone to take care of you when you're sick? Now we've got to find a way to let Negroes get what most white folks already have. At least the chance to get it. As I see it, the problem isn't so much hatred as fear. The white worker fears the Negro's going to take something away from him—his job, his house, his daughter. Well, we ought to do something about that. Now, we can't do everything at once, but we can make people feel a little guilty about not doing it. We've got the biggest pulpit in the world up here, and we ought to use it to do a little preaching. Why don't you see what you can do? You're my regular alter ego.

Goodwin, stunned by the scale of the issues the president was skimming over so easily, found himself dismissed.

Goodwin was no doubt perceptive enough to recognize that the president's flattery with the designation "alter ego" was calculated. Johnson had first anointed Goodwin as "my voice, my alter ego, like Harry Hopkins [had been to Franklin Roosevelt]" late in March 1964 as the Kennedy transition was still in process. This elevation had come as Johnson summoned Goodwin into the bathroom adjacent to the Oval Office mid-defecation, a typical Johnsonian test to see whether it would flummox an observer. As Goodwin noted in recalling this first call to be Johnson's "voice," the praise was "characteristic Johnson hyperbole . . . At least five staff members had already been promised the Hopkins role." Along with choreographed bathroom encounters and the president's uncanny ability to monitor three television networks and still dominate a conversation, yet another "shock" tactic in the range of behaviors that form part of what historians often describe as the "Johnson treatment" was to take advantage of his superior height in the White House swimming pool, —wading to a depth where he could stand comfortably but where hapless shorter aides and acquaintances were forced to tread water for long stretches of time.[36]

With little more than the president's vague charge, colorfully issued in what might be reasonably called "ranch speak," Goodwin began to plan the speech. Although he retained primary authorship, he worked with White House aides Jack Valenti and Bill Moyers and especially with the Department of Labor's Daniel Patrick Moynihan. "Research materials were accumulated," Goodwin wrote, a revealing use of the passive voice, for the speechwriter's memoir only indirectly acknowledged Moynihan's central role in the genesis of the speech: collating the research that formed the statistical underpinning to the address and supplying some of its principal arguments and even language.[37] Goodwin wound up drafting the speech beginning late in the afternoon of June 3, working through the night and into the early morning hours and having the text delivered, along with the president's hearty breakfast, on the very day of the Howard commencement.

In a cover memo, Goodwin suggested that by demonstrating his concern for the bleak economic conditions of the urban poor, Johnson might reduce the chances of a second summer of rioting. (The year 1964, as will be seen, had witnessed major disturbances in Harlem and several other cities in the Northeast.) Even more important, both Goodwin and Bill Moyers felt that the speech would break the established cycle, most recently demonstrated by Selma, of civil rights crises forcing impromptu White House responses. For once, with the domestic political horizon apparently clear, Johnson would deliver a "pathbreaking speech . . . [that] will put us ahead of the trends." Johnson usually found such an offer of one-upmanship irresistible. Some months later, a White House aide confidentially shared with two investigators his clear memory that LBJ and his aides hoped the speech would "leap frog the [civil rights] movement." Goodwin had himself heard the president express a similar desire to play the piper, calling the tune for once, instead of scrambling to catch up with the latest civil rights crisis. In 1964, the president, in vowing not to compromise on civil rights legislation, had boasted to Goodwin, "Those civil rightsers are going to have to wear sneakers to keep up with me."[38]

A Johnson insider once characterized three possible responses from the president to a speech draft: "He would throw it in the wastepaper basket and say, 'This is no God-damned good, I want something different'; or he'd say, 'This is fine,' and deliver it; or in some instances, he'd do some editing on it— and he's a very good editor." Goodwin stood anxiously by while the president read the draft over breakfast, penciling in a few comments before pronouncing his verdict: "That'll do just fine, Dick."[39]

Goodwin wondered aloud whether, given the bold message of the speech and with the "leapfrog" dimension in mind, the president should check out the speech with a handful of civil rights leaders "to make sure it doesn't get us into trouble." A distracted Johnson turned to face the always flickering multiple television screens in his bedroom and nodded vague assent: "If you'd like to." The calling list Goodwin worked from over the next two hours was short and telling; after hearing the speechwriter's machine-gun-paced delivery of the speech's highlights over the telephone, Roy Wilkins of the National Association for the Advancement of Colored People (NAACP), Whitney Young of the Urban League, A. Philip Randolph of the Brotherhood of Sleeping Car Porters, and Martin Luther King Jr. of the SCLC all voiced strong support.[40]

The tight time frame and extremely limited circulation of the speech in the twenty-four hours before its delivery were not unheard of but were unusual for a significant presidential address. The earlier voting rights message accompanying the submission of administration legislation had undergone a far more exhaustive process of preclearance and vetting, involving legislators, Department of Justice lawyers, civil rights leaders, and several speechwriters, although the language remained largely Goodwin's, subject to Johnson's editing. Deliberate delay, up until the last minute, Goodwin recalled, was a tactic that prevented other White House staff speechwriters and especially line-level bureaucrats from "trying to substitute their literary judgment for mine."[41]

The ultimate decisions to limit advance warning of the Howard speech and to allow Goodwin to complete the speech at the last moment were Johnson's. "Unpredictability was a political weapon" savored by the Texan, according to one biographer, and "premature revelations of presidential intentions were 'impediments' to the Great Society." Unpredictability had its downside, though. Without at least some advance leaking of an important address— smoke signals—there was little way to guarantee media exposure or to shape the coverage that would follow.[42]

At Howard the president appeared to seek a sounding board for ideas about a fundamental transformation in the way Americans thought about equality. But, as Daniel Patrick Moynihan later insisted, Johnson's audience "was not in the least prepared for such a speech, nor was the press." Moynihan, who had contributed many of the basic premises of the presidential address, suggested that the media—and as a result, the public—had been distracted by the Gemini 4 flight. Television coverage of the Howard speech was perfunctory. *Newsweek* did include several excerpts from the speech, but most of the next week's editions of major newsmagazines made only brief, if any, mention of the Howard speech. And in the next morning's papers only a handful of commentators grappled with the interwoven strands of the address's principal arguments.[43]

In the days that followed, however, editorials and opinion columns did appear in several of the nation's most influential daily newspapers, as commentators belatedly began to alert their readers to the broader implications of the speech. Marquis Childs, writing for the *Washington Post*, suggested that the speech would ultimately be recognized as a "landmark that promises to divide one era from another." Political logic, Childs reflected in wonder, dictated that Johnson should have been content to rest on his civil rights laurels, with the administration's voting rights bill seemingly assured of passage. In light of this, the risk-taking approach was all the more remarkable. C. B. Powell, the editor of the *New York Amsterdam News*, found the Howard speech to be without historical precedent, and, in language welcome to Johnson, obsessed as he was with his ultimate place in history, Powell mounted a detailed argument that Johnson had outshone previous White House occupants, including Lincoln, FDR, Truman, and Kennedy.[44]

Tom Wicker of the *New York Times* agreed. The Howard speech was "remarkable in the history of the Presidency, as well as of the civil rights movement." In his second treatment of the speech, appearing three days after its delivery, in a "News Analysis" column, Wicker compared the sociological underpinnings of the Howard address to the rationale of the Supreme Court in the 1954 *Brown v. Board of Education* school desegregation decision. Johnson was grappling, the columnist believed, with "the problem . . . [of] the acceptance of the Negro as an equal human being rather than a 'separate but equal' human being." Wicker's column implied that if dramatic policy changes followed from the premise set forward in the address at Howard, they could bring serious political and social repercussions for both blacks and whites.[45]

Perhaps most interesting, Wicker wrote a third piece in the *New York Times* that appeared on June 6 in which he was one of only a handful of commentators to pass on a claim the White House press office was anxious to have repeated. This was the "first major Presidential speech on civil rights that had not been made under the direct pressure of some racial crisis," the reporter noted. But the *Times* buried Wicker's assessment on page forty-three with a headline that gave no obvious indication that the article concerned the address at Howard.[46]

Arguably reaching even fewer readers, Douglas Kiker of the *New York Herald Tribune* anticipated Wicker in observing the frequency with which each crisis deliberately created by civil rights activists forced a response from the administration. Kiker's column on June 6 accurately reflected the tenor of White House discussions of "leapfrogging" civil rights leaders, with the reporter speculating that the Howard speech represented the president's "effort . . . to move quickly and get ahead of civil rights leaders who currently are looking about, to see where and how the rights movement should be directed."[47] The divergent emphases in written commentary suggested how different columnists could hear different things. Rustin's article in *Commentary* four months earlier may have informed some of the news analysis, but columnists never mentioned him by name.

Even before the newspapers had gone to bed late that Friday night after Johnson's speech at Howard, the telegrams began to arrive at the White House. Although by White House standards the mail response hardly constituted an avalanche, several dozen letters followed in the ensuing days, with return addresses from the heads of the major civil rights organizations, prominent labor leaders and academics, and previously unknown constituents.[48] Minutes after watching highlights of Johnson's speech on her television, a Mrs. Oscar D. Stern of Chicago, obviously moved, sat down and scribbled her thoughts on a postcard: "President Johnson: Dear Sir: I must follow this impulse. You just talked on our TV and your face under the mortarboard—your voice, the words you said, touched me, and I'm not in the mood to skip over this moment to say a huge 'bravo'—I'm all on your side." Civil rights leaders, including Martin Luther King Jr., Roy Wilkins, and Whitney Young, who had heard the major points of the speech in advance from Goodwin, responded in overwhelmingly positive fashion (although, interestingly, none of the major civil rights leaders devoted his weekly newspaper column in the African American press to the Howard address in the weeks following).[49]

Conservative politicians and media organs gave little or no indication that the speech had registered with their concerns, and the silence from urban political leaders whose depressed urban cores were deeply implicated in the speech was striking. Individual letter writers did demonstrate, however, that the contents of the address had touched a sensitive nerve. Charlotte Webb, a white woman from Massachusetts, wrote to complain that the speech was unfair to southern whites, whom she perceived to be "the champion of the Negro." "Whites have 'loved' and cared for the Negro," she noted, a paternalistic historical relationship that had only recently soured as a result of the "Civil Rights confusions."[50]

A terse note from a white native of Sumter, South Carolina, advised Johnson, "time permitting," to direct his attention to Strom Thurmond's speeches in Congress on known communistic tendencies in the civil rights movement: "Then have a long consultation with Mr. J. Edgar Hoover" of the FBI. Ernest C. Arnold, a white-collar worker from Muskogee, Oklahoma, in the oil and gas industry, wrote as though from the historical perspective of Reconstruction — albeit laced with a dram of Cold War anticommunist rhetoric. He lambasted Johnson for pushing whites to employ blacks in greater numbers and implied that the Howard speech portended a grave political crisis: "You surely do not think that after a bunch of Negroes and white carpet-baggers have made themselves as obnoxious as possible, that those who have not only been insulted and abused, but have also had much of their property ruined or stolen; are going to turn their other cheek and employ them. I just can't bring myself to believe that you are that devoid of understanding of human nature. You, King, Brother Bobby, and others of your click are unknowningly [sic] but bull-headedly leading us straight into Communism via a revolution."[51]

On the day following the Howard address, Kenneth McFarland, of Topeka, Kansas, wrote to Johnson in more circumspect language. He requested a copy of the speech from the White House to verify if the wire services had printed the text correctly, and noted that he was "deeply concerned" about Johnson's use of the words "opportunity" and "achievement." "The key word in America has always been 'opportunity.' Equality can never mean more than equality of opportunity."[52]

David Lawrence, the influential founder and editor of U.S. News and World Report magazine and the nation's most widely read conservative columnist, generally avoided overtly racist comments, even as he consistently supported southern segregationists on "constitutional grounds." But he caustically dismissed the Howard remarks as nothing more than another "pro-Negro speech." In his syndicated column, published in 350 newspapers around the nation, he complained that the "President blamed almost everything on the white population, praised the Negroes for their demonstrations, and, in effect, gave them the signal to go ahead with more of the same." It was an argument that precisely anticipated many whites' responses to the escalation of urban riots in and after 1965.[53]

Lawrence's implicit suggestion that LBJ's address was a segregated, "pro-Negro" speech intended for primarily black consumption was troubling, but the White House sent a strong signal on June 5 that the commitment to an expanded battle for civil economic rights was an "integrated" effort on the part of the entire administration and a message intended for audiences on both sides of the color line. Vice President Hubert Humphrey's commencement speech before a primarily white audience at the University of Maryland echoed each of the themes of Howard as he challenged whites to join a second stage in the civil rights struggle. Like Johnson, Humphrey cautioned his audience about the complexity of the problems facing both blacks and whites: "The most difficult and challenging days for America lie just ahead." But as vice president, Humphrey's reworking of the Howard message before a white audience received almost no coverage beyond the Beltway. It was a galling reality that Johnson could certainly appreciate from his own three years on the periphery of the Oval Office.[54]

In March, the administration had linked its fortunes with those of the civil rights movement when Johnson dramatically declared, "We Shall Overcome." Just three months later, the Howard University speech called for greater economic justice. The ideas the president presented there were not entirely original, but Johnson articulated them with eloquence. And with the weight of the White House behind them, the speech's complicated messages reached millions, even if the audience proved somewhat inattentive. Johnson's rhetorical expansion of the vista of civil rights and economic justice seemed a natural marriage of the discourses of civil rights and the War on Poverty. It is thus tempting to view the president's speech at Howard University as yet another peak in the administration's public commitment to civil rights and economic justice for the poor.

Yet any peak derives its tapering nature from the steepness of multiple slopes. And so came the inevitable fall.

In retrospect, it appears that the Johnson White House began a gradual disengagement from the civil rights agenda beginning in the summer of 1965. A number of distinguished historians as well as other participant observers have long speculated on the reasons for this repositioning. In all but a few cases, in writing of the fate of the "next and more profound stage of the battle for civil rights," these chroniclers have concluded that there was retreat, withdrawal, loss of will, and even betrayal. Writing from the vantage point of 1970, journalist John Herbers typified this trend when he wrote of a "rush of history" in the spring and summer of 1965. He identified the Howard University speech as "the high mark" in a "watershed year of the social revolution" and argued that "the nation was approaching a solution to its racial malady in the 1960s and need not have experienced the violence, polarizations, cynicism, and 'backlash' that now make a solution very difficult to effect."

Herbers prefaced his elegiac account of "the lost priority" of civil rights with a terse thesis: "It took a long time to make the Negro revolution of the 1960s. It took only a few months, weeks really, to do it in."[55]

In his own memoir of the period, Richard Goodwin interrupted the chronology detailing the composition of the Howard speech to lament that what should have served as a prelude instead became an epitaph. Goodwin's treatment of both the commencement address and Johnson's earlier "We Shall Overcome" televised voting rights message to Congress and the nation is rooted in the Greek dramatic tradition of hubris as he describes "the tragedy—the terrible, irrevocable tragedy" of Johnson's rhetorical reach in contrast with a perceived subsequent failure of political will. Johnson, the victim of inexorable historical tides, "might have gone a long way towards his intent had his passage not been swept up in the turbulent eddies that so violently disrupted his public course and his own mind, mercilessly sweeping the journey toward unforgiving rocks." For many historical observers, hostile and sympathetic alike, Johnson stood at the center of a drama mythic in its dimensions. Like Icarus, it seems, the overambitious Texan had flown too close to the sun.[56]

Here, then, are the basic elements of the tragic narrative: Two weeks after the Howard speech, 8,000 American Marines landed in Vietnam. By summer's end, tens of thousands more were on their way and the United States was mounting its devastating B-52 bombing raids against North Vietnam.

The chorus of praise that had greeted the Howard address fell silent as Americans were riveted by the explosion of Watts. On August 11, just one week after Johnson signed the Voting Rights Act into law and a wave of Justice Department registrars fanned out across the South, rioting erupted in the southern Los Angeles community, killing thirty-four and resulting in millions of dollars in property damage. Smaller riots broke out in Chicago, Philadelphia, and other cities. Public debate raged over the Moynihan Report, the "Case for National Action," which focused on the "tangled pathology" of the inner city, dividing erstwhile allies in the liberal civil rights coalition and poisoning the planning for the fall White House conference that had been called for in the Howard speech. (The confidential Moynihan Report was leaked by hostile bureaucrats over the summer but only trumpeted in the press after Watts.) Public awareness of the relationship between the Moynihan Report and the Howard address remained limited, and the mainstream media confused the issue further by erroneously linking the production of the Moynihan Report with the rioting in Los Angeles. "After Watts," one historian concludes, "the legions of moderate whites who had so recently demanded justice for the meek, Christ-like demonstrators at Selma began melting away."[57]

The slope descends from the summer of 1965 to the bitter months of 1968. The events of that latter year are deeply etched in the American historical memory. In January came the horrific violence of the Tet offensive in Vietnam. In the ensuing months, the Kerner Commission prefaced its disturbing findings on urban disorder by suggesting that America had become "two societies . . . separate and unequal," and that "white racism" was largely to blame. Lyndon Johnson withdrew from the presidential race, and only days later an assassin took the life of Martin Luther King Jr. Within hours, dozens of additional cities went up in flames. Robert F. Kennedy fell to a second assassin's bullet, and late that summer a police riot broke out amid the chaos and political theater of the Chicago Democratic Convention. The whole world was indeed watching, as protesters chanted with a mixture of anguish and euphoria. Many in the national audience were sickened and saddened by the violence and anarchy; others were simply angry.

The logic and power of this tragic narrative have become so familiar as to become self-reinforcing—the handful of events neatly strung together, clutched and counted with the intimate familiarity of well-worn rosary beads. Nicholas Lemann has described the summer of 1965 as a hinge for an entire decade.[58] The metaphor is apt in at least one way, for many historians and observers of the period have been eager to slam the door after 1965, to foreclose examination of events that do not fit the tragic narrative, or to muse—however eloquently—on divergent possibilities, progressive visions of what might have been: But for the Lorraine Motel balcony in Memphis in April 1968. But for the Hotel Ambassador kitchen in Los Angeles two months later on June 5, with another assassin's bullets flying within hours of the third anniversary of the Howard speech. But for Mayor Richard Daley's heavy-handed approach to dissent in Chicago. But for the Democratic candidate, Hubert Humphrey, waiting until the eleventh hour to declare his independence from the Johnson administration on Vietnam.

There are, however, alternative narratives. We should not forget that the Marines who landed on the beaches in Da Nang that spring (the public was not informed until a larger June deployment) bolstered a sizable presence of U.S. advisers already "in country," some with nearly a decade's experience in Indochina. Despite their alleged role as noncombatants, these Americans had tasted serious action, sharing the burden of a defeat and suffering heavy casualties as 1964 drew to a close with fighting in Binh Gia near Saigon and in the capital itself when the Viet Cong bombed a hotel housing American officers. The bombing of North Vietnam late in the summer of 1965 constituted a resumption of an earlier campaign.

In 1964, a full year before Watts, extensive rioting had shaken Harlem and Rochester in New York; Jersey City, Elizabeth, and Paterson in New Jersey; Dixmoor, a poor suburb of Chicago; and Philadelphia, where two people were killed. Whitney Young, Kenneth Clark, James Farmer, and other civil rights leaders and public intellectuals had publicly and privately expressed concern about the deteriorating status of many black families—as had E. Franklin Frazier a generation before—well before Daniel Patrick Moynihan grafted Labor Department policy research onto the debate and unwittingly helped to trigger a bitter controversy on urban and racial pathology.

White House attempts—both overt and clandestine—to understand the roots of unrest in the nation's urban centers from 1964 forward helped to generate the cumulative momentum for the establishment of the National Advisory Commission on Civil Disorders, with its more immediate catalyst, the Newark and Detroit riots of July 1967. The Kerner Commission Report has served as a chronological and ideological benchmark in the debate on the destiny of the nation's inner cities. Thus, the Johnson administration's attempts to understand, forestall, and, ultimately, contain urban unrest raise important questions about the limits of articulating, and the possibilities of realistically fulfilling, a civil rights agenda committed to economic justice against a backdrop of urban poverty.

"Nothing is inevitable until it happens," historian A. J. P. Taylor reminds us. In reality, there was no single line of descent from Howard to the chaos of 1968, no seamless web of historical circumstances. There were efforts, typically disjointed, by some in the administration, the FBI, and other agencies in the federal government to contain, subvert, or actively oppose the agendas of certain black leaders and organizations. But there was no systematic conspiracy on the part of the Johnson administration to sabotage the expanding agenda of the civil rights revolution and ensure defeat in the "next and more profound stage of the battle for civil rights." The reality was far messier, tangled skeins of severed threads, abortive connections, and seemingly aimless wanderings.

In the three years following the Howard speech, there were both haphazard advances and disorganized retreats by many of the parties most interested in the outcome of the battle declared at Howard's commencement. The relationship between LBJ's civil rights policy and grassroots social insurgency took the form of an erratic dialogue, typically unacknowledged and increasingly unpredictable. Miscommunication and misunderstanding frequently meant that this dialogue took place in several different languages without the benefit of adequate translation. To complicate matters even further, the Johnson administration was selectively hearing impaired. Whom its officials chose to hear and who encountered deafness when trying to communicate with the administration revealed a great deal about the White House's restricted vision of political empowerment.

The critical role of media coverage of civil rights demonstrations in pricking the national conscience and laying the groundwork for the landmark civil rights legislation of 1964 and 1965 has been well documented. Sit-ins, Freedom Rides, fire hoses and police dogs, gas-masked figures on foot and on horseback against a silhouetted steel structure swinging nightsticks amid roiling clouds of tear gas—these and other images form the iconography of the civil rights era.

The years 1965 to 1968 can stake their own claim as the era of the media-defined watershed. Events playing out in the news appeared all the more stark and all-determining because of heightened expectations. As events were recast in print, and especially as they were refracted through the camera lens and manipulated at editing consoles in television network newsrooms, the fundamental and seemingly ever-growing power of reportage to shape public perception, even public discourse, was more and more evident. The medium of television in particular was becoming increasingly revolutionary. "Like nothing else before it," one historian has suggested, TV "exposed the contradiction between liberty and white supremacy."[59] It could circumscribe or—less often—open up avenues of initiative within the federal government and the broadening spectrum of civil rights movements. Arguably more than at any time in the past, the media in and after 1965 played a critical role in fashioning national political culture and delimiting the perceived boundaries of political possibilities and agendas for reform. Television had furthered the goals of the southern-based civil rights movement up through the Selma campaign in 1965; in the three years that followed, it would increasingly fuel white backlash with its coverage of urban rioting.

At Howard, Johnson articulated the concept of equality of results and implicitly made a political commitment to achieving that objective. Broadening even further the ambitious scope of Moynihan's case for national action, the president warned of the corrosive effects of allowing "another nation" to fall further behind. Johnson offered an impassioned plea to commit the full energies of government to the battle ahead: "This will be a chief goal of my administration, and of my program next year, and in years to come. And I hope, and I pray, and I believe, it will be a part of the program of all America."

Gareth Davies has described the Howard speech as an "initial breach [that] opened the door to subsequent and more wide-ranging critiques of the nation's underlying principles." Those critiques gathered momentum "on Capitol Hill, in academe, and within [Johnson's] own administration," Davies argues, to the president's increasing discomfort.[60] But many others were contemplating that breach as well. The Howard address had ostensibly championed those African Americans "buried under a blanket of history and circumstance," trapped behind "invisible," "gateless" walls. How would those seemingly far removed from the corridors of power in Washington and the sectarian debates within university departments respond?

As the eyes of the federal government and many of the southern-based civil rights organizations appeared to be turning to the problems of the great cities of the North, the shooting death of O'Neal Moore, the black sheriff's deputy in Bogalusa, Louisiana, came as a tragic reminder that racism in the hearts and minds of many white southerners had not been overcome (indeed, it had grown stronger among some)—that civil rights legislation in and of itself could not prevent murder. The inability of local authorities to prosecute Ernest Ray McElveen successfully—the alleged murderer was charged but never tried— demonstrated that federal protection of civil rights in the rural South was still pitifully weak. News of the murders in Bogalusa jockeyed for column space with longer articles drawing attention to the Louisiana-based Deacons for Defense and Justice, part of a deeper tradition of "rifle clubs" and advocacy of armed self-defense among African Americans in the South that had only occasionally drawn white attention, as when Robert F. Williams had championed the power of "Negroes with guns" or Malcolm X spoke of the dichotomy of "the ballot or the bullet."[61]

The Johnson administration would soon grapple with the challenge of dealing with "Negroes with guns." But it would also confront black preschool children armed only with crayons and coloring books when they staged an invasion of Capitol Hill. The seemingly innocuous issue of a preschool education program—planned by a committed group of blacks and whites at Mount Beulah Junior College near the tiny hamlet of Edwards, Mississippi—would rise to the level of high politics. Local people were unwilling to let Edwards, Mississippi, and Bogalusa, Louisiana, go unnoticed by those above.

L ooking down as he stepped back beyond the reach of the microphones at Howard University on June 4, 1965, the president waited for a response. Richard Goodwin recalled looking out anxiously at the thousands of expectant black faces as Johnson prepared to begin his remarks, fearing that they

*The president greets the enthusiastic crowd at the conclusion
of his speech. Courtesy of the LBJ Library.*

looked upon the president as "the honkie intruder on black ground." But as
Johnson concluded, the waves of applause built and crashed against the ros-
trum and the facade of the Frederick Douglass building behind it, only to crest
again. The Howard choir began to sing "We Shall Overcome." Sensitive to the
demands of the president's busy schedule, the graduation planners had made
arrangements for Johnson to leave immediately following his address. But as he
walked from the stage, his phalanx of secret servicemen could make no head-
way through the crush of onlookers eager for a presidential handshake. Basking
in the ovation, Johnson waded out into the predominantly black crowd to press
the flesh and, to the dismay of his security detail, was soon surrounded.[62]

Ever sensitive to Johnson's deep insecurities, Goodwin had appended to the
Howard speech draft's cover memo what he later called a final paragraph of
"grotesquely exaggerated rhetoric." Effectively stroking and stoking the Johnsonian ego with the same words, Goodwin wrote: "You received almost all the
Negro vote. You have fulfilled the expectations of that support. But both Bill
[Moyers] and I agree that a speech like this might well help toward making
you 'The Great Emancipator' of the twentieth century." John Herbers offered
a similarly hyperbolic—and implicitly paternalistic—analysis of the day's significance when he later wrote: "Not since Lincoln signed the Emancipation
Proclamation had Negroes been offered such hope." To those observers and

others present after the graduation exercises, the physical tableau—a tall white president being hemmed in on all sides by black well-wishers—presented an eerie reflection of Lincoln's visit to a liberated Richmond, one-time capital of the dying Confederacy, an even century before.[63]

That day at Howard was one of the last times that the irrepressible Johnson was able to interact with an uncontrolled crowd without enduring the heckling and abuse of antiwar sentiments following 1965. In the middle of hundreds of smiling faces, crossing his arms at the elbows to shake with both hands, the Texan reveled in the place and the moment. Johnson, who observers noted had never once smiled during the address, could not stop beaming. Captured by a *Washington Post* photographer, the normally unflappable secret serviceman nearest Johnson finally cracked a wide grin himself as he watched his chief work the exuberant audience, enduring the cacophony of staccato shouts: "Mr. President! Mr. President!"[64] The security detail and Howard University's newest honorary degree holder moved along slowly in the collective embrace of the crowd. The line of limousines could wait.

CHAPTER TWO

Romper Lobbies and Coloring Lessons

Poverty Wars and the Child Development
Group of Mississippi

In the Howard University speech of June 1965, Lyndon Johnson insisted that opening the "gates of opportunity" was not enough: "All our citizens must have the ability to walk through those gates." The creation of the Child Development Group of Mississippi (CDGM) that same year highlighted the connections between the president's civil rights and economic justice policies and cast a spotlight on the troubled relationship between the White House and grassroots civil rights and antipoverty activists. Lyndon Johnson's War on Poverty, authorized by the Economic Opportunity Act of 1964, would spark political controversy nationwide, even as its programs unquestionably helped improve the lives of thousands of America's poorest citizens in attempting to close the yawning gap between haves and have-nots. As Mississippi's white political establishment angrily responded to the poverty wars in their state by bitterly attacking CDGM, this relatively minor program became a critical test of the administration's resolve to live up to the promise of Howard.[1]

The commitment to quality preschool education for children of all racial and socioeconomic backgrounds reflected the sweepingly optimistic rhetoric of Johnson's speech at the June 1965 Howard University commencement ceremony, although the OEO had already undertaken plans for the summer programs in the spring of that year. One of the War on Poverty's most popular programs, Head Start reflected the belief that early, positive intervention in the lives of prekindergarten four- and five-year-olds, particularly those from disadvantaged backgrounds (the language of OEO), would improve their educational and employment prospects in the future.

Head Start was initially funded under the Community Action Program

(CAP) of OEO with a start-up budget of $17 million for the first year and projections of $150 million in 1966. Under the leadership of Head Start director Julius Richmond, OEO hoped to reach 100,000 four- and five-year-old children in 300 communities during the first summer of programs in 1965. The men and women who envisioned Head Start saw it as a way of providing broad social services and medical care for poor children and their families. Parents would be involved in their children's education as paid or volunteer workers, and childhood socialization would be a critical component of the program's mission. Initially, Head Start met little resistance; Lady Bird Johnson was a vocal and enthusiastic supporter of a concept that seemed comfortably mainstream.[2]

But these programs came to be more than a reflection of contemporary national thinking on early childhood education, certainly the case in Mississippi. The earliest concept for CDGM originated with self-avowed "New York Jewish radical" Thomas (Tom) Levin, a psychologist who had organized a team of doctors to provide medical support to civil rights activists participating in the 1964 "Freedom Summer" project in Mississippi, which was led by the Council of Federated Organizations (COFO). The ideology of SNCC, with its concept of the "beloved community" and its commitment to decentralized and inclusive leadership, particularly impressed Levin. The "Freedom Schools" set up in many areas during the Mississippi voter registration campaigns in the summers of 1963 and 1964 also influenced the New Yorker.

Fifteen years later, Levin would claim that he intended to establish a "Lenin School to set up black revolutionaries." The local black Mississippians who ran the program "would be the kamikaze revolutionaries that would change the self." Despite Levin's later recollection, there is little evidence that other founders of CDGM were shaped by Lenin's theories of revolutionary cadres, and although Levin's role was central, Head Start was fundamentally a collaborative and community-based effort. Head Start organizers' ideas sprang directly from their experience in the trenches of the civil rights movement, with its emphasis upon the connections between politics, participatory democracy, and the role that education could play in alleviating the sense of despair that had shackled generations of young black Mississippians. For many black adults in the state, the program provided a chance to break the cycles of poverty and submission that had marked their lives. There were "some real good people teaching our children," one mother of CDGM preschoolers would relate, "and they give us food for them, and a woman like me, they've given me a job, not sweeping after Mrs. Charley for five dollars a week . . . but a *real* job and one that pays me good to *do what's important for me and my family.*"[3]

CDGM offered children preschool education, access to medical services, and two hot meals, which some of the poorest youngsters might not otherwise receive. It also promised far better salaries to teachers and teachers' aides than were available in the wage-depressed economy in which most of the state's poorest African Americans were trapped.[4] And there were larger goals. The Freedom Schools served as a model for what would become CDGM's preschool alchemy of politics and grassroots democracy, self-esteem building, and early education.

In the words of one advocate, the Freedom Schools would "fill an intellectual and creative vacuum in the lives of young Negro Mississippians," emboldening them "to challenge the myths of our society, to perceive more clearly its realities and to find alternatives and ultimately, new directions for action." They were an example of what a scholar of the "organizing tradition" in Mississippi Delta has termed "education for activism." Among the range of movement activities, work in the Freedom Schools was at times devalued and has too often been overlooked historically. In part, this was because it lacked the dramatic intensity and risk of "direct action" represented by sit-ins and marches and also because women played a central role in this aspect of movement organizing and as a general rule women's contributions to social activism were not accorded a proper degree of respect.[5]

Often employing the Socratic method, volunteer teachers in the Freedom Schools instructed black youngsters and adults alike on a range of traditional academic topics, at the same time encouraging nonviolence in deed and thought. The teachers, some with professional experience but many simply volunteers eager to work in education, also posed far more sweeping questions about societal inequities and the extent to which African Americans should seek "material things" or "soul things"—whether they should pursue assimilation into the dominant white culture or preserve community traditions and avoid the temptations of materialism.[6]

By teaching black history, black traditions, and an early version of "black pride," the founders of CDGM followed the pattern established by the Freedom Schools in their expressions of faith in the transformative potential of preschool education and the importance of reaching the children before the daily insults of life in Mississippi's racial caste system had taken their toll on self-image and psyche. Such assumptions clearly echoed the sociological rationale for the *Brown v. Board of Education* decision in 1954 abolishing segregation in public education. In Mississippi, of course, as in most of the Deep South, whites' "massive resistance" had effectively thwarted meaningful desegregation for over a decade. Encouraged by Jule Sugarman, a sympathetic OEO administrator who directed the newly created Head Start programs in the South,

Levin envisioned that federal funding of the Economic Opportunity Act of 1964 might eventually be used in Mississippi to subvert white control over black education at the state and local levels.[7]

According to one contemporary account, Levin took the Economic Opportunity Act's language mandating "maximum feasible participation" by poor Americans at face value. He was also taking a long view of racial and economic change in Mississippi, a state that would have no public kindergarten for its children—black or white—until the early 1980s. Levin envisioned CDGM as a potential vehicle for advancement for all the state's poorest citizens. In applying in the spring of 1965 for funding from OEO for a seven-week session of summer preschools for poor children, he wrote: "A primary purpose of the summer is to stimulate communities to function autonomously so that the program can continue permanently with or without outside help."[8]

Thus, the language of "kamikaze revolutionaries" and "Lenin schools" was absent—not surprisingly—from the initial proposal seeking federal funding. Moreover, the idea of creating a self-perpetuating program seemed fundamentally in keeping with the language and intent of the Economic Opportunity Act in a period when much of the federal government and the wider public perceived a diversity of local approaches to be one of the antipoverty program's signal strengths and the key to ensuring its longevity and success over time.

To workers processing the flood of grant applications to the OEO in its first year of operation, the CDGM proposal initially appeared to offer both a well-thought-out program and the chance for a public relations bonanza. Sargent Shriver, the director of the Peace Corps and brother-in-law to the Kennedy brothers whom LBJ had appointed to head the OEO from its inception, was hungry for headlines in the early months of the War on Poverty. CDGM—at least as it appeared on paper—represented a CAP without any hint of involvement by former segregationists, a rarity in the Deep South. Like Levin, some OEO officials envisioned CDGM as a vehicle to make a federally funded end run around the fiscal and political stranglehold on black education imposed by Mississippi's white state authorities.

The legislation that created OEO allowed local antipoverty groups to work through independent, nonprofit, third-party agencies and organizations. When civil rights mainstay Tougaloo College conducted an about-face under external pressure from influential white northern benefactors and backed away from its earlier plan to serve as the conduit for Head Start funding in the state, OEO administrators and Mississippi activists ultimately settled on Mary Holmes Junior College, a small, historically black Presbyterian college located in West Point, Mississippi, to administer and supervise the federal grants.[9]

With little internal deliberation, the OEO awarded $1.4 million to CDGM in May 1965—a record sum in the early months of the War on Poverty and especially noteworthy given the relatively modest scale of the program Levin and other Mississippians initially proposed. The CDGM grant represented approximately one-third of all the federal funds initially appropriated for Head Start programs statewide in Mississippi.

In a remarkably short period of time, Levin and others on the fledgling organization's board designed and implemented a seven-week summer program with centers in more than seventy-five communities across the state that served more than 6,000 preschool-aged children, almost all of them black. Their success in large part stemmed from their ability to build upon the elaborate human infrastructure built up by COFO over the course of nearly four years, which had made 1964's Freedom Summer such a remarkable experiment in indigenous movement building. Relying on those courageous activists and using the talents of some of Mississippi's poorest citizens, many of them black female farm laborers, CDGM became the largest and best-known Head Start program in the country.

Its preschool education was directed at meeting more than the conventional expectations of early childhood education. As with the Freedom Schools, there was clearly a component of esteem-building, which was very much in keeping with the overall goals of civil rights activists, who were intent on African Americans affirming their humanity and dignity. Because of the heavy involvement of local blacks in the day-to-day management of the CDGM centers, community members suddenly felt a proprietary sense over their youngsters' educations. They drew a sharp distinction between the CDGM educational experience and the education their children received in still-segregated public schools. African American schoolteachers and administrators had to navigate carefully in fiscal and political waters dominated by white segregationists; such an environment stifled assertiveness, creativity, and risk-taking on the part of both educators and their charges.

CDGM, one parent remembered, was something new: "Head Start is to put life back in the community, to give us something to run for our children the way we want it run. We will not teach the children to hate themselves and their people as the schools do. We will teach the children to be proud. Nothing you know is worth anything if you don't first know to be proud of yourself."[10]

A twenty-six-year-old African American staff worker and occasional teacher in CDGM, known fondly to preschoolers and their parents as "Mr. Peter," tried to distill the message being related daily in ramshackle Head Start centers in and beyond the Mississippi Delta: "We try to show [the children] that we respect them, as children, as human beings. We aren't forever comparing them to some white face in a white child's book. We show them the strength and value of their *own* words, their own tradition—they are the children of workers, who built this whole state, with their sweat and tears and shortened lives. We tell the kids that, and they listen."[11]

For involved local parents, CDGM seemed an immediate success story for themselves and for their children. But over the course of the next two years, CDGM shifted in the public imagination—in Mississippi and beyond—from one of the OEO's most acclaimed successes to one of its most controversial and divisive grants. For Sargent Shriver, and ultimately for Lyndon Johnson, a momentary public relations bonanza became a long-term public relations nightmare as Mississippi's white political establishment reacted to the funding of CDGM in the same way that it had responded to any hint of interference or criticism by "outsiders" for well over a century.

Led by the two most prominent members of the state's powerful congressional delegation—archsegregationist U.S. senators John Stennis and James Eastland—whites in the Magnolia State lashed out against CDGM. When they assailed the men and women of CDGM as "radicals," "subversives," and "outside agitators," they drew upon a toxic historical mythology surrounding the Reconstruction era and a powerful vocabulary of more contemporary anticommunism.

Mississippi's governor, Paul Johnson Jr., was seen as more moderate than his predecessor, Ross Barnett, but this initially seemed more a matter of style (and intelligence) than substance. In his January 1964 inauguration, he had insisted that "hate, or prejudice, or ignorance will not lead Mississippi while I sit in the Governor's chair." We are "Americans as well as Mississippians."[12] But he quickly showed that his moderation had limits. In the wake of the disappearance of the civil rights workers in 1964, for example, Johnson had repeatedly insisted that the three slain workers (who had been buried under a Mississippi earthen dam) were enjoying a vacation at the expense of the people of Mississippi. When reports surfaced that the men had been seen alive shortly before the discovery of their bodies, reporters questioned Johnson about the reports as he joined Alabama's governor George Wallace at a white supremacy rally held in Jackson. With a smile and a conspiratorial wink, the Mississippi governor told newsmen that "Governor Wallace and I are the only two people who know where they are and we're not telling."[13] His insensitivity on issues of race would be further demonstrated when he responded in 1967 to well-documented accounts of malnutrition among African Americans in Mississippi. "Nobody is starving in Mississippi," he retorted. "The nigra women I see are so fat they shine."[14]

Although the governor was not in a position to cause as many problems for LBJ as members of the state's congressional delegation, he proved to be a powerful foe of CDGM, repeatedly attacking the organization. In the first weeks of the grant period, Governor Johnson wrote Sargent Shriver an angry letter describing CDGM as little more than a front for "extremists and agitators" seeking "to subvert legal authority in Mississippi and to create division and dissension between the races."[15] Johnson and other Mississippi political leaders found ample material for their continuous attacks in the secret reports of the Mississippi State Sovereignty Commission.

In the late 1950s and early 1960s, even as congressional committees like the House Un-American Activities Committee in Washington, D.C., drew fewer national headlines, most of the Deep South states created what historian Jeff Woods called "little HUACs and little FBIs" to investigate, expose, and harass any individual or group sympathetic to civil rights. None was more far-reaching—or ruthless—than the Mississippi State Sovereignty Commission, created in 1957 and given the power to perform any "acts . . . necessary . . . to protect the sovereignty of the State of Mississippi . . . from encroachment . . . by the Federal Government." The commission staff interpreted this mandate broadly, gathering information on civil rights activists, spying on them and using that information to discredit their activities with the public.[16]

Although there is no evidence that the commission directly organized acts of physical violence against individuals, staff members clearly did nothing to stop, and indeed sometimes encouraged, such assaults so long as they took place behind closed doors. After investigating a surging civil rights movement in Grenada, Mississippi, during the fall of 1966, commission investigator Tom Scarbrough insisted that the only solution to the problem was to "get rid of the rabble rousers, which are SCLC workers." Local officials cooperated by arresting five SCLC staffers and dispatching them to Parchman, the state penitentiary, where highway patrolmen removed their identification badges and savagely assaulted the five men, with special attention given to the most outspoken of the group, Robert Johnson. ("They are really working him over," Scarbrough reported with apparent satisfaction.) Johnson was held even after bail was posted, "because he's so beaten up he couldn't get up to get out."[17]

The commission suggested to some employers that they fire targeted activists; in other cases, they arranged for local draft boards to draft "troublemakers" into the army in order to remove them from the state. The commission conducted jury research on behalf of white supremacist Byron de la Beckwith in his trial for the murder of Medgar Evers, and it also furnished Neshoba County deputy sheriff Cecil Price with the license plate number for the blue station wagon of civil rights workers James Chaney, Michael Schwerner, and Andrew Goodman. Price arrested and then released the three before stopping them a second time and turning them over to Klan murderers.[18]

Within weeks of its formation in 1965, CDGM came under constant scrutiny by paid informants and staff investigators. By July, Mississippi State Sovereignty Commission director Erle Johnston reported to Governor Johnson that he had successfully planted in Levin's office a secretary who would "furnish us copies of all correspondence, memoranda, etc." Over the next eighteen months, the commission received dozens of internal memos, reports of meetings, copies of financial records, and anything that could be used to discredit the Head Start program, eagerly forwarding any potentially damaging information to senators Eastland and Stennis to be used in their attacks against the OEO in general and CDGM in particular.[19]

The commission's reports simply reinforced the conviction of most white Mississippians that the Head Start program was a shadow organization fronting for SNCC, the Mississippi Freedom Democratic Party (MFDP), the Delta Ministry, and other remnants of the strained COFO coalition. One journalist seeking to pinpoint the source of white anger toward CDGM suggested that whites clearly identified the Head Start program as the "residual legatee of 'the movement.'" All the "SNCC operations were located in the same area that the [CDGM] Head Start People were," said one of Senator John Stennis's top aides. And they were, he claimed, "one and the same people."[20]

From its inception, CDGM had in fact been hard-pressed to secure locations for its Head Start centers. Already established meeting places for civil rights activists became the most likely sites in which to locate centers, but this quickly opened CDGM to allegations on the part of white segregationists that it was a "front" organization: "One of the first tasks of CDGM was to get facilities to meet in," Kenneth Dean remembered. "The shortest solution to that problem was to turn the Freedom Centers that had been used by civil rights groups into Headstart centers. . . . I don't think anybody was naive enough to think that there wouldn't be opposition from this because most of these centers didn't measure up to guidelines but they were all that they could get."[21]

Although there were indeed close connections among CDGM and SNCC and the larger COFO umbrella, whites chose to ignore SNCC's fundamental wariness of the role OEO might play in co-opting civil rights movements through federal largesse, a concern publicly stated on numerous occasions. SNCC's relationship with CDGM was in fact uneasy from the start. The civil rights organization had refused to endorse Levin's proposed Head Start program during a staff meeting in Waveland, Mississippi, and although a number of SNCC staff members did participate in CDGM-related activity, they seldom sank deep roots in the organization. In many cases SNCC veterans resented what they perceived to be the institutional and bureaucratic straitjacket imposed by the guidelines of the poverty program, and one observer noted that some civil rights activists "deplored the development of the poverty program and Headstart and CDGM because they saw it as the government's way of capturing and killing the civil rights movement." CDGM benefited tremendously from allies, many of them white, in ecumenical religious groups like the Delta Ministry and the National Council of Churches, but these groups were no more welcomed by state segregationists than the dedicated civil rights organizations.[22]

Even before the 1954 *Brown* decision, southern political leaders had railed against communism as the principle source of racial unrest; red-baiting had long had a symbiotic relationship with race-baiting. In the late 1950s and 1960s, however, segregationists joined hands with a larger national conservative movement in using anticommunism as a potent rhetorical weapon to demonize any individual or group challenging the racial status quo. If Mississippi's whites linked their anti-CDGM arguments to the national vocabulary of anticommunism and internal subversion, their rhetoric was still rooted in the traditional fears of "racial amalgamation" and "mongrelization." After local townspeople became "quite disturbed regarding the reports of drunken sex orgies at Mt. Beulah," state investigators ramped up their investigation of the main CDGM headquarters and training facility, which had formerly served as an all-black junior college. As the *Jackson Daily News* argued in a 1965 editorial, the Head Start program as a whole was "one of the most subtle mediums for instilling the acceptance of racial integration and ultimate mongrelization ever perpetuated in this country."[23]

To be sure, a gradual shift in language had begun. Explicit references to "race-mixing" featured less prominently than they had in whites' hysterical responses to interracial participation in the 1964 Freedom Summer. Accusations of wild sexual orgies in dormitories at CDGM's training center were couched in race-neutral terminology, but many whites made the connections between race, sex, and radicalism. In foregrounding sexual anxieties in its early May editorial attacks against CDGM—before the Head Start program was even up and running—the *Jackson Daily News* also sounded Cold War themes: "The most frightening parallel of these so-called Head Start programs . . . are some similar programs which have been a part of some anti-American countries for years."[24]

Whites also were quick to compare the federal government's sponsorship of black-controlled Head Start programs to the harrowing narrative of "Black

Reconstruction"—more commonly known as "Negro Domination"—which was enshrined in white regional mythology. "Not since the days when Mississippi was occupied by scalawags after the War between the States have we been subjected to such an obnoxious group of people as those who operated the Child Development Group of Mississippi," complained Mississippi governor Paul Johnson Jr. in one of his typical attacks on antipoverty activists. Governor Johnson, it must be noted, muddled his high school history lessons. Scalawags—by definition "natives" who betrayed their home region—could not logically be "occupiers." But it was effective, nevertheless, as part of that "unholy trinity" of "carpetbaggers" and the black representatives of "Negro Rule" who had shaped the thinking of white Mississippians since the 1870s.[25]

In echoes of the "Redemption" campaign of the 1870s, white Mississippians once again embraced a mythology in which sexual fears, race prejudice, and hostility to any challenging ideas overlapped and became mutually reinforcing. Bidwell Adams, the longtime chairman of Mississippi's Democratic Party, pointed to the "black and unholy pages of history" that marked the Reconstruction era, when whites struggled under the heel of radicals like "Thaddeus Stevens, living in Washington with Lydia Smith, his mulatto mistress," and were beholden to former slaves in the state's legislature, who "could only vote by making an 'X' behind their names."[26]

And beneath the hyperbole of rampant interracial sex, communist subversion, and a second Reconstruction, white antipathy toward Head Start in Mississippi had its own inherent logic and rationality, grounded in economic fears and white resentment of a civil rights activism that had been building in the state since World War II. Leaders of CDGM—black and white—had in fact always worn their civil rights sympathies on their sleeves, and they found the notion of a clear-cut distinction between preschool activities and politics to be artificial. Both arenas offered great transformative potential. Under the OEO grant, CDGM teachers made up to sixty dollars a week, whereas many planters paid only three dollars a day to black laborers to chop cotton plants. As Tom Levin recalled, "We were not disturbed by [the opposition of] Senator Stennis. He showed good judgment in considering us a danger to the status quo in Mississippi. We *were* a danger."[27]

CDGM infuriated Stennis and other white Mississippians because it directly jeopardized their economic control over the livelihood of blacks in the state. White Mississippians had always welcomed the massive annual infusions of government capital for military bases, improvements of the levee system along the Mississippi River, and agricultural subsidies to white plantation owners. But federal involvement in the Magnolia State, especially programs intended to benefit its impoverished African American population, had nearly always been brokered—and not infrequently misappropriated—by members of a white ruling class. Now that control was directly threatened.[28]

Mississippi officials did not restrict their harassment to words. At times, it seemed little had changed from the state's deeply rooted climate of violence and intimidation that had exploded during Freedom Summer the preceding year. Overall violence declined, but only marginally, as officials and vigilante groups repeatedly harassed CDGM. City, county, and state police issued more than $1,000 in traffic tickets to the organization's workers in the first week the centers were open. Landlords threatened to evict agricultural laborers affiliated with the new Head Start group. Local whites burned crosses, aimed shotgun and rifle shots into Head Start centers, and on one occasion ran Tom Levin off the road as he drove from one site to another. Volunteers saved Second Pilgrim's Rest Church, location of one of the CDGM centers, by frantically removing burning materials that local white opponents had ignited underneath the building's exposed footings. As innocuous as preschool education for underprivileged children would seem to be, Kenneth Dean remembered that the controversy over CDGM produced "one of the most hate-filled atmospheres that I have ever known about. People wanted to kill CDGM as much and as strongly as the Ku Klux Klan wanted to kill the three people [James Chaney, Andrew Goodman, and Michael Schwerner] that they put under the dam."[29]

OEO officials in Washington, well aware of the harassment faced by CDGM workers in Mississippi, repeatedly pressured the FBI to take action. But Hoover had made his position clear the previous year when he had briefly visited the Mississippi field office and conducted a news conference for local newspaper reporters. After criticizing the "harsh approach toward Mississippi" taken by the Justice Department, he said: "We don't guard anybody. . . . The FBI can't wet-nurse everybody who goes down and tries to reform or educate the Negroes in the South." Hoover's attitude clearly percolated down to FBI agents in the field. When a group of Klansmen shot up a car carrying CDGM workers in the summer of 1965, OEO general counsel Donald Baker asked the FBI to investigate. Three months later, Baker received a report: "Random hunter's shots! That was their opinion! They put it in writing, for God's sake."[30]

Lyndon Johnson and key members of his administration saw Governor Johnson and other local Mississippi officials as a nuisance. Senators James Eastland and John Stennis, by contrast, were serious players in congressional politics. Eastland, head of the Senate Judiciary Committee, held unassailable credentials as race-baiter, red-baiter, and archsegregationist. He had labeled the Supreme Court's *Brown* school desegregation decision "illegal, immoral, and sinful," and he was among the shrillest voices promoting the massive resistance movement and a favorite of Mississippi's powerful Citizens' Council movement. In the early 1950s, the genteel but acerbic Alabama civil rights advocate Virginia Durr joined a group of white Methodist churchwomen lobbying for abolition of the Magnolia State's poll tax. After listening to their petition, the wealthy Delta planter and lawmaker exploded with anger. "I know what you women want," he said, "black men laying on you!" Eastland, concluded Durr, was as "common as pig tracks."[31]

John Stennis chaired the Senate Finance Committee's Sub-Committee on Appropriations and, despite his archsegregationist views, had managed to remain influential with conservative lawmakers on both sides of the aisle — to a considerable degree because of the leverage his seniority allowed him to wield on several key committees. And Stennis was not reluctant to remind the president of his power as an arbiter of federal spending. When militant civil rights demonstrators staged a sit-in at an abandoned Greenville, Mississippi, air force base early in 1966, Stennis would demand that Johnson have the protesters evicted or, he bluntly warned, "my only recourse will be through the HEW [Housing, Education, and Welfare] appropriations bill."[32]

The courtly Stennis proved to be the more effective of the state's two senators in mounting a campaign against CDGM. Beginning in August of 1965, he engineered a scathing series of attacks on the fledgling antipoverty organization through the pages of the *Jackson Daily News* and *Jackson Clarion-Ledger*, two of Mississippi's most conservative papers in a state not noted for its liberal media establishment. Stennis used his regular press briefings in the Senate as an effective pulpit, echoing and embellishing the charges of those whites most upset by the early success and apparent promise of the CDGM Head Start program. The senator and Mississippi's leading dailies accused CDGM of being a "front" for "radical" civil rights groups, a beachhead for the Kremlin in the Mississippi Delta, even a nesting ground for interracial sex "perversion."

Governor Johnson dispatched Rev. M. L. Young, a black Methodist minister friendly to the governor, to the Mount Beulah campus where training for CDGM staff was taking place. Young reported that he had found "excessive drinking" and "lewd behavior" to be rampant among "so-called civil rights workers . . . who spend more time on bottles and pleasures than in working for the best interest of our race."[33]

Relying on such "intelligence" gathered by the Mississippi State Sovereignty Commission, opponents of CDGM also accused the organization of harboring communists and other extremists among its staff, of diverting OEO funds into the coffers of radical civil rights organizations, and — most ironically given the Magnolia State's segregationist past—of practicing reverse discrimination by serving only a tiny minority of white preschoolers and by having few whites on its board and staff—most of them originally from outside Mississippi. Local directors of CDGM projects had, as it happens, vigorously sought the enrollment of white children, with predictably meager results. The handful of families of native white participants endured threats of economic and physical reprisals.[34]

To some of the state's more progressive whites, the antics of the Mississippi State Sovereignty Commission and its investigators invited ridicule. Maverick journalist Bill Minor once mocked the commission as a "cornpone Gestapo," an incompetent "KGB of the cotton patches," which cobbled together gossip, inaccurate information, and paranoia concerning an impending communist takeover. One memorandum by Erle Johnston Jr., director of the commission throughout much of the 1960s, reported that he had been "reliably informed" that the "rate of venereal disease is 39.2 per cent" among supporters of the MFDP.[35]

Mississippi Human Relations Council executive director Kenneth Dean remembered being urgently dispatched by Erle Johnston, who seemed "real nervous and scared" as he urged Dean to investigate a gathering taking place at the local Ramada Inn. A meeting of radical Revolutionary Action Movement members had been convened on Mississippi soil, Johnston confided, with extremists out of both Detroit and Chicago "running guns."

The commission had been following the group for months: "One of their men had them under surveillance." Dean reluctantly agreed to investigate "because we had agreed that we would be opposed to violence." Upon arrival at the Ramada, he found that indeed "there were cars from out of town. . . . There were a bunch of blacks and whites being seen in the lobby and in the dining rooms . . . meeting and plotting and planning." But the "revolutionary" gathering was a board meeting "for people who were trying to get . . . the Headstart program off the ground." As Dean deadpanned, "This gives you . . . a fair assessment of the intelligence apparatus within the Sovereignty Commission."[36]

Patt Derian, a white Mississippi liberal, agreed that the leaders of the commission "were the biggest bumblers in the world. . . . They were dumb and terrible, like the Keystone Cops." Claiming firsthand knowledge, she described the commission's practice of fabricating allegations against key civil rights leaders or personalities, then "ambl[ing] over" from their offices to place the information in the hands of sympathetic editors at the *Jackson Clarion-Ledger* and *Jackson Daily News.* "It would appear in the paper, then they would clip it out and put it in a file. The Sovereignty Commission," she continued, "is really such a joke that if they ever stumbled on something that was fact it was purely coincidental."

Derian's mockery was leavened by an appreciation of the devastating impact of the commission's generous payroll for CDGM informants and other organizations deemed subversive. And for those who suspected—often correctly—that they were within the commission's investigation sights, even bumbling investigative techniques might have sinister consequences. Erle Johnston boasted that his organization patterned its filing and information-gathering after the FBI, and he shared its most sensational intelligence with Hoover's national intelligence apparatus, assuring the Magnolia State a prominent place in the FBI's bulging "Racial Matters" files.[37]

In July 1965, Senator Stennis dispatched one of his staff members and an accountant hired under contract to ferret out examples of fiscal irregularity or radical politicking that might discredit CDGM with the OEO. They first met with the staff of the Mississippi State Sovereignty Commission and promised that all materials unearthed in their investigation would be funneled "unofficially" to the commission. They passed on information from FBI files purportedly showing that Levin had been a "member of several [communist] front organizations." Under prodding from Stennis, the Senate Appropriations Committee had appointed a special investigating subcommittee to look into OEO projects less than a month after the first antipoverty funds had been disbursed, the "fastest creation of an inspection division by Congress in the history of the United States," according to Shriver.[38]

Responding to Stennis's accusations and demands, the OEO launched its own internal investigation and audit of CDGM in the midst of the seven-week Head Start summer program in 1965—the first of many. Auditors did uncover irregularities, but the problems seldom involved fraud or the theft of funds. In some cases, white merchants, although willing to sell supplies, refused to furnish receipts since they did not want to leave a paper trail that would come back to haunt them.[39] In other instances, auditors detected what they described as "conflicts of interest" when CDGM supporters obtained contracts to provide service. Officials of the new Head Start organization responded that traditional white vendors and suppliers would not provide those services. Similar occurrences fueled charges of rampant "nepotism." (Ironically, the OEO would sometimes fault CDGM for its "go-it-alone policy." Protagonist Yossarian from Joseph Heller's novel *Catch-22* would surely have sympathized.)

Ultimately, the audits found that funds unaccounted for made up less than 1 percent of CDGM's total grant. Unfamiliarity with red tape and an unprecedented degree of decentralization resulting in poor communication between central board and neighborhood Head Start centers and staff probably explained most of the lapses. OEO investigators concluded that there was no evidence of a systematic abuse or misappropriation of funds by CDGM. Instead they pointed to a general pattern of "fiscal amateurism" punctuated by some "unfortunate" decision-making.[40]

Despite the relatively positive report of OEO auditors, Shriver responded to pressure from Mississippi's senior senator, Stennis, who had earlier demanded that CDGM expel its "radical" leadership and move its headquarters from Mount Beulah, the abandoned black college campus that had also been used as the offices of the Delta Ministry in a region dominated by MFDP activists. At the behest of Shriver and Stennis, Tom Levin, considered to be the most radical member of CDGM, was forced to resign his post atop the organization. His frequently abrasive managerial style and his reluctance to soften his opinions in deference to the political sensitivities of others had won him few allies in CDGM's ranks. Even a sympathetic observer characterized Levin as "an outraged Yankee who didn't feel the least compunction when attacked, to attack right back." Ultimately none of CDGM's other leaders were willing to risk having the entire program grant scuttled solely out of allegiance to the New Yorker. John Mudd, a twenty-six-year-old white Harvard graduate who had first worked in Mississippi in 1964, took the helm of the embattled organization on the eve of the OEO's decision to withhold funds from CDGM, effective September 1, 1965.[41]

Not satisfied by the findings of the OEO audit, the decision to dismiss Levin, or the fiscal constraints now facing CDGM, Stennis continued to attack the Head Start grantee and to criticize Sargent Shriver and the entire antipoverty program in hearings before his subcommittee in October 1965. The director of OEO had failed to carry through on his earlier commitment to move the organization away from Mount Beulah, which Stennis viewed as the center of radical activities in Mississippi. (OEO did ultimately require that CDGM move its administrative headquarters to the state capital in Jackson, where the Head Start program experienced the oddity of sharing an office building with the newly reinforced Mississippi branch of the FBI.)

Increasingly, Stennis won a sympathetic audience among both southern Democrats and congressional Republicans. Many among the latter group alleged—with some justification—that they had been excluded and silenced at each step in the formulation and implementation of antipoverty legislation by Democrats. Moreover, many Republicans, committed to laissez-faire economics, remained fundamentally hostile to the expanded role of the federal government in Johnson's War on Poverty. According to one commentator, they viewed antipoverty legislation as "a computerized version of the New Deal, and . . . reacted accordingly."[42]

By this point, CDGM had become, in many ways, the symbolic battleground of the administration's entire antipoverty program. As one observer pointed out, Stennis's Senate Subcommittee on Appropriations, in reviewing the OEO's request for approximately $1.5 billion for 1966 during hearings in October 1965, spent three hours examining the $1.4 million CDGM summer grant, and only one hour on all of the rest of the agency's budget.[43]

Blacks in the Mississippi movement had played by the ground rules of social protest laid down by the Kennedy administration. Working through the Voter Education Project, at the urging of Attorney General Robert Kennedy and others, they had attempted to register to vote. The Kennedys had hoped voter registration would remove the civil rights crisis from the streets, where it was an unwanted—and very visible—embarrassment. But civil rights activists, despite methodical organizing efforts and heroic sacrifices, had made only limited progress in expanding the black electorate, and local whites had verbally and physically attacked them for their efforts, often with the undisguised collusion of local white authorities.

And officials of the federal government—which civil rights workers believed had given them assurances of protection—stood by as the FBI and the Department of Justice insisted that the restraints of the nation's federalist system made it impossible to intervene on their behalf even when confronted with evidence of flagrant violations of universally accepted civil rights. Activists had come to expect indifference, occasionally even outright hostility, from the FBI, but they had placed faith in the implied promises of the Kennedys and others in the Justice Department. Blacks were thus "doubly disillusioned" by the repeated failures of the Department of Justice to offer protection in Mississippi.[44]

Bitter memories over the way they had been treated at the Democratic National Convention in Atlantic City in 1964 reinforced mounting black estrangement from the federal government at the midpoint of the decade. In August, as the climax to the Freedom Summer project, a virtually all-black MFDP had challenged the "regular" all-white Mississippi delegation to the national convention. Lyndon Johnson—obsessed with having nothing mar what he saw as his convention—had delegated Hubert Humphrey, on penalty of losing the nomination for the vice presidency, to negotiate a settlement that would avoid a noisy, divisive, and potentially televised floor fight.

LBJ's heavy-handed tactics reflected the assumption on the part of whites that they could dictate an outcome to black civil rights activists. Under the resulting proposed compromise, members of the MFDP were offered two seats as at-large delegates. Whites on the credentials committee promised integrated delegations at the 1968 convention, but they told black delegates they should be content with the two seats and agree to sign loyalty pledges to the national party. To add insult to injury, Johnson's forces then selected the two token MFDP representatives. Fannie Lou Hamer, a former sharecropper-turned-civil-rights-activist, had electrified the nation by posing the question "Is this America?" as she exposed the brutal realities of Mississippi in nationally televised testimony. Faced with the take-it-or-leave-it offer tendered by the president's emissaries, she expressed the outrage and disillusionment of many in SNCC and the MFDP: "We didn't come all this way for no two seats." Despite strong pressure from some of the more moderate members of the MFDP and the pleas for compromise from prominent national civil rights leaders like Martin Luther King Jr., the vast majority of the insurgent delegation supported Hamer in rejecting a compromise that sounded like "trickle-down democracy."[45]

Black Mississippians' experiences of "black and white together" during Freedom Summer followed by their rebuff at the 1964 Democratic Convention left a bitter aftertaste. That intense period established a critical benchmark for measuring African American civil rights activists' growing disillusionment with the Johnson administration and with white liberals who claimed to be allied with the movement. Despite what they saw as a betrayal of trust by the national party, blacks in the MFDP declared their willingness to campaign for Johnson in Mississippi, even as many whites in the state's seated delegation made no effort to conceal their preference for the Republican presidential nominee, conservative Arizona senator Barry Goldwater.[46]

Julian Bond, who served as communications director for SNCC, later remembered that fellow activists often asked each other, "Didn't what happened in Atlantic City turn you against regular politics?" Bond came to believe that this estrangement from traditional politics (and from the Johnson administration) gradually emerged "more in retrospect than it did at the time." James Farmer, leader of the Congress of Racial Equality (CORE), believed the White House posture in Atlantic City was less sinister than "stupidly handled" and "a grave tactical error." The compromise that was offered "smacked of . . . an attempt to pick the leaders . . . [which] was bound to go down the wrong way." As Farmer perceptively noted, "There had been too much of a tradition of the establishment picking our leaders, and saying, 'We'll pat this one on the head and oppose this one.'"[47]

It is clear, however, that the events of 1964 helped to erode any sense of deference CDGM members had in dealing with politicians, whether from Jackson, Mississippi, or Washington, D.C. And that frustration and defiance boiled over in February 1966 when CDGM executed a well-staged publicity coup in Washington as they battled for reinstituting funding for their beleaguered organization. In an event that the press described as a "romper lobby," two busloads of African American preschoolers made the long trek from Jackson to the nation's capital, singing freedom songs and other popular anthems with modified lyrics along the way: "Glory, glory, hallelujah, we want our Head Start school!" Wielding crayons, paste, scissors, modeling clay, and "a live mouse in a cage," the diminutive members of the Mississippi delegation descended on a House office building hearing room to demonstrate the benefits of Head Start education under the guidance of their CDGM teachers.[48]

There the forty-eight children—accompanied by twenty-three adults playing dual roles as chaperones and lobbyists—sang "Who stole the cookie from the cookie jar?" and listened to New York Democratic representative Joseph Resnick as he scolded his Mississippi colleagues. In 1964 Resnick had ridden Lyndon Johnson's coattails to a stunning upset of a heavily favored Republican incumbent in New York's Hudson River valley. Although he had few black voters in his district, the wealthy self-made businessman enthusiastically supported Johnson's civil rights activism, and he welcomed the preschoolers and their chaperones to the congressional subcommittee hearing. "I'm very sorry that members of your congressional delegation are not here to greet you," he told them. "Your state representatives, congressmen and senators, instead of cooperating with you and working with the OEO, have thrown up blockades and roadblocks and done everything they could to stop the [Head Start] program."[49]

Given the growing opposition to CAP from white southern politicians and other opponents of the War on Poverty (increasingly, with northern mayors and congressional Republicans prominent among them), Shriver and other officials at OEO had been tempted to deny additional funding to CDGM for a continuation of the initial seven-week Head Start experiment that had been conducted in the summer of 1965. But the children's presence proved that advocates of CDGM could still mount pressure from the Left.

Ultimately, the OEO offered a deal, supported reluctantly by a majority of CDGM board members. The organization was to enlist the accounting service of Ernst and Ernst's local Mississippi office as financial auditors. CDGM would also retain the prestigious Washington, D.C., management consultant firm of Klein and Saks to improve its administrative procedures. Finally, CDGM pledged to seek to include more whites on its board. As a consequence of these concessions, CDGM received a $5.6 million grant to fund more than 120 Head Start centers and 9,000 children, with funding to run from February through the early fall of 1966.[50]

Tom Levin, who had been ousted as director at the first sign of pressure from Mississippi's political leaders, felt intense bitterness as he realized how little—at least in his perception—political capital the executive branch and antipoverty officials in Washington were willing to expend in a conflict with the powerful congressional delegation from Mississippi. "We had anticipated," Levin recalled, "that OEO would not be likely to wage a war on the established state of Mississippi, but we had not anticipated that it would fold this near the starting line. . . . The nightmarish quality of it was that we thought OEO people were our friends. We were trying so hard to be their best program." In Levin's estimation, CDGM had bent over backward in attempting to respond to accusations and to satisfy the concerns of sympathetic auditors and hostile critics, but each effort seemed only to generate further demands. In Levin's words, "It was Kafkaesque."[51]

An African American mother whose children attended a CDGM center and who worked there herself as an aide, captured the sense of frustration—and defiance—felt when the federal government put her organization into funding limbo. "We're not scared, but *they* are in Washington, D.C.," she told an interviewer. "I guess they gave up on us a long time ago; so when they gave us the Headstart program they thought it would be a real-quiet like thing." But, she observed, it didn't take long for Mississippi whites to "figure out we was up to no good. . . . We was being 'uppity.'" Astutely, she put her finger on the thing that most outraged whites. African Americans had seen CDGM as "*ours*, and we were somebody, and not people they'd throw us something, so that they could go home and feel better." What was worse, from the standpoint of whites, was the willingness of blacks to cast off the cloak of deference and submission. "They probably saw that they got us going too fast, and that we'd be real, honest-to-goodness practicing citizens of the U.S.A., and they never have allowed that here, and maybe up in Washington they're not ready for it either."[52]

Veteran Mississippi civil rights activist Lawrence Guyot later reflected that CDGM was a way of "creating [an] indigenous leadership composed of people who had never led anything. . . . It was about making empowerment as contagious as possible." As with the MFDP, "that was what made [it] threatening" to white Mississippians, and even to the federal government. Poverty wars would continue in the Magnolia State. In Washington, D.C., hostile and sympathetic observers alike were soon distracted by other issues, but CDGM loyalists would continue to fight for an organization whose development they had so tenaciously nurtured.[53]

CHAPTER THREE

The Cocktail Hour on the Negro Question

The Watts Riot, the Moynihan Report, and the Search for a Scapegoat

In the year following Lyndon Johnson's delivery of the Howard University speech, as antipoverty activists in Mississippi struggled to make children's voices heard in the corridors of power in Washington, the Johnson administration attempted to make sense of the shifting landscape of civil rights. Against the backdrop of the Watts riots, the Moynihan Report controversy, and the planning for and carefully stage-managed denouement of the White House Conference on Civil Rights in 1965 and 1966, key White House leaders alternately sought to define, reach out to, anoint, and ultimately contain different black leaders. Gone was the easy self-assurance present in the summer of 1965 when administration insiders had spoken confidently of "leapfrogging the movement." If anything, in 1965 and 1966 the administration would often appear to be like a cork bobbing unpredictably along in the shifting currents of events.

The underlying logic of the Howard University speech—which had appeared to puncture the bubble of complacency and self-congratulation in the realm of race relations—offered a compelling framework for making sense of the controversies and crises in the year following its delivery. But the relentless pace of events eroded any White House resolve to stay on message in following up on the promise of Howard. Increasingly preoccupied with the escalation of U.S. involvement in Vietnam, Johnson left far more of the micromanagement of his civil rights policies to aides and to the cabinet agencies than during the first two years of his presidency. Executive branch policymakers balanced dual imperatives, seeking to be proactive while at the same time attempting to "keep the lid on" multiple racial issues that they began to refer to as "social dynamite."[1]

In early June 1965, however, a mood of triumph still prevailed at the White House, with the ebullience of the president and his aides fueled by positive mail from prominent constituents. The civil rights leadership had praised Howard with near unanimity, but the words in one letter from John Kenneth Galbraith dovetailed even more perfectly with Johnson's concerns. Writing from his position at Harvard University, the distinguished economist and former diplomat heralded the Howard speech as a "masterpiece . . . as penetrating a social document as any President has ever presented." Johnson's endorsement of fundamental changes in American race relations resonated around the world, said Galbraith, particularly among the people of color in Africa and Latin America, and strengthened the nation in its ideological struggle with communist revolutionaries. As though he had been privy to internal White House debates about "leapfrogging" in the days surrounding the delivery of the speech, Galbraith argued that Johnson's position "moves the government from a little behind the civil rights movement, where it always has been, to a long step ahead. And it points it in exactly the right direction." He encouraged the administration to ensure that the commencement address was "widely circulated," reasoning that "speeches like this are far too important to waste."[2]

White House aides had similar objectives. In the days immediately following Johnson's speech at Howard University they were determined to get additional political mileage out of the address. Media-savvy Jack Valenti wrote LBJ and suggested that the administration assemble a glossy pamphlet featuring the text of the speech. There was some disagreement about whether the publication should feature pictures of notable civil rights leaders as a means of "globalizing" Howard's message or restrict the graphics to pictures of the president with Howard students at the event itself, thus enhancing Johnson's role.[3]

Ultimately, Richard Goodwin and Jack Valenti, in cooperation with Louis Martin, African American Democratic Party stalwart and head of minority affairs for the Democratic National Committee, oversaw the distribution of thousands of copies of the speech, especially to black Democrats. Johnson and unnamed Howard graduates dominated the accompanying photographs.[4]

A celebratory mood reigned in the White House as the Voting Rights Act cleared Congress, with organized opposition from diehard white segregationists a faint echo of the "bitter end" intensity of the preceding year. Several dozen Dixie legislators even broke ranks to support the administration's legislation. With the bill headed for passage in undiluted form, Johnson sent a written message on August 3 to the SCLC's 9th Annual Conference, closely

On August 6, 1965, the day he signs the Voting Rights Act into law, President Johnson challenges civil rights leaders, including SNCC's John Lewis and CORE's James Farmer, to move beyond protests and demonstrations. Courtesy of the LBJ Library.

patterning his remarks on the language of the Howard speech. As he had in the commencement address two months before, Johnson called on the cooperation and leadership of African Americans in consolidating gains and offering "vision" in "a new phase in this revolution for civil rights" to improve the lives of "those Americans who have been crippled and confined by decades of denial." The president's address centered on the need "to balance the scales of opportunity," but noticeably absent was the promise of "equal results" from two months earlier.[5]

Three days later, on August 6, at the ceremony for signing the Voting Rights Act in the Capitol rotunda, Johnson's speech to the assembled notables focused on the "responsibilities" of blacks to translate the promise of the ballot into meaningful political reforms and to encourage a greater degree of responsiveness in policymaking by all levels of government. The Voting Rights Act was "not only a victory for Negro leadership . . . [but] a great challenge to that leadership . . . which cannot be met simply by protests and demonstrations."

It is instructive to compare the themes and rhetorical strategies of the March 1965 "We Shall Overcome" voting rights message, the June Howard University speech, and the remarks of the president upon signing the Voting Rights Act in August 1965. In March, Johnson had adopted the anthem of the movement—"We Shall Overcome"—as the rallying cry for his own administration's push for ambitious voting rights legislation. In some ways, the Howard speech can be seen as a bridge, a midpoint between the shifting emphases in the two bracketing voting rights messages. There were extensive similarities, in particular, the March speech's metaphor of access: "So we want to open the gates of opportunity. But we are also going to give all our people, black and white, the help that they need to walk through those gates."[6] The metaphors of violence and disfigurement resurfaced too, as Johnson spoke of "the wounds and the weaknesses . . . the inward scars which diminish achievements," laying the blame on American society.[7]

Even as he spoke eloquently to the assembled supporters of the measure, the president revealed a striking capacity for pettiness when he deliberately passed over civil rights leader James Farmer of CORE as he distributed ceremonial pens at the signing of the Voting Rights Act. Farmer, a native of Marshall, Texas, had angered Johnson when he refused to agree to impose a moratorium on civil rights demonstrations by CORE during the 1964 presidential campaign. Whitney Young of the Urban League, Roy Wilkins of the NAACP, A. Philip Randolph of the Negro American Labor Council, and Martin Luther King Jr. of the SCLC had all accepted the administration's position that demonstrations would only serve to aid Republican candidate Barry Goldwater. (SNCC's John Lewis was similarly reluctant to abandon protests, which strained that organization's relationship with the White House.) As Farmer moved close for one of the pens, Johnson pointedly ignored his fellow Texan in favor of congressional and other civil rights leaders. Roy Wilkins of the NAACP and then Whitney Young of the Urban League, Farmer remembered, had repeatedly beseeched the president as Johnson studiously ignored CORE's leader, "looking right at me." "Here's Jim, Mr. President. Jim Farmer. He hasn't got a pen yet." The chief executive reluctantly yielded a souvenir. In Farmer's recollection, "I just walked up and practically took one out of his hand."[8]

Although White House aide Joseph Califano made no reference to the Farmer snub, he later recalled that Johnson, as he passed out the pens, exhorted King and other civil rights leaders to "shift their energies 'from protest to politics.'" As he had in the Howard speech, the president was echoing the sentiments of African Americans like Bayard Rustin who earlier in 1965 had spoken of the importance of shifting "from protest to [coalition] politics."[9]

In June and July, while Johnson and his congressional liaisons applied a legislative full-court press to secure passage of an undiluted Voting Rights Act and then prepared to take the first steps toward its implementation by dispatching federal registrars to problem areas in the South, a handful of other administra-

*Members of the Big Six, here pictured in an Oval Office meeting with Johnson
early in 1964. From left to right, Martin Luther King Jr. of SCLC, President Johnson,
Whitney Young of the Urban League, and James Farmer of CORE. Roy Wilkins
of the NAACP, another member of the Big Six, was present for the discussion
of the administration's civil rights priorities. Courtesy of the LBJ Library.*

tion officials began to wrestle with the organizational challenges of planning
the White House Conference on Civil Rights called for in Johnson's Howard
University speech. Louis Martin, from his position on the Democratic National Committee, expressed concern that limiting participation might leave
key administration allies feeling wounded if they were passed over. One solution to this perplexing problem might be to have one large plenary session that
would include the broadest possible cross section of African American leadership and white civil rights supporters. Then, presumably, the substantive work
of the conference would be accomplished among more selective company,
especially the "Big Six" civil rights leaders.[10]

Harry McPherson's reminiscence about the Johnson era suggested just how
sweeping was the administration's assumption that a handful of black leaders
could speak for the aspirations of "their" people: "It was like bringing George
Meany and Walter Reuther and four labor leaders in [to the White House]
to talk for labor. . . . You had the six in to talk for the Negroes."[11] Throughout
the first two years of the Johnson administration, the group had consisted of
James Farmer of CORE, Martin Luther King Jr. of SCLC, John Lewis of SNCC,

A. Philip Randolph of the Brotherhood of Sleeping Car Porters, Roy Wilkins of the NAACP, and Whitney Young of the National Urban League. Although the "Big Six" as a linguistic construction failed to include Dorothy Height of the National Council of Negro Women, a noteworthy civil rights leader in her own right, Johnson did often include Height in meetings.[12]

Amid all the attention to Johnson's invocation of the phrase "We Shall Overcome," commentators and critics gave little attention to that portion of his March 1965 address to a Joint Session of Congress that called for voting rights legislation. He urged each of his listeners to "look within our own hearts and our own communities . . . [and to] put our shoulder to the wheel to root out injustice wherever it exists." The freedom struggle was being waged "in Buffalo as well as in Birmingham, in Philadelphia as well as in Selma," and the president warned against the temptation of "any section [to] look with prideful righteousness on the trouble in another section." "There is no Negro problem," the president declared to the assembled lawmakers and a television audience of millions. "There is no Southern problem. There is no Northern problem. There is only an American problem."[13]

But Johnson's comments proved at least partially prescient as the largest urban riot of the post–World War II era rocked the West Coast. On August 11, 1965, five days after the signing ceremony for the Voting Rights Act, African Americans in the Watts area of southern Los Angeles rioted following an altercation between a black motorist and officers of the notoriously racist police department. The rioting, which wound down only on its sixth day, ultimately claimed the lives of thirty-four individuals, three-quarters of them black, and left nearly 1,000 others injured. The riot led to as many as 4,000 arrests, destroyed 232 businesses, and damaged over 600 others, with resulting property damage climbing well over $30 million.[14]

The outbreak of rioting in Watts shocked Johnson and fueled emotions that careened between rage and profound depression. He initially hunkered down at the ranch in Texas where news of the conflagration in southern California reached him. After an initial warning to White House aides to steer clear of any involvement in Los Angeles, he drove around the sprawling ranch for hours, refusing to take telephone calls, even from close aide Joseph Califano, for several days. Aside from a brief press release from Bill Moyers expressing presidential disapproval of the use of violence to seek remedies for grievances and the usual rhetoric labeling the unrest "tragic and shocking," the White House remained uncharacteristically silent.[15]

The timing of the Watts uprising just days after the passage and signing of sweeping voting rights legislation struck the president forcibly, a coincidence that journalists and historians would spend the next three-and-a-half decades etching into the nation's cultural memory of the 1960s. Help was on the way to the poorest of America's poor, Johnson had been insisting, yet Watts indicated that some African Americans were driven to take what he called "unwise actions out of frustration, impatience, and anger."

On Sunday morning, Johnson finally began telephoning for updates on events in Los Angeles. "How is it possible . . . after all we've accomplished? How could it be? Is the world topsy-turvy?" the president would ask his closest aides. A common theme running through each of their recollections was a sense that Johnson felt betrayed after "all that [he] had done" for black Americans.[16]

The politically savvy Johnson instinctively knew that the rioting in Watts would alienate the many whites who felt that the civil rights struggle had been won, jeopardizing any further legislative agenda, which was already viewed by this constituency as either unnecessary or misguided. And, like most white Americans of his generation, he saw in the history of the Reconstruction era a warning of the dangers posed by black excesses. Even as National Guard units struggled to bring the riot under control, LBJ told his new aide, Joseph Califano, that Watts was history repeating itself. According to Califano, who had left his Pentagon post under Robert McNamara only weeks earlier, Johnson saw parallels between the rioters and the way impatient freedmen had taken rash actions in the era of Radical Reconstruction in the South.[17] If Watts was any indication of what African Americans would do as they were emboldened by newly passed legislation guaranteeing their rights, Johnson lamented, "Negroes will end up pissing in the aisles of the Senate." It was a vision he clearly associated with the racist historical accounts of "Negro Rule" following the Civil War, and one which evoked the worst iconography set in celluloid in D. W. Griffith's 1915 epic *Birth of a Nation*, in which barefooted drunken black legislators had desecrated southern statehouses.[18]

The intensity of the Watts uprising came as a surprise, but the possibility of urban unrest had preoccupied the administration for months. In early May 1965, one month before the Howard speech, Special Counsel to the President Lee White, a Kennedy holdover, had strongly urged the president to respond affirmatively to Roy Wilkins's request that Johnson consider addressing the annual NAACP convention in Denver. In White's opinion, this would "strengthen Roy's hand" and bolster his "somewhat weakened position in his own organization." The timing—the end of June—and symbolic value of a major address to a primarily black organization would be desirable as well, White noted, "in view of the fact that we will then be in the midst of our 'long hot summer.'"[19] Johnson ultimately chose the Howard University venue as his forum, but White's memo offers compelling proof that at least some within the administration were well aware that the potential for urban disturbances existed in the summer of 1965 and were seeking ways to forestall it.[20] In an interview in *Look* magazine at the beginning of June, for example, Attorney General Nicholas Katzenbach focused on the dangers of teen unemployment. He warned: "Unless communities work hard to look at their problems and see how young people can be employed during the summer, and unless they face up to their slums . . . we could have trouble in any one or more of 25 to 30 cities this summer."[21]

Administration insiders' use of the phrase "long, hot summer" was a direct outgrowth of a spate of urban disorders in July and August of 1964.[22] The first had occurred in Harlem only two weeks after Johnson signed the Civil Rights Act into law, when police arrested more than 480 "rioters" during five consecutive days of unrest following the New York Police Department's fatal shooting of a fifteen-year-old named James Powell.[23] Spreading like brushfires, riots subsequently erupted in Rochester, New York; Jersey City, Elizabeth, and Paterson, New Jersey; Dixmoor, Illinois, a mixed-race suburb of Chicago; and Philadelphia, Pennsylvania. Following an extensive FBI study of the different outbreaks, J. Edgar Hoover relayed to Lyndon Johnson his conclusions that the riots were part of a growing problem of juvenile delinquency. (James Powell, the shooting victim in Harlem, was described in internal FBI correspondence as "a young colored hoodlum.") Although the infamous Red-hunter assured Johnson that members of the American Communist Party had been involved in the rioting in different cities once it developed, he reluctantly conceded that there was "no systematic planning" or "official instigation" by the "agitators." And he was emphatic that the riots were "not a direct outgrowth of conventional civil rights protest."[24]

In the spring of 1965 the president had created the Task Force on Urban Problems, chaired by LeRoy Collins, former Florida governor and director of the Community Relations Service (CRS), in the Commerce Department, and including Attorney General Nicholas Katzenbach, Sargent Shriver of the OEO, and other cabinet-level heads. The task force had arranged meetings with mayors of nearly one dozen major metropolitan areas deemed to be "hotspots"—the less incendiary CRS euphemism was "target cities"—in an effort to reduce tension levels in advance of the summer months.

On June 4, 1965, the same day President Johnson had addressed black graduates at Howard University, a diverse cross section of black New York City leaders met with Mayor John Lindsay and Governor Nelson Rockefeller. A host of problems, they argued, had not been addressed since the Harlem riot of the previous summer. The *New York Times* reported that urban officials in cities across the state — including Rochester — were working "to settle Negro grievances in advance of what might be called the summer deadline."[25] (Los Angeles officials, including Democratic Mayor Sam Yorty, rebuffed the task force, a point which CRS representatives were quick to point out, both privately and ultimately publicly, in the immediate aftermath of the Watts rioting.)[26]

The task force operated under the President's Council on Equal Opportunity (PCEO), which was created by executive order early in February 1965 and chaired by Hubert Humphrey. The PCEO was to serve as a clearinghouse for programs of the various federal agencies dealing with civil rights–related issues. The vice president served as what Johnson himself called a "point man." At the time, Humphrey already headed the President's Committee on Equal Employment Opportunity (PCEEO), having inherited the position in which Johnson had labored — usually without much public acknowledgment — during the Kennedy administration.[27] (The virtually identical acronyms, PCEO and PCEEO, caused considerable confusion among those observers seeking to make sense of the myriad of task forces and agencies charged with overseeing civil rights administration and policy coordination.)

On May 13, seeking additional means to reduce tensions, Johnson announced in a cabinet meeting the creation of the Youth Opportunity Campaign, a special initiative intended to increase by over 500,000 the number of summer jobs for teenagers. The president simultaneously juggled the books and reallocated other antipoverty appropriations to expand the War on Poverty's Neighborhood Youth Corps by another 50,000 jobs. Adding to the vice president's duties, the president appointed Humphrey as chairman of still another special task force to coordinate plans for this additional summer employment. The Minnesotan invested a tremendous amount of energy in seeking the cooperation of private industry, asking thousands of companies to hire one or more summer "trainees," depending on their size.[28]

Ultimately, Humphrey's task force managed to secure an infusion of $15 million of antipoverty funding to support CAP efforts and another $20 million in support of 31,000 jobs created under the Neighborhood Youth Corps.[29] Both programs fell under the jurisdiction of the OEO, and director Sargent Shriver endorsed Humphrey's efforts. In late July 1965, with his penchant for seizing upon any favorable press for the OEO, he forwarded a news story to the president arguing that "the most significant single thing combating potential riots this summer is your war against poverty."[30]

In the days and weeks following Watts, the Johnson administration and civil rights activists engaged in a limited amount of finger-pointing and mutual recrimination, with both sides claiming the other was more shaken, more at a loss.[31] But a fair amount of introspection took place as well.[32]

Less than two weeks after the riot ended, Johnson's press secretary, George Reedy, struggled to understand the meaning of the riot and its consequences for the Johnson administration antipoverty and civil rights programs. There would be endless debates about the causes of the riot, said Reedy, but they seemed self-evident to him. One need only drive through the impoverished and desperate slums ("I did two weeks ago") to understand that "the mere existence of a segregated community in modern society creates a 'we and they' — a 'friend and enemy' — psychology. . . . People are not going to live peacefully under such circumstances unless they are cowed[,] and this country has passed the point where Negroes can be cowed even if the majority of whites desire to do so."

As Johnson's press secretary, Reedy was also aware of the way in which the new media shaped public responses to the issue of civil rights. It was not simply that the camera had begun to shift its gaze from long-suffering black victims to angry and apparently unthinking rioters. It was also the way in which the powerful images of urban disorder threatened even the most respectable middle-class black activists. "Unless they are extraordinarily careful, the Civil Rights leaders run the risk of identifying their movements with ordinary hooliganism and savagery," warned Reedy. And white Americans would increasingly see black America through the prism of civil disorder and violent cities.[33]

At the same time, many civil rights leaders privately — and occasionally publicly — concluded that the rioting was an indictment of their own personal and organizational failures to reach out to a broader black constituency that would include the poorest of the poor in the cities of the North and West. CORE's James Farmer put it most bluntly: "Civil rights organizations have failed. . . . No one had any roots in the ghetto." For Bayard Rustin, the rioting in Los Angeles was a sobering reminder that "coalition" politics was an issue that had little resonance for the urban poor, especially angry teenagers. "We must hold ourselves responsible for not reaching them," he said. "Roy [Wilkins], Martin [Luther King Jr.], and I haven't done a damn thing about it. We've done plenty to get votes in the South and seats in the lunchrooms, but we've had no program for these youngsters."[34]

Johnson's first extensive public response to Watts was calculated to please those concerned that the White House might seem to be endorsing urban unrest as a form of legitimate social protest. On August 20, the president deliberately linked the actions of rioters with those antiblack extremists: "A rioter with a Molotov cocktail in his hands is not fighting for civil rights any more than a

Klansman with a sheet on his back and a mask on his face. They are both . . . lawbreakers, destroyers of constitutional rights and liberties, and ultimately destroyers of a free America." This was the public "get-tough" response, and running beneath the surface of the president's rhetoric were undercurrents evoking the language of insurgency and counterinsurgency, usually reserved for events falling under the purview of the State Department and the Pentagon.

Behind the scenes, however, Johnson quickly directed Califano and White House counsel Lee White to prepare a wide range of "ameliorative" federal responses. The programs were to be targeted carefully at families so that there would be no perception of directly rewarding the activities of the rioters themselves.[35] The same public relations high-wire act of dealing with the rioters while acknowledging the bleak circumstances faced by black urban residents would be repeated again and again in succeeding summers.

For any critics tempted to suggest that the Watts riot was the by-product of the War on Poverty, the administration could argue that it had not made its way to some of the poorest sections of Los Angeles due to the recalcitrance of powerful Democratic mayor Sam Yorty.[36] The Watts area had received almost no antipoverty funding in the period before August 1965. That soon changed, as an astonishing number of antipoverty programs in Watts began to take off literally overnight when the president approved the recommendations of a task force created for the express purpose of funneling money into Los Angeles.[37]

Still, the dissonance between Johnson's tough public pronouncements and the less-publicized crash program of antipoverty aid created a problem of appearances. Robert Weaver, administrator of the Housing and Home Finance Agency (and soon to be named secretary of the newly created department of Housing and Urban Development), identified this tension in a memo in late August as an avalanche of federal dollars began making its way to selected programs in South Central Los Angeles: "We should avoid giving the impression that riots pay off." Weaver, one of the highest-ranking black officials in the Johnson administration, urged that federal antipoverty aid be spread across greater Los Angeles as a preemptive response to expected charges that the administration was "rewarding the rioters."[38]

This was certainly the view of a growing number of white Americans. On June 8, 1965, C. Harrison Mann, an Arlington member of the Virginia House of Delegates, had written to the president to express his dismay over the Howard University commencement address. The speech constituted "one of your more demagogic efforts thus far," he scolded Johnson, identifying the core theme of the president's message as "the preaching of hatred and racism." If Johnson were to persist in a similar vein, it would "just [be] a matter of time before everyone questions your judgment on every matter, which would be most regrettable." White House aide Hobart Taylor penned a perfunctory reply using the standard language of "the president acknowledges receipt of your views," language usually reserved for "kook" mail and implacably hostile constituents.

Two months later, following the Watts riots, Mann sent a follow-up to Johnson aide Bill Moyers. The explosion of urban unrest in southern Los Angeles was proof in the Virginian's mind that the "sentiments" of the Howard address "and similar pronouncements are coming home to roost." Mann enclosed a news clipping quoting a black businessman in Los Angeles, who stated, "When the President of the United States tells you you have a hard time that sort of makes it official. Now you give that thought to men who are not prepared and you have trouble." "Regrettably," Mann concluded, "Mr. Johnson's statement following the riot simply took the blame off these people and makes the situation worse. . . . I suggest [that the president] pipe down."[39] His private words echoed Los Angeles Police Department chief William Parker's very public dig at the president's overall civil rights policies. While the flames were still roaring in the Watts district, Parker told reporters that the violence stemmed from a climate where "you keep telling people they are unfairly treated and teach them disrespect for the law."[40]

If August 1965 had been a month of elation and shock with the signing of the Voting Rights Act followed so closely by the Watts riot, September proved to be a time of transition. Speechwriter Richard Goodwin took an indefinite leave of absence from the White House and gravitated toward the Robert Kennedy camp. What ordinarily would have been seen as the ultimate act of disloyalty in the eyes of Johnson was softened to an extent by Goodwin's authorship of many of the president's speech-making triumphs. Goodwin had indeed fulfilled LBJ's expectations that he serve as "regular alter ego." And the president valued the rich collaboration he and the John F. Kennedy holdover had shared and — perhaps more importantly — the eloquence that had sprung from Goodwin's pen but that was associated in the public mind with Lyndon Johnson.[41]

September also witnessed a major shake-up in the organization of civil rights oversight in the executive branch. The vice president's Youth Opportunity Campaign, under the auspices of the PCEO, had enjoyed mixed but generally positive results, thanks to Humphrey's fanatical devotion and energetic follow-through. But part of the original charge given to the PCEO — or so Johnson later claimed — was to examine the possibility of "recommending consolidations and elimination of . . . numerous inter-agency committees and bodies" related to civil rights, attempting to streamline enforcement and policymaking.[42] The president had given Humphrey a relatively free hand, and the vice president was eager to make the PCEO a vital and leading player in the administration's overall civil rights strategy.

By May, Humphrey was speaking of the necessity of "consolidation" of all the federal government's civil rights functions, but the exact nature and extent of such a reorganization remained unclear.[43] The White House, too, was canvassing at least some of the different agencies and executive departments involved in civil rights policy and enforcement for recommendations and ideas about ways to reorganize and streamline a bureaucratic flowchart of ever-increasing complexity. LeRoy Collins, director of the CRS within the Department of Commerce, responded to this White House request by calling for a single civil rights office within the executive branch to be known simply as the Agency for Civil Rights.[44] The new tendency toward "consolidation" was all the more striking because from the passage of the Civil Rights Act of 1957 up until 1965 the dominant trend in the executive branch's response to civil rights had been one of proliferation. But all such speculation about a shake-up in the organizational structure of the administration's civil rights effort was hypothetical until Johnson elected to act.

In the middle of September, Hubert Humphrey, following up on a desire to open better lines of communication between the administration and major civil rights organizations, convened a meeting on board the presidential yacht *Honey Fitz*. Attendees included the SCLC's Martin Luther King Jr. and Andrew Young; Floyd McKissick, a rising leader in CORE, who would take over the directorship from James Farmer early in 1966; Whitney Young of the Urban League; and Clarence Mitchell of the Washington NAACP, arguably the single most influential black lobbyist on Capitol Hill.[45]

Anticipating a harmonious discussion, Humphrey and his staff members instead were effectively blindsided in a heated exchange that in the memory of one participant "almost turned the boat over." The civil rights leaders took the administration to task for its shortcomings in implementing and enforcing the Voting Rights Act more vigorously. Floyd McKissick raised pointed questions about the Moynihan Report—so influential in the drafting of LBJ's Howard University speech but now receiving heavy media attention in the aftermath of the Watts riot because of its focus on the destabilizing influence of "pathology" in "the Negro family."[46] Humphrey was taken aback by the intensity of the civil rights leaders' criticisms, but the meeting served its purpose: the vice president felt it was more important than ever to strengthen ties between the White House and civil rights organizations, and the most logical forum for such a renewal would be the proposed White House Conference on Civil Rights.

Near the end of September, the vice president urged Johnson to convene the White House conference in November in order to fulfill the promise of the Howard speech. But the ground was shifting under Humphrey. On September 18, 1965, Johnson indicated privately to Joseph Califano that he planned to remove the responsibility of serving as civil rights "point man" from the vice president's shoulders, telling his assistant, "[Humphrey's] got enough other things to do." After only seven months in existence, both the PCEO and the older PCEEO were to be dismantled. Working with Attorney General Katzenbach and White House counsel Lee White, Califano frantically put together a reorganization proposal moving civil rights enforcement into various bureaucratic line agencies with ultimate oversight residing in the attorney general's office.[47]

Hubert Humphrey was on his way to Washington's National Airport for a trip home to Minnesota when Johnson unceremoniously summoned him to the White House. There the president informed him of what was already a fait accompli and asked for his blessing of these new plans "to strengthen our new civil rights efforts."[48] In Joseph Califano's vivid memory of the Oval Office meeting—surreal even by the Texan's standards—Johnson distanced himself from the demotion he was announcing by adopting the third person as he worked over the vice president: "*They say*, Hubert . . . that the best way to . . . speed up Negro rights would be to fold up a lot of the responsibilities you've got and put them on the Attorney General's shoulders. . . . Hubert, this is the kind of thing *they* have been recommending to me. But I didn't want to move on it without talking to you and getting your views. Do you think it's a good idea to strengthen our civil rights efforts this way?" The meeting was effectively over, and at its conclusion Califano remembered that everyone in the Oval Office "knew [Humphrey had] just been castrated."[49]

In his oral history of his years in the White House, Harry McPherson argued that Johnson "had tremendous love and affection for Hubert Humphrey . . . immense admiration for his heart and for his brains." But there was also an undercurrent of the contempt of the strong for the weak. McPherson and Johnson shared a belief that the vice president "was not tough enough. . . . He's not capable of the kind of ruthlessness that a great politician needs to have. He's too gentle with people, and he's too inclined to say yes to too many people. Mrs. Humphrey once said, 'It's a good thing he wasn't born a woman, because he can't say no.'"[50]

The acid-laden repetition of "*They say*, Hubert" was Johnson the manipulator and bully at his worst, and to compound the awkwardness of the vice president's dismissal Johnson struck upon the idea of having Humphrey publicly suggest that the impetus for the reorganization grew from his own ideas. LBJ pressured Califano to draft a memo along these lines for Humphrey's signature. Humphrey chafed at the indignity but ultimately complied, lending his name to a document that reasoned that "interagency committees and other interagency arrangements would now only diffuse responsibility."

In further recommending that the responsibilities of the overarching PCEEO be reassigned, Humphrey (or, rather, White House staffers directly commissioned by the president to write a memo for the vice president's signature) acknowledged Johnson's "deep personal attachment . . . for the work of the Committee" and his earlier tenure at its head. But abolishing the committee and parceling out its duties would "result in more effective operation." The memo concluded: "I am especially pleased and proud . . . to recommend these consolidations and terminations to you."[51] With his signature, the vice president gave his blessing to the dismantling of both the PCEO and the PCEEO and vastly diminished his authority as the administration's civil rights "point man."

Realizing that the sudden demotion of Humphrey might give the appearance of a top-down palace coup, Califano and Johnson sought to allay the fears of key civil rights principals. Califano reached out to Louis Martin and planned to call LeRoy Collins to "get him aboard." Clearly concerned, Califano also mused aloud about "which, if any, Congressmen and Negro leaders should be notified" in advance of the press release concerning the reorganization. CORE's James Farmer remembered receiving a call from White House counsel Lee White on the day that Humphrey announced his own demotion. "The President wants you to know that this in no way indicates downgrading of civil rights at all," White insisted. "It's just to better organize things here." Farmer entertained suspicions that White was essentially reading from an Oval Office script: "I felt that he protested too much after he raised the question."[52]

Wiley Branton posed another potential problem. Throughout the spring and summer of 1965 Branton had served as the executive secretary of Humphrey's PCEO. From 1961 to 1965, the well-respected civil rights veteran had directed the Voter Education Project under the auspices of the Southern Regional Council in Atlanta. His program had helped add hundreds of thousands of African Americans to the voting rolls of the South. The eradication of any executive agency with a black member in a prominent position—particularly someone as respected as Branton—threatened to become a public relations nightmare. Early on the morning of September 24, the White House directed Humphrey to inform Branton of the reorganization and to summon him to a White House meeting scheduled in Califano's office with the president in attendance. In briefing Johnson for the meeting, Califano drolly noted that "Branton will suspect that the vice president's recommendation that the Council be terminated may not have been entirely his own idea."[53] Califano and other White House aides sought to reassure Branton that the elimination of the PCEO was in fact the logical fulfillment of its function—it had in part been charged with reorganizing the executive branch's approach to civil rights—and not an indication of Johnson's disapproval of the PCEO's track record. Branton, accordingly, was to be offered a job as a "special assistant" to Attorney General Nicholas Katzenbach, charged with working to increase black levels of voter registration in response to the Voting Rights Act.

From the White House perspective, the meeting went smoothly. Hearing successively from Califano and then the president that he was "just the man to get the job done"—the prelude to full-blown application of the "Johnson treatment"—Branton wisely accepted his new appointment. With the PCEO sinking behind him, he hardly had a fallback position. He packed up his desk for the move to the Justice Department.[54]

Having thoroughly humiliated the vice president in private and then dispatched his underling, Califano, to gain Humphrey's signatures on documents to which he bore no authorial relationship, Johnson was still not through with the Minnesotan. Once again, Califano would play the hatchet man. He worked into the early morning hours of September 24 to line up the choreography. Later that day the president would expect Humphrey to appear at a White House briefing hastily arranged by Bill Moyers in the Cabinet Room. Instead of Johnson informing the public of the reshuffling of civil rights responsibilities, Humphrey, brave captain of a sinking ship, would break the news that the PCEO, which he headed, had just been "consolidated" out of existence and that the PCEEO was now defunct. Dutifully following the script, at the press conference he awkwardly delivered the news of his own ouster. Reporters peppered him with questions: "You no longer have an official title?" "That is correct," Humphrey replied, "except for Vice President."[55] The cheeky edge to the answer was the only hint of departure from what one historian has aptly described as "a posture of loyal humiliation."[56]

The rationale for the reorganization could be justified as an attempt to remove the "middleman"—in this case Humphrey, in his capacity as head of the PCEO—and streamline the coordination of civil rights responsibilities, with cabinet officers now reporting directly to the president.[57] But civil rights leaders and their liberal allies could not help but be suspicious as they witnessed such a fundamental restructuring. And the White House's over-anxious efforts to justify the civil rights reorganization did little to remove their qualms.

The rioting in Watts and the White House civil rights reshuffling took on additional overtones as a full-blown public relations crisis developed following the unofficial release of the ill-fated Moynihan Report. Harry McPherson first sensed the potential for trouble when he was laid up in the hospital recovering from a minor surgical procedure in the spring of 1965. He remembered one visitor especially vividly: Daniel Patrick Moynihan arrived with a bottle of scotch and a bound report entitled "The Negro Family: The Case for National Action" and emblazoned with the words "For Official Use Only." After reading through the material and talking with its author, McPherson felt the security classification probably was insufficient. The document, he recalled in classic understated fashion, "was politically charged."[58]

Moynihan had been compiling research for the report as early as December 1964. He was influenced by Stanley Elkins's controversial 1959 work *Slavery*. In an explosive comparison, Elkins had argued that slavery had "infantilized" blacks much as the Holocaust had reduced the Jews in Nazi Germany's concentration camps to a state of dependency. Moynihan had received a copy of Elkins's work from Nathan Glazer four years after its publication and was instantly drawn to its bold, sweeping arguments.[59] The book appeared to offer further corroboration of E. Franklin Frazier's work on the harmful impact of slavery on African American families. Moynihan was similarly drawn to Kenneth Clark's newly published *Dark Ghetto*, in particular to a chapter on the breakdown of black families.[60]

Relying heavily on Elkins and Clark, Moynihan was thus predisposed to view nontraditional black family structures in terms of "damage" or "pathology." If a long history of racial oppression, particularly in the slavery era, had served to weaken "the" Negro family, resulting in a higher number of out-of-wedlock births and a matriarchal family structure, then Moynihan had powerful ammunition for his arguments that preferential treatment for blacks might be in order, to compensate for past injustices. From a bureaucrat's "empire building" perspective, surely the Labor Department would play a role in fashioning programs to remedy the problems.

Moynihan and his staff researchers' revelatory moment evidently occurred when—in the course of studying data related to employment and welfare—they noticed what appeared to be a statistical anomaly in the first years of the 1960s. As unemployment figures began to drop, applications for welfare were rising sharply. According to the reigning economic models and past experience, these two data tracks were supposed to rise and fall together. But something had changed. At the time the Labor Department researchers spoke in terms of the numbers "disaggregating." More than two decades later Moynihan was able to express the disjuncture in more accessible language: "The numbers went blooey on me."[61] His attempt to explain what was happening became the Moynihan Report.

The preface to "The Negro Family: The Case for National Action" anticipated, although in a more anxious tone, the rhetorical tenor of the Howard University speech that Johnson would deliver just weeks later: "The United States is approaching a new crisis in race relations." "The fundamental problem," Moynihan wrote, "is that of family structure. The evidence—not final, but powerfully persuasive—is that the Negro family in the urban ghettos is crumbling."[62]

The chapters of the Moynihan Report that were ultimately to draw the most consistent fire were the second, "The Negro American Family," and the fourth, with its more eye-catching title "The Tangle of Pathology." (The author borrowed the latter from Kenneth Clark's *Dark Ghetto* chapter entitled "The Pathology of the Ghetto.") Moynihan concluded his bleak appraisal with a metaphor suggesting strangulation: "the tangle of pathology is tightening."[63]

In fact, his data showed two diverging tendencies. Moynihan wrote on the very first page of the report of "a middle-class group [that] has managed to save itself," a group that was making steady progress. The weight of his rhetoric, however, emphasized the negative trends, focusing on the lives of those blacks who were losing ground. For "vast numbers of the unskilled, poorly educated city working class the fabric of conventional social relationships has all but disintegrated," he wrote. "So long as this situation persists, the cycle of poverty and disadvantage will continue to repeat itself."[64] Moreover, the lack of comparative data on white families from similar socioeconomic backgrounds fueled the suspicions of those who thought that Moynihan—like earlier writers—sought to demonstrate that the great majority of African Americans were "beyond the melting pot."[65]

As had E. Franklin Frazier's *The Negro Family in the United States*, Moynihan committed the grievous tactical error of implying a singular cause for the multiple problems of black Americans. By implication and extension, this universalized the discussion of "pathology" and dysfunction, removing it from the confines of the "ghetto" and linking, in the minds of the white public, the very idea of *the* black family with crippling family problems.[66]

The report made a "case for national action," but the contours of a plan of attack were not mapped out. Thus it was easy for Moynihan's opponents to label the report a diagnosis—and a flawed one in the minds of the critics—with no prescription for cure. The report vaguely called for "a national effort towards the problems of Negro Americans," to be focused around "the question of family structure": "The object should be to strengthen the Negro family so as to enable it to raise and support its members *as do other families*. After that, how this group of Americans chooses to run its affairs, take advantage of its opportunities, or fail[s] to do so, is none of the nation's business."[67]

Debate still rages among scholars and historical participants about whether and when Moynihan's findings were to have been made public. Moynihan himself has resolutely insisted that he did not intend for the report to be immediately publicized, at least not in the form in which it initially circulated in the executive branch. And he defended the report's lack of prescriptive solutions, concerned that arguments over remedies (and even preemptive bureaucratic "turf battles" over which agencies would be most involved in administering them) would dilute the statistical impact of his bleak prognosis. "The Negro Family: A Case for National Action" was first and foremost intended to be just that, a wake-up call and a rallying cry for further debate. It also would provide a statistical baseline against which any future policies and programs and their ameliorative impact might be measured. Moynihan reasoned that if he could convince Johnson and the White House's inner circle of policymakers of the dire circumstances of black families the president might endorse aggressive policies to begin addressing the perceived crisis.[68]

Whether or not the Moynihan Report was truly intended for only a handful of influential policymakers, once Moynihan's findings began to be discussed in the press many African Americans interpreted the "wake-up call" as a stinging slap in the face. A number of prominent black critics soon attacked the report as the worst kind of "blaming the victim."[69] James Farmer later captured this mood in his regular newspaper column, "The Core of It." The civil rights leader and CORE national director fumed in response to the debate over the Moynihan Report: "I'm angry . . . really angry and I intend to spell out this anger in just one more effort to convince somebody, anybody, down in the places of power that the cocktail hour on the 'Negro Question' is over and that we are sick unto death of being analyzed, mesmerized, bought, sold and slobbered over while the same evils that are the ingredients of our oppression go unattended."[70]

Although the Moynihan Report attracted the most scrutiny by the press and interested constituencies *after* the Watts rioting in early August, copies of "The Case for National Action"—stamped "For Official Use Only"—had in fact found their way into the hands of the press as early as mid-July, several weeks before the unrest in Los Angeles erupted. The White House seems to have approved of the Labor Department's leaking of the report. In retrospect, that decision appears incredibly shortsighted, but it is an indication of just how variable were the political and ideological winds in the summer and fall of 1965. A trickle of articles soon began to appear summarizing the overall thrust of Moynihan's research.[71] The first, written by John D. Pomfret, appeared in the *New York Times* less than a week after the first public discussion of how the White House Conference on Civil Rights would approach the agenda detailed in the Howard University speech. By prearrangement with the president's staff, Pomfret did not reveal Moynihan's authorship, instead attributing the report to a White House "study group."[72]

It took the Watts riot to direct widespread attention to the controversial research.[73] Reporters made frequent reference to Moynihan's findings as they attempted to explain to a shocked American public the roots of the anger among urban blacks that might produce such a violent outburst. (The fact of the general public's relative amnesia concerning earlier outbreaks of urban violence in 1964 bears repeating; in some respects it tracked Lyndon Johnson's own selective memory and led to the sense of "shock" when the Watts riots broke out.) The coincidence in media coverage of Watts with Moynihan's research produced an understandable but erroneous linkage in the minds of many whites and blacks, that somehow the report was a direct federal response to the urban crisis in southern California.[74] As scholars Rainwater and Yancey conclude, "Because of the newspaper coverage, the Moynihan Report was taken as the government's explanation for the riots. . . . Watts gave the Moynihan Report new meaning."[75]

Moynihan had been massaging his statistical data for a period of months, although the extensive urban unrest in 1964 must have been in the back of his mind, and the author later noted that Watts represented "dramatic confirmation of my bet that things were going to hell at the bottom."[76] Most of the early criticisms of the Moynihan Report occurred without the critics having read the document in its entirety. Instead, rumor and innuendo and the media's penchant for quoting Moynihan's conclusions without caveats or context fueled an atmosphere in which the anger expressed by James Farmer and other critics, particularly in the black community, was both predictable and understandable.

In his Howard speech in early June, Johnson had referred to the problem of fractured black family life, but the majority of journalists had made only passing reference to this portion of the text. There were a handful of notable exceptions. An editorial in the *Economist* had noted that "the President departed from the conventional civil rights speech . . . in talking frankly of a subject which liberals prefer to skirt: the breakdown of the Negro family." The

Economist hoped that the White House conference Johnson had called for would be "fruitful" precisely because of the president's "willingness to speak about the unspeakable."[77]

In a similar vein, Mary McGrory of the *Washington Star* had argued that the Howard speech struck "an authentic new note," a dramatic departure because—according to her reading of the text—Johnson was asking African Americans "to help find the remedy for their own social plight." McGrory, one of the first prominent female journalists of her era, had been widely praised for her reporting of the Army-McCarthy hearings; and she would win a Pulitzer Prize for her columns on the Watergate scandal. "The core of the Johnson speech," she argued in her nationally syndicated column, was "the failure of Negro family life." African Americans speaking out on "this hitherto most delicate subject" "have run the risk of being called 'Uncle Tom.'" In addressing this charged topic, the president was essentially creating a "safe" space for debate, thus freeing those whom the *Economist* editorial had categorized as "the more responsible Negro leaders" to weigh in on the topic with a measure of political cover. Commentators Rainwater and Yancey subsequently described the tenor of McGrory's article as the "they-should-pull-up-their-own-socks" school of "self-improvement."[78]

Even within the black community, there was often praise for the president's concerns about the problems of black family life. Aminda Wilkins, the wife of NAACP director Roy Wilkins, wrote Johnson an effusive letter five weeks later, prompted by an article in the *New York Times*. A reporter who clearly had access to Moynihan's "Case for National Action" had focused on White House plans to make black family life a central part of the planned White House Conference on Civil Rights. Aminda Wilkins related to the president how she had drawn together African American women earlier in the decade to draft a "Call to Action for the Negro Community," focusing on the "deterioration of Negro family life and the failure of organized groups to do anything about it." The report argued that "the Negro community itself should be concerned and take action." The women had presented their recommendations to Whitney Young of the Urban League and to the NAACP leadership. In Aminda Wilkins's recollection, "While their executives were in sympathy with our idea, their Boards felt that they could not, in effect, admit that there were social lags in the Negro community."[79]

Throughout the summer of 1965, before the public outrage from black civil rights leaders and academics across the spectrum became widespread, civil rights leaders gave several Moynihan-like pronouncements. Although the deterioration of black families was hardly the centerpiece of the speech, Whitney

Young's address to the fifty-fifth annual conference of the Urban League spoke candidly of disproportionately higher numbers of female-headed households in African American communities before declaring emphatically that "the crucial element in any crusade designed to strengthen that family . . . is the Negro male!" The ensuing language described a matriarchal black family forged in a history of hostility and the corresponding "psychological castration" of black men. Speaking with conviction about a gendered universe that shared essentially the same matriarchal patterns described by Moynihan, Young concluded that "in the Negro family, as is true in all others, strength and stability must emerge from a father who can share the responsibilities within the family, as provider and as an appropriate role model."[80]

In the first days of August, on the eve of the Watts uprising, all indications had been that the White House Conference on Civil Rights would focus heavily on "Negro family structure."[81] But as acrimony over "The Case for National Action" mounted, administration staffers grew increasingly reluctant to use the Moynihan Report as the basis for the panel on the black family. Harry McPherson recalled hearing rumors that the event would be picketed.[82] Capitol Hill columnists and perennial administration critics Rowland Evans and Robert Novak devoted their August 18, 1965, "Inside Report" to the debate over Moynihan's motivations. Their analysis emphasized that the document was the outgrowth of the preceding summer's urban unrest. They traced the influence of Moynihan's research on the development of the Howard speech but emphasized that in the aftermath of the rioting in Watts the administration had come to see the Moynihan Report "as a political atom bomb certain to produce unwanted fallout."[83]

Historian Walter Jackson has noted that part of the reason African Americans chafed at the implications of the Moynihan Report was that it seemed once again to relegate them to a passive role. Having worked mightily to maneuver a succession of reluctant chief executives—Kennedy and Johnson most successfully of all—into pushing for sweeping civil rights reforms and transforming the national debate, they had a firm appreciation of their own agency. With the publication of "The Case for National Action," Jackson argued, "blacks reacted viscerally against the image of themselves as patients surrounded by social scientists taking their pulse and probing their pathologies." African Americans stood ready to offer their own diagnoses and their own prescriptions. Moreover, their collective memory was of a federal doctor who had often been extremely reluctant to apply consistently the remedies he valued so highly in the abstract.[84] And the question of costs was another matter altogether. The Moynihan Report's failure to discuss possible policy approaches to untangle black "pathology" left undetermined the issue of who would foot the bill for the cost of healing "the scars of centuries."[85]

As the Moynihan Report increasingly came to be viewed as radioactive, White House insiders—and former insiders like speechwriter Richard Goodwin—worked to prevent "The Case for National Action" from tainting the rhetoric of the Howard presidential address. Goodwin has consistently minimized Moynihan's contribution to the speech. Although his attempt to downplay Moynihan's role in the language and ideas underlying the Howard speech may be politically rational, it is empirically untenable. Careful comparison of the first page of the Moynihan Report, titled "The Negro American Revolution," with the opening lines of the Howard speech instantly puts the issue to rest. The themes and architecture of the Howard speech overlap stylistically and substantively. Goodwin's optimistic tone and rhetorical skills made Moynihan's grim data more palatable, but the latter's report had its own stylistic elegance, and portions unmistakably found their way into Goodwin's successive drafts of the Howard speech.[86]

The critical distinction between the Howard speech and the Moynihan Report was the envisioned targeted audience. As scholars Rainwater and Yancey have pointed out, in the case of the internally circulating "Case for National Action," "the argument rests less on moral considerations than it does on a certain kind of high-level administrative rationality." The Howard speech, on the other hand, "places the same views in the context of justice and morality." Johnson's June 1965 commencement address, concluded Rainwater and Yancey, "gave a public face to a then confidential . . . report." The danger came when the Moynihan Report "crossed over" to a wider audience, for the language of bureaucracy could appear "almost heartless if considered outside of that context of frank internal policy debates."[87]

It would not be too much of a stretch to argue that Moynihan set the stage for Johnson's moment of rhetorical glory, with Goodwin tailoring the script to the occasion. Goodwin survived the donnybrook unscathed, and the president's scars were minimal, but Moynihan increasingly looked like the sacrificial lamb. Although Catholic, Moynihan himself might have identified with a different animal: a scapegoat, after the Jewish Yom Kippur tradition in which a goat is sent into the wilderness bearing the symbolic sins of the people upon its horns.[88]

The White House staff faced a daunting theatrical challenge: how to stage the White House Conference on Civil Rights in the aftermath of the Watts riots, the unceremonious ouster of Hubert Humphrey as civil rights "point man," and the Moynihan Report controversy, while convincing their audience that the drama revealed an administration that remained fully committed to winning a victory in the "next and more profound stage of the battle for civil rights." After the turbulent politics of the summer, the stage lights were blinding, and an increasing number of actors were displaying little interest in reciting their lines and taking direction from above.[89]

CHAPTER FOUR

Bomb Throwers and Babes in the Woods

The White House Conference on Civil Rights

Joseph Califano vividly recalled a meeting between Lyndon Johnson and White House conference planners shortly after the Howard University speech that captured Johnson's heady aspirations for the conference yet in retrospect served as a gauge of how dramatically the conference diminished in importance in the months following its announcement in the Howard speech. In attendance at the meeting, along with the president and Califano, were Berl Bernhard and Morris Abram. Bernhard, a former director of the staff of the Civil Rights Commission, was slated to serve as executive director of the White House Conference on Civil Rights in charge of day-to-day planning. Abram would cochair the November 1965 planning session for the conference. (Missing that day were Abram's cochair, African American lawyer William Coleman of Philadelphia, and A. Philip Randolph, who in October 1965 was named to serve as honorary chairman of the gathering. Randolph was ultimately less involved in the day-to-day planning, often delegating his duties to his close associate at the A. Philip Randolph Institute, Bayard Rustin.)

Johnson laid out for Abram and Bernhard his vision of a successful conference:

> In the hill country in the spring, the sun comes up earlier, and the ground gets warmer, and you can see the steam rising and the sap dripping. And in his pen, you can see my prize bull. He's the biggest, best-hung bull in the hill country. In the spring he gets a hankering for those cows, and he starts pawing the ground and getting restless. So I open the pen and he goes down the hill, looking for a cow, with his pecker hanging hard and swinging. Those cows get so Goddamn excited, they get more and more moist to receive him, and their asses just start quivering and then they start

quivering all over, every one of them is quivering, as that bull struts into their pasture.

According to Califano, at the end of Johnson's bawdy foray into the genre of the pastorale, "Abram's and Bernhard's jaws were ajar, just as the President wanted them." After a theatrical pause, Johnson broke the suspense to explain the connection between this bovine pornography and his plans for a gathering that would fulfill the Howard promise: "Well, I want a *quivering* conference. . . . I want every damn delegate quivering with excitement and anticipation about the future of civil rights and their future opportunities in this country."[1]

Aside from its visceral shock value, Johnson's resort to animal husbandry suggests that the president, subconsciously or not, viewed himself by late 1965 as having an originative—given LBJ's penchant for animal husbandry, seminal—relationship to civil rights reform. Although Johnson had been quick to recognize the contributions of civil rights leadership and the impact of grassroots events, the quote suggests the hubris of paternity.

The committee charged with organizing the planning session devoted significant energy to the necessity of more rigorously implementing preexisting civil rights legislation. But Morris Abram argued that over time, in Johnson's mind, the White House Conference on Civil Rights became something other than an opportunity to map out strategy for the "next and more profound stage of the battle for civil rights" called for in the Howard speech or more systematic enforcement of legislation already on the books. It was also to serve as an opportunity for "a celebration, a justified celebration, of *his* achievement."[2]

In late September, just one day after Humphrey's painfully awkward press conference announcing the demise of the PCEO and the PCEEO, Califano reported to the president that "civil rights circles" had accepted the reorganization, in large part because of the seeming promotion of Wiley Branton to the new position in the Justice Department. But Califano urged Johnson to expedite planning for a "preliminary conference," to be followed by a full conference "early next year," in order to help soften criticism that the reorganization was reflective of waning White House interest in the civil rights agenda.[3]

Watts certainly had an effect also, but evidence suggests that the simmering controversy over the Moynihan Report more than any other factor delayed planning for the full-blown conference, which the Howard speech had initially promised would take place in the fall of 1965. To give the appearance of keeping to the suggested timetable, administration officials, including Clifford Alexander at the White House, elected to convene a much smaller planning conference to set an agenda, which would then be taken up by a larger gathering, most likely early the following spring. (The full conference ultimately convened on June 1, 1966.) This strategy dramatically whittled down the invitation list from well over 2,000 for the anticipated larger conference to several hundred.[4]

Disagreements over the agenda for both proposed conferences quickly emerged, however, in early meetings between officials representing the Johnson administration and a cross section of civil rights leadership. In August 1965, meetings with James Farmer, Whitney Young, A. Philip Randolph, Martin Luther King Jr., John Lewis, LBJ, and his aides appear to have been as concerned with determining the meaning of the rioting in Watts and side-stepping any connection with Moynihan's research as they were with charting a course for the White House conference, the ostensible purpose for meetings with the civil rights leaders.[5]

Some observers within the administration were convinced that Johnson's ardor for the proposed conference had cooled considerably. From his vantage point as former acting director of the CRS, Calvin Kytle recalled a period in late summer and early fall 1965 when high-ranking staff members of the bureaucratic line agencies involved with civil rights "would write memoranda to their counterparts at the White House. When are we going to get the word on the conference? How are we going to organize it? Who will staff the thing? Who will be invited?" And from the White House: "No response at all." Kytle, who had been euphoric about the Howard speech and had sought to broadcast and promote its message through the media relations division of the CRS, was now pessimistic: "You had the feeling that Johnson or somebody at the White House was having second and third thoughts not only about the conference but about the [Howard] speech itself, the intent of the speech." Little direct communication took place between the White House and civil rights leadership during the period from early August through early September, when Humphrey drew the ire of civil rights leaders aboard the *Honey Fitz* yacht. To learn that A. Philip Randolph had been appointed honorary chairman of the White House conference only upon reading about it in the newspapers was exceptionally frustrating to most of the civil rights hierarchy.[6] One leader, who wished to remain unnamed, expressed his opinion to two researchers investigating the Moynihan controversy: "The whole thing was a bit of a mess. We could not find out who was running the conference."[7]

Organizing the White House Planning Conference finally began in earnest in early October. At the end of that month, Lee White, Harry McPherson, and Clifford Alexander attended a meeting with Morris Abram, Bill Coleman, and Berl Bernhard, along with SCLC representatives Roy Wilkins, Whitney Young,

James Farmer, Dorothy Height, Ralph David Abernathy, and Walter Fauntroy, SNCC member Marion Barry, and Bayard Rustin, sitting in for honorary conference chairman A. Philip Randolph. The group convened in the Indian Treaty Room of the Executive Office Building (one reporter, tongue in cheek, renamed it the "Negro Treaty Room"). "The purpose of the meeting," Lee White assured the president, "was to let this leadership group know where we stood and to ensure that they did not either take away control of the conference from your designated co-chairmen or withdraw their support from it." White was particularly concerned that Bayard Rustin might attempt to redirect the agenda, but Rustin was "quite cooperative," and administration stalwart Roy Wilkins was "the most impressive and was of great assistance in establishing a total atmosphere of cooperation and understanding."[8]

Bayard Rustin had largely coordinated the daunting logistics of the 1963 March on Washington, first proposed by Randolph, and in 1966 he headed the day-to-day operations of the A. Philip Randolph Institute. But in the week immediately preceding the conference planning session, powerful voices in Washington cautioned that Rustin's public involvement in the conference would raise questions of an ideological capitulation to the Left and might run the risk of incurring a major public embarrassment for Johnson. White House secretary Marvin Watson, who was in part charged with protecting the president from just such embarrassment, was worried over FBI reports on Rustin.[9] Hoover's FBI was engaged in a long-standing and particularly sordid smear campaign against Rustin on both ideological and "moral" grounds. Rustin's ties to a number of groups that the FBI classified as "Communist front" organizations made him poison to Hoover, and Rustin's homosexuality enraged the director (Hoover's own sexual habits have since been the subject of intense speculation).[10]

Lee White's endorsement of Rustin's inclusion in the conference — conveyed in a secure wire to Johnson's "gatekeeper," Marvin Watson — was guarded. He plaintively related "Harry McPherson's recollection . . . that there has never been any charge that [Rustin] has ever been or is currently a card carrying member of the Communist Party." The rhetoric, straight out of the 1950s, illustrated that the culture of anticommunism still reigned supreme, certainly in the FBI but also in other major branches of government as well.

White's insistence on Rustin's ongoing involvement in the White House Conference on Civil Rights was mainly pragmatic. Barring Rustin from the conference was not a "totally free choice," noted the White House counsel, and any such action would not go unnoticed. A. Philip Randolph had made his intention plain. He would pull out of the conference if Rustin were not included. Some White House insiders believed that the labor leader was engaged in a tactical bluff, although few were willing to call it. But for the honorary chairman to boycott the gathering would create a public relations nightmare and would "blanket" any positive coverage of the event, White cautioned. Rustin himself might "make a fuss" if excluded, so admitting him to the conference was the "least bad" of "two undesirable alternatives."

White outlined a strategy to keep Rustin's participation "low-key." "We have taken every precaution to insure that Rustin will not play a leading role." Along with keeping Rustin from making a formal address to the delegates and from leading any panels, the pettiness extended to the "refus[al] to place [Rustin's] name on materials being circulated to the Conference participants."[11] In retrospect, the rebuff seems all the more stinging given Rustin's prominent role in planning the conference. In addition to drafting A. Philip Randolph's opening remarks to the planning conference, he had attended many of the planning meetings, often as Randolph's appointed stand-in, and on several occasions Rustin had supported administration positions and had drawn favorable comparison with Roy Wilkins for the NAACP leader's reliability for toeing the line on most civil rights issues.

Even as anticommunism and Cold War homophobia shaped the quiet debate over the issue of Rustin's participation, other civil rights leaders sought to distance themselves from the conference planning process. Martin Luther King Jr., a member of the executive committee charged with the task of setting the agenda for the larger spring conference, often sent SCLC subordinates Walter Fauntroy or Rev. Ralph David Abernathy as his surrogates to planning meetings in the fall of 1965. Morris Abram remembered: "[It was] damn hard to get [King] to come."[12] And the SCLC minister was not alone in his reservations. In the weeks immediately preceding the planning conference even stalwart administration defenders like Whitney Young publicly voiced their unease about whether Johnson intended to live up to the rhetorical promise and commitment of Howard. In addition, the bureaucratic reorganization and Humphrey's ouster alarmed civil rights leaders, despite White House assurances that the shake-up of executive branch responsibilities did not represent a "downgrading" of the administration's civil rights agenda.

The formal planning conference, with approximately 200 participants, was finally scheduled to take place in Washington on November 17 and November 18, 1965. Abram and his staff had set an agenda and defined areas of study and action to be debated and commented upon by the larger and presumably more inclusive White House Conference on Civil Rights to follow early the next year, although clearly the administration intended the larger conference primarily to rubber stamp the outcomes of its predecessor. In the November planning conference, individual panels were to consider eight broadly defined topics: jobs and employment security, administration of justice, voting rights and citizenship, health and welfare, "The Family: Resources for Change," housing and neighborhoods, community institutions, and education.[13] Whether the black family would be included on the agenda for the larger conference was a recurring and divisive issue. Most of the civil rights leaders opposed its inclusion—the Moynihan Report was still casting a long shadow.

Nevertheless, Morris Abram felt Daniel Patrick Moynihan deserved a place at the planning conference, but he knew he would likely lack allies in this effort. Abram faced stiff resistance from the White House for a variety of reasons, including concerns that the inclusion of Moynihan might "offend" civil rights leaders on the executive committee for the planning conference. Whatever the merits of the report and beyond any question of Moynihan's sincerity or intent in producing it, the author had "opened a Pandora's box," Abram recalled. If the report, or the conditions in the black family it purported to describe, seemed to "expos[e] a nest of worms," then to roll out the presidential red carpet to Moynihan—or even to suggest letting him slip in by a back door—was like "trying to invite a polecat." Nevertheless, Abram persisted.[14]

Ultimately, the White House gave the green light, albeit reluctantly. White House staff aides may have reasoned that to bar Moynihan would only have attracted further media scrutiny. But White House officials were walking a tightrope, according to the perceptive analysis of scholars Lee Rainwater and William Yancey: "The conference was convened under the authority of the President's Howard University speech which had spoken of the special nature of Negro poverty and of family problems as central to this special nature. Too vigorous a repudiation of Moynihan could be taken as a criticism of the government, no repudiation as part of a government plot to do in the movement."[15]

Moynihan was, for his own part, incredulous when he found out he was persona non grata; the self-described "academic" clearly had a proprietary feeling toward the conference, harking back to the contested authorship of the Howard speech. If Johnson subconsciously envisioned himself as the strutting, rutting bull at the conference, Moynihan clearly also felt he should have a central role. "Hell," he told Abram when the invitation was finally, reluctantly, extended, "there wouldn't be any [White House] conference *had I not written that into the Howard University speech*. Here I am the father of the conference and I haven't received any invitation."[16]

As plans continued, there was still the danger that the "radioactivity" would finally contaminate the still-untainted Howard address. In the days leading up to the planning conference, a group of civil rights activists and liberal clergy members met in New York and called upon Johnson to remove the issue of "family stability" from the scheduled agenda.[17]

The night before the official opening of the White House Planning Conference, Johnson welcomed the delegates in the White House East Room with well-crafted remarks that received a prolonged ovation. Still, however eloquent, they were a pale echo of the rhetorical intensity of his Howard University speech. In the very sentence in which he spoke weightily of the history of race relations as an "American dilemma," tipping his hat to Gunnar Myrdal as he had on other occasions, the president somehow also felt it necessary to mention that First Lady Abigail Adams had "once hung out her wash" in the same East Room. The speech combined a progress report on advances in the civil rights movement with Johnson's pledge that "we must do more. We will do more." Anticipating civil rights legislation to be introduced in Congress early in 1966, Johnson made it clear that among the administration's priorities would be laws striking down discrimination in jury selection in both federal and state cases.[18]

As at the Voting Rights Act signing ceremony in August, the president emphasized the limitations of the federal government. Legislation could not solve everything; there was "no single easy remedy," and African Americans and likeminded white allies would need to continue to work for implementation and enforcement of preexisting statutes and for broadening opportunities for blacks in the economy. The White House Conference on Civil Rights, to be held the following spring, could continue the Howard speech's promise "To Fulfill These Rights," with its nod toward Harry Truman's civil rights commission. But there would be a new thrust as well: "From Opportunity to Achievement."[19]

Johnson's speech had an antiphonal quality, a sense of preoccupations divided between a familiar obsession with inequality in the rural South and the growing perception of the extent of problems in urban America, especially in the North and West. The president spoke of the "millions . . . trapped in ghettoes and shanties . . . discouraged and hopeless . . . as far from sharing in the promise of America as if they really inhabited another planet." And Johnson was mapping out the middle ground ideologically as well, striving to form a consensus behind a centrist approach to racial advancement, in part by defining that middle ground against the extremes: "The tide of change is running with the Negro American. . . . Neither the ignorant violence of the Ku Klux Klan nor the despairing violence of Watts can reverse it."[20]

With the Moynihan Report clearly on everyone's mind, conference executive director Berl Bernhard attempted to turn its painful conclusions into levity at the opening session of the planning Conference. "I want you to know that I have been reliably informed that no such person as Daniel Patrick Moynihan exists," he told the delegates with a deadpan expression.[21] The White House had been perfectly willing—perhaps even eager—to have authorship of the Moynihan Report ascribed to a White House "study group" in the first days after its release. By late October, the administration wanted nothing to do with the report, characterizing it as, like Athena, having sprung fully formed from Moynihan's head.[22]

Moynihan was absent from the opening plenary session, but Morris Abram later remembered his colleague being "thoroughly trashed," "roundly criticized," and "beaten" by the other participants during the two-day event. That may have been the case in private conversations, but the public reality was somewhat less dramatic. Moynihan participated in the panel on the family but was uncharacteristically low-key and did not say a word during the first day's session. On the second day, he engaged in a muted debate. Claiming a "point of personal privilege," he defended his rationale for authoring the report—it had been written with a "tactical" end in mind. African American sociologist E. Franklin Frazier, he reminded those who criticized his conclusions, had put forth a similar thesis with the publication of *The Negro Family in the United States* in 1939. With both sides in the debate claiming that Frazier would support their side—Frazier had passed away three years earlier—it was a classic case of academics speaking for the dead, but more importantly of scholars, policymakers, and scholar-activists miscommunicating among themselves. Still, a thin veneer of civility prevailed, despite the clearly irreconcilable views, and it was hardly the confrontation many observers seem to have expected (and in some cases hoped for).[23] Instead, the controversy over the report bubbled in the background and at least to some extent cast a pall over the November gathering.

Although few in number, some African American leaders reacted to the Moynihan Report with ambivalence. Certainly most condemned the way in which the research was cast, but they also sensed that the controversy prevented any further discussion or substantive debate over the fate of the African American family. As NAACP legal counsel Robert Carter noted, the Moynihan Report "taught us things that we already knew but were not thinking of."[24] The climate had been poisoned by the timing and context of the report's release; the fact that it emanated from on high evoked a painful history of white scrutiny and proscriptive oversight of black America, what James Farmer had bitterly referred to as the national "cocktail hour on the 'Negro Question.'"

Moynihan had submitted his resignation as assistant secretary of labor to Johnson in mid-July before public debate over his findings turned bitter and had announced his intentions to campaign for the presidency of New York's city council. When he fell short of realizing that goal, Moynihan later accepted a one-year faculty appointment at Wesleyan University.[25] From his post there and in subsequent years Moynihan often railed against the bureaucracy—the "Permanent Government"—whose members, he argued, had had a "savage reaction" to the report. At the goading of "Welfare administration types" in the Department of Health, Education, and Welfare who felt it threatened their bureaucratic turf, government officials had turned against the rationale underlying the report. As Moynihan reconstructed events, these same bureaucrats must then have hastened to contact civil rights leaders to warn them that the report was "inaccurate, insulting, misleading and dangerous to the interests of the movement."[26]

Any anticipated disagreements over the Moynihan Report were unexpectedly upstaged at the White House Planning Conference by honorary conference chairman A. Philip Randolph, who stunned the gathering in mid-November when he called for a "Freedom Budget" for black Americans that he likened to a domestic Marshall Plan. The price tag was certainly calculated to attract attention—Randolph threw out the number $100 billion. Explicitly referring to the debate over the Moynihan Report, Randolph shied away from blaming "pathologies" of black families. The real culprit was the physical entity of the ghetto itself, which would need to be reinvented or eradicated altogether.[27] The debate over the Freedom Budget continued in the ensuing months and years, but few could get their minds around a figure like $100 billion, and, given the growing fiscal sinkhole of Vietnam, the discussion seemed an exercise in the hypothetical.[28]

McPherson's retrospective account of the November White House Planning Conference elliptically referred to how "the planners vied with one another in demanding more and more extreme reparations for the Negro's wrongs." Elsewhere he characterized the delegates' debates as "sulfurous language, a good deal of bickering back and forth," which the White House "played . . . down as much as possible, because we didn't want it to be seen as the conference itself."[29]

Although the dialogue was hardly incendiary, a number of grassroots delegates who knew the naked realities of racism and power in the Deep South did complain over what they saw as the lukewarm implementation of the newly enacted Voting Rights Act. Why promise new laws when existing legislation was not being adequately enforced, they asked. Attorney General Nicholas

Katzenbach admonished Floyd McKissick in a panel discussion on voting, when the African American CORE leader asked for more proactive federal involvement in aiding potential black registrants. Katzenbach questioned whether civil rights leaders and their organizations were "really doing your job." If they were, Katzenbach asserted, "a great many people would be participating" in the political system. When McKissick argued that blacks were being asked to shoulder too much of the burden of voter registration, Katzenbach had a quick reply: "The burden is on people, in a democracy that is where the burden is."[30] But many black delegates refused to accept such a pat answer. Ronnie Moore, another CORE leader who had traveled from Louisiana to attend the planning session in Washington, argued that Justice Department officials' Voting Rights Act implementation efforts typically failed to take into account the glaringly discriminatory realities blacks faced.[31] However powerful and eloquent the voices of black grassroots activists, the media gave little coverage to their complaints.

As for Johnson, after his welcome to the delegates he seems to have withdrawn and remained largely above the fray. The whole affair confirmed his worst opinions about the hair-splitting tendencies of academia and "experts." Given the president's mounting sense that the "liberal media" was out to "get him," he must have found it miraculous that his Howard speech was *not* regularly dredged up along with the Moynihan Report for public pillory; its timing and its glowingly optimistic rhetoric may have protected it from criticism, but Johnson was ill-accustomed to such good fortune. As the tumult over the report subsided, Johnson is reputed to have admonished his press secretary, Bill Moyers: "I don't know what was in there, but whatever it was, stay away from it."[32]

And even though there had been no major public relations embarrassments, the lesson of the planning conference was that the "militants"—whom McPherson referred to in his memoir as "a small army of abrasive men"—were running the risk of shattering Johnson's "liberal consensus." The vanguard of this extremist army disparaged the leadership of "moderates" like Roy Wilkins of the NAACP and Whitney Young of the Urban League. Without the moderates of all races, progress would be impossible, according to McPherson's thinking.

Referring specifically to the Howard speech's rhetoric, Johnson's aide concluded: "If we were to move on to the next stage, the leadership would have to be returned to the centrists, to the sensitive establishment—to business, labor, [Roy] Wilkins, and [Whitney] Young." This, McPherson argued, was the rationale behind Johnson's decision to appoint Chicago and Northwestern

Railway chairman of the board and Johnson supporter Ben W. Heineman, a white man, to head the anticipated spring White House Conference on Civil Rights. Heineman, the president hoped, would bring a number of businessmen on board. Although McPherson approved this choice, he was sensitive enough to appearances to note the incongruity of these elite white corporate chiefs "flying in aboard private jets to talk about people whose children ate the paint off windowsills."[33]

The selection of Heineman raised concerns among some who had high aspirations for the follow-up conference, finally scheduled to begin on June 1, 1966. Certainly he was considered to be friendly to the cause of civil rights, but his credentials were far less obvious than those of a Morris Abram, a Berl Bernhard, a William Coleman, or any number of other civil rights proponents with close ties to both civil rights leadership and the Johnson inner circle. Abram felt that Johnson's decision to tap him as chair the previous fall had sent a strong signal that he would be given a high-profile leadership role in the spring. But the president "decided that he would get rid of . . . me," Abram remembered. He reasoned that Johnson "wanted more control" over how the conference would be run; he "could run herd on [Heineman] better, and maybe he could." The president may well have believed that Heineman, who lacked close personal ties to the major civil rights leaders, would be a "safer" choice than other possibilities.[34] Certainly Johnson's decision to appoint a businessman as chairman may have served as a good indication of how far he had traveled from his earlier expressed hopes for a "quivering" conference; the emphasis now seemed to be on the managerial rather than the inspirational.

As a signal of the priority he assigned to the upcoming convocation—if only to preventing its becoming a public relations disaster—Johnson assigned oversight duties to top White House aide Harry McPherson, to be assisted by high-ranking African American administration insiders Clifford Alexander, newly appointed HUD secretary Robert Weaver, and Louis Martin. Martin was charged with carefully handpicking the attendees.[35] That none of these talented individuals nor African American administration allies outside the government evidently received serious consideration for chairing the conference and that Johnson instead opted for a white executive without extensive civil rights credentials is noteworthy. The sheer number of delegates—ultimately as many as 2,500 invitations were extended—allowed him a striking degree of latitude in shaping the racial and ideological complexion of conference attendees, but it was also a staggering task.

The result of such strict oversight and preemptive "damage control" was that some delegates did not receive their invitations until days before the gathering convened in Washington.[36] Anna Hedgeman, an African American woman affiliated with the National Council of Churches' Commission on Religion and Race (and later one of the founding feminists in the National Organization for Women), would reflect as the 1966 conference drew to a close: "I have a feeling I've been taking LSD. . . . This Conference is unbelievable. My invitation didn't come until the 23d of May. I don't know if they thought that Negroes don't have appointment calendars."[37]

Following Johnson's lead with the selection of Heineman, Martin made certain that business and industry officials figured prominently. Along with bureaucrats of the "permanent government," state and local government officials were also well represented. "Civil rights groups" and "poor and grassroots organizations" drew fewer invitations; Martin had turned the doctrine of "maximum feasible participation" on its head. Asked whether the invitation list was rigged, Ramsey Clark hedged. "It wasn't rigged, but you only invite people that you know, and our acquaintanceship was very thin. It was middle class, upper middle class, and only secondarily . . . people really involved personally and daily in the misery of racism and poverty."[38]

In stacking the invitations deck with government personnel, Martin was responding in part to Johnson aide Bob Kintner, who had stressed that these representatives of the various executive branch agencies should be encouraged to share with nongovernmental conference participants the "inspiring story . . . of progress during the sixties. . . . This will give balance to a conference that otherwise will tend to talk only of what the government ought to do next." That such talk of what to do "next" was precisely what Johnson had called for in the Howard speech was evidently lost on Kintner.[39] By the spring of 1966, some simply wanted the assembly to be a celebration of Johnson's leadership of past civil rights efforts.

Building on the work of the planning conference, a new council made up of thirty members met regularly throughout the spring. In the weeks prior to June 1, it distributed a 100-page book laying out the meeting's agenda, with Johnson's Howard speech language "To Fulfill These Rights" stenciled prominently below the gold leitmotif of the standard American eagle seal with its optimistic slogan of "E pluribus unum." Referring to the president's description of a "seamless web" of problems facing American blacks, the council's report freely conceded that the agenda its members had mapped out was far from comprehensive.[40] But the polished volume sent an implicit message that the work of the conference had been largely done in advance. Attendees might discuss the issues, but the administration was attempting to limit the parameters of debate; the delegates' primary job would be to attend panels on the selected subject areas and then endorse the resolutions and research accomplished and then assembled by others.[41]

The Watts riots and the ongoing controversy over the Moynihan Report, in Morris Abram's memory, cooled Johnson's enthusiasm for the gathering as it became more and more likely that the dominant tenor of the conference would be something other than celebratory adulation.[42] Johnson's desire for a "quivering" conference—indeed, his desire for any kind of conference—had waned dramatically in the months between the Howard speech and the reorganization of the administration's civil rights bureaucracy in September. The November planning conference had done little to reignite his passion. "Why do we have to have the damned thing?" the president asked, only half-jokingly. When McPherson suggested "it would look worse" to cancel it after LBJ's bold announcement at Howard, Johnson agreed, but retorted, "You boys have gotten me in this controversy over Moynihan, so I've got to get somebody like Heineman to get me out of it." He was "quite right in doing that. Absolutely right. Because . . . at this point we were just over our heads," said McPherson. "We didn't know how to deal with it."[43] The president was offering little guidance.

Notably missing by the time the conference actually convened was a delegation from SNCC. Stokely Carmichael and other members of the organization's Atlanta Project had ousted John Lewis as SNCC chairman following exhausting internal debates in May 1966, and whites, too, were on their way out of the organization.[44] Simultaneously launching criticisms of "colonization" and American involvement in Vietnam, SNCC appeared to be making a hard turn to the left, particularly when viewed from the vantage point of a White House increasingly sensitive to any criticism of American involvement in Southeast Asia. Julian Bond, who had directed public relations work for SNCC since its inception in 1960, confided to John Lewis following Carmichael's ascension, partly in jest: "The crazies are taking over."[45]

Lewis's involvement in the planning stages of the White House Conference on Civil Rights in the spring of 1966 actually served as one of the pretexts for rejecting his leadership, as some critics within SNCC suggested that with Lewis at its head the organization would no longer remain on "the cutting edge of the civil rights movement." Lewis recalled "being taken to task by my own organization [SNCC] for being too 'chummy' with the White House and President Johnson."[46]

Lewis's perceptions were not far off the mark. The former SNCC leader had been, to some extent, an irritant to both White House occupants in the 1960s. He had fought tenaciously against Kennedy officials' censorship of his remarks at the August 1963 March on Washington and had toned down his strident rhetoric with great reluctance following a personal plea from A. Philip Randolph. During the 1964 election campaign, he had hardly endeared himself to the new president when he and CORE leader James Farmer refused to endorse the Johnson administration's proposed "moratorium" on civil rights protests when Democratic stalwarts feared such demonstrations might enhance Republican Barry Goldwater's chances. Nevertheless, the White House—although leery of SNCC's historical unwillingness to be "led"—still found Lewis "restrained" enough to merit inclusion in administration planning. As Harry McPherson recalled, during the interval before Stokely Carmichael assumed leadership, "SNCC was still an organization that you could invite to the White House without getting a hand grenade thrown through the window before they came."[47] When SNCC pulled out of the conference, the administration was spared the discomfort of having to determine whether a group that was increasingly perceived as "radical" should be invited. As historian Steven F. Lawson has argued, "The withdrawal of SNCC actually pleased administration strategists interested in preserving harmony." Given the organization's increasingly strident rhetoric, White House staffers now had good reason to fear "hand grenades," at least of the figurative variety. But so long as SNCC members and other "extremists" remained outside the White House conference, they would—in the words of one Johnson associate—"provide a kind of foil that may reassure middle-ground, well meaning people that the conference is not altogether kooky."[48]

Harry McPherson either misremembered or chose not to dwell on SNCC's withdrawal in his account of the White House conference published in his memoir, *A Political Education*. There were certainly fears of SNCC militants somehow "infiltrating" the final dinner—McPherson spoke of "rumors to this effect." On May 19, less than two weeks before the convening of the full assembly, Louis Martin and other administration insiders charged with ensuring that the conference not be marred by any unpleasant surprises met with J. Edgar Hoover at the FBI. Relaying to the FBI director their "concern about elements that are seeking to disrupt the White House Conference on Civil Rights," they also expressed their keen interest in having him use his investigative expertise to "learn of the sources of revenue which enable these bomb throwers to carry out their programs." Hoover, not surprisingly, was eager to comply and assured his visitors he would gather information and draw up a detailed report for the president. Louis Martin also sent Johnson his assurances that he was using his own extensive network of "personal contacts in an effort to keep things under control for the conference."[49]

But they did not really need Hoover's assistance. Martin had assiduously prescreened the delegates. Cultivating his wide-ranging contacts, he had, in addition, arranged for a number of "attractive young women in formal gowns" from nearby Howard University "to serve as hostesses." "That'll make those SNCC boys think twice about raising hell," McPherson remembered Martin saying.[50] It was an odd choice of words given that SNCC had pulled out of the conference.

Given such anxieties and meticulous planning, the conference itself threatened to become an anticlimax. Approximately 2,400 delegates converged on Washington's Sheraton Hotel and Conference Center for the full meeting of the White House Conference on Civil Rights when it convened on June 1 and June 2, 1966, almost exactly one year from the date that Johnson had initially announced his plans for such a gathering in the Howard University speech.

As a measure of how much the political and ideological landscape had been reconfigured in just one year since the president's bold commitment at Howard, as late as three days before the full conference began it was still unclear to White House insiders whether Johnson would make an appearance, and if he did, whether he should deliver a major speech. Harry McPherson and others were still concerned that "possible public disagreements" might tarnish the president's image, and White House Secretary to the Cabinet Bob Kintner suggested that Johnson wait until the last minute, allowing one day of the conference to pass uneventfully, before making the final decision on whether to speak.[51]

Undoubtedly, they recalled the embarrassment Sargent Shriver had suffered only six weeks earlier when he had attempted to speak to a Washington conference on poverty, only to be shouted down. Militant delegates had accused him of being a "liar" and had complained that the War on Poverty was "one big laugh" that had done nothing to help the poor. Front page stories in the *Washington Post* and the *New York Times* described how Shriver had barely managed to finish his brief talk because of the jeers and heckling. Aides had hurried him out of the convention hall after he was jostled by angry demonstrators.[52]

Bob Kintner noted that conference participants would certainly expect the president to put in an appearance but legalistically offered, "I gather no commitment at all was made."[53] There appeared to be serious doubt as to whether the "prize bull" would even leave his "pen" or whether the delegates in the "pasture" were sufficiently "excited . . . to receive him."

With the conference only thirty minutes from the opening gavel, Ben Heineman called Johnson in the White House residence to make his case for a presidential appearance in the opening plenum session. You could "make a brief statement and then leave," Heineman argued. In his best judgment, there would be "minimal risk" of any unpleasant reactions from the audience. And even though he was unwilling to write off the conference, he expressed his concern that it was beginning on a "dispirited" note. An encouraging statement from the president would "galvanize the conference."

But Johnson was clearly apprehensive. "I'm quite depressed at the headlines and the attitudes of the McKissicks and . . . the SNCC people," he replied. In what seems to have been a reference to the backlash against post–Civil War Reconstruction, he continued, "I'm very fearful that they'll drive us back to where we were a hundred years ago." Unspoken was his fear that the more radical members of the conference would heckle his appearance. "The press keeps saying that I'm expected to appear," said Johnson. "Do we gain enough to justify the chance of unpleasantness?"

When Heineman insisted that there was little chance of a hostile reaction, Johnson suddenly took up a second line of argument. Hubert Humphrey was scheduled to open the conference, and the president expressed concern that this "good man" would be made to look as though he were playing second fiddle. Given the fact that Johnson had publicly humiliated Humphrey by stripping him of his civil rights leadership the previous September, the argument was less than convincing, but it gave the president an out for adopting a wait-and-see attitude to see how the conference evolved.[54]

The president ultimately decided to address the opening night's dinner, on June 1, adopting a secondary role as host and introducing the evening's keynote speaker, Thurgood Marshall, whom Johnson had appointed as solicitor general in July 1965. (Many observers saw the appointment of Marshall to this post as a "stepping stone" to a future Supreme Court appointment, and, indeed, LBJ did nominate the distinguished jurist to the highest federal bench in 1967. Characteristically, Johnson kept even his close associates second-guessing his decision. When the president—in apparent innocence—asked new White House aide Larry Temple to recommend an African American for appointment to the Supreme Court and Temple suggested Philadelphia jurist A. Leon Higginbotham, LBJ sprung his trap: "Larry, the only two people who ever heard of Judge Higginbotham are you and his momma. When I appoint a nigger to the bench, I want everyone to know he's a nigger."[55])

In his opening remarks, the president cautioned against a "go it alone" attitude among blacks. His references to Black Power became less elliptical when he insisted that historically "those who have whispered the counsel of despair—the counsel of separatism—have been ignored." Johnson instead paid tribute to African Americans who had first displayed the courage to demand an "awakening" and to the whites who had "joined the cause of justice."

Although he alluded to the administration's efforts in civil rights, voting rights, and the War on Poverty, Johnson avoided his standard recitation of a laundry list of concrete accomplishments and registered a note of humility, acknowledging that "in these efforts we have made mistakes." More mistakes would be made, he predicted, "for we know our weaknesses. We will arouse hopes as we have already done, that cannot be quickly fulfilled." Johnson then doffed his hat to the large contingent of businesspeople in attendance, heralding the efforts of individuals and the private sector to narrow the gaps in income and opportunity. Urban problems and the ongoing potential for additional urban unrest were clearly weighing heavily on his mind as he opted for an organic metaphor to describe the challenges facing urban America. Johnson called on all those attending the conference to "plant . . . a whole row of seeds" whose sowing would one day—"years from now"—yield "a harvest of hope, where there might have been a howling desert of despair and bitterness."

There was perhaps a trace of defensiveness and certainly a rare acknowledgment of the boundaries of political possibility as Johnson shifted from his peroration to the closing portion of his speech: "Do not expect from me, or any man, a miracle. Do not expect us, even together, to put right in one year or four all that took centuries to make wrong." But the tone of the message was optimistic and belied the behind-the-scenes efforts to keep the conference a cosmetic and subdued affair. The administration's efforts in the battle for civil rights were ongoing, and Johnson vowed to devote his own time and "such talents as I have been given" to the daunting task at hand. Once again improvising on the riffs of civil rights freedom songs, he insisted: "We are moving. We shall not turn back."[56]

As the president yielded the podium to Thurgood Marshall, the audience broke into a round of applause that was long and appeared heartfelt. Johnson intimate Harry McPherson remembered the atmosphere as "convulsive," with "people . . . on their feet yelling, 'LBJ! LBJ!'" Despite all the earlier worries of a surprise demonstration by the president's opponents, the dinner (with the exception of the enthusiastic applause for Marshall and Johnson) had proved to be "as restrained as a Chamber of Commerce convention."[57] Harry McPherson recalled of Johnson in the parking lot after the speech: "His eyes were large and his face almost incandescent with the pleasure of an unexpected and flawless triumph. It was about the last one he would have."[58]

Some White House allies, including the Urban League's Whitney Young, believed that Johnson's speech set the stage for a more productive second day of the conference.[59] Other civil rights leaders were skeptical. Martin Luther King Jr., in particular, felt snubbed by conference planners. Relegated to only a brief appearance on one of the many panels, the Baptist minister was reportedly annoyed that Roy Wilkins was the only major civil rights leader on the speakers' list for the final banquet on June 2 and felt that Thurgood Marshall had given short shrift to the impact and necessity of protest in his remarks on opening night. A gossipy column written by Rowland Evans and Robert Novak described how "King sulked in his hotel room the final day of the conference," excusing his absence by claiming illness. Seeking to avoid the embarrassment of not having the SCLC leader in attendance on the final evening's gathering, conference chairman Ben Heineman cleverly recruited Coretta Scott King to sing the national anthem for the dinner audience. Her outmaneuvered husband put in an obligatory appearance.

King's lieutenants were outraged by what they felt was a calculated effort on the part of the administration to keep him on the sidelines. Columnists Evans and Novak bolstered these suspicions when they suggested that King had been barred from the final dinner speakers' platform "out of realistic fear that he would eloquently invoke opposition to Viet Nam." Despite the growing intensity of his public pronouncements against the war in Southeast Asia, on this occasion King left Washington without addressing U.S. foreign policy or making public comments about bruised feelings he may have had.[60]

Evans and Novak were not far off the mark. Along with concerns about militant disruptions related to a critique of the Johnson administration's enforcement of civil rights and voting rights statutes—a repeat of Humphrey's grilling on board the *Honey Fitz* presidential yacht perhaps, but this time in full view of the media spotlights—administration allies stood ready to fall on the Vietnam hand grenade if necessary. King had opted, for the moment, to allow a distinction between civil rights and antiwar positions, even though he had publicly stated that he felt the dichotomy was artificial.

With SNCC "bomb throwers" boycotting the conference, Floyd McKissick, who had succeeded James Farmer at the helm of CORE, became the most prickly burr in the saddle, and the administration moved quickly to end that irritation. When McKissick attempted to introduce a resolution seeking a unilateral American withdrawal from Vietnam, Howard University president Nabrit ruled CORE's leader out of order with a brusque, "I don't want to put the albatross [of Vietnam] around the civil rights movement." Delegates upheld his ruling by a large majority. Whitney Young, Roy Wilkins, and Clifford Alexander, as though reading from the same White House script, all used the same language in declaring that Vietnam was "not germane."[61]

A number of delegates did make allusions to Vietnam, comparing the Deep South to that troubled country. Juanita Jackson Mitchell, president of the Maryland NAACP, argued that "in the South peace-keeping is needed, as we are doing in Viet Nam to assure the exercise of constitutional rights by the people." The growing chorus of critics of the war in Southeast Asia might have disagreed with her assessment of American policy "on the ground" in Vietnam, but her statement was certainly calculated to capture the attention of the White House and tweak the administration's nose for a double standard of ignoring abuses of democracy at home while spending billions to "defend democracy" abroad.[62] As the Reverend James F. McCree, a civil rights leader from Canton, in Madison County, Mississippi, said to a burst of applause, "If the federal government can try and protect people in other countries, in Southeast Asia, in the Congo, why in the hell can't the federal government protect its citizens in Mississippi?"[63]

Among the great majority of grassroots participants, however, there was very little vocal criticism of U.S. policy in Vietnam. Louis Martin's carefully chosen invitation list proved to have been a shrewd move.[64] Even self-described militants like Philadelphia's Cecil Moore sought to protect the firewall between discussion of civil rights and Vietnam. When McKissick made the increasingly common argument that blacks and the Vietnamese people experienced a common oppression based on their shared identity as "colored" peoples, Moore refused to be sidetracked: "Hell, we may be colored, but we're Americans and we want responsibility in this thing like anyone else. . . . To confuse Vietnam with civil rights is all wet."[65] As the two-day affair wound down, a bitter McKissick dismissed the entire civil rights gathering as "a hoax."[66]

In the aftermath of the White House Conference on Civil Rights, newly installed CRS director Roger Wilkins expressed misgivings, writing a memo about growing "Negro skepticism" toward government promises: "There is widespread belief among Negroes . . . that there will be no significant follow-up to or implementation of the recommendations of the Conference."[67] He accurately gauged the mood of several "grassroots" representatives from the Deep South who had attended the conference:

"We want action," insisted a black woman from Mississippi. "We are tired of promises and want action now or we're going to have Watts all over the country. We in the South are ready. We have been in slavery. We want our freedom just like everybody else wants theirs. We want you—Washington—to do something now. . . . and stop just talking about it. Will action take place or not?"

"Some of the people I know can count the chickens without going inside," said another African American delegate from neighboring Alabama, who argued that "fair housing" should take a backseat to ensuring housing of any kind for America's poorest citizens: "We've gone about as far as we can without getting into the streets and raising hell for what's supposed to be ours," he suggested, then concluded, "This conference isn't going to be any good for us."[68]

Many of their complaints focused on the ongoing lack of protection against white violence. Judson King, an African American delegate from near Rocky Mount in North Carolina, spoke of how blacks "are so exposed in rural areas" and uniquely vulnerable to economic retaliation and threats of physical violence: "We can't hide in the crowd." Whites in the local power structure were well aware of "who owes how much money, and what kind of shotgun shells you might have bought. . . . How do you get protection in a situation like that?"[69]

Hartman Turnbow, a sixty-one-year-old Mississippi farmer from Tchula in Holmes County, had survived white vigilantes shooting into his home and a firebombing. Mississippi authorities' response was to jail him on charges of arson. At the conference, the MFDP veteran activist took the floor in a panel and declared: "If anybody will tell the truth about what is happening in Mississippi, I will. In Mississippi, as far as law is concerned, we have none, not for the Negro. As far as justice is concerned for the Negro, there is not any." Token gains were no longer enough: "The only way that I feel that the Negro in Mississippi will ever get justice, get halfway justice, is if there were some kind of way to have some Negro jurors, some Negro highway patrols and some Negro police, and let him not be put there by the Mississippi whites. Let the Negroes put him there, because if the whites pick a police or pick a jury, he is just a black white man and he is going to do you worse than the whites do."[70]

Grassroots delegates also pressured government representatives at the conference for more vigorous implementation of desegregation in public education. A father of eleven from Mississippi described smelling what he and his friends called "molasses bread" emanating from white homes as a child. "But all we did was smell it. Now I've been smelling education all my life. I'm tired of smelling it. We want education—across the board."[71]

Mrs. Geneva Tracy, from St. George Island in Dorchester County, South Carolina, demanded that the federal government deliver "action, and not just promises." The mother of four, with two of her children in newly desegregated schools, cataloged the discrimination her family had faced as a direct result of their dramatically visible involvement in school desegregation efforts.[72] Her complaints, like those articulated by numerous other grassroots delegates, prompted a *Washington Post* reporter to reflect upon the declining stature of representatives of the federal establishment in the eyes of grassroots activists: "The local Federal administrator is often cast in the role of villain once reserved for the club-swinging Southern policeman."[73]

A number of black southerners in attendance appear to have made a conscious decision to piggyback onto the northern concerns with urban unrest. As they saw it, the media had turned the spotlight on the Watts rioting and other manifestations of urban unrest. Black southerners were playing a distinct second fiddle to the dynamic of the urban powder keg, what A. Philip Randolph referred to at the conference as "socio-racial dynamite."

Race-related problems in housing and education, two issues that were by 1966 often debated mainly as "northern" dilemmas, had southern versions as well. Henry Reaves, of Holly Springs, Mississippi, described the impact of agricultural mechanization and pointed out that the replacement of increasing numbers of blacks by machinery in the southern agricultural labor force led to a steadily mounting wave of migration to urban areas. With an instinctive awareness of White House concerns, he warned that "we can expect a lot more Watts."[74]

Albert Turner, a bricklayer turned civil rights worker and would-be politician, from Marion, Alabama, argued that the crisis in northern cities was inextricably linked to depressed conditions in the South: "It's like taking medicine after you get a cold to work on this problem in cities like Cleveland. . . . That cold started in Mississippi and Alabama, and I'm asking you to give us the aspirin [in the South]. . . . You can talk about Watts and Harlem . . . but if you want to solve those problems, go to Alabama and help those people—*and keep them here.*"[75]

Federal officials and those charged with running the conference choreography typically failed to engage with these critiques directly, falling back on "Robert's Rules of Order" and always pointing to the clock. Word had come down from the Oval Office that administration representatives were there at the conference "to listen and not to talk," but salient critiques from the grassroots delegates largely were ignored. Andrew Kopkind, the radical journalist writing for the *New Republic*, assailed the White House Conference as a "strictly controlled March on Washington" and suggested that in the short term it "had the effect of anesthetizing the movement."[76] The intensity of the language emanating from the "grassroots" representatives, however, suggested that the patient had refused to go under.

A spirited black activist from Bogalusa, Louisiana, where African Americans had waged a spirited freedom struggle against a resourceful and often brutal white power structure, informed a reporter covering the gathering that the constituents he represented would be "peeved. They spend $500 to send me to this big show, this come-on, this waste of time. I hoped I would come back and tell them some kind of action would be taken immediately." From his perspective, the conference represented a step backward to the kind of gradualism and ameliorative approach that had typified White House responses to problems in race relations for nearly all of the post–World War II period.[77]

So how did White House insiders perceive the role of grassroots participants at the 1966 conference? Excerpts from a subsequent oral history with conference chairman and businessman Ben Heineman are revealing:

> INTERVIEWER: Other than just being symbolic presences, did the grassroots people contribute?
>
> HEINEMAN: I would think that they contributed credibility, and they had the opportunity to contribute. I don't think they contributed substantively, no! . . . After all, I would have been a little dismayed if after all that planning . . . we had arrived there and found a whole lot of new ideas that hadn't occurred to us—it would reflect on the planning.[78]

The chairman's embedded condescension spoke volumes about the blinders that were in place as the Johnson administration grappled with shifting currents in the linked struggles for civil rights and economic justice.

The range of verdicts on the White House Conference on Civil Rights issued by grassroots attendees and notable civil rights leaders was as diverse as the delegates themselves. The SCLC's Andrew Young compared the gathering to "a nice tea party where we can renew old acquaintances, but it's not much more than that." Other African American delegates sought to break through the decorum with pointed questions. Septima Poinsette Clark had pressed those managing the conference with the pragmatic, and insistent, query: "Can you give me something I can take back home to Selma, Alabama?" James Meredith—only days away from embarking on his "March against Fear" in Mississippi—archly inquired as to the "purpose of my being here. . . . I'm sure you didn't ask us here to waste our time."[79] But in at least one interview after the conference he was less caustic, describing the significance of the gathering as "the recognition for all these people who have been through a lot."[80]

Asbury Howard, a grassroots delegate from Bessemer, Alabama, was also circumspect as he left Washington: "I don't know what'll come of these resolutions or those good-sounding ideas . . . but these people came to Washington, they heard the President, the Vice President. . . . They heard their words and the tone in which they said them, and they'll go home now feeling a confidence and spirit they've never felt before. Now doesn't that mean something?"[81] But there was little evidence that the White House was in a mood to understand the significance of the words of grassroots delegates and "the tone in which they said them" or to draw inspiration from what one delegate called their confidence and spirit.

Aaron Henry, elder statesman of the Mississippi civil rights struggle, returned home to the Magnolia State with mixed emotions. The airing of grievances by a range of grassroots representatives had been a worthwhile goal, he later observed. He professed to realism about what the federal government was capable of. But in response to conference chairman Ben Heineman's genial but cutting dismissal of grassroots activists—"I don't think they contributed substantively, no!"—Aaron Henry offered a gently worded rebuttal: "No one person has the answers to all the problems," Henry stated. "There's no panacea. . . . There are no guidelines, there are no rules, and anybody's idea might be right. . . . I don't care whether you came from Morehouse or no house," he continued, cleverly sounding the double entendre. "That doesn't give [you] any more of an opportunity to be right than any other person. Many people who live on the farms, who aren't educated and certainly those who have gone to college and are educated, have ideas about how we can get out of this box we're in. And I think it will do us well to listen to all of us."[82]

As the delegates left Washington, the White House staff's relief at having weathered the conference without a public relations debacle was palpable. Most had abandoned their earlier aspirations. A few aides boasted of having scored positive media coverage "while sitting on a number of kegs of dynamite." Others seemed eager to simply put the conference behind them.[83]

The wounds of misunderstanding had been sustained by all sides. Moynihan, by then a private citizen, continued to defend the report against its critics and to place its call to action at the heart of Johnson's Howard University speech. At least publicly, he still seemed to expect that the White House might undertake a major policy initiative on addressing family problems nationwide, and he sought to defuse the swirling controversy over his findings by downplaying the originality of his thesis. He and his critics were on precisely the same page when it came to the necessity of addressing the crisis of unemployment and underemployment among poor urban blacks and the critique of inadequate investment in the nation's "ghettos," he insisted.

Over time, Moynihan increasingly turned his sights on those who had attacked him from the left, especially "liberal" white academics. They had shattered a consensus that had seemed to prevail at the heady moment of the Howard speech on the necessity of—if not the recipe for—addressing the problems of the ghetto. Privately he seethed at what he felt were unfair attacks on his research and willful mischaracterizations of his findings. He complained in a letter to White House aide and friend Harry McPherson that the criticism he was enduring was comparable to having "my head . . . sticking on a pike at the South West Gate to the White House grounds."[84]

The results of the conference were less than awe inspiring. In a series of resolutions, delegates called for increased low-cost housing expenditures, guaranteed employment, additional investment in public works, improvement of inner-city educational facilities, and higher welfare benefits. The price tag might not have been as high as the $100 billion figure introduced with Randolph's Freedom Budget at the November White House Planning Conference, but it was clear to most astute political observers—and certainly to Johnson—that Congress would be in no mood to foot the bill for such ambitious social expenditures. At a time when Vietnam appropriations were consuming an ever-growing share of the federal budget, hostile opponents in Congress had new ammunition for their ongoing assault on federal antipoverty programs.

Among the many issues debated by the delegates attending both fall planning and the spring full conference was a widely expressed concern over perceived sluggishness in federal enforcement of existing statutes and executive orders. In summing up the significance of the conference, McPherson spoke of general concern over an "enforcement gap" and further suggested that an "information gap" meant that at the local level neither federal nor state and local officials were fully apprised of the details of policies and legislation adopted in Washington, D.C. If such incomplete communication of the latest federal directives was a generalized pattern, it certainly made implementation of existing legislation every bit as pressing a concern as the enactment of new laws.[85]

Harry McPherson and Clifford Alexander chaired an interdepartmental committee, which included John Doar, Roger Wilkins, and LeRoy Collins, charged with implementing initiatives endorsed by the conference. They continued to meet as late as 1968, but over time, in McPherson's memory, their meetings became less frequent and "less purposeful."[86] In the week following the conference, McPherson wrote to Johnson suggesting that once Ben Heineman's council had drafted a final report on the gathering the president should arrange to receive it directly; anything else "would be taken amiss by the civil rights groups." McPherson warned that in the months to come both the press and civil rights groups would want to know the outcome of the conference's recommendations. "What is vital," McPherson wrote, "is that the work of this conference not become a dead letter—a stone dropped into the still waters of government." But Johnson's associate went on to make the distinction between appearance and reality, between professions of commitment and actual follow-through. "We will have to show that we have taken the recommendations seriously . . . and that we have taken some aggressive and visible action on them." Undercutting that sentiment, however, McPherson assured Johnson: "Certainly we do not need to show that we have adopted them."[87]

At the end of August 1966, the president had Ben Heineman, A. Philip Randolph, and other conference notables present the report of the White House Conference on Civil Rights to a regular cabinet meeting. There would be no special ceremony, no Rose Garden celebration. Randolph and Heineman listened as Johnson issued a perfunctory thank-you. The meeting's business then quickly turned to a briefing on the Vietnam situation by Robert McNamara and Dean Rusk, whereupon Johnson abruptly stood and left.[88]

In October 1966, Bayard Rustin and A. Philip Randolph attempted to present Johnson with a copy of their revised Freedom Budget, a detailed forty-page proposal that had grown out of ideas conceived as early as the fall 1965 planning session for the White House conference. Seeking to position the report in a light that would seem favorable to Johnson, Rustin told White House aide Clifford Alexander that civil rights leaders supporting the Freedom Budget would be happy to say publicly that the proposal was a direct outgrowth of the White House conference. Envisioning well in excess of $100 billion in spending, the report offered a blueprint to eradicate poverty by 1975. Part of the appeal of the report was its color-blind approach, emphasizing that nearly three-quarters of those meeting the definition of poverty in the United States were white. (To the extent that the War on Poverty had succeeded, its appeal had been grounded in a similar argument that poverty knew no color.) The authors of the Freedom Budget warned of "volcanic . . . eruptive potential . . . seething just below the surface in portions of almost every large city" in America, and asked, "Can we afford another Watts, and more than one more?"[89]

Johnson's lieutenants clearly wanted to avoid the chief executive receiving a copy of the Freedom Budget in any sort of ceremony with all the media fanfare that such a situation would inevitably attract. No matter what the president said, such an occasion would give the appearance of a White House blessing for the ambitious document. (Bayard Rustin no doubt had just such a public relations scenario in mind.) Although Clifford Alexander, Louis Martin, and other administration insiders may well have been sympathetic to the goals of the Freedom Budget, they agreed with Harry McPherson's judgment about political timing. With White House staff aides casually tossing around the moniker of "bomb throwers" and classifying the problems of the nation's cities as "social dynamite," the more than $100 billion price tag of the Freedom Budget was assuredly "fiscal dynamite." Timing was critical. Rustin wanted the Freedom Budget to be debated publicly in the weeks leading up to the midterm elections, and White House staff members consumed by fears of a white backlash at the polls were desperate to prevent an airing of any discussion of recommendations for billions of dollars in additional federal expenditures.[90] McPherson adopted a strategy of buying time, asking Rustin to provide the White House with additional copies of the Freedom Budget so that they could then have experts in the various cabinet departments give it careful study.

At the beginning of November 1966, A. Philip Randolph and Bayard Rustin went public. No longer harboring any illusions that the White House would be coming on board, they circulated a mass mailing calling for a nationwide campaign to enact the Freedom Budget's recommendations. Rustin had deftly played on Johnson's fear of Robert Kennedy's candidacy—the "Bobby factor"—by casually noting that if the president were not eager to receive the Freedom Budget publicly "it would be his desire to present it to Senators [Robert] Kennedy and [Jacob] Javits."[91] But the White House refused to take the bait.

B oth stages of the White House Conference on Civil Rights revealed growing fissures between the civil rights movement and the administration, and Johnson's enlistment of moderate leaders to pour oil on "militant" waters exacerbated fault lines between grassroots activists and more prominent civil rights allies. More ominously, the White House Conference on Civil Rights revealed an apparent erosion of the commitment of the Johnson administration, not so much to the civil rights agenda as to making the civil rights agenda the centerpiece of its efforts.

Conference planner Morris Abram's sense of the significance of the gathering was tepid: "The most you can say is that there [were] no disruptions. Everyone was afraid of a disruption." Johnson, who saw Watts as a personal insult, was similarly tempted to view the two conferences as a slight, a sign that the public had once again failed to recognize his contributions to racial progress. Certainly the two meetings in Washington were less dramatic and traumatic than the explosion in South Los Angeles, but the lack of recognition for his efforts still smarted. "I think [the President] thought that if we had orchestrated [the conferences] properly he would have gotten the applause that he deserved," Abram reflected.[92]

But perhaps there was a degree of naïveté in those who envisioned the White House Conference on Civil Rights as more a celebratory event than a difficult threshing out of the overwhelming array of issues now facing advocates of social and economic change. In hindsight, said Abram, Johnson "was a babe in the woods for . . . call[ing] that conference, because he thought he was going to celebrate himself."[93] Instead of a celebration, the White House Conference on Civil Rights revealed planners and participants navigating a minefield while trying to create the appearance of a casual stroll through the park.

Off the record, an unnamed civil rights leader echoed these sentiments as he told Washington reporters Evans and Novak that the conference was "better than nothing."[94] In the tradition of "damning with faint praise," such remarks were hardly the resounding endorsement Johnson had imagined in the heady weeks after delivering the Howard University speech in June 1965. The president had wanted "every damn delegate quivering with excitement and anticipation." Instead of the passionate congress Johnson so eagerly sought, the White House Conference was, according to one reporter, a "carefully neutered" affair.

New York Times reporter John Herbers later described the two conferences as "full of sound and fury but little else."[95] Johnson's associates had worked assiduously to ensure that any such drama was minimized and contained, protecting the president from political fallout. Although there had been no clear-cut plan for waging the "next and . . . more profound . . . battle for civil rights" announced at Howard, there had at least appeared to be a unifying clarity of purpose. Mixing Shakespeare's language of idiocy and incoherence with the ultimate fable of garbled communication in Genesis, journalist John Herbers suggested that in the aftermath of the White House Conference on Civil Rights "what earlier . . . had been high purpose and promise was now babel and confusion."[96] And Johnson was not alone in his inability to keep his bearings amid a thicket of interconnected and unexpectedly thorny issues. Abram freely conceded: "I would say that we were all babes in the woods."[97]

CHAPTER FIVE

Mississippi Is Everywhere

The Meredith March and CDGM's Last Stand

Policy analysts Lee Rainwater and William Yancey found little to admire in the White House's handling of the two conferences on civil rights. The Johnson administration had exercised "benign Machiavellianism" to modulate, moderate, or silence debate, depending on the degrees of convergence or divergence with its own priorities. White House advisers even seemed on occasion to derive satisfaction from the emergence of more sharply evident fissures within the civil rights movement. In one of the most sweeping statements of his riveting and at times polemical account of the "unraveling" of American liberalism in the 1960s, historian Allen J. Matusow went even further. "The real meaning of the [White House] conference was this," he insisted. "So far as the president was concerned, the civil rights movement was over."[1]

Lyndon Johnson, his allies inside as well as outside of the administration, and many other civil rights advocates would certainly have appealed Matusow's verdict, even if many feared it held a kernel of historical truth. The president's attention to domestic affairs might have diminished, but he clearly hoped to continue and even expand his antipoverty programs. Although issues concerning the war in Vietnam had dominated his State of the Union Address in January 1966, several White House advisers were quick to note that he had brought moderate and liberal members of Congress to their feet with a plea that the nation not use the war as an excuse to "sacrifice the children who seek learning, or the sick who need medical care, or the families who dwell in squalor."[2]

The administration's approach to civil rights policy certainly appeared to be badly adrift and hesitant at times, but there is no evidence that the White House actively sought disengagement. The operations and programs of the nation's growing civil rights bureaucracy did not suddenly disappear. Throughout the offices of the "permanent government" and in the White House itself, individuals continued to focus on domestic policy issues directly related to civil rights and economic justice agendas. And, despite its manifold shortcomings, the White House Conference on Civil Rights still convened in June 1966, after more than six months of intensive preparations.

Even though movement activists across a broad spectrum of diverse organizations and ideologies probably appreciated historian Allen J. Matusow's comparison of Johnson to Machiavelli's "The Prince," individuals working at the grass roots had continued to organize in the northern cities and the rural South. "The" movement had not collapsed, but the scope, depth, duration, and bias of mainstream media coverage had changed dramatically.

Reporters had often neglected grassroots protests, especially in the remote areas of the rural South and in the unfamiliar geography of the urban North. In 1965 and 1966, ongoing organizing by MFDP activists in Mississippi and by the Lowndes County Freedom Organization in southwest Alabama failed to attract major media attention except in moments of crisis or when the local intersected with the national. Racially motivated acts of violence were always assured column space, especially if the victims were white. But few reporters or their readers dwelled on the discrepancy between massive coverage of the deaths of the "Mississippi Three"—two of them white—in 1964 and the reportorial silence about the unsolved murders of three additional African Americans in the Magnolia State that season. Similarly, in neighboring Alabama, James Reeb, Viola Liuzzo, and Jon Daniels became household names, while black martyr Jimmie Lee Jackson—whose killing in the town of Marion jump-started the most well-known stage of the Selma area movement—was all but forgotten. Despite scathing attacks by state newspapers, CDGM had survived, largely because of its liberal northern allies' ability to mobilize journalistic attention, especially in print media and opinion journals. And, in 1966, Mississippi was once more in the camera's eye.

In the first week of June 1966, less than seventy-two hours after departing the White House Conference on Civil Rights, James Meredith began to walk south from Memphis to Jackson, Mississippi, the capital of a state that many activists and historians had called the "iceberg" of race relations. Given the sweltering reality of Mississippi's summer and racial climate, the metaphor seemed odd but not inappropriate in terms of the magnitude of a "thaw" that would be required to reshape white attitudes. Meredith chose U.S. Route 51, what he called "the classic route of the Mississippi Negro, a concrete river heading away from home," during the Great Migrations to the fabled "Promised Land" of the North. He told newsmen he planned to complete a 220-mile, sixteen-day, reverse pilgrimage. Meredith, the first African American to integrate the University of Mississippi in the fall of 1962, hoped that this new personal example of courage—which he dubbed a "March against Fear"—might encourage others to break the grip of psychological intimidation that underlay black disfranchisement and segregation in the Magnolia State. Nearly two years after passage of the Civil Rights Act and ten months after passage of the Voting Rights Act, large numbers of white Mississippians still openly flouted the federal legislation. "Colored" and "White" signs and practices were commonplace, especially in rural areas and small towns and hamlets, and the work of registering thousands of African American voters was still far from complete. Meredith also hoped by this example to embolden large numbers of blacks to participate in a statewide primary scheduled for June 7, 1966.

On June 5, just under four years shy of his integration of Ole Miss, Meredith departed from Memphis carrying an African walking stick, the gift of a Sudanese chief, and wearing a pith helmet, which he ironically noted "had once been the hated symbol of the white man in . . . 'darkest Africa.'" Twenty-four hours later, on the second day of the march and only a few miles into Mississippi near the small town of Hernando, a white man from Memphis named Aubrey James Norvell abruptly emerged from where he had been concealed and called Meredith twice by name. Then, as reporters and a handful of individuals sympathetic to the civil rights activist scattered, Norvell fired his shotgun three times. His assault left Meredith stunned and bleeding on the ground, with buckshot wounds to his back and neck.[3]

Both federal and state law enforcement agents witnessed the ambush, and Mississippi State Troopers quickly arrested the suspect. Other officials rushed the barely conscious civil rights activist to Bowld Hospital in nearby Memphis. The first media reports erroneously indicated that Meredith's wounds were critical, perhaps even fatal. Amid a welter of conflicting rumors, a veritable "Who's Who" of African American civil rights leaders representing most of the national organizations converged on Memphis, and several leaders made preparations to resume the march from the point where Meredith had fallen.

Senator John Stennis insisted to the president—who wasted no time in labeling the shooting "an awful act of violence"—that the full weight of the state's law enforcement would be devoted to ensuring that Meredith's assailant would be "fully prosecuted," but he urged Johnson to "use your vast influence to call upon all extremists to stay out of Mississippi." To allow the new marchers to proceed would be a grave threat to the maintenance of "law and order" in the Magnolia State. Governor Paul Johnson grudgingly assured reporters that local law enforcement and state forces "will be used to see that these demonstrators get all the marching they want, provided they behave themselves, commit no acts of violence nor take a position of provocative defiance." In contrast to earlier episodes in which Washington officials and southern politicians had traded public accusations, the Johnson administration took pains to keep contacts between the Justice Department and Governor Johnson confidential.[4]

As preparations for a resumption of Meredith's march by the major civil rights organizations went forward, the white leadership of the Magnolia State scrambled to avoid the kind of national condemnation that had marked earlier civil rights confrontations. Governor Johnson's press release two days after Meredith was wounded emphasized the fact that the assailant was from another state, boasted of state law enforcement's role in Norvell's quick capture, and assured a nationwide audience that "all Mississippians" "deplored" the attack on the civil rights activist. At the same time, the governor trained his sights on the new detachment of marchers already heading southward. These "agitators" were attempting to stage "a big production to foment strife and hate . . . for the purpose of whipping up civil rights laws." He referred to the 1966 civil rights package then being debated in Congress—legislation that in the governor's eyes would never successfully deter those bent on violence. The governor beseeched white Mississippians to exercise "forbearance and restraint" until the "exhibitionists" "complete their show."[5]

Stokely Carmichael, Cleveland Sellers, and Stanley Wise of SNCC were among the first civil rights leaders to arrive in Memphis, determined to continue Meredith's effort, and they were joined there shortly by Martin Luther King Jr. of SCLC and Floyd McKissick of CORE. McKissick had been among the most outspoken voices of dissent just days before at the White House Conference on Civil Rights. Failing to take up the march in Meredith's stead, the activists pointed out, would fatally undercut the message of assertiveness that Meredith had sought to dramatize. Weighing such decisions in the aftermath of violence was all too familiar to many movement veterans whose individual activist histories dated back to direct action campaigns, including the Freedom Rides and the Birmingham protests and voter registration work in Mississippi, Alabama, and elsewhere. Two of the three organizations were undergoing important transitions. McKissick had succeeded James Farmer as director of CORE in January 1966, and SNCC had boycotted the conference entirely after Stokely Carmichael's election to replace John Lewis as chairman in May.

Lewis, fresh from his "de-election," engineered by a faction whose power in SNCC was growing, was himself far more skeptical about the advisability of continuing the march, in part because of his doubts about Meredith. The man who had integrated the University of Mississippi was a figure of considerable symbolic significance, said Lewis, but in his estimation Meredith had never been a part of the movement in the collectivist sense of that term. "He was a strange bird from the beginning. . . . One day he'd be in Hawaii, and the next he'd announce that he was going to run for the president." Lewis was also concerned about the improvisational nature of the civil rights movement leaders' response to Meredith's shooting. The "situation was different from Selma, where the march was a culmination of a long campaign with a particular focus." Freelance journalist Paul Good agreed that the Meredith March lacked the "clean lines of purpose, national backing and surface unity of the Selma to Montgomery March." But the black activists who were the mainspring of the march were "one year deeper into frustration and disillusion," a frustration that created a showcase for a very public debate that had been simmering within various quarters of the civil rights movement for months, and in some cases, years. Despite his misgivings, Lewis eventually joined the march in progress.[6]

King, McKissick, and Carmichael visited Meredith in the hospital on June 7 to discover to their relief that his wounds were not nearly as serious as had initially been feared. They joined Meredith's marching route on that very afternoon, walking three abreast in the thick heat along the winding Mississippi highway and leading an improvised column of a dozen-and-a-half other marchers, mostly African Americans and with a small contingent of increasingly uneasy whites. Within minutes, Mississippi state troopers unceremoniously shoved them to the shoulder of the road, knocking SNCC's Cleveland Sellers to the ground and almost provoking Carmichael to violence.

King later recalled hearing "words [that] fell on my ears like strange music from a foreign land." Angry African American marchers urged their leaders to make the affair an "all-black march" and declared, "We don't need any more white phonies and liberals invading our movement." "If one of these damn white Mississippi crackers touches me," threatened one demonstrator, "I'm gonna kick the hell out of him." King hoped the singing of the benedictory anthem "We Shall Overcome" would restore a degree of harmony, but the volume of the singing fell appreciably during the stanza "Black and White Together." "This is a new day," a marcher told him as the afternoon progressed. "We Shall Overcome" was a passive modality, a gentle hymn, out of step with the tenor of the times. The lyrics should be rewritten: "We Shall Overrun."[7]

Both Whitney Young of the Urban League and Roy Wilkins of the NAACP had initially been reluctant to travel to Memphis and join the leaders of SCLC, SNCC, and CORE. The two moderates distanced themselves from plans to continue the march, however, as it became increasingly obvious that the ideological contours of a protest with heavy participation by SNCC members were not to their liking. Young and Wilkins wanted the march to become a lobbying vehicle for the president's proposed civil rights legislation. SNCC, CORE, and—to a lesser extent—King and the SCLC he represented had a different set of priorities.

Stokely Carmichael, SNCC's new chairman, deliberately antagonized Wilkins and Young, refusing to agree that the march would be conducted in a spirit of unconditional nonviolence and clearly signaling that in no way would the protest be co-opted by the president's legislative agenda. At a mass meeting with as many as a thousand people packed into Rev. James Lawson's Centenary Methodist Church in Memphis on the evening of June 7, Floyd McKissick expressed his lack of faith in the president's 1966 civil rights agenda and updated his "hoax" charge to label as "rigged" the White House Conference on Civil Rights from the previous week. CORE's national director drew an even more raucous response from the crowd when he offered the colorful symbolic suggestion that the most honest treatment of the Statue of Liberty would be "to break that young lady's legs and throw her into the Mississippi [River]." Charles Evers drew cheers as he evoked the virtues of frontier western-style gunplay in retaliation for the assault on Meredith, and King was only marginally successful in his appeals for nonviolence, arguing that armed militancy would play directly into the hands of white racists.[8]

"I started cursing real bad," Carmichael recalled later of the tense exchange with his more moderate civil rights rivals at the Lorraine Motel that took place following the public mass meeting (the same Memphis landmark would later enter the martyrology of the movement). SNCC deliberately "played out the image of militancy, knowing full well Wilkins and Young would find it unpalatable." Carmichael's angry profanity cemented the decision of the NAACP and the Urban League to withdraw. The NAACP leader finally snapped and, in his own recollection, left "in disgust" when Carmichael referred disparagingly to Lyndon Johnson as "that cat the President." When Wilkins announced his intention to pull out, along with the NAACP, one SNCC staffer remembered, "We used that opportunity to say to Roy Wilkins what people in our organization had been wanting to say for so long—that is, to retire, to teach in a college and write a book about his earlier days." Wilkins's parting words came in the form of a condolence for King, who had telegraphed his intention to remain and have SCLC play a role in the planned resumption of the march: "Dr. King, I'm really sorry for you."[9]

SNCC had taken a more judicious approach to handling SCLC. Carmichael and his lieutenants recognized that without King's participation the march would not only lose the charismatic leader's crowd appeal but would also run the risk of a media blackout. SNCC's new leader was involved in a Machiavellian exercise of his own: "We wanted to pull [King] out to the left." Rid of the "right wing"—his dismissive description of Roy Wilkins and Whitney Young and the venerable organizations they represented—Carmichael was convinced that "King would have to come to the left." At this point, he and the new leadership of SNCC argued that white participation should be deemphasized and marchers should be protected by the Deacons for Defense and Justice, a group whose membership had expanded in Louisiana after it publicly advocated the doctrine of armed self-defense. A clearly uneasy King and a slightly less anxious Floyd McKissick of CORE agreed to allow the Deacons to guard the march.[10]

Stokely Carmichael and other SNCC staffers had occasionally left the path of the Selma to Montgomery March in Alabama the previous year in forays that laid the foundations for SNCC's return to Lowndes County and the ongoing development of the Lowndes County Freedom Organization. Soon after the resumption of the Memphis to Jackson march, leaders of the participating organizations drew up plans to register black voters along their route and to stage acts of civil disobedience if these registration efforts encountered white opposition. In a joint manifesto, they called for 600 federal registrars in Mississippi and castigated the Johnson administration for its failure to protect civil rights workers in the exercise of constitutionally guaranteed rights.

Paul Johnson had provided a substantial Highway Patrol escort for the activists during the first week of the march, but as the demonstrators advanced through the state and grew more assertive in their speeches and demands, the governor dramatically reduced the size of the state law enforcement presence, from twenty state troopers to four, leaving the protection of the group in the hands of local lawmen, who were notorious for their racist and iron-fisted treatment of blacks, especially civil rights activists. "I'm not going to wet nurse a bunch of showmen," he said, in defending his decision to reduce the level of state protection. The fact that the timing of that reduction coincided with the marchers' successful registration of over 1,000 new African American voters in and around the town of Grenada in one two-day period seemed unlikely to be a coincidence.[11] Ultimately, organizers added 4,000 new African American voters to registration rolls, with more than twice that number joining the column of marchers for at least part of their journey, despite the appearance of fissures among the march's leaders and their lieutenants.[12]

The initial manifesto signed by the leaders of CORE, SCLC, and SNCC had papered over ideological differences, and the righteous indignation greeting Meredith's shooting helped to foster a common sense of purpose. But with each passing mile, the differences among the civil rights groups grew more apparent. As the relatively small group of marchers wound their way deeper into Mississippi, they traveled through areas that had previously been SNCC strongholds under the umbrella of COFO. At nightly rallies, the three major organizations and their leaders competed for support. They were engaged in a balancing act, appealing for black unity while simultaneously staking out subtle and not-so-subtle differences—programmatic and ideological—refracted through the lens of powerful and charismatic personalities. McKissick and Carmichael took more radical stands. King argued for the ongoing relevance of nonviolence, reiterating SCLC's insistence on a philosophy of "redemptive love" and "soul force." "Power," Carmichael rebutted, "is the only thing that is respected in this world, and we must get it at any cost."

With these internal debates growing increasingly heated, Carmichael dispatched SNCC staffer Willie Ricks to act as advance man along the projected march route, drumming up interest among local audiences and seeking to ensure large crowds at the nightly rallies. Ricks reported back to Carmichael that his use of the paired words "Black Power" guaranteed a tremendous response at various churches and community gatherings.[13]

SNCC and its leadership awaited the proper opportunity to put Ricks's research to the test. On June 16, when Carmichael was arrested in Greenwood, Mississippi, for putting up tents in a local black schoolyard without permission, he posted bond and then returned to the march. At the evening rally, Carmichael told followers that "every courthouse in Mississippi should be burnt down tomorrow so we can get rid of the dirt."[14] He continued dramatically, "This is the twenty-seventh time I have been arrested—and I ain't going to jail no more!"[15]

Blacks who had been pleading for freedom for six years and had, from their perspective, made few gains embraced the new vocabulary of protest: "What we gonna start saying now is 'Black Power'!" Willie Ricks had correctly anticipated the readiness of this audience. When Stokely Carmichael yelled the question "What do you want?!" the crowd exploded in unison: "Black Power!" Though different from the call-and-response litany that Martin Luther King Jr. established with his audiences, the new antiphon was no less powerful, and in this case even more participatory. That the appearance of spontaneity had been carefully crafted was largely lost on most observers. Camera flashes lit the gathering, and national reporters hurried to file stories about a slogan that many whites would soon see as incendiary and menacing, though its genesis was rooted in countless acts of white violence.

Journalist Paul Good, covering the march as a freelance writer, was disgusted by what he saw as shallow and superficial media coverage. At the first

sign of conflict between marchers, wire service reporters and television cameramen "shoot from the[ir] truck[s] like flushed quail," wrote Good. Mile after
mile, open bed trucks filled with black field hands passed by, "heading for their
$3 a day in the sun, serfs in a cotton industry receiving a billion a year in federal
subsidies." But the newsmen showed little interest in this or in the hundreds of
dilapidated shacks "where the essence of the march was made flesh in the lives
of Negroes whose median income was $600 a year, whose atrophied political
instincts were still held in check despite the Voting Rights Act, by threats of
dispossession from the land, firing from job, or other retaliation." Too often,
reporters could only see dissension as they stared "straight through the realities
of a Deep South that was changing grudgingly and only when pressure grew
too great to bear, pressure sometimes instigated by the federal government but
most often by the understaffed and overextended civil rights groups."[16]

Thus, "Black Power"—with its overtones of black militancy—became the
focus of news coverage of the march, diverting attention from its goal—to
register new black voters—and its earlier symbolic focus on blacks' refusal to
be cowed by a state legendary for its climate of institutionalized intimidation
and racism. Even though King, McKissick, and Carmichael struck a bargain
agreeing to forgo the use of the slogans "Freedom Now" and "Black Power"
during the remaining stages of the march, the genie was out of the bottle, and
both SNCC and headline-hungry white media would find the new story line
irresistible.[17]

On June 21, as the civil rights caravan moved deeper into the Delta, King
and a small group of twenty marchers made a three-hour detour across the
state to Philadelphia, Mississippi, where local whites had murdered Andrew
Goodman, James Chaney, and Michael Schwerner two years earlier. When
King tried to lead a small rally of 250 black Neshoba County residents onto the
courthouse lawn, sheriff's deputy Cecil Ray Price, still not indicted two years
after his role in the infamous murders, blocked the group. As angry whites
surrounded the marchers and began shouting and heckling a shaken King,
he called out, "I believe in my heart, the murderers are somewhere around
me at this moment." A smirking Price responded quietly: "You're damn right,
they're right behind you right now."[18] As he led his dispirited followers back to
the black section of Philadelphia, whites pummeled and kicked several of the
marchers and beat two white photographers who had been covering the rally.

Philadelphia was only a dress rehearsal. Two days later, marchers tried to
pitch their overnight tents on the grounds of a black elementary school in
Canton, Mississippi, and in an eerie replay of the Selma bridge incident, state
troopers and local police confronted the marchers, ordered them to leave, and

then donned their gas masks. When the crowd stood silently, lawmen fired off dozens of canisters of tear gas and waded into the marchers swinging their billy clubs. As one journalist said, this was more than an attempt to disperse a crowd—police, state troopers, and sheriff's deputies "came stomping in behind the gas, gun-butting and kicking the men, women and children. They were not arresting, they were punishing." Dr. Alvin Poussaint, a representative of the Medical Committee for Human Rights, accompanied the march, and he and another doctor were up all night treating the victims. It was, he said, like a war zone in the aftermath of a battle.[19]

Had they happened just one year earlier, the brutal beatings in Canton might have ignited national outrage. But in 1966, the incident barely registered among most whites. Far more interesting to white readers were the fault lines in the movement, which grew sharper as marchers ignored their leaders' unity agreement and chanted "Freedom Now" and "Black Power" in a competitive black antiphony. What could have been heard as alternating theme and response now sounded like jarring and deliberate dissonance. As he watched the events of the Meredith March against Fear unfold, John Lewis quietly began to sever his ties with the six-year-old SNCC. In the aftermath of the Canton police riot, despite growing philosophical differences with Carmichael, Lewis briefly joined demonstrators out of a sense of solidarity. When he addressed a rally and spoke about nonviolence, however, he found his audience drifting away. The veteran of countless direct action campaigns in the South thought that the Meredith March was in many ways a disaster; he felt that its spontaneity, which some observers saw as an asset, left little chance for the kind of coherent programmatic focus the Selma to Montgomery March had achieved.

Governor Paul Johnson, anticipating that his state would weather what he repeatedly derided in press releases as "the so-called Civil Rights march," was in a self-congratulatory mood as the march drew to a close.[20] Plagued by renewed police brutality and a steady stream of physical and verbal attacks by whites, the march finally ended on June 26 with a rally at the state capitol. Meredith joined the final leg of the triumphant procession, and Carmichael addressed the assembled crowd of approximately 15,000—easily the largest of the entire march but noticeably lacking the appearance of group unity and solidarity that had characterized earlier mass gatherings in Washington, D.C., in 1963 and Montgomery in 1965. Blacks, Carmichael declared, should "build a power base . . . so strong that we will bring [whites] to their knees every time they mess with us."[21]

SNCC militants realized they had lost any meaningful political leverage over the administration of Lyndon Johnson after pulling out of the White House

Conference on Civil Rights weeks earlier, but in the waning days of the Meredith March, CORE's Floyd McKissick, King, and other participants had sought to paint the administration into a corner, citing Mississippi governor Paul Johnson's only half-hearted attempts to restrain violent law enforcement and attacks from white bystanders in Canton and Philadelphia, Mississippi.

Other civil rights leaders and march sympathizers joined McKissick in demanding that the president dispatch federal protection to "lawless Mississippi." But Johnson refused to accede to such requests. During the Selma to Montgomery March, George Wallace had refused to guarantee the safety of the marchers and thus had forced the administration's hand into federalizing the troops. Governor Paul Johnson, on the other hand, offered empty assurances of his determination to fulfill his duties, just as the very law officers charged with protecting the marchers swung billy clubs at them and lobbed tear-gas-filled grenades into their midst. So long as Mississippi's chief executive at least verbally remained committed to the rule of law, the White House was determined not to become further embroiled in the controversial march. Martin Luther King Jr. refused to keep silent about the self-evident charade, pointing out the behavior of "the very state patrol . . . that President Johnson said . . . would protect us. Anyone who will use gas bombs on women and children can't and won't protect anybody."[22]

The White House did maintain steady contacts with leaders on the Meredith March, primarily through the Department of Justice's John Doar. During his service to three successive administrations, Doar had always displayed a knack for placing himself in the middle of difficult civil rights confrontations. He functioned as the administration's "point man" for the Meredith March, operating as a liaison between civil rights activists, Mississippi state government officials, and the White House, an unenviable job. Through Doar, King repeatedly asked President Johnson for federal protection, following attacks on civil rights marchers at various points along the march route. "I've heard nothing from President Johnson," King acknowledged from the march route. "It's terribly frustrating and disappointing. I don't know what I'm going to do."

Inside the White House, Harry McPherson urged LBJ to respond personally to King, even as he recommended that the president publicly abjure additional federal involvement. The White House aide's logic spoke volumes about the administration's attempts to navigate its way through the roiling currents of civil rights leadership and suggested that the increasingly strained relationship between the White House and the SCLC leader was not beyond salvaging. "King is useful to us," McPherson asserted, "and needs the prestige of a reply by you."[23]

LBJ evidently felt otherwise. The White House press secretary announced that LBJ had "no specific reaction" to the violence in Canton. Preoccupied throughout the entire month of June by mounting U.S. casualties in Vietnam, he was authorizing a sharp escalation in American bombing. In a private dinner with Georgia senator Richard Russell, the president divulged classified information about his evolving strategy in Southeast Asia and alluded to the events of the Meredith March as though they were karmic retribution for his having parted ways with his longtime friend Russell on the question of civil rights. In between speculating about the likelihood of King being assassinated and noting King's difficult balancing act in sharing the stage of the march with the more militant Carmichael, the president actually praised Mississippi law enforcement for having practiced relative restraint, this just days after the mayhem in Canton.[24]

King had tried to walk a tightrope through the Meredith March. He recognized the inherent dangers of the slogan—he would label "Black Power" "an unfortunate choice of words"—but was aware that the new militancy might potentially be used for leverage as he broadcast a warning to LBJ and whites in America: "The government has got to give me some victories if I'm gonna keep people nonviolent," King said. "I know I'm gonna stay nonviolent no matter what happens. But a lot of people are getting hurt and bitter, and they can't see it that way any more." The SCLC leader's entreaties that blacks remember "that some white people in the United States are just as determined to see us free as we are to free ourselves" seemed almost anachronistic.[25]

White House aide McPherson had painstakingly drawn up a series of answers to questions about the federal government's hands-off attitude toward the Meredith March that he expected Lyndon Johnson might face in a press conference. The proposed replies laid the responsibility for law enforcement at Governor Paul Johnson's doorstep, and McPherson urged the president to walk his own tightrope in any responses to the ideological tenor of the march or to the growing appearance of a vocal minority espousing racial separatism. Johnson was to stress the theme that "real progress cannot be achieved in an atmosphere of intolerance and hatred—either of the white for the Negro, or of the Negro for the white." If asked directly for his response to the charged phrase "Black Power," McPherson's script called for Johnson to stress his advocacy of "democratic power—[with a] little 'd.'" To achieve a greater measure of equality in employment, housing, and education would require the "vision and . . . hard work of every individual. It is going to take working together—not in two armed camps."[26]

ike it or not, "Black Power is now a part of the nomenclature of the national community," King would subsequently suggest, in *Where Do We Go from Here: Chaos or Community?*, a meditation published in 1967 in which the SCLC leader openly debated how best to follow up on the victories of the civil rights era's heyday, recent triumphs that nevertheless now threatened to enter the realm of distant nostalgic recollection. To understand Black Power, "one must look beyond personal styles, verbal flourishes, and the hysteria of the mass media to assess its values, its assets and liabilities honestly."[27]

Stokely Carmichael had needed the presence of Martin Luther King Jr. to ensure that the resumption of James Meredith's "March against Fear" received significant media coverage, but the Black Power slogan had quickly eclipsed even King's considerable star power. The SCLC leader's assessment of the growing "hysterical" tendencies of coverage of American race relations was not much of an exaggeration. Still, King would seek to maintain his reputation as the principle advocate of nonviolence while spelling out the perils of ignoring the pleas of his seemingly more militant rivals.[28] The dynamic interplay between the leaders of the two organizations was not unlike the pas de deux King had danced with earlier militants, such as Robert Williams of Monroe, North Carolina, and Muslim leader and brilliant polemicist Malcolm X.[29] Just as King *needed* white antagonists like Eugene "Bull" Connor and George Wallace (SCLC insiders in fact regularly joked that Connor was the "best friend" the movement had ever had), so too did he need rhetorical and ideological foils within the African American community.

When King emerged into the limelight during the Montgomery Bus Boycott, he became, according to movement historian Charles Payne, "the inheritor of momentum that other people established. . . . Other people constructed the stage, but once he stepped into the role of movement spokesperson, his charisma, broad appeal, and personal growth allowed him to project the message of the movement in ways that virtually no one could have predicted in 1956."[30] In Mississippi, a decade later, King could not always play the lead role. He was continually upstaged, not necessarily by Stokely Carmichael, but by an idea: Black Power.

King reasoned that the slogan would "confuse our allies, isolate the Negro community, and give many prejudiced whites, who might otherwise be ashamed of their anti-Negro feeling, a ready excuse for self-justification." But Carmichael and other SNCC and CORE leaders represented an increasingly vocal constituency, one committed to a movement in which blacks would call the shots and unite under a powerful—and to most audiences a novel—rallying cry.

The preceding summer, on the eve of Johnson's Howard University speech, Nicholas Katzenbach had reflected on the "danger of too much militancy" among civil rights activists. He worried that extremism "would alienate liberal white support, without which we can't do what we are doing. But without militancy, you would not have had the Mississippi Summer Project [of 1964]. It's a very delicate balance."[31]

"Mississippi is everywhere," argued James Meredith. He had debated whether to carry a gun on the march. His grandfather, he decided, would have found foolhardy his decision to bring a family Bible instead. Within weeks after the march, Meredith wrote a piece for the *Saturday Evening Post*, arguing in a mournful tone that "nonviolence is incompatible with American ideals. . . . America is a tough country, and a man has to look out for his own. . . . To ask Negroes to support nonviolence is to ask them to be . . . something alien in their own country."[32]

In the aftermath of the Meredith March, the Black Power slogan resonated far beyond Mississippi's highways. Governor Paul Johnson called it "the greatest threat to law and order and domestic tranquility ever heard in this country," a response shared by most whites across the nation, who reacted as though struck by a thunderbolt. These unfamiliar new militants and their sloganeering drew white media like moths to a flame. A Herblock cartoon in the *Washington Post* depicted Black Power as a "Dangerous Genie." For its part, *Time* magazine wasted little time in labeling the slogan the clarion call of "the new racism." Two perceptive writers spoke to the heart of the matter when they described Black Power as a "fright concept" that deeply divided civil rights activists and alarmed white moderates who saw it as a form of reverse racism.[33]

The Black Power slogan may have represented a rhetorical escalation, but it was not the first time a civil rights catchphrase had alarmed whites. In July 1963, Vice President Lyndon Johnson's aide George Reedy had written to Johnson warning that the rallying cry "Freedom Now" and the very meaning of the word "integration" made whites uneasy, or even conveyed a sense of unimagined horrors just around the corner. For African Americans, integration reflected the desire for access to public institutions "which are essential to economic survival in modern competitive life," but, according to Reedy, to many whites, the concept "invokes nightmares of mulatto children; wild sex orgies; and the inability to spend a quiet evening at home with a few friends."[34]

For African Americans, the new slogan summoned emotions rooted in their long search for self-determination and self-identity. It also represented *new* dimensions of anger and bitterness at the failure of the United States to respond to their entreaties for civil rights. The potency of the phrase overshadowed

King's usual monopoly of the limelight and thrust a young Stokely Carmichael into the glare of national media attention. Following the advent of the Black Power slogan, SNCC's new chairman increasingly faced the dilemma of having his rhetoric become divorced from the organization's long-standing commitment to grassroots organizing. As with King, the media fueled this obsession with style over substance, but the irony was striking, given the withering criticisms that SNCC staffers had on occasion leveled against King and other SCLC leaders in the past. One SCLC staffer captured Carmichael's dilemma succinctly: "Stokely didn't get a chance to give any meaning to black power. He threw the words out, and before he could explain it the press had taken it and used it as a bludgeon."[35] In its conceptual elasticity, the slogan was bigger than Stokely Carmichael, bigger even than the memory of Malcolm X.[36]

For every voice that championed the slogan, a chorus of leaders—white and black—spoke out against its use. The White House was especially eager for "moderate" African American civil rights leaders to lead the way in condemning its use, reasoning that their disapproval would be seen as somehow more legitimate or authentic. Roy Wilkins gamely played along. As the Meredith March concluded in July, Wilkins circulated within the NAACP a letter condemning the march's failure to spotlight passage of the still-pending Civil Rights Act as a "civil rights tragedy." The NAACP leader spoke acidly of the near impossibility of cooperating "with groups . . . which may very well be pursuing certain goals that have nothing to do with civil rights at all."[37]

The phrase "Black Power" placed Wilkins and some of Johnson's other African American allies in a difficult rhetorical predicament, and later in the summer of 1966 the depth of Wilkins's anger became evident at the NAACP annual convention in Los Angeles. He spoke out against the new slogan, arguing that in the end the concept equated with "black death." "Black Power" was "a reverse Mississippi, a reverse Hitler, a reverse Ku Klux Klan . . . the father of hatred and the mother of violence."[38]

O n August 24, the *Jackson (Miss.) Clarion-Ledger* reported that CDGM had offered its facilities to civil rights marchers for food preparation. In the article, unnamed investigators—undoubtedly working for the Mississippi State Sovereignty Commission—also claimed that "Black Power" signs were clearly visible in a number of CDGM Head Start centers. CDGM officials freely conceded that some signs advertising upcoming meetings were there and noted that the centers often doubled as community centers by night. The centers, they pointed out, were often the only buildings available for use by unpopular groups such as those that had organized the Meredith March.[39]

In January 1966, civil rights activists had staged a sit-in at an abandoned air force base near Greenville, Mississippi, to draw attention to the plight of the growing numbers of homeless agricultural laborers in the state, many displaced by the increasing mechanization of the cotton industry. The air force base occupation proved to be an irritant to Mississippi politicians and to the Johnson administration. The group of black activists drafted a manifesto that sought to force Lyndon Johnson off the fence in his dealings with the state's white political establishment: "Whose side are you on—the poor people's or the millionaires?"[40]

Mississippi politicians were convinced that the sit-in's leaders were associated with CDGM. When Governor Johnson found out in early February 1966 that CDGM was to be partially refunded by OEO, he bypassed Shriver and fired off an outraged telegram to the White House charging that the CDGM staff was part of "the same group that broke into the Greenville Air Force Base, flaunted the federal laws, defied federal authorities, and spoke openly of overthrowing our national government." Having pointedly emphasized ties between CDGM staff and calls by some civil rights leaders in Mississippi to resist the draft for the Vietnam War, the governor demanded that the president bring an end to this "shameful situation."[41]

Echoing Governor Johnson's earlier charges that CDGM served as a "front" for civil rights groups, Senator James Eastland took to the Senate floor and lashed out at the junior college grantee, Mary Holmes Junior College, as being "a shadow organization" that allowed an end run around the state governor's veto power. He scornfully attacked the motives of CDGM staff. The "education [of preschool children] is the furtherest [sic] thing from their minds," he told his fellow senators. The entire antipoverty granting process had become little more than "a device to funnel funds into the extreme leftist civil rights and beatnik groups in our state, some of which have definite connections with Communist organizations." Eastland warned that if CDGM's funding were not revoked, it would taint the poverty program nationwide.[42]

Even with CDGM funding for the immediate future apparently secure, rumors circulated within the civil rights community that Lyndon Johnson had offered a "quid pro quo" to Stennis: OEO would rein in CDGM in return for the senator's blessing of appropriations for the escalating American commitment in South Vietnam. Supporters of CDGM nationwide also suspected LBJ and his allies of attempting to muster a "third force" in Mississippi politics—the group that came to be known as the Loyalist Democrats—against the segregationist "regulars" and the embattled remnants of the MFDP.[43]

The rumors were not far from the truth. Through friendly administration contacts in Mississippi, LBJ and his lieutenants — Harry McPherson prominent among them — kept close tabs on the unfolding CDGM controversy and, in line with the administration's emphasis on consensus, sought damage control at every step. White House aide Harry McPherson held a less than charitable view of CDGM, accusing it in his memoir of being "riddled with nepotism" and subscribing to the view that it had misused funds and government automobiles and that its response to official inquiries had been "evasive."[44] Given the president's aversion to bad publicity about OEO programs, Shriver and the bureaucrats who administered grants scrambled to squelch internal reports that might be interpreted as failures in the War on Poverty before they became public. One of OEO's biggest divisions, in fact, was its public affairs office, run by Herbert J. Kramer, a veteran of corporate advertising, who made no bones about his division of OEO being patterned after "an in-house advertising agency." According to this logic, the more CDGM threatened to discredit the War on Poverty brand, the greater the likelihood it would be removed from the product line. But in-house efforts to exercise political damage control inevitably strengthened the hands of conservatives, who simply raised the level of their attacks.

By summer 1966, barely more than two years since the president's declaration of an unconditional war on poverty, bureaucratic competition and infighting over shrinking appropriations for social programs had intensified problems for those within the OEO who were most committed to the concept of "maximum feasible participation" of the poor. In the first heady months of the War on Poverty, Sargent Shriver had warned of the consequences of backdoor political compromises. "The danger of politics," he told the General Assembly of the United Presbyterian Church, "is that we will . . . reduce demand, lower expectations, temporize, and delay." None of this would take place out in the open. "We are too clever, we are too crafty, we are too wise in the ways of the world for that." Instead, the men and women who sat in their offices in Washington would "say all the right words. We will take all the right stances, and we will make the right gestures," assuring those struggling in these new programs that "we are doing our best. . . . But we will fail . . . to add the significant words, *on our own terms*."[45]

To Lyndon Johnson, whose whole life was politics, every program had to be weighed and evaluated from exactly those practical considerations. As he later confided to biographer Doris Kearns, "I wish the public had seen the task of ending poverty the same way as they saw the task of getting to the moon, where they accepted mistakes and failures as part of the programs, admitting that some were working better than others." But, he added, "I knew the moment we said out loud that this or that program was a failure, then the wolves who never wanted us to be successful in the first place would be down upon us at once, tearing away at every joint, killing our effort before we even had a chance."[46]

The bitter controversy in 1965 and 1966 over funding for CDGM erupted against the backdrop of the Meredith March and new press "exposés" of radicalism in Mississippi's Head Start program. Stennis and other state politicians continued to hound CDGM for what they called its "subversive" activities, and they increasingly gained new allies from both sides of the aisle and from both sides of the Mason-Dixon Line. Senate and House conservatives joined the hunt and intensified their scrutiny of CDGM and other vulnerable War on Poverty CAP grants in the rural South, as well as the urban North.

In late September 1966, CDGM's critics received powerful new ammunition from Donald Baker, of the OEO's in-house Office of Inspection, who penned a savage indictment of the Head Start organization's "deficiencies" in a memo to Shriver. Baker, who had served as staff director for the House Committee on Education and Labor before moving to the newly created OEO, strongly supported the Johnson antipoverty agenda. As one of his friends later explained, Baker saw himself as caught between "sea monsters on all sides": ideologues on the right who wanted to destroy the program entirely and those on the left who wanted to use it for broader political purposes. For Baker, Head Start was a childhood education program best run by professionals. Instead, he concluded, in "many areas it was converted from a child-oriented program" to a "public employment program" for "illiterate, untrained Negroes" who did little more than "baby-sit the children." What was worse, in Baker's estimation, CDGM had become a "tool of the black militants. . . . The fact of the matter is, a lot of our money went to pay for the automobiles and to feed the marchers" participating in the Meredith March against Fear. Only a complete overhaul of the organization "from top to bottom" could remedy the deficiencies he had described, concluded Baker. Clearly he knew that no one thought such an overhaul likely.[47]

As Robert Levine, an OEO friend, acknowledged, Baker was a political pragmatist who saw his role as advising Shriver on how to "work out that [CDGM] mess" in order to avoid being "cut off at the pass by the Congress." Whatever Baker's rationale, his report simply gave segregationist politicians additional ammunition for their vendetta against these and other antipoverty programs. In its wake, Mississippi's senator Stennis issued an ultimatum demanding that the Head Start program not receive additional funding.

Lyndon Johnson was already anxious about the 1966 midterm elections and concerned that he would lose large portions of the South in 1968 to Republicans or third-party challengers like George Wallace. White House aide and fellow-Texan Harry McPherson, who closely monitored the electoral pulse, told the president: "Moderate friends in Mississippi warned me that CDGM's political activities would destroy any chance the national Democratic party might have to carry the state in 1968."

At least one historian has suggested that the "Bobby factor" made Johnson acutely aware of the status of the CDGM controversy. Since Robert Kennedy had been among the Mississippi Head Start program's champions, CDGM may have "activated another of Johnson's obsessive fears as well, the fear of being politically and morally upstaged by Kennedy." The president often expressed concerns about Shriver's leadership of the OEO, unable to shake his suspicion that Kennedy's brother-in-law was secretly working to help Bobby gain the White House in 1968.[48]

Initially, in encouraging the establishment of CDGM and generously funding it, OEO had seen itself as making an "end run" around Mississippi's segregated political establishment. But by the middle of the summer of 1966, Shriver and the bureaucrats who administered grants—mindful of the president's hostility to adverse publicity about OEO programs and the increasingly negative political fallout—were ready to abandon a program they had praised only months earlier.

Even before the Donald Baker memo, Shriver had begun to engineer an escape from what was increasingly seen as a political liability. In mid-August of 1966, he summoned Mississippians Hodding Carter III and state NAACP president Aaron Henry to the OEO offices in Washington. "We met with Sarge [Shriver]," said Carter, the white editor of the iconoclastic *Greenville (Miss.) Delta Democrat Times*, "and Sarge said: 'I need somebody to get my ass out of this sling. I gotta dump this one [CDGM].'" As Aaron Henry recalled the conversation, Shriver said, "Either we'll shut it [Head Start] down, or we start a new organization that will follow the rules."[49]

In the changing political climate within Mississippi, Shriver saw an opportunity to jettison CDGM without completely caving in to Stennis and the state's reactionaries. As the scope of the federal grants grew steadily, a growing number of self-defined white "moderates" and a handful of predominantly middle-class blacks emerged, anxious to play a dominant role as brokers in the distribution of federal largesse in the state. In his meeting with Carter and Henry, Shriver urged them to recruit a biracial board incorporating "more conventional black and white leadership" to form a new Head Start entity to compete with CDGM for the lucrative CAP grants.[50]

The result of Henry's and Carter's efforts was the creation of Mississippi

Action for Progress, Inc. (MAP), a new community action program whose twelve-member board, as initially constituted, was three-quarters white, all-male, and without a representative from the state's poorest population. (Patt Derian was later drawn into the organization, but the new organization appeared to represent a sharp turn away from CDGM's emphasis on female leadership and empowerment.) MAP touted participation by whites as prominent as Hodding Carter III, Yazoo City industrialist and Baptist lay leader Owen Cooper, and Leroy Percy (a cousin of author William Alexander Percy). Many of the leaders on the board of the new CAP were veterans of a group known as the Mississippi Young Democrats, which had hoped as early as 1964 to receive the blessing of the Democratic National Committee and in so doing to displace the nascent MFDP.[51]

MAP had two other political assets: it lacked SNCC and MFDP involvement and it had the imprimatur of the state's increasingly "moderate" NAACP. In this context, Aaron Henry's declaration of allegiance to MAP was of critical importance, for his long-term civil rights credentials were assumed to be above reproach by many in the state's African American communities. Ironically, Henry had been—according to Tom Levin—barred from the original CDGM board by OEO on the grounds that his politics were too radical. But times were changing in Mississippi.

Aaron Henry insisted at the time and also later that he harbored no grudge against CDGM (despite its admittedly lukewarm embrace of NAACP activists within its ranks).[52] In a later oral history, the NAACP leader suggested that one of CDGM's major weaknesses had been its reluctance to engage in subterfuge in its accounting procedures, which were so meticulously scrutinized by an army of auditors, many of them bringing clear political biases along with their adding machines. Referring to allegations that CDGM had lent its resources— essentially automobile transportation and some meals cooked at Head Start centers—to Black Power advocates during the racially charged Meredith March in the summer of 1966, Henry insisted that CDGM board director John Mudd should have been more "creative" in record keeping to avoid providing the Head Start agency's critics with political ammunition. "John was honest. He would say where he was and what he did. But that ain't no way to run a ball game."

Personally, said the long-time NAACP activist, he didn't "give a damn" how many people Mudd and his staff had driven to the Meredith March. But they knew that they were under heightened scrutiny, with auditors peering over their shoulders, said Henry. And "any time a son-of-a-bitch writes on [a] god-damn trip ticket, 'Meredith March!' he's a crazy son-of-a-bitch." Henry claimed

Mudd had told him that "just because they [the federal government] put their money down here, they can't tell me how to spend it." Aaron had no sympathy for such attitudes. "I said, 'John, you're crazy like a son-of-a-bitch! [laughter] They *can* tell you how to spend it.'"

Ever the pragmatist, Henry saw it as a simple equation: if you wanted to get federal funding for black kids in Mississippi, you played the game according to the rules in force. And Mudd's unwillingness to do so meant that he had "become my problem, you see." For Henry, the alternative was clear. He and other practical-minded moderates should "move toward organizing a new unit that would hire a director who would do right."[53]

Working quietly behind the scenes, MAP began preparing an application for its own Head Start program. Top OEO officials expedited the request at every step of the way, with one remembering that the application was "written in considerable degree by members of our own staff."[54]

Several of the original MAP board participants genuinely believed in the Head Start program's benefits for Mississippi preschoolers, and defenders of the new grantee have since stressed that it was OEO and President Johnson that demanded creation of a rival organization, not so-called moderates in Mississippi. Board members surely must have recognized the tremendous potential for distribution of political patronage that would exist under a program with an unconditional federal blessing. All those on the appointed board of MAP had worked for Democratic factions that had challenged the MFDP for recognition by the national party, and they recognized the legitimizing impact such patronage would provide and the political dividends that would accrue.[55]

As the MAP proposal moved forward, OEO officials simultaneously approached officials at the historically black institution, Rust College, located in northwest Mississippi. The small Methodist college, founded in 1866 by the Freedman's Aid Society of the Methodist Episcopal Church, had earlier applied for antipoverty funds and had been turned down. But OEO officials encouraged the college to apply for a $1.2 million Head Start grant and quickly threw together the grant proposal within the offices of the Washington agency. The OEO did not tell CDGM that "deficiencies" and irregularities had placed the organization's funding in jeopardy.[56]

The secrecy ended on September 30, 1966. When CDGM supporter Kenneth Dean learned from a sympathetic OEO official of the secret move to displace the organization's Head Start program, he leaked the story to the right-wing *Jackson (Miss.) Daily News*. In interviews, Senators Stennis and Eastland told the reporter that they had "unconditional and authoritative assurances *from the administration* that CDGM would not be funded." Forced to go public, the

OEO officially informed CDGM four days later that its grant had been revoked "on grounds of fiscal irresponsibility."[57]

A week later, the OEO issued a press release describing in glowing terms what MAP would mean for Mississippi. Announcing the Rust College grant, Shriver was quoted as saying: "We intend to diversify the sponsorship of Head Start and other War on Poverty programs in Mississippi. We intend to move as fast as possible away from de facto racially segregated programs," explicitly including CDGM in this grouping, despite the group's unsuccessful attempts to recruit white children. The Rust College grant would be a model. Critics were convinced that the flood of federal money into Mississippi coinciding with the creation of MAP and the approval of the Rust College grant was no accident. By dispersing all of the state's allotted antipoverty funds, any subsequent battle over CDGM funding would be entirely symbolic; there would be no money left to fight over.[58]

The NAACP, Mississippi's oldest civil rights organization, now appeared to many whites to be more palatable than the MFDP. Governor Paul Johnson's eagerness to sign the MAP charter (he secretly signed it on the same day it was drafted) represented something of a political evolutionary leap for the newly proclaimed racial "moderate." On the gubernatorial campaign trail in 1963, Johnson had told his audiences that the initials NAACP stood for "niggers, alligators, apes, coons, and possums." By 1966 he was ready to endorse MAP, even with its substantial NAACP involvement.

Presumably, objections by Stennis and others in the state's most ardent segregationist wing would be far more muted in confronting this lesser of two evils. The perceived radicalism of Aaron Henry's earlier apostasy—casting his lot with the upstart MFDP challenge in 1964—might be forgiven (if not forgotten) by whites in the interest of exploiting shifting state political realities.[59]

But many whites in the state continued to attack the new MAP Head Start organization with much the same language they had used against CDGM. In a regular feature in the *Jackson (Miss.) Daily News* one gossip columnist blasted Head Start as a bloated "nursery project" and referred to a "local wit" who had suggested the necessity of a training manual for Head Start programs, to be entitled "The Care and Feeding of Pickaninnies." The book, suggested columnist Tom Etheridge, could be written by Owen Cooper and Hodding Carter III, key figures in MAP; the logical publisher would be the "NAACP Press."[60]

But the real damage came from the bitter internal struggles these events unleashed. The defection of Aaron Henry and other established black leaders from CDGM was hardly surprising. Some members of the black community—particularly NAACP activists—defended MAP. Winson Hudson, president of the NAACP in Leake County since 1962, admitted that "a lot of people said that Aaron was up in Washington compromising too much, but, at the same time, if we ever went to Washington, you'd find old Stennis and Eastland treating us like white folks for the first time. They were afraid of Aaron." Aaron did a "lot of compromising to keep us eating bread, and that was important, because if they had closed down Head Start, a lot of us wouldn't be here now—would've had to leave Mississippi," she argued.[61]

As the predominantly middle-class black leaders lined up behind the new MAP, however, long-standing internal tensions within African American protest communities came to the surface. MAP leaders were, in many cases, genially dismissive of the men and women who had run and staffed CDGM. Supporters of the original Head Start program responded with anger and a deep sense of betrayal. Some recognized that there had been benefits and liabilities associated with their organization. As one African American woman from Lauderdale County said: "'Course CDGM's good. . . . 'Cept the things about it that's bad. There's a lotta good folks come here to help us. 'Course there's a lot just come to cause a fuss too. And the federal government's finally recognized us down here—'course sometimes that ain't so good, 'cause for every smile it gives us, it gives us a kick too. Well, at least it's got us colored peoples workin' for oursel's. . . . It's great for the kids. On'y thing, it's kinda hard on 'em when they get to real school and it ain't like our school."[62]

Most CDGM veterans and supporters of the MFDP were far less ambivalent. They angrily accused those blacks who were throwing their support to the newly created MAP of being latecomers to the civil rights movement "who couldn't care less" about the struggle for lasting social change.[63] When 2,000 "angry and disappointed" CDGM supporters crowded into Jackson's old city auditorium on October 8, speaker after speaker assailed Aaron Henry and other black Mississippians who had supported the new Head Start organization as "Uncle Toms." And civil rights activist Fannie Lou Hamer showed the same eloquence that had nearly swayed the credentials committee at the Atlantic City Democratic National Convention in 1964. "The [white] people on those [MAP] boards," she charged, "are the same people who were shooting at us in '63 and '64." Certainly this was not an accurate description of the MAP board, but Hamer's frustrated rhetoric mirrored the disillusionment of activists who had embraced CDGM as their own. As the rally wound down, members passed a resolution calling on the national office of the NAACP to request that their local officials "withdraw their support from MAP" and "support CDGM and the poor people of Mississippi." There would be no reply from the national organization.[64]

Two weeks later, in a stinging article in the *Nation*, CDGM activists John Mudd (who had replaced Tom Levin as head of CDGM) and Marvin Hoffman accused OEO and its Mississippi allies of trying to create a new structure that followed the historic hierarchy of social relations in the Magnolia State. In the "New Plantation," said Mudd and Marvin, Mississippi's white moderates would play the role of "boss man," and the white moderates' black middle-class allies would collectively serve in the capacity of "head nigger." In a variation of this theme, a CDGM flyer warned supporters that MAP was "trying to make a *political plantation* out of Mississippi, run by Paul Johnson, Sen. Stennis, Sen. Eastland, Douglass Wynn, and Hodding Carter for *Lyndon Johnson*." And, in an unmistakable reference to the events of the post-Reconstruction era, the flyer reminded readers: "Our grandparents were sold out in the same way many years ago."[65]

As participant scholars — and subsequently historians — have argued with near unanimity, African Americans in the Mississippi Delta and across the state displayed a clear preference for the CDGM approach to preschool education over that of MAP. The new organization's administrators, despite the enormous influx of federal dollars, initially struggled to recruit preschoolers and staff. Many, perhaps most, MAP supporters and staffers were well-intentioned. They believed their Head Start program — whether born in the spirit of compromise or in the crucible of political expediency — could offer a means to the desegregation of the state's public school system once the force of massive resistance had exhausted itself. (Such a hope looks naive in retrospect, given the rapid growth of white private schools in the next decade.) But to working-class African Americans at the grass roots it was difficult to view the circumstances surrounding the origins of the new Head Start agency as anything other than a poisoned well. Operating under a grant of $3 million in the closing months of 1966, MAP's board was able to start only five Head Start centers in just two counties, offering preschool education to approximately one hundred Mississippi children, many of whom came from secure economic backgrounds, hardly the targeted demographic of the War on Poverty.

Meanwhile CDGM, deprived of federal funds and staffed almost wholly on a volunteer basis by "local people," managed in the short run to keep sixty Head Start centers open, with four thousand preschoolers in attendance.[66] Despite the hardships they faced with so few concrete resources, this was exactly the sort of self-perpetuating activism that Tom Levin had imagined the organization might cultivate. Ironically, it was only when the government defaulted on its initial commitment to Head Start in Mississippi that "maximum feasible participation" was allowed to run its logical course. Patt Derian, an MAP board member who retained an admiration for CDGM, was quick to concede the issue of "regimentation," which she saw as one of her program's signal weaknesses in comparison with the creative and improvisational spirit of CDGM Head Start centers.[67]

The national coalition of liberals that had supported civil rights was fraying, but CDGM was not without its allies. The Citizens Crusade against Poverty, a national nonprofit agency, headed by Walter Reuther, created a special board of inquiry that argued the case for the embattled Mississippi antipoverty program. "CDGM is not simply a collection of isolated child care centers," argued the board of inquiry. "It is an organization that belongs to the people of Mississippi. It is a program that makes child development the symbol and the point of embarkation for a life of dignity for children and parents and community." The report noted that this proprietary sense was not contingent upon federal funding, for during the period between 1965 and 1966 when Stennis had succeeded in temporarily denying them funding, African Americans in Mississippi had created over four dozen preschool centers. Even without federal funding or formal ties to the antipoverty grant, they still insisted on naming them "CDGM Centers."[68]

On October 19, four days after the board of the Citizens Crusade against Poverty had issued its report, a full-page advertisement in the *New York Times* sought to shame the head of OEO for his role in the suspension of CDGM funding with the banner headline: "SAY IT ISN'T SO, SARGENT SHRIVER." Among those individuals and organizations most prominent in the publicity campaign designed to pressure OEO to reverse itself were A. Philip Randolph, Walter Reuther of the United Auto Workers, Joseph Rauh of the Americans for Democratic Action, former OEO official Richard Boone, the Citizens Crusade against Poverty, and the National Council of Churches. The signers of the advertisement represented constituencies Johnson could ill afford to alienate.

The adverse national media exposure and an ongoing campaign on behalf of CDGM from the pages of the influential *New Republic*, accusing Shriver of being Stennis's "patsy," eventually resulted in the head of OEO offering a scaled-down grant extension to CDGM. The final grant was a substantial one, $8 million, but by this point the cumulative toll of being in funding limbo and the sense of having been abandoned by erstwhile Washington allies had caused significant damage to the state's first Head Start grantee. Although CDGM would continue for a time, bureaucratic wrangling and uneven allocations in the ensuing months left its supporters demoralized and MAP with a clear-cut victory.[69]

The more fundamental problem was that fewer and fewer antipoverty dollars remained as Americans assumed greater responsibility for the fighting in South Vietnam. Sargent Shriver learned that the Pentagon had assured Johnson that with an appropriation of $20 billion the United States could end the war in Southeast Asia by December 1966. Shriver later reflected: "The idea was that we had to fight *this* war [in Vietnam] this year. Next year we'd get to the war on poverty. I think I knew then that 'next year' wasn't going to come."[70]

The story of CDGM as much as the more well-known CAP controversies in the Democratic cities of the urban North and Midwest revealed the hazards of interpretation inherent in the ambiguity of the phrase "maximum feasible participation," the underlying rationale behind the War on Poverty's community action programs.[71] The Johnson administration's response to CDGM reflected a fundamental dissonance between its professed commitment in the Howard University speech to "equality as a fact and . . . as a result" and the more familiar and politically palatable abstraction of "equality as a right."

When Senator John Stennis, others on the Mississippi congressional delegation, and conservatives attacked CDGM, they grounded their charges in ongoing concerns about "radicalism." In a climate of growing white unease over perceived separatist tendencies within the civil rights movement, their shrill charges came to be seen as less extreme. Facing legislative decrees, executive orders, and reverses in the federal courts that threatened all-white schools and white domination of state politics, proponents of massive resistance were soon directing their formidable energies to ingenious (albeit constitutionally suspect) vote dilution strategies and to the creation and maintenance of a parallel educational establishment, its standard-bearer the all-white "seg academy," a privatized institutional echo of Jim Crow's segregated schools.

White private school founders sometimes strip-mined the public schools of fiscal resources. In a number of communities, they actually absconded with desks and chairs and even entire science labs from public schools, in a sordid process of dubious legality that historians are only now beginning to document. The Head Start pattern of having ostensibly integrated educational settings quickly gave way to virtually all-black spaces, which, in practice, offered an eerily accurate forecast of public school demographics in many areas of Mississippi following court-ordered integration at the start of the 1970s.[72]

Those who had built CDGM from the grass roots up had seen in preschool education for the state's poorest children the potential for a transformative experience, one that would instill powerful social values of community and lead to self-improvement, self-empowerment, and self-respect. Historian Charles Payne has concluded that "what they got under MAP was an educational program dominated at best by a traditional social-welfare mentality. Let's-have-some-experts-do-something-for-poor-people."[73]

Contrary to depictions within CDGM's inner circle, Sargent Shriver was not an evil man. He was a politician, who, like Lyndon Johnson, lifted his finger to the political winds and made political decisions accordingly. By the time Mississippi's Head Start funding had been reallocated, however, Shriver's duplicity had been established, leading to serious charges of a "credibility gap" at the OEO that mirrored the administration's growing problems in accounting for lack of military "progress" in Vietnam.

Shriver, and presumably many others within the Johnson administration, had played a number of different sides in a complicated political equation. Some of these bureaucrats could comfortably separate their commitment to prosecuting the War on Poverty as a whole from their willingness to beat a strategic retreat when political circumstances dictated. From their viewpoint, CDGM was seen as expendable if it became a stumbling block to larger goals of the War on Poverty. And to Johnson and other Democratic strategists who were increasingly convinced that federal civil rights initiatives might permanently damage the Democratic Party's fortunes in the South, the CDGM controversy was connected to a partisan political agenda; MAP appeared to point the way toward a blueprint for the creation of political alternatives to what were seen as the extremes of the MFDP and all-white "Regular" Democrats in the politically charged climate of Mississippi.

Fundamentally, both OEO leadership and increasingly hostile "armchair generals" seeking to direct the War on Poverty from the hallways of Congress and city halls around the country failed to perceive events as they were seen at the grass roots among Mississippi's African American poor, or perhaps they appreciated all too well the sweeping reformist visions of the foot soldiers of the state's overlapping antipoverty program and civil rights movement. The greatest failure lay in the reluctance of the White House to connect the CDGM episode with a tortured history of similar political compromises and shattered promises in the War on Poverty nationwide. CDGM had come to represent far more than preschool education for mostly black toddlers in the Magnolia State. In the words of one contemporary observer, "the poor of Mississippi . . . had become an allegory of the poor elsewhere."[74] Local people who had staffed CDGM centers or had enrolled their children had seen the dramatic impact of early education in broadening the intellectual vistas of the young. And they had come to feel a sense of ownership in the Head Start program they had built from the ground up. Over and over again, in viewing the events from 1965 through 1967, they could claim: "It was ours."

For many blacks in the United States, that pattern of bold federal pronouncements, half-hearted commitment and implementation, and ultimately quiet retreat was laden with historical echoes stretching back to the first Reconstruction. And nowhere was the analogy more powerful than in the state of Mississippi. In the fall of 1875, facing a conservative resurgence and widespread intimidation of black voters and their white Republican allies, Mississippi's Republican governor Adelbert Ames had wired President Ulysses Grant, requesting federal troops to be sent to guarantee the safety and security of members of his party amid the growing atmosphere of conservative white violence. Grant's attorney general relayed back the message: "The whole public are tired with these annual autumnal outbreaks in the South, and the great majority are ready now to condemn any interference on the part of the Government." Grant refused to dispatch additional federal troops, and white conservative "Redeemers" swept into power across the state.[75]

Ninety-one years later, there were no troops to be withdrawn, and the threat of widespread bloodshed appeared less imminent, despite ongoing brutality like that witnessed in Canton during the Meredith March against Fear. But the same weariness, the same sense of lost national resolve, shaped the politics of Lyndon Johnson's administration. Monthly public opinion polls tracked the dwindling support of white Americans for federal activism on behalf of civil rights and antipoverty initiatives.[76] Faced with these unpalatable political realities, Shriver and the OEO shifted support from CDGM to MAP and moved from a position ostensibly endorsing a grassroots economic insurgency to an orientation that might best be described as political containment. To many inside the Washington Beltway, CDGM represented a skirmish, one of many in an ongoing series of battles over how best to interpret such elastic clauses as "maximum feasible participation."

Nor was there any sense of just how important this shift had been in igniting submerged conflicts within the civil rights and antipoverty community rooted in class, gender, organizational and personal rivalry, and ideology. Increasingly, after the split between CDGM and MAP, it was difficult for black Mississippians to chart a unified strategic and tactical course for future protest and reform. An observer from California, who had participated in CDGM during its first year of existence, wrote what might have been an epitaph for Levin's vision of "kamikaze revolutionaries": "You can't run a radical program on government money," he said. "You can't develop grass roots democracy on a timetable set in Washington or structure freedom by the same regulations that organize a bureaucracy."[77]

As Aaron Henry and his allies consolidated their control over Head Start antipoverty funds, CDGM supporters continued to attack those blacks who had backed MAP as "Uncle Toms" and "office Negroes." The federal government, argued one black Forrest County activist, was at least partially accountable for pitting blacks against each other. "You can't blame 'em for being dumb," he said bitterly, "they're just a bunch of federal jerks." But he did blame them for "being a bunch of dirty, dishonest politicians playin' with us little people."[78]

African Americans' anger, historian William McFeely has written, "may derive as much from the broken promises of Reconstruction as from slavery itself." Slavery promised nothing, noted McFeely. "Then, with emancipation and Reconstruction, official, public promises were made—and broken. Expectations rose and were dashed."[79] As the ideological "middle ground" shrank in 1965 and 1966, the recriminations and the sense of betrayal that divided moderate and more radical Mississippi civil rights and antipoverty activists emerged in different contexts across the nation. Those divisions, and the mounting suspicion that the federal government was a reluctant ally at best, fueled speculation over whether the ultimate fate of the "Second Reconstruction" would be any different than the first.

CHAPTER SIX

The Unwelcome Guest at the Feast

Vietnam and the Political Crisis of 1966

Through the spring and summer of 1965, Lyndon Johnson's advisers continued to relay bleak news over Vietnam. As the South Vietnamese government grew weaker and the antigovernment insurgency bolder, several of the president's closest advisers and administration insiders concluded that the United States should begin withdrawing and accept the inevitability of a unified Vietnam under the leadership of the North. Even the U.S. ambassador to Vietnam, Maxwell Taylor, doubted that the government could survive without massive American support. Johnson peppered the hawks in his administration with skeptical objections, many of them based on a secret seventy-five-page memo written by Undersecretary of State George Ball, which had called for America's withdrawal.

The president was also conscious of the dangers that massive military intervention would pose to his domestic policies. Those "damn conservatives" like Mississippi's John Stennis would insist they weren't against the poor, said Johnson, but they "are . . . going to use this war as a way of opposing my Great Society legislation," he told a group of White House visitors in late 1964. The war? Oh, "they'll like the war. They'll take the war as their weapon."[1]

Despite Lyndon Johnson's private misgivings, he moved the United States step-by-step toward a wider involvement in Vietnam, initiating a bombing campaign in February 1965, then approving ground troops to guard American bases, and finally authorizing combat units to move out of their defensive enclaves to engage the enemy. Trapped by his belief in the domino theory of communist expansion in Southeast Asia, as well as by his own insecurities, he assured Martin Luther King Jr. in a July telephone conversation that he was not a warmonger but that he had no intention of leaving Vietnam with his "tail between his legs."[2]

In a White House meeting, South Dakota's first-term senator George McGovern, who had a Ph.D. in history, pointed out that the Vietnamese had been resisting the Chinese for more than a thousand years; there was little danger of Vietnam becoming a satellite of the Chinese, he argued. "Goddamn it, George," responded Johnson, "you and Fulbright and all you history teachers. I haven't got time to fuck around with history . . . when there are boys out there who might die before morning."[3]

Most of the nation rallied behind the president's decision. But in a June 6, 1965, column, just two days after Johnson had declared his commitment to waging "the next and the more profound stage of the battle for civil rights," influential *New York Times* columnist James Reston warned of a growing uneasiness on the part of Americans. He questioned whether the administration "is willing or able to provide the means to achieve the exalted aims it proclaims." Without public policy follow-through on eloquent words, promises rang hollow. And just as Johnson had done in the opening of his Howard University speech, Reston made the connection between social revolutions at home and political unrest abroad. At a time when the still-simmering crisis in the Dominican Republic was weighing far heavier on many Americans' minds than the ongoing conflict in Southeast Asia, Reston made direct reference to Vietnam. Domestic policy, always seen as Johnson's forte, Reston warned, ran the risk of mirroring his foreign policy, where the president was increasingly receiving poor marks. Johnson had no clear strategy in place for achieving the victory he came so close to assuring must be imminent, Reston concluded. "On this question, as on Vietnam, the disparity between ends and means is startling and disturbing."[4]

Walter Heller, whose work on the nature of poverty had been influential in shaping both Kennedy's task force and Johnson's antipoverty program, wrote the president in December 1965 to express his concern that increased Vietnam funding might choke off antipoverty efforts. Even if it meant a slight rise in taxes to pay for Vietnam, the president had to continue to give top priority to the funding of Great Society programs or risk the "political . . . disaffection of key groups of beneficiaries." Against the backdrop of a booming economy, the nation's wealthy could easily absorb a marginal tax increase to fund the war, but cutbacks in antipoverty expenditures would hammer the poor. Heller concluded, "It's another case of the hound who's only running for his dinner against a hare who's running for his life."[5]

A. Philip Randolph had become a strong supporter of Johnson, but he warned against allowing "guns" to win out over "butter." Other members of the liberal consensus, including Randolph's friends in organized labor, pressed Johnson not to allow escalation in Vietnam to obscure the necessity of ongoing support for Great Society programs.[6] At the same time, more conservative forces were pressuring the administration to go slow on antipoverty programs. Some, like Mississippi's John Stennis, had even threatened to hold Vietnam appropriations hostage.[7]

The administration clearly felt it faced a challenge in gaining support from black America for the Vietnam War, and the conflict cast a long shadow over the relationships between the Johnson administration and black protest movements in this period. Creating gaping fissures in Johnson's larger "liberal consensus," Vietnam became one of many litmus tests defining acceptable black leadership in the eyes of the White House. As early as the summer of 1965, Martin Luther King Jr. had begun to call for a bombing halt and a negotiated settlement in Vietnam. After enduring censure from longtime foes, as well as allies, he muted his criticism, but he defended his right to move beyond domestic civil rights issues and to address the nation's foreign policy. "I'm much more than a civil rights leader," King insisted.[8]

In late August 1965, Bill Moyers wrote to the president to relay Roy Wilkins's concerns that he was spending an inordinate amount of energy "keeping the 'Peace in Viet Nam movement' from becoming too big a factor in the civil rights movement." Moyers had also spoken with a representative of *Jet* magazine, who urged the president to devote more publicity to the heroic black soldiers and airmen in Vietnam, in order to blunt blacks' sense of disengagement.[9] That same month, with Watts still fresh on his mind, Louis Martin proposed that Johnson speak to the National Newspaper Publishers Association, the professional organization for African American press leaders. Martin argued that the president could persuade these influential opinion makers "to go out and sell their people" on the administration's accomplishments in the arenas of civil rights and antipoverty efforts. He added, "They could also get the Negroes solidly behind us on Viet Nam."[10]

During these hectic months, Martin played a critical role in advising Johnson. He had begun his career in the late 1930s as the crusading editor of the *Michigan Chronicle*, the black Detroit newspaper founded by the publisher of the *Chicago Defender*. Martin passionately supported Franklin Roosevelt's New Deal; he also enthusiastically backed Walter Reuther's United Auto Workers at a time when most of Detroit's black leaders were reluctant to take on the city's powerful industrialist, Henry Ford. And in his news coverage and editorials he focused on the problems of the growing black Detroit ghetto. His warnings proved prescient when the city exploded in the 1943 race riot, which left thirty-four people dead. No "single experience in my life made greater impact on my outlook and philosophy," he later wrote.[11]

By the 1960s, Martin was a major political power, regularly consulted by white politicians anxious to gain the support of black political leaders and voters. He had been an important figure in the 1960 Kennedy presidential campaign and continued to work closely with the White House and with the Johnson administration after Kennedy's assassination. Publicly, he was a loyal Johnson soldier. Privately, he often argued with the president, who depended upon his knowledge of urban issues and his deep connections to a broad range of black leaders.[12]

As full-blown combat operations began in Vietnam, Johnson had seemed most concerned over the limited role that African Americans might play in the war. The army offered an opportunity for poor blacks to move out of the ghettos, he told former CIA director John McCone. The army rejected more than half of black draftees because of health and lack of education. As a result, Johnson said ruefully, the "white boys are doing all the fighting [in Vietnam]."[13] Daniel Patrick Moynihan had made much the same argument a month earlier in a memo encouraging LBJ to relax screening standards for War on Poverty programs like Job Corps that would simultaneously better prepare minorities for service in the military: "The biggest opportunity to do something about Negro youth has been right under our noses all the time. . . . The down-and-out Negro boy needs to be inducted into the male, American society."[14]

As the fighting increased, however, the administration confronted an unexpectedly different problem. African Americans were dying in disproportionate numbers, dramatizing the unwelcome connection between civil rights and the war in Vietnam. Administration officials meticulously documented this trend and, after analyzing casualty reports for the years 1961–65, concluded that the statistical anomaly resulted from African Americans' disproportionate assignment to combat roles. Highlighting the potential problems with U.S. Army testing, the research showed that fully 90 percent of African Americans were assigned the designation of "mental groups III and IV" based on testing, and as a result "more Negroes tend to be assigned to the combat arms, while fewer tend to be assigned to such fields as electronics."[15] The ultimate Catch-22 came when Pentagon data tabulators and public relations officers claimed, without flinching, that figures on black casualties in Vietnam merely demonstrated "the valor of the Negro in combat."[16] Thus the disproportionate carnage merited no apology. Affirmative action in the rice paddies of South Vietnam meant giving more African Americans a chance to prove their manhood by placing themselves in harm's way.[17]

Civil rights activists saw on every hand the racial inequities in the mobilization for the war in Vietnam. While draftees filled the ranks of combat units, the National Guard—which was 98 percent white—was never called up for duty in Vietnam and became a haven for young men seeking to avoid the war. (Whites, who were far more likely to attend college, also benefited from the deferment system through the early stages of the war.)

And the selective service system itself hardly inspired confidence. Louisiana's Ku Klux Klan's Grand Dragon chaired that state's largest draft board until 1966, and all-white draft boards in the South had a disconcerting predisposition to call up civil rights activists and antiwar dissenters, a practice encouraged by General Lewis Hershey, head of the Selective Service System. Southern draft boards targeted a number of prominent African Americans, like boxer Muhammad Ali and SNCC activists Cleveland Sellers and Julian Bond. (The chairman of Atlanta's draft board openly expressed his regret that he had not been able to draft "that nigger" Bond.) A New Orleans board drafted the son of civil rights activist Jeannette McDonald and, when he failed to appear for his induction, indicted him for failure to register for the draft. With some embarrassment, they had to drop the charges after they learned that James McDonald, a thirteen-year army veteran, was stationed in Germany.

Members of the Johnson administration had displayed sensitivity to their chief's desire for loyalty on the Vietnam issue when debating what elements to include in the civil rights legislative package of 1966 before it went up to Capitol Hill. William Taylor, staff director of the U.S. Commission on Civil Rights, supported a federal statute guaranteeing the protection of civil rights workers in the exercise of their constitutional rights, but he was at pains to stress that only those "speech actions" "directed at obtaining equal treatment" be protected. "Excluded from coverage would be public protests . . . such as a demonstration on Vietnam."[18]

In an attempt to hang on to many of his liberal supporters, Johnson dispatched Joseph Califano, Douglass Cater, and other domestic policy advisers to canvass for ideas among academics and others outside the Washington Beltway in May and June 1966. They were to search for input on sweeping questions: "Where should the Great Society go from here? What needs have we left unmet?" A number of the historians, professors of government, and economists, clearly flattered by the attention from White House insiders, drafted laborious and lengthy letters outlining their ideas and suggestions for Johnson to follow. Others cut to the chase. When Columbia University historian William E. Leuchtenburg and other prominent scholars met with Califano and Cater in New York, Leuchtenburg called attention to the "one thing wrong with the meeting. . . . Like Banquo's ghost," he remembered, "Vietnam was the unwelcome guest at the feast. . . . I think all of us hoped it would go away, and permit us to concentrate on fulfilling the Great Society."

The Democrats would be battered by the Republicans in the upcoming congressional elections, the historian predicted, in large part because Johnson's hawkish policies in Vietnam had "sabotaged his own programs. . . . The attention of the country has been directed away from the Great Society and toward a holy war against the Reds." (Nicholas Katzenbach said as much when he left the Justice Department for a posting in the State Department. Aside from Vietnam, he noted, "everybody else is playing marbles."[19]) Now, Leuchtenburg suggested, Johnson was alienating his core constituencies, the building blocks of the Roosevelt coalition, who until this point had chosen to support him despite increasing doubts about foreign policy. "But the mask is off." No longer was it possible to blame Vietnam escalation on Pentagon figures like Dean Rusk or Robert McNamara. Johnson had "placed himself at the head of the war crowd, and made clear his contempt for anyone who continues to believe in the policies he voiced when he asked for support in 1964."

Whether or not they really intended to put the recommendations of the academics to use—and there is little indication that Califano did anything other than file the letters and memos away—the soliciting of suggestions evoked Roosevelt's famed "Brain Trust." Clearly, officials hoped to enlist the support of liberal academics and intellectuals in supporting the overall objectives of the White House, and increasingly those objectives demanded loyalty to the administration's policies in Vietnam. Leuchtenburg would have none of it. He concluded bluntly: "Count me out."[20]

Vietnam had become "Johnson's tar baby," said *New York Times* correspondent John Herbers. And while "the President was aiming his first blow at the tar baby, the civil rights leaders began to get out of line."[21] African Americans across the political spectrum were asking hard questions about the Vietnam War: Why were so many blacks dying to rid South Vietnam of communism when the commitment to fight racism appeared to be waning?

On January 6, 1966, SNCC had become the first of the major civil rights organizations to come out against the war. The SNCC resolution called on all Americans to do civil rights work "as an alternative to the draft." SNCC chairman John Lewis read from the statement: "We believe the United States Government has been deceptive in its claim of concern for the freedom of the

Vietnamese people, just as the Government has been deceptive in claiming concern for the freedom of colored people. . . . The United States Government has never guaranteed the freedom of oppressed citizens and is not yet truly determined to end the rule of terror and oppression within its own borders." The document was calculated to tweak the administration's nose further. It compared U.S. government failure to oversee free and fair elections in Vietnam with its failure to enforce voting rights at home, and it linked the draft for the army with a domestic battle being waged: "We ask, where is the draft for the freedom fight in the United States?"[22]

The controversy that erupted soon enveloped SNCC's communications director, Julian Bond. While attending Morehouse College early in 1960, he had helped to stage sit-ins against Atlanta's segregated public facilities. One of the founding members of SNCC, Bond became a charismatic and articulate spokesman for the organization's goal of cultivating black leadership in black communities. His extensive media contacts helped to ensure at least a sporadic spotlight on the physical brutality and psychological trauma SNCC workers and local blacks endured as they organized in remote areas, which was often overshadowed by the choreographed campaigns of more established civil rights groups.

In 1965, Bond had won a seat in the Georgia legislature as a Democrat representing black Atlantans, but his unwillingness to disavow SNCC's antiwar statement brought retaliation. Hostile white legislators, citing "disloyalty," barred him from taking his seat, then excluded him again when constituents promptly reelected him. In 1966, during a third successful campaign, Bond resigned from SNCC. Its new leaders, he felt, had let ideological preoccupation supplant grassroots mobilization, but he refused to criticize the organization publicly. White attempts to crush Bond's nascent political career ironically catapulted him to national prominence as a civil rights cause célèbre, a status cemented when a unanimous Supreme Court ended Bond's legislative limbo and restored him to his seat in the Georgia statehouse.[23]

SNCC's antiwar resolution did not immediately result in a complete rupture with the Johnson administration. Three months after its passage, then-chairman John Lewis attended a White House meeting to discuss the prospects for civil rights legislation in 1966 and other issues, including concerns about urban unrest during the upcoming summer.[24] But SNCC's declaration clearly unnerved administration officials, who grew concerned about how other civil rights leaders would respond. The president was immensely gratified when Roy Wilkins and Whitney Young publicly distanced themselves from SNCC's manifesto. Louis Martin immediately activated his contacts with black publishers, clearly fishing for denunciations of SNCC's action in their editorial columns. Clifford Alexander wondered aloud about the possibility of recruiting the half-dozen African Americans in Congress to speak out "expressing the whole-hearted support of the Negro people for our actions in Vietnam." He worried privately about "the most difficult part of the equation . . . what Martin Luther King will do next."[25] Alexander and Louis Martin planned to talk to Andrew Young, seen by the administration as representing SCLC's more conservative, "sensible" wing, "to impress upon him the seriousness of the [SNCC] statement and the over-all negative consequences of it for the civil rights movement."

Johnson's growing estrangement from other former members of the Big Six civil rights leaders became even more obvious when James Farmer dashed off an impassioned and uncharacteristically blunt telegram to Sargent Shriver at OEO in the first days of July 1966 and carbon-copied his remarks to the president. After his replacement by Floyd McKissick as head of CORE earlier in the spring, Farmer began to draw up plans for a nationwide literacy project to target African Americans, Puerto Ricans, Mexican Americans, American Indians, and other minorities.

Farmer had spoken with the White House about his ideas as early as 1965, and Johnson had initially sent favorable signals. "The President was backing it 100 percent and urged me to proceed," Farmer later remembered.[26] (Indeed, some media accounts offered compelling evidence that the president had called for just such an anti-illiteracy effort by civil rights leaders in the first months of his term.) Believing that he had a green light from the executive branch, Farmer had applied for funding through OEO. A story leaked to the press on Christmas Day, 1965, hinted that CORE's leader planned to step down and suggested that White House approval of his proposed literacy project all but assured a favorable hearing by OEO. A friendly contact inside the headquarters of the War on Poverty relayed to Farmer the news that the proposal was "on Shriver's desk for signature. This went on for weeks and weeks. And my contact . . . would tell me . . . 'This is the day . . . that he signs [it.]'"

As weeks stretched into months, Farmer asked Johnson intimate A. Philip Randolph to inquire about the status of the proposal and was told to get in touch with Democratic congressman Adam Clayton Powell, the powerful African American chairman of the House Education and Labor Committee from New York. Powell refused to return Farmer's calls, and when a sympathetic Martin Luther King Jr. finally reached the congressman, Powell reportedly replied: "I have nothing against Farmer's proposal. . . . But the President asked me to axe it."

The former CORE director now scorned Shriver—and implicitly the larger

Johnson administration—for having kept the literacy program in limbo. Such indecision, Farmer acknowledged, was "your administrative privilege," but the silence from OEO in the face of repeated inquiries about the status of the anti-illiteracy project's grant request was inexcusable: "Your failure to communicate with me in any way whatsoever is far more than a personal affront; it is another broken promise [to] millions of Americans who are more and more outside the mainstream of the nation's life." The entire episode, he wrote, "raise[d] serious questions about the current direction of the antipoverty effort." Farmer closed by angrily informing Shriver and Johnson that he was withdrawing his proposal and would seek nongovernmental sources of funding.[27]

Although evidence suggests that Farmer's grant may have died as a result of opposition in prominent city halls and in Congress rather than in the executive branch, the complete lack of candor left him deeply embittered. The sense of being passed over evoked painful memories of the Voting Rights Act signing ceremony just eleven months earlier, when Johnson had deliberately attempted to slight Farmer by denying him one of the ceremonial signing pens.

The *New York Times* ran a piece on the denouement of Farmer's grant proposal that supported Adam Clayton Powell's claim that Johnson himself had played a prominent role in having the grant "killed." The president had detailed aide and media relations expert Robert Kintner to warn Sargent Shriver in no uncertain terms about stopping any leaks of internal OEO decision making: "Get tough," Johnson had urged Kintner.[28] When the story blew up, the incident further fueled Johnson's suspicions that Shriver was less than loyal to the White House.

Johnson biographer Robert Dallek has argued that as early as the end of 1965, Johnson held the "conviction that organizing efforts among the poor would become a launching pad for a Robert Kennedy presidential campaign." Reports of conflicts between democratic mayors and antipoverty activists affronted him on a number of levels, but at a bare minimum they fueled perceptions of an eroding liberal consensus.[29] In mid-October 1966 Shriver appeared on NBC's *Today* show, and a reporter put him on the spot by asking whether he felt that OEO's budgetary appropriation should be increased by $750 million, as Kennedy was demanding in the Senate. Shriver hedged by agreeing that "of course the poor needed more money than was recommended but that only the president could judge the various needs of the country."

White House aide Robert Kintner wasted no time in relaying the television exchange to his chief: "I think it is wrong politically to put the President on the spot of being the one who is not willing to give the most money to the poor." The media relations expert reserved his most telling point for his memo's conclusion. Shriver's lukewarm defense of Johnson's prerogative to determine funding priorities created an on-camera impression of "letting Senator Kennedy have the position that he wants to take care adequately of the poor." Kintner could hardly have stirred Johnson's charged feelings about the "Bobby factor" more cunningly.[30]

In spite of the administration's strained relationship with CORE — both with ex-director Farmer and the vocal McKissick—and its mutual estrangement with King, contacts with both groups continued. Johnson sent warm personal messages to the SCLC annual convention, which, in a symbolic statement of the dramatic changes under way in the South, met in Jackson, Mississippi, in the weeks following the conclusion of the Meredith March.[31] But questions about the administration's commitment to the Howard University speech's "dual agenda" persisted. As early as December 1965, momentum was building within certain sectors of the federal bureaucracy to dismantle OEO and farm out its programs to other cabinet-level agencies, in particular to the secretary of Housing and Urban Development.[32] Speculation continued to mount throughout 1966, with detailed plans circulating throughout the executive branch that were reminiscent of similar schemes to "streamline" civil rights agencies the preceding summer and fall, some of which had been leaked to the media.[33] Predictably Johnson was livid when wire reports in mid-August indicated that he had "secretly ordered the Budget Bureau to begin a quiet survey that may be the first step toward the dismantlement of the anti-poverty program as it now exists." Even though the media speculated that "spinning off" War on Poverty programs into the line agencies of the "permanent government" would actually shelter them from congressional cuts, Johnson was always furious when such "leaks" sought to second-guess his priorities, which restricted his range of political options.[34]

OEO and the Bureau of the Budget were also engaged in mutual recriminations. Antipoverty planners accused officials in the executive office of the Bureau of the Budget of attempting to micromanage the War on Poverty and threatening to withhold funds from the OEO. Budget director Charles Schultze vigorously denied the accusations, and the president issued a stern directive through Califano ordering both sides to adhere to a cease-fire: "Stop fighting each other through the press." Johnson's displeasure was closely tied to his political need for "consensus." Airing the dirty laundry of the executive branch in the mainstream media would make it harder to convince the public of the desirability of continuing the War on Poverty.[35]

Schultze had warned in fall 1965 that the federal government "ought not to be in the business of organizing the poor politically." "Maximum feasible participation," as he construed it, should be limited to involving the poor "at the actual working level in the poverty program." Powerful urban mayors would not be happy about this since it created tensions with the entrenched social welfare bureaucracies at the city level, but they could learn to tolerate such friction. But for community action and maximum feasible participation to move into the realm of conventional urban politics was beyond the pale. The mayors, Schultze cautioned, "won't stand for what appears, to them, at least, as the Federal creation of competing political groups in their own cities." The budget director urged Johnson to rein in OEO and require that its personnel "soft-pedal . . . its conflicts with local officials over heavy representation of the poor on planning boards."[36] Johnson, in typical abbreviated form, penciled "OK, I agree," on the memo. (Schultze was astute enough to realize that such a stance of "soft-pedaling" on the issue of "maximum feasible participation" would likely produce "friction with civil rights groups," but the mayors were seen as an even more powerful and valuable constituency.)

By late 1966, the overselling of the OEO—present from its inception in overly specific timetables for the eradication of poverty—had come back to haunt supporters. Shriver had expended tremendous amounts of energy and significant capital outlays "advertising" the successes of the Johnson programs with what one media columnist called the "characteristic zeal of a toothpaste salesman."[37] In seizing on every glimmer of positive coverage for his program, Shriver looked to feather the president's nest as well as his own. Only if Johnson remained identified with the successes of the effort, and not just with its controversies, Shriver reasoned, would the War on Poverty stand a reasonable chance of enduring amid the increasingly dire fiscal realities imposed by a tight-fisted Congress and Johnson's ever-expanding commitment to the war in Southeast Asia.

In the first two years following passage of the Economic Opportunity Act in 1964, Shriver was not alone in his enthusiasm. Bill Crook wrote an effusive letter to Bill Moyers at the White House in early May 1966 arguing that "the mayors of all of our southern cities are purring like kittens asking for another bowl of milk" and crowing that "unless my radar is on the blink completely, this [antipoverty] program is becoming one of the administration's greatest assets—and more."[38] Six weeks later, Shriver directed a memo entitled "Now Is the Time to Strike" to the president: the GOP assault on the War on Poverty "has 'peaked'—they have run out of ammunition," he asserted. The administration should tout the War on Poverty among its chief accomplishments in campaigning for Democratic candidates in the upcoming off-year elections.[39]

But by the end of the summer, Shriver's relentless optimism appeared to be wearing thin. After rioting broke out in the Hough district of Cleveland, in eastern New York, in Jacksonville, Florida, in Omaha, Nebraska, and in Mayor Richard Daley's Chicago, the War on Poverty seemed less likely to be a strong selling point for the Democrats in the November off-year elections. Although administration defenders could plausibly argue that only a broadening of efforts could forestall additional urban unrest, for many critics the War on Poverty was increasingly linked to images of angry—and now emboldened—blacks willing to make their case through mayhem. Alarmed mayors who lined up for funds in the hope of avoiding the lightning strike of rioting during the "long, hot summer" had to be told the OEO's coffers were running low. An analysis in *Newsweek* in the first week of August, three weeks after rioting in Chicago, described the War on Poverty as "the will-o'-the-wisp of American politics," visible in glimpses all over the nation with "driblets that helped some of the poor some of the time" but ephemeral and nowhere sufficient to lift large numbers of Americans out of poverty.

Newsweek suggested that "the buck—and the blame—ends with Lyndon B. Johnson." Surely the legislative genius could squeeze more funds from Congress if he were willing to commit himself. But Johnson, more and more observers noted, increasingly chose to focus on Vietnam. Shriver offered lukewarm assurance: "The President believes . . . we are meeting an appropriate amount of the needs of the poor at this time." When pressed by the media on whether the United States might "win the war in Vietnam and lose it in Hough [Cleveland]," Shriver was less diplomatic, employing rhetoric usually used to justify extraordinary measures in response to threats to national security: "Yes. . . . I think that is a present danger."[40]

Eight months earlier, Hubert Humphrey had identified another political vulnerability for OEO—Shriver and his staff were facing a mayoral whipsaw. Urban mayors, although eager to criticize controversial programs and to charge the federal government with fomenting an insurrection of the poor in their own backyards, nevertheless responded angrily when faced with fiscal cutbacks to the antipoverty programs they found more politically and ideologically palatable. Humphrey anticipated across-the-board budget cuts in War on Poverty programs in the months to come. If Head Start and employment programs fell under the congressional budgetary axe, the vice president predicted that both mayors and their constituents would be as angry about that as the momentary divisions over controversial CAP efforts.[41]

Shriver defended his program in two separate sessions of testimony before the Senate in the summer of 1966. The urban crisis was twofold, he insisted; its victims were first and foremost the poor themselves—"there is no crisis on

Park Avenue." And in Shriver's mind, "democracy based on full participation of the poor offers the only viable solution to that crisis." Even after months of attack, Shriver still appeared to be pledging at least rhetorical allegiance to the principle of "maximum feasible participation."

Evoking the bleak metaphor of the French play *Huis Clos* without mentioning Jean-Paul Sartre, OEO's director spoke of cities that "have become prisons for the poor. . . . There is no exit for most of those who live there." It was no longer practicable to reply to the angry cry of "Burn Baby Burn!" with the counsel "Wait Baby Wait." "I stand before you today as an advocate" of the poor, "partial, biased, impatient. Not so much afraid of this violence and discontent as I am of our temporizing, timidity, and lack of faith in democracy." Shriver recited the closing stanza of T. S. Eliot's "The Hollow Men," concluding with the familiar: "This is the way the world ends / Not with a bang but a whimper." Beseeching Congress not to cut Johnson's already lean appropriation request, Shriver lamented, "There is more to be feared from the whimper than the bang."[42]

Despite the growing opposition to antipoverty programs and additional civil rights legislation, in early January the brutal slayings of Vernon Dahmer in Mississippi and Sammy Younge in Alabama (both civil rights activists) emboldened Johnson to stress the necessity of additional laws to protect civil rights workers in his 1966 State of the Union Address later that month.[43] Between September and December of 1965, all-white juries in Alabama had refused to convict the murderers of civil rights martyrs James Reeb, Viola Liuzzo, and Jonathan Daniels. And there were other acquittals in less-heralded cases in which the victims were African Americans. The state of Alabama, for example, did not even bother to investigate the state trooper who had killed Jimmie Lee Jackson and inadvertently created the rallying point for the Selma to Montgomery March. Taken together, these events sent a powerful signal that neither state statutes nor color-coded administration of justice afforded adequate protections to black and white civil rights activists, although it was telling that the deaths of the white victims—Reeb, Liuzzo, and Daniels—resulted in legal proceedings while the death of Jackson, an African American, drew far less condemnation from Alabama's white authorities and citizens alike.[44]

The question then became one of timing and priorities. In a period when many whites felt that the most glaring injustices had been redressed—that the movement had already, in effect, succeeded—the prospects for additional civil rights legislation appeared bleak.[45]

As February passed, civil rights leaders and their allies grew restive, despite the administration's assurances that the Department of Justice was busy draft-

With Attorney General Nicholas Katzenbach of the Department of Justice looking on in the background, Vice President Hubert Humphrey discusses prospects for civil rights legislation in March 1966 with the civil rights leadership, including Roy Wilkins, John Lewis, and Martin Luther King Jr. Courtesy of the LBJ Library.

ing the legislation. (Civil Rights Division lawyers were doing just that, but they probably could have completed the task more quickly if the chief executive had applied his famous "Johnson treatment.") The president's meeting with civil rights leaders in mid-March of 1966 to discuss the prospects for legislation in the upcoming congressional session was a calculated exercise in dampening expectations.[46] Nicholas Katzenbach's briefing memo urged his chief to shift most of the lobbying responsibilities to the civil rights groups themselves, warning that to secure Senator Everett Dirksen's support and that of other Republican allies would be far more difficult than in 1964 and 1965. "Even supporters of civil rights are apathetic," Katzenbach noted, and the sense of moral urgency that had driven passage of landmark legislation in the two preceding congressional sessions was noticeably absent.[47]

Despite such lowered expectations, the delay in introducing the legislative civil rights package raised eyebrows in all quarters as March passed with no action.[48] Finally, in late April 1966, the president forwarded his proposals to Congress, but when Joseph Califano sent a memo to the president outlining strategies to achieve "decent press coverage" of the package, Johnson circled that phrase and scribbled the ominous interrogatory, "Who wants more coverage?"[49] After meeting briefly with the civil rights leadership and affixing his signature on his message to Congress, Johnson left Washington for his Texas ranch, taking with him many members of the White House press corps who might otherwise have elected to cover the reception of the president's new civil rights proposals on Capitol Hill.

The proposed legislation and the accompanying message delivered to Congress on April 28 focused on four areas: protection of civil rights workers in the exercise of constitutionally protected activities; guarantees of nondiscrimination in jury selection in both state and federal courts; the strengthening of the attorney general's discretionary power and authority to bring lawsuits against recalcitrant school systems still resisting the implementation of desegregation; and a call for a national policy barring racial discrimination in housing, to encompass both rental and saleable real estate.[50] Any one of the recommendations would have drawn strong opposition in Congress, but the fourth area on housing discrimination proved to be particularly divisive. Senator Sam Ervin, North Carolina's master of soft resistance to racial reform, shrewdly predicted that northern colleagues who had been strong allies of civil rights legislation targeted at abuses in the benighted South would become less enthusiastic "now that other than Southern oxen are being gored."[51]

Mississippi Democratic congressman William Colmer railed against a bill that he warned knuckled under to threats from black militants promising "another long, hot summer." Some of his northern colleagues, he noticed, "now find it difficult . . . to vote for a bill which . . . would adversely affect their own constituents. This proposal . . . is not a pistol pointed at one section of the country. Rather, it is a scatter gun aimed at all sections."[52] His remarks were an implicit invitation to northern whites to jump on board the bandwagon of states' rights, a strategy that both George Wallace and Richard Nixon were already using to good effect.[53]

The bill's opponents had additional ammunition. The June Meredith March against Fear and the emergence of cries of "Black Power" were soon followed by dozens of urban racial disturbances, notably in Chicago and Cleveland in mid-July. Although these uprisings proved less extensive than Watts, the dramatic television coverage of armored personnel carriers rumbling through the city streets while rioters burned and looted seemed to confirm the worst fears of whites.

In the aftermath of the Chicago riot, Martin Luther King Jr. led a series of open-housing marches through all-white neighborhoods in suburban Cicero, which provoked violent assaults from angry whites. As King biographer Taylor Branch observed, the events during the summer of 1966 — particularly the vio-

"We are all . . .
Mississippians."
Whites protest
integration attempts
led by King and
others in Chicago
in 1966. Copyright,
Benedict J. Fernandez.

lence against peaceful marchers in Cicero—had nationalized the issue of race. Comparing white northern racism with its more familiar southern cousin, SCLC lieutenant Andrew Young suggested that southern violence was typically authored by a "rabble element." In Chicago, he was stunned to note the presence of "women and children and husbands and wives coming out of their homes [and] becoming a mob. . . . In some ways it was far more frightening." After being struck by a rock "as big as [a] fist," during one Chicago march, an exhausted King remarked that he had "never seen as much hatred and hostility on the part of so many people." Glumly, the editors of the *Saturday Evening Post* acknowledged: "We are all, let us face it, Mississippians."[54]

Civil rights legislation had bogged down in various House committees, but the outbreak of the Cleveland and Chicago riots brought legislative matters to a head when a Florida Republican congressman tacked an "anti-riot" amendment onto the president's civil rights bill. Congressmen who had made careers out of damning federal intervention in local affairs suddenly championed the majesty of the national state with a legislative rider that would make it a federal felony if state lines were crossed to perpetrate a riot. The House adopted the rider by an overwhelming margin and, after dramatically weakening the housing section of the civil rights measure, sent the legislation on to the Senate.

Debate in the upper chamber the following month sounded eerily familiar. Louisiana senator Allen J. Ellender and North Carolina senator Sam Ervin both expressed the conviction that the civil rights legislation passed in 1957, 1964, and 1965 had come about only through blackmail, with senators "yielding to intemperate demands from pressure groups."[55]

Governor Paul Johnson, leery of the jury antidiscrimination provision of the legislation as well as its commitment to federal protection for civil rights workers, pleaded with white Mississippians to avoid further incidents that might galvanize support for the bill. Martin Luther King Jr. had plans to appear in the Mississippi town of Grenada following a white mob's assault on black students attempting to integrate the local high school. After the brutal beating of several of the students (and three reporters), Paul Johnson had sent state troopers to halt the violence. Fearing that the Magnolia State would once again be catapulted into national headlines, the governor called for patience and restraint. He reminded whites of the "clear obligation of all law-abiding citizens to preserve the peace" in a September 18 press release, and he emphasized the practical as well as moral reasons for his call for law and order. Only a "violent incident which focuses the spotlight of unfavorable publicity on the South can salvage this vicious [civil rights] legislation."

He need not have worried. As with the brutal assault on civil rights marchers in Canton just weeks before, white violence that once would have triggered national indignation seemed to elicit the equivalent of a national shrug.[56] As historian Steven F. Lawson has noted, "On this occasion, there were no Birminghams or Selmas to spark a civil rights victory." That Canton and Grenada are not today household historical references suggests how the tenor of American race relations had shifted since Lyndon Johnson had pledged that the nation would overcome racism and discrimination in Alabama's Black Belt and far beyond.[57]

On September 19, 1966, one day after the Mississippi governor's appeal, a Senate cloture vote failed. The violence directed against civil rights activists both during and after the Meredith March in June had been nearly completely eclipsed by the furor over the Black Power slogan. Not least, the recurrence of urban unrest in forty-four cities in 1966, twice the number of cities that had seen serious unrest the previous year, all but guaranteed the legislation's defeat in the Senate. Unable to recruit Illinois Republican and Senate minority leader Everett Dirksen to their cause, as they had in 1964 and 1965, the administration and civil rights lobbyists faced an intransigent coalition of white southern Democrats and enough Republicans to make a cloture vote a hopeless cause. That the "anti-riot" amendment went down to defeat along with the larger omnibus bill offered only a small measure of comfort. Those who had supported the administration measure, those who had vocally opposed it, and those who had been conspicuous for their silence—returned to their home districts two weeks later to wage the fall election campaign.[58]

One day after the bill's defeat, Harry McPherson bleakly concluded that "it would have been hard to pass the emancipation proclamation in the atmosphere prevailing this summer."[59] Late summer polls by Louis Harris and George Gallup had only documented what was obvious to any casual observer. Public support for additional civil rights measures had declined sharply, particularly among low-income whites. The Harris survey concluded that the "sense of being relegated to the backwash of American life, half-forgotten and left to fend for themselves, pervades low-income whites." Many felt that "much of the Great Society of the 1960s has passed them by." Both the president and the established civil rights leadership faced an evaporating consensus, McPherson confided to Nicholas Katzenbach, and how the administration wrestled with this "principal dilemma" would dictate the possibilities of executive-initiated social reform in both the immediate and the long-term future.[60]

Even before the final defeat of the 1966 civil rights legislation, McPherson had already prepared his postmortem. In one of his patented no-holds-barred memos, he argued to Johnson that the faint prospects for passage were probably doomed by the breakdown of the civil rights coalition. "The civil rights movement is obviously in a mess," concluded Johnson's longtime Texan associate. He warned that the nation stood at a crossroads in race relations: one road led to additional violence and white repression; the other direction was "uncertain," but its outcome depended on ongoing cooperation between civil rights constituencies and the administration, and on whites and blacks "working *within* the American system, not against it."[61] Black alienation was becoming increasingly evident, in part because "breakthroughs in political rights," with the successful passage of civil rights legislation in 1957, 1960, 1964, and 1965, had raised hopes among African Americans nationwide. But deeply entrenched economic inequalities, de facto school segregation, and barriers to equal access in housing were proving to be far more intractable issues.

What was striking about McPherson's memos was the absence of any reference to civil rights leaders' growing uneasiness over the war. Most mainstream leaders had remained silent, out of a sense of loyalty to Johnson and a concern

Vietnam drives a wedge between King and Johnson. Courtesy of the LBJ Library.

that criticizing him would jeopardize the Great Society legislative agenda or, most important, would discredit the civil rights movement as disloyal. King himself had swallowed his deep misgivings, but Johnson was well aware of the views of others of the nation's best-known civil rights leaders. It was a rift that King's opponents often sought to exploit. John Roche, the Brandeis academic who had replaced Eric Goldman as the resident White House intellectual, was a passionate hawk who ingratiated himself with Johnson by stoking the president's paranoia over Robert Kennedy. He seldom lost a chance to remind Johnson of King's opposition to the war.

For the most part, however, the president avoided criticizing King outside his most immediate circle. In the wake of the 1966 July riot in Chicago, Mayor Richard Daley warned the president that the "good doctor" (as he sarcastically referred to King) is "not your friend. He's against you on Vietnam. He's a goddamn faker." But in a long telephone conversation, Johnson repeatedly refused to take the bait and ignored Daley's outburst.[62] He could be petulant in his hostility at times. When Nicholas Katzenbach urged him to respond to a King telegram with a personal reply ("King is useful to us"), Johnson ignored the advice. Still, he understood that even a King who was weakened politically was a useful ally. And although many observers were convinced that King had become persona non grata in the White House, it was in fact the SCLC leader who began to cancel meetings with LBJ. As late as March of 1967, Johnson directed an aide to "ask Louis Martin why he hasn't brought [King] in. He's canceled two engagements with me and I don't understand it."[63]

McPherson certainly saw the need to continue working with King, as well as with more supportive black leaders. Still anxious to take charge of the issue, he urged Johnson to call a meeting with a group of major civil rights leaders to "strengthen the[ir] resolve" and to undercut the growing influence of black militants. Playing on Johnson's ego and evoking the former confidence in White House charisma so in evidence at the time of the Howard University speech, McPherson called on the president to "reassert what is undeniable, as well as inescapable — your leadership of the civil rights movement." Warning that urban rioting was fueling a backlash, he argued that if Johnson could convince a broader cross section of African American leadership to "speak out for order" it might help to lessen the anticipated electoral damage to the Democrats in the upcoming midterm elections. McPherson proposed an invitation list headlined by A. Philip Randolph, Martin Luther King Jr., Roy Wilkins, and Whitney Young. A quick and decisive sentence at the bottom of the list spoke volumes when it stated flatly: "There is no longer any need to have SNCC and CORE represented."[64] The Big Six had been whittled to the Big Four.

McPherson optimistically insisted that there was "a stirring in the Negro community now for moderation. Stokely Carmichael, Floyd 'McKissack,' [sic] and their people are jeopardizing the Negroes' future."[65] McPherson's misspelling of CORE's newly installed national director, although assuredly innocent, may reinforce the axiom that familiarity breeds contempt. Perhaps more than any other delegate, McKissick had proven to be a troublesome ally at the full meeting of the White House Conference on Civil Rights earlier in the summer of 1966 for his outspokenness on the issue of Vietnam and his overall unwillingness to follow the administration's script for the two-day gathering. If McPherson's list reflected a shrinking Big Six, his suggested inclusion of black Philadelphia minister Leon Sullivan, Texas state senator Barbara Jordan, Dorothy Height of the National Council of Negro Women, and African American jurists Juanita Stout and Leon Higginbotham indicated the administration's evolving vision of acceptable black leadership. If nothing else, the

Roy Wilkins increasingly serves as Johnson's closest ally among the nation's civil rights leaders, but the proximity of the head of the NAACP *comes with a price. Courtesy of the* LBJ *Library.*

list was significantly more diverse in terms of gender than that of many earlier high-profile civil rights meetings. Some form of presidential initiative was vital, said McPherson, who concluded with the admonition: "If you do nothing to exercise your leadership . . . you will be damned by the Negroes, who will turn increasingly toward extremist leaders."[66]

After reading the memo, Johnson initialed his approval for a meeting and suggested adding black Philadelphia lawyer William ("Bill") Coleman's name to the list of invitees. But Johnson made his blessing conditional, "subject to Nick's approval." And Katzenbach carefully rebutted McPherson's suggestions. The attorney general rejected the timing of such a meeting as inauspicious and implicitly criticized the proposed invitation list as too centrist. Each time that Johnson met with members of the "established Negro leadership," Katzenbach argued, civil rights leaders like Roy Wilkins and Martin Luther King Jr. "are made to appear [the President's] lieutenants or apologists . . . pacific captives of the administration." This establishment "taint" undercut more moderate leadership and strengthened the appeal of "extreme groups." For Johnson to create the appearance of pressuring civil rights leaders to speak out even more forcefully against violence and urban unrest, as McPherson's memo was suggesting, would further tarnish them as administration lackeys.[67]

Katzenbach, ever the political pragmatist, argued that if Johnson convened the meeting as proposed, the civil rights leaders would have no choice but to criticize the administration for its lackluster enforcement and implementation record in key areas of concern to black leaders. Although the attorney general did not spell out such a critique, he knew it might include a number of troubling questions. Why had so few federal registrars been dispatched to counties in Mississippi where local officials were clearly flouting the provisions of the Voting Rights Act? How did the president explain the appearance of a loss of will in the War on Poverty and tolerate the congressional slashing of already-lean proposed antipoverty appropriations? To avoid the potential for acrimony if such charges were raised publicly, Katzenbach recommended that any meeting be put off until after the November congressional elections. At that point, the president could convene not only the Big Four civil rights leaders, but a cross section of labor and religious leaders to begin to chart the legislative agenda for the 90th Congress.

In the next installment in the lively, and increasingly strained, exchange of opinions, McPherson argued in a September 20 memo to the attorney general—one surely intended for Johnson's eyes as well—that he still thought the president should meet with civil rights leaders in advance of the elections. He agreed with Katzenbach's assessment of the political liabilities inherent in Johnson's appearing to favor Wilkins and Young, whom some insiders half-mockingly referred to as "the Roy and Whitney Show." If Johnson were only to meet with the leaders of the NAACP and the Urban League he would compound their problems, fueling innuendo about their being "Uncle Toms." But McPherson still thought it advisable for the president to invite King and the broader ideological and generational cross section of leadership he had proposed in his initial memo. (He now upped the ante by colorfully labeling state senator Barbara Jordan "a militant in Texas terms.") Such a high-profile meeting, McPherson reasoned, would appear to dilute the influence of Wilkins and Young, thus enhancing their stock among a broader spectrum of blacks and "tak[ing] the curse of 'President's boy' off Whitney and Roy."[68]

Against the backdrop of these frank exchanges, presidential speechwriter Ben Wattenberg began to draft a major presidential address, which bore as its unadorned working title the heading, "Negro Speech." Although Wattenberg described himself as a domestic "moderate" in the mid-1960s, he was fiercely anticommunist and an unwavering defender of LBJ's Vietnam policies. Always sensitive to what he saw as shifting political moods, he had become convinced by mid-1966 that the American people were unwilling to support the more far-reaching aspects of Johnson's antipoverty program, an argument he supported in his influential 1970 book, *The Real Majority*. Although he always insisted that he remained an "old Democrat," he would ultimately serve in the Reagan administration, where he worked closely with other neoconservatives like Irving Kristol, Norman Podhoretz, Midge Decter, and Jeanne Kirkpatrick.[69]

Wattenberg's draft emerged in part as a response to recent summer riots, in particular the flare-up in the Hough district of Cleveland. It clearly reflected a preemptive approach to limiting losses in the November elections. Though originally entitled "Negro Speech," it clearly had among its intended audience those white voters increasingly being tagged as "backlash." Wattenberg, adopting the president's voice, decried the discourse of the preceding year "when the dominant public words describing the Negro have all been in the language of crisis and chaos." He rattled off a vocabulary list of "riots, slums, . . . illegitimacy, crime, cultural deprivation, ghettos, narcotics, poverty—and more."[70]

"The language of crisis and caricature," Wattenberg reasoned, had fueled both the phenomenon of backlash and the currency of Black Power. The two concepts were linked in the speechwriter's mind, with the former grounded in a stereotyped vision of black America and the latter reflecting an equally two-dimensional appraisal of whites. Wattenberg's speech called for Johnson to herald the sacrifices of black infantrymen in Vietnam—he cited the figure of blacks representing 18 percent of all Americans killed in action in Southeast Asia—and to stress that their heroics were "far more typical of the attitudes of Negroes in America today than what a handful of hoodlums . . . have caused in some of our cities this past summer." Wattenberg was careful to attribute the label "hoodlum" to NAACP leader Roy Wilkins. In doing so, he insulated Johnson from direct responsibility for the use of such disparaging and racially charged vocabulary, but had the speech been delivered as written it could hardly have helped to bolster the impression of Wilkins's political independence from the White House.

The proposed speech concluded with a series of stern admonishments to both whites and blacks and seemed tailored to the "extremists" of both races. It praised an American tradition of diversity and implicitly argued that blacks were not "beyond the melting pot" but instead had been forcibly excluded by whites from avenues to full assimilation. Wattenberg's language sought to undercut the appeal of backlash politics by insisting that blacks sought no special favors: "The Negro American—hard-working, as decent as the next man, and just as anxious to advance himself on his own merit—poses no threat to anyone."

The final section of the "Negro Speech" sought to assuage the fears of anxious whites and to serve notice to African Americans of things to come. Its language looked forward to a race-blind marketplace in the near future where "a Negro engineer will not . . . be held back . . . by his color" but where that job candidate would sink or swim strictly "on the basis of his ability." "For the graduate of a Southern Negro college today may well be competing with a graduate from Harvard or MIT within the next few years, and the race will go to the swift." All of the metaphors of the Howard University speech were in evidence, but Wattenberg was reinventing their meaning. The proposed "Negro Speech" sounded a clear retreat to the classical notion of equal opportunity: "Overcompensation is only a momentary occurence [sic]," he wrote. "To the Negro in America today I have only one message," read the draft's blunt language: "A fairer America will bring no gifts upon silver platters." Where Johnson in the lead-up to the Howard University speech had likened the daunting task of assuring "equality as a fact and equality as a result" for African Americans to "converting a crippled person into a four minute miler"—but welcomed the challenge—Wattenberg appeared confident that blacks would soon be left to run the race unassisted.[71]

Having weathered the long, hot summer of 1966, Johnson ultimately opted for a wait-and-see approach on civil rights. Heeding the advice of his attorney general over that of White House aide Harry McPherson, the president did not convene the proposed meeting of civil rights leaders. Ben Wattenberg's "Negro Speech" circulated among top administration domestic advisers, including Bill Moyers, Douglass Cater, Harry McPherson, and Clifford Alexander, but it ultimately died a quiet death, undelivered, in the bulging cabinets of the White House file system.

On October 10, 1966, an article in the *National Observer* described a forthcoming manifesto by Martin Luther King Jr., Roy Wilkins, A. Philip Randolph, Dorothy Height, and Whitney Young, warning of the consequences of Black Power rhetoric. As the article's author noted, with apparent satisfaction, CORE's Floyd McKissick and SNCC's Stokely Carmichael had not been consulted. Four days later, a full-page ad appeared in the *New York Times* under the headline "Crisis and Commitment." Sponsors of the ad affirmed their faith in the "democratic process" and the "force of law and its fulfillment in the courts," a pointed reference to the failure of Congress to pass the jury reform measure in the administration's 1966 civil rights omnibus bill. Although King was noticeably absent from the statement's signers, at the heart of the manifesto was an appeal for the ongoing relevance of nonviolence, implicitly a rejection of the militancy of the Meredith March and the violent rage of both Watts and

Hough. "We repudiate any strategies of violence, reprisal or vigilantism," read the text, "and we condemn both rioting and the demagoguery that feeds it, for these are the final resort of despair, and we have not yielded to despair."[72]

"It is not condoning riots to cry out against the conditions in the Negro ghettos," the ad continued. Signers of the statement argued eloquently that those using urban unrest as an excuse to derail additional civil rights reform demonstrated not only a fundamental shortsightedness but also a lack of proportionality. "Has the nation forgotten," asked the advertisement, in cadences that might have been inspired by the rhythmic balance of King's oratory, "that for every Negro youth who throws a brick, there are a hundred thousand suffering the same disadvantages who do not?" And the signers telegraphed their intent to remain loyal to Johnson's faltering consensus on the Vietnam War—perhaps explaining King's absence from the signatories—when they reminded readers that "for every Negro who tosses a Molotov cocktail, there are a thousand fighting and dying on the battlefields of Vietnam."

A thinly veiled subtext scolded congressmen and senators who had compromised the strength of the year's civil rights legislation before allowing it to die in the Senate chamber. Although the opposition of certain congressmen was a foregone conclusion, to watch "sometime friends pulling back in full retreat and yielding to the battlefield scavengers ground which could have been held if it had been fought for" was a painful reminder that all political alliances are transitory. But the manifesto's signers were unwilling to let the deserting coalition members slink away without a history lesson.

Martin Luther King Jr., in his famous 1963 address to the March on Washington, had spoken of a "promissory note" that the nation had defaulted upon, "a bad check which has come back marked 'insufficient funds.'" But the signers of the October 14, 1966, advertisement harked back to the nineteenth-century loss of will that presaged the demise of Reconstruction: "Then, as now, the voices of temporary liberalism sounded discouragement and disillusionment with the capacity of the freedmen for full citizenship. Then, as now, the South capitalized on Northern weariness with the 'race problem' and was enabled to shut off the hope of freedom. But the 'race problem' remained, and today we are paying for yesterday's default."

The advertisement, an impassioned plea for forward momentum, reflected the weight of an oppressive cyclical history: "We are determined that this history shall not repeat itself and we call upon all our countrymen, black and white, of all faiths and origins, to move with us."[73] Critics looking to explain the failure of the administration's proposed 1966 legislation could point their fingers in any number of directions, but the self-evident erosion of the pro–civil rights coalition, which had been so effective in securing passage of sweeping reforms in 1964 and 1965, was cause for grave concern. Along with legislative woes, the major civil rights organizations in 1966 were also facing an uphill battle to attract donors to replenish their treasuries. Even the foundations could not fill the fiscal gap. Solicitor Thurgood Marshall wrote the president worriedly in the early weeks of January with reports of foundation support for civil rights organizing drives drying up: "Too many contributors feel that the job is now completed."[74] When many of the same northern churches that had offered critical moral support to the Civil Rights Act in 1964 and the Voting Rights Act in 1965 failed to close ranks behind the 1966 civil rights package, reporter Mary McGrory observed, "The music has gone out of the movement."[75]

But the real bang came on Election Day, 1966. Gaining forty-seven seats in the House, Republicans substantially reduced the Democratic majority. Although the Republican Party remained a distinct minority in the Senate (64 to 36), it gained three seats in the upper chamber and won eight governorships. The Republicans' working alliance with conservative southern Democrats, moreover, placed them in a position to stymie virtually any legislation they targeted.[76]

It would be easy to exaggerate the sweeping nature of the 1966 elections. Incumbent administrations typically lose ground in such off-year campaigns, and the rebound from the Democrats' overwhelming victory of 1964 exaggerated the appearance of a massive backlash. And, despite ongoing violence and intimidation at the polls, at least ten African Americans won election to public office in rural areas of the Deep South, a development not seen since Reconstruction.[77]

But antipoverty and civil rights partisans found it hard to find a silver lining in the aftermath of the elections, as Congress reduced Johnson's already-lean $1.75 billion antipoverty appropriation request by $138 million. The cities and CAPs bore the brunt of the cutbacks. The normally diplomatic Shriver was uncharacteristically blunt in assessing the impact of congressional tightfistedness: "The poor will feel that they have been shortchanged. They will feel they have been double-crossed. The poor will feel that democracy is only for the rich."[78]

Poll data released by the Louis Harris Survey indicated an erosion of support for both OEO and the War on Poverty. Although African Americans in the inner cities favored antipoverty programs by a 5-to-1 margin, "only 3 in 10 low income whites with opinions think the War on Poverty has been a success."[79]

Civil rights activists roundly condemned the budget shortfall, and James Farmer, ex-director of CORE, staged a rally attended by approximately 1,000 blacks and whites in Washington's Lafayette Park. He called for an "antipoverty march" of massive proportions "that will make all previous marches look like child's play and a picnic." Congress was "afraid of the poor organizing," Farmer insisted, and took Johnson to task for his fiscal priorities. Ruth McKall, a neighborhood activist, took the podium to ask rhetorically: "Why is it so much more important to spend $20 billion on the war in Vietnam when the most important war of all, the war on poverty . . . is being fought right here under your nose to the piteous tune of $1.7 billion?" (Her numbers did not take into account Congress's slashing of the budget to approximately $1.6 billion.) "Your Great Society has too soon become the forgotten society," she said, taking Johnson to task as a truant guardian. But a "massive" march seemed unlikely to materialize. (Rally organizers predicted a turnout of as many as 5,000 and got approximately one-fifth that number. Joseph Rauh Jr., Walter Fauntroy, and other Washington D.C. activists with a national profile made impassioned remarks but appeared somehow forlorn.)

A group of picketers left a black box decorated with a white bow in front of the White House Christmas tree, explaining to the media that it was "a box of nothing . . . because that's what we feel the President has given us."[80] Canvassing their Washington, D.C., area sources, White House aides found little evidence that plans for a "massive march" were under way. Robert Kintner dismissed the former CORE director's chances of successfully staging such a protest: "Mr. Farmer does not have a political base."[81]

Lyndon Johnson made clear his feelings about the verdict of the nation's voters within days of the election when he sent his greetings to the Urban League as they observed the tenth annual Equal Opportunity Day. Looking back on the last year, Johnson admitted, it was tempting to slip into pessimism. "But we have survived more perilous periods of reaction," Johnson insisted, "and with your help we will also survive the treachery of today's false prophets."[82]

Shriver tendered a handwritten letter of resignation to LBJ during the president's Christmas vacation at the ranch. No political neophyte, he had his own sources of intelligence and no doubt realized Johnson's growing animus against the OEO and himself. At the core of the problem was the president's obsession with "loyalty" and "disloyalty" and the thorn of genetics. Johnson would never be able to forget—or forgive—that Shriver was brother-in-law to both Kennedys, and Johnson became more and more convinced over time that Shriver would be backing a presidential bid by Robert Kennedy in 1968.[83]

Shriver justified his resignation by reasoning that the OEO needed "a new face and a new image" in order to succeed with appropriations in Congress and insisted that his political leverage was "exhausted" in Congress: "I am out of IOU's up there [on Capitol Hill]. . . . Someone needs to come in with different friends and different enemies than I have."[84] Johnson had been warned by Califano that a fundamental shake-up of the antipoverty effort would be politically hazardous, and the president told Shriver that his resignation would lend ammunition to critics from both the left and right. Conservatives would be delighted with the upheaval, and liberals would see the director's departure as evidence that the administration had abandoned the War on Poverty in favor of the war on communism in Southeast Asia.[85] Apparently outmaneuvered, Shriver succumbed to the still-potent "Johnson treatment" and agreed to remain. The agency limped along to the dirgelike cadence of T. S. Eliot's "whimper."[86]

Surveying the landscape in mid-December 1966, McPherson urged Johnson to shift the agenda from more programs to more effective coordination and management of the myriad existing programs: "I think we have about all the social programs we need. . . . We may have too many. . . . What is needed is some generalship." Seeking to ignite the president's political instincts, McPherson warned that inaction on the administration's part would erode public confidence in the ability of the Democratic Party to lead the country. He called on Johnson to shake up his cabinet officers by asking them to justify whether the dollars they spent on their respective department's programs were cost-effective. The president was surrounded by a "tired cabinet," in McPherson's opinion: "They are good men, but they are beyond asking the hard questions now. They are just trying to make the old machine go."[87]

The same fears at OEO that had circulated late in 1965 now took on added urgency. Donald Radler, the agency's congressional liaison officer, reported that the setbacks in the 1966 election were prompting rumors on Capitol Hill "that the 90th Congress will dismember OEO and parcel out its programs to the 'horse and buggy agencies,'" line agencies like Housing and Urban Development and the Department of Health, Education, and Welfare. Since Congress was already contemplating such a radical move, suggested Radler, perhaps Johnson himself should undertake a dramatic restructuring of the bureaucracy—the Economic Opportunity Act of 1964 gave the president such broad authority.[88]

Aide Harry McPherson was thinking in terms of damage control. Looking ahead, he felt certain the slimmer Democratic majority that would take up the reins of government in the new 90th Congress in January of 1967 would lack the votes necessary for cloture on any civil rights legislation; it would be exceedingly difficult to pass open-housing legislation in the Senate. Roy Wilkins and administration insiders gave some consideration to liberalizing the Senate rules, and although McPherson considered success in this regard unlikely, Johnson's adviser thought "making some noises about preferring a less restrictive cloture rule . . . would make it more difficult to nail us with neglect when no civil rights act emerges from the 90th Congress."[89] Johnson and his advisers were concerned about the growing white backlash against their policies, but the immediate threat was from the liberal left, those who were "trying to put the monkey on our back." As 1966 ended and 1967 began, searching for political cover seemed to be the order of the day.

The Johnson administration's fears proved well-founded when King gave his famous Riverside Church speech on April 4, 1967, exactly one year before his assassination. "As I have walked among the desperate, rejected and angry young men I have told them that Molotov cocktails and rifles would not solve their problems," said King. "But they asked—and rightly so—what about Vietnam?" I knew at that point, he continued, "that I could never again raise my voice against the violence of the oppressed in the ghettoes without having first spoken clearly to the greatest purveyor of violence in the world today—my own government." "[I] cannot be silent," he said. "I speak for the poor of America who are paying the double price of smashed hopes at home and death and corruption in Vietnam." His statement was arguably a requiem for the "Double V" campaign of the "Good War," World War II.

For a time, recalled King, it "seemed as if there was a real promise of hope for the poor—both black and white—through the Poverty Program." But the buildup in Vietnam had "eviscerated" such programs, "and I knew that America would never invest the necessary funds or energies in rehabilitation of its poor so long as adventures like Vietnam continued to draw men and skills and money like some demoniacal suction tube."[90]

King had feared and expected strong criticism for his stand against the war, but he was unprepared for the savage attacks that followed. John Roche, White House aide and the former head of Americans for Democratic Action, wrote in an "Eyes Only" memo to Johnson the following day that "King—in desperate search of a constituency—has thrown in with the commies." Roche suggested that "Communist-oriented 'peace' types have played him . . . like [a] trout," strongly implying that communists had in all likelihood ghostwritten the Riverside speech. King, he argued, was "inordinately ambitious and quite stupid (a bad combination)."

The civil rights movement, Roche told the president, was "shot—disorganized and broke." By attacking the Vietnam War, King was only "painting himself into a corner with a bunch of losers." In speaking out against the war, concluded the memo, King might gain standing as a "folk hero" among "alienated whites" but would suffer a loss in standing among both "the great bulk of the Negro community (who are solid, sensible supporters of the administration)" and "black nationalists." The latter group viewed King as a rival and would see his increasingly strident antiwar pronouncements as encroaching on their ideological turf.[91]

According to one close associate, LBJ "flushed with anger" upon first reading an executive summary of the "Beyond Vietnam" address.[92] Though he refrained from publicly questioning King's patriotism, the Riverside speech marked the final break between the two. This time there would be no reconciliation. Later in the year, the SCLC issued a fund-raising appeal under King's name, criticizing the administration's war policy and its failure to fund antipoverty measures. The administration and Congress had "offered nothing better than an iron lid for the ghettos," read the letter (which had actually been written by King's close friend, Stanley Levinson). Johnson ordered Sheldon Cohen, the commissioner of the Internal Revenue Service, to investigate SCLC to see if its tax-exempt status might be revoked. He also enlisted tax lawyer Carol Agger, the wife of his old friend and Supreme Court justice Abe Fortas, for advice. Agger and Cohen concluded that it would be impossible to make a case against the SCLC.[93]

White House assistant George Christian reached out to Carl Rowan, the African American who headed the U.S. Information Agency. Rowan assured Christian that "everyone in the Civil Rights movement has known that King has been getting advice from a communist." In Rowan's opinion, "most Negroes" did not share King's opposition to the war in Vietnam, but "many of the less educated will go along with him."[94] Most ominous of all was the reaction of J. Edgar Hoover. Already convinced that the civil rights leader was a "notorious liar," the FBI director warned Johnson that "it is clear . . . [King] is an instrument in the hands of subversive forces seeking to undermine our nation."[95]

The civil rights leader had gone over to what embattled insiders clearly viewed as the other side. Clifford Alexander dismissed King's "peacenik efforts" as reflective of a more general pattern of "very little creativity within the [civil rights] movement itself" but urged Johnson to press Roy Wilkins for the NAACP leader's assessment of the response of other civil rights leaders to King's statement. The NAACP's national board, on April 10, had voted and artfully dodged the issue of support for or opposition to the war, but they had unanimously ruled that a hypothetical merger of civil rights and peace movements represented a serious tactical mistake. The vote further solidified Wilkins's position as an administration stalwart and more than met Johnson's high expectations of personal loyalty.[96] Whitney Young carefully distanced himself from King

King's increasingly vocal critique of Johnson's Vietnam War policy in the spring of 1967 angers the president and leads to accusations from administration insiders that the civil rights leader has subversive leanings. Copyright, Benedict J. Fernandez.

initially, but even the ever-reliable Urban League was restive on the subject of Vietnam. At their annual conference in August, an internal movement challenged the organization's position that its primary focus should remain domestic issues, not international ones. Ultimately, the Urban League had adopted several "statements of concern," one of which noted that if faced with "a choice . . . between supporting guns or butter, the Urban League would support butter." The good news for Johnson was that the Urban League leadership insisted that for the time being there was enough money to fund *both* guns and butter.[97]

The intense and often vitriolic criticism that greeted his most decisive antiwar speech to date saddened and wounded King, but he denied he was condemning the war abroad out of a sense of frustration with the progress of the civil rights agenda at home. "I do it not out of anger . . . [but] out of a great anxiety and agony and anguish." Vietnam was "basically a war of colonialism," and to separate the struggle against American colonialism abroad from the fight to eradicate racism and economic injustice at home was completely artificial. The two battlefronts were inextricably bound together. The Great Society, he concluded, had "been shot down on the battlefields of Vietnam."[98]

CHAPTER SEVEN

Scouting the Star-Spangled Jungles

The White House, the Community Relations
Service, and the Dilemma of Urban Unrest

Exactly two years after the flames of the Watts riots had been extinguished, Martin Luther King Jr. appeared before the yearly convention of SCLC, on August 16, 1967, to deliver his annual report. The nation had weathered four successive years of urban disturbances, culminating in the conflagrations in Newark and Detroit the preceding month. In addressing the question "Where Do We Go from Here?" the SCLC leader referred specifically to Watts and argued that some African Americans "contend that . . . riots in various cities represented effective civil rights action." "But those who express this view always end up with stumbling words when asked what concrete gains have been won as a result. At best, the riots have produced a little additional antipoverty money allotted by frightened government officials and a few water sprinklers to cool the children of the ghettos. It is something like improving the food in the prison while the people remain securely behind bars."[1]

King was not the first Baptist minister to grapple with the dilemma of the riots. Just days after the passage of the Civil Rights Act in 1964, which created the CRS, prominent evangelist Billy Graham had turned down Lyndon Johnson's offer to serve as the chairman of a Citizens Committee that would advise the CRS on how best to play its role as a mediation agency resolving civil rights disputes in local communities. Using logic that must have appeared strange to some at the time, Graham wrote Johnson: "It is my opinion that the South will solve its racial problems long before the North does. I believe the explosive areas are in our great cities in the North."[2]

Less than two weeks later, extensive rioting had broken out in Harlem, followed by outbreaks of unrest in Rochester, New York, and in several other cities. In response to the uprisings in New York, White House aide Douglass Cater urged Johnson to consider using the CRS but reminded him that the agency had yet to receive appropriations from Congress. J. Edgar Hoover had dispatched FBI agents to the scenes of the disorders, but Cater noted that the difficulty of communicating effectively with rioters was hamstringing the federal response: Hoover's informational networks were less well developed in the inner city than elsewhere. The White House could take some measure of comfort from the fact that the problem transcended the color line. "Even the younger Negro leaders" were unable to make meaningful contact with the African Americans—disproportionately teenagers—who made up most of the rioters, Cater believed.[3]

The administration had largely avoided direct involvement in responding to the summer disturbances of 1964, choosing to focus its efforts on "fire prevention," with stepped-up youth employment opportunities and other similar initiatives. In 1965, the luxury of nonintervention evaporated. In the hours immediately following the outbreak of rioting in Watts, Johnson had broken his ominous silence only to warn White House aide Joseph Califano to keep the federal government from being embroiled in what he desperately wanted to remain a local crisis: "Not one of our people sets foot there [in Los Angeles] until you talk to me." But when the president refused to take Califano's subsequent calls to the ranch, Califano, who felt the crisis in Watts was out of control, authorized the Pentagon to deploy air force C-13s to ferry supplies and equipment to California National Guard troops operating under state command. This clearly ran counter to Johnson's desire to keep the federal government as far removed from the political fallout of the riot as possible. Later, LBJ angrily chided Califano: "Remember you work for your President," adding, "and damn sure not for Yorty," the Democratic mayor of Los Angeles.[4]

Following the rioting in 1964 and 1965, the administration had begun to take stock of how little it knew about a segment of the African American community that was often unrepresented by the "moderate" civil rights leadership with whom Lyndon Johnson had grown so accustomed to working. Although events like the White House Conference on Civil Rights still revealed a relatively restricted vision of black leadership, administration officials and allies began to take tentative steps to broaden their range of contacts. In one of the initial overtures, Morris Abram remembered how black Philadelphia lawyer Bill Coleman—"there was no more establishment figure on earth"—went to a meeting of "black militants" at the Bellevue Stratford Hotel in the downtown area of his home city in December 1965. Known to some by the nickname

"Pomp"—he wore a vest with his Phi Beta Kappa key prominently displayed—Coleman, an editor of the *Harvard Law Review*, had once clerked for Supreme Court justice Louis Brandeis. For Abram, the memory of Bill "Pomp" Coleman and his rendezvous with Philadelphia militants "was funny. Bill went out to find them."[5] That Abram found the anecdote so noteworthy was a revealing indication of how unusual it was for the administration to reach out to non-traditional black leaders.

Coleman found those who were gathered in the City of Brotherly Love "outrageous." He good-naturedly referred to the self-described "militants" from Philadelphia, New York, Chicago, and as far away as California as "nuts"—individuals whom more moderate civil rights leaders like "Roy [Wilkins] would have had no use for" and those on the margins or entirely beyond even Johnson's broadly defined "consensus." But Coleman and an associate, Carl Holman, agreed to meet with the group, and a wide-ranging conversation took place over the span of about six hours. Equal employment programs came under withering fire, and the urban leaders also called for "much more imaginative loan programs" "to break the hold of the loan sharks." One local activist acknowledged that it was difficult to distinguish authentic grassroots groups from organizations hastily created to apply for antipoverty funds, but he and other West Coast representatives lambasted the operation of antipoverty programs—in high gear in southern Los Angeles in the aftermath of the Watts destruction—calling the poverty program "a joke." "It would be better to stand on the street corners and hand out the money to the poor," one leader said, "than to use [antipoverty funding] as a political football."[6]

Virtually all of the leaders in attendance argued that urban political machines were using the welfare programs "as a political instrument and the poverty programs . . . as a political plum." The politicization of federal funding targeted at lower-income urban dwellers was stifling grassroots organization, and frustrated blacks in the poorest neighborhoods were opting for disorder, out of economic need and out of the belief that only through rioting could their voices break through the insulating barrier separating them from meaningful contact with the federal government. As one Chicago activist told White House aide Bill Graham, there were no antipoverty programs operating in his neighborhood because of the absence of riots. "We may have to import some rioters from another neighborhood," he sarcastically concluded. Over and over again, leaders called on the representatives of the Johnson administration to revitalize the War on Poverty and to redouble its commitment to the doctrine of "maximum feasible participation" of the poor.[7]

If the "nuts" and "militants" Coleman described in the Philadelphia gathering of December 1965 had been included more fully in the White House Conference on Civil Rights the following summer, it would have been "disruptive" or worse, in the memory of conference planner Morris Abram. "Given LBJ's desire for order and desire for praise," he recalled, "it would have been a disaster" to house a meeting "under the White House eaves . . . that was cussing him, that was using dirty words about him, that was negating everything he'd done."[8] However, the same careful choreography that made for a relatively bland White House Conference on Civil Rights in June 1966 may actually have prevented the ever-sensitive Johnson from disengaging with the issue of civil rights and shifting entirely into a bunker mentality.

Lyndon Johnson and a growing number of progressive activists were increasingly preoccupied by America's metastasizing involvement in Southeast Asia, but racial matters were seldom far from their minds in the latter half of the 1960s. In the year following Watts, the administration stepped up its efforts to monitor the shifting currents of black protest, particularly in urban areas. On the first Saturday in September 1966, when Adam Clayton Powell convened a "Black Power Planning Conference" in the Sam Rayburn office building on Capitol Hill, LBJ stalwart Louis Martin represented the Oval Office's eyes and ears. Although he downplayed his connection to the White House, his status as one of the administration's few high-ranking African American insiders became an asset when the handful of whites in attendance, along with the white media representatives, were asked to leave following a nearly unanimous vote by the overwhelmingly black attendees. Three of Adam Clayton Powell's own white staff assistants were among those politely ejected.

Martin delivered a bleak report to the White House: "The majority . . . of the delegates seemed to be 'visionaries' who had no real appreciation of the realities of American life save for the suffering that Negroes experience." But his impressions of the assembled "militants" reflected not so much any great antagonism as a kind of bemusement and disdain for what he saw as their naïveté and a kind of fruitless and slightly screwball "idealism." They were like "so many romantics who are ready to ride like Don Quijote [*sic*] against the windmills of racism."[9]

However dismissive administration insiders might have been of the "visionaries," the White House antennae were up, and the administration's responses to the threat of riots in American cities *before* and *between* the eruptions of the "long, hot summers" merit every bit as much sustained attention as its more reactive crisis management in the midst of some of the worst riots. As the courageous demonstrations that had provided moral currency for the civil rights legislation of 1964 and 1965 receded in the headlines and yielded to sensational coverage of urban riots in the succeeding three years, Lyndon Johnson confronted what might be termed an "intelligence problem."

By 1967 and 1968, urban rioting had become a quintessentially public spectacle, with a familiar and nearly ritualized choreography: appeals for federal assistance, the deployment of troops under federal command, urban crises that in turn fueled "political" crises (perhaps most famously in the case of the Detroit riot in July 1967). In that summer and again in the spring of 1968, television screens offered viewers the drama of armored personnel carriers on downtown streets as a counterpoint to less-often-documented Molotov cocktails and sniper fire. These images projected a stunning visual backdrop for political bickering among powerful urban mayors, police chiefs, governors, federal bureaucrats, the White House, and often exuberant spokesmen for Black Power.[10]

But off-screen a far less visible scenario unfolded. The Johnson administration's responses to both the possibility and the reality of urban unrest repeatedly shifted in the turbulent period preceding the establishment of the Kerner Commission in the summer of 1967. After the cataclysm of Watts, in August of 1965, and riots in the Hough district of Cleveland and in Mayor Richard Daley's Chicago and elsewhere in the summer of 1966, in early 1967 the president dispatched staff members to more than a dozen of the nation's most depressed urban areas to identify African American leaders, to measure the pulse of unrest, and to predict cities "most likely to riot."

The quiet forays received next to no attention from the mass media; indeed, the White House took elaborate precautions to ensure secrecy. Yet these efforts at scouting the "star-spangled jungles"—as one presidential aide later referred to the poverty-stricken inner cities—played an important role in shaping Johnson's civil rights policies and his responses to the unfamiliar dimensions of black urban poverty.[11] The attempts to explore new channels of communication and gather "intelligence" illuminate the larger contours of Johnson's civil rights and antipoverty policies in the three years following passage of the Voting Rights Act.

As early as the months preceding their chief's landslide electoral victory over Republican presidential candidate Barry Goldwater in 1964, Johnson associates had been uneasy over the prospect of urban unrest and possible white backlash. Some Democrats, in the typical gallows humor of campaign insiders, in fact dubbed the riots that broke out in the summer of 1964 "Goldwater rallies."[12] Flushed with victory at having secured passage of the Civil Rights Act, the president and administration officials nevertheless began to grapple with a "Negro problem"—as they defined it—whose contours were far less familiar than the ongoing struggle for civil rights in the South.[13] The second of the most formidable legal bulwarks of racial discrimination had fallen with passage of the Voting Rights Act in August 1965, but many civil rights activists warned that legislative breakthroughs might do little to address the persistent economic gap between whites and African Americans, a gap nowhere more evident than in the nation's inner cities.

The Watts riots in August 1965 stunned most white Americans, not just Lyndon Johnson. The president saw Watts as an act of collective political "betrayal" by black America: "How could they do that to me after I had given them so much?"[14] Historians as well as contemporary observers on all sides of the political equation—including some high-ranking administration officials—have placed too much emphasis on the rioting in Los Angeles as an explosive departure in social protest, a watershed. According to this view, Watts effectively "blind-sided" the administration in August 1965 in the immediate afterglow of the passage of landmark voting rights legislation. The chronological proximity of the two events has proven difficult to disentangle from issues of causality. But as early as the summer of 1964, when rioting had shaken Harlem and Rochester, New York, key aides and administration allies had voiced grave concerns about the deteriorating state of the nation's cities. George Reedy and African American administration ally Louis Martin were among those who warned that the urban "problem" might ultimately prove to be far more intractable than the headline-dominating southern freedom struggle.

Many civil rights activists, too, had suggested that the long-desired legislative breakthroughs, however invaluable, would do little to close the economic gap between whites and African Americans. In fact, the overall income gap between blacks and whites was narrowing, in a noteworthy statistical trend that would continue until the 1980s, as more blacks rose to middle-class status and in many cases followed whites to the suburbs. But riots in Harlem, Rochester, Jersey City, and Philadelphia showed that economic improvements were too little, too late—and far from the norm for those still trapped in the most depressed black communities of America.[15] White House aide Hobart Taylor wrote privately of his fears that a major riot was the one event that might derail the president's chances of claiming a mandate from the 1964 election. Anticipating trouble, Taylor's memo to Johnson urged black federal officeholders to fan out and establish "regular lines of contact" with urban blacks, including "that whole area of leadership not controlled by the national [civil rights] organizations."[16]

Some played the role of Cassandra, but others were less prescient. Ramsey Clark, later to serve as attorney general, noted that before Watts the dimensions of the urban crisis were far from apparent to those serving in the Justice Department. "We just didn't see it," he remarked. "I can't say that we felt any real sense of responsibility," he continued, his admission of a collective failure of perception in the Justice Department offering an unwitting paraphrase of Robert Kennedy's candid admission—offered only in retrospect—about the relative importance of civil rights in the early days of the Kennedy administration: "We didn't lie awake nights worrying about it."[17] For Clark, as for countless others, Watts *was* a wake-up call, offering a crash course in the realities of urban poverty.

Even before the riot had ended, California governor Edmund D. ("Pat") Brown announced plans to establish a state investigatory body to examine the causes of the unrest and the responses to the riot by state and local politicians and law enforcement—from his own office to Los Angeles mayor Sam Yorty to the city's chief of police, William Parker. Johnson moved quickly to have a federal hand in the pot. He demonstrated his political judgment in successfully lobbying the governor for ex-CIA director John McCone to chair the state commission—soon to become known as the McCone Commission. (McCone, a conservative Republican, had resigned in April, but he maintained good relations with Johnson.) As the riot wound down, on August 17, Johnson confided to Nicholas Katzenbach his belief that the uprising had been planned and carried out at the instigation of radicals. ("See to it that Hoover is in it up to his ears in Los Angeles," he told Katzenbach. "If you'll go after the leaders it can be stopped.") But he quickly shifted gears, concerned that conservatives would attribute the riot to communist subversives. As he told Joseph Califano, "If [McCone] says no communist conspiracy [existed] and describes the conditions in Watts, we'll be able to help those Negroes out there."[18]

That was clearly the direction from which he wooed McCone when he called on August 18 to urge him to accept the chairmanship of Brown's commission. In a torrent of words that left McCone overwhelmed, Johnson gave his explanation for why the riots had erupted. "These groups have got absolutely nothing to live for—forty per cent unemployed—they sleep with rats—from broken homes and illegitimate families and narcotics and we've isolated them in certain areas and when they move in, we move out." Even the army was not a possibility for redemption, he told McCone; more than half of black inductees were rejected for reasons of health and lack of education. "The white boys are doing all the fighting [in Vietnam]," he exclaimed in one aside.

By the end of the conversation, McCone—who had initially insisted that he was "considering" accepting the appointment—had assured the president he would agree to Governor Brown's request. The "Johnson treatment" could be nearly as overwhelming over a telephone line as when the Texan actually towered over his hapless victim.[19]

Roger Wilkins proved to be invaluable in helping to facilitate direct face-to-face contact between high-ranking federal officials and "everyday" local people from Watts and the surrounding areas. When the president dispatched Ramsey Clark to head a second task force charged with reporting on the underlying factors precipitating the Watts uprising, Wilkins helped to arrange for a meeting between Clark—whom he had only recently met—and African American residents in the Watts area. Wilkins, certain that Clark would spend a few moments dispensing platitudes about the federal government's concern for the destiny of minorities and the poor, had been tempted to dismiss Johnson's emissary. Instead, Clark *listened.* The Justice Department official sat for hours and took copious notes while those in attendance, their indignation often coming out, shared accounts of all the problems—most notably police brutality—they faced in Watts. The lengthy meeting was the beginning of a remarkable relationship between the two men and a transformation in Clark's understanding of the problems of the nation's inner cities. Before Watts, the leadership in the Justice Department was "so consumed with the South and there was so much to be done there," Ramsey Clark later recalled, that "when we thought of the North, we didn't think of civil rights. . . . We really didn't."[20]

Ramsey Clark's note taking transcended politics and bureaucratic etiquette—he was clearly moved by what he had heard—and it informed the meticulously researched report he and Roger Wilkins began to compile. Los Angeles's poorest residents were largely "voiceless," and "inadequate communication between the segregated societies" prevented meaningful attempts to close both economic and cultural gaps. Clark's report described two communities "drifting apart," with the riots widening the fissures.

"Traditional goals of the civil rights movement have not been particularly germane," the task force concluded. Blacks in Los Angeles were preoccupied by different issues and drawn to different leaders. "It is vital that the white community realize that a new type of leadership has emerged in the Negro community," Clark wrote, "a leadership which is new, untested and relatively unknown. . . . It is a matter of the greatest importance that these new leaders be understood."[21]

Clark's conclusions were sobering: the riots in Los Angeles, like the ones the preceding summer, were "manifestations of defects in our development as a democratic society." It was critical to address the problems, but their complexity meant that "there is no easy solution. The problems will not go away."

Ramsey Clark's report, however, did eventually "go away," prematurely buried by larger political concerns. Although dozens of bureaucrats within the "permanent government" reviewed Clark's findings in the early winter of 1965 and were impressed with the carefully reasoned language of the task force, the White House issued a strict embargo, which precluded any public release of the report. Ultimately, several copies wound up filed in an undated brown envelope labeled "Confidential Reports which we have announced have never been prepared. Do not give out to anyone, or acknowledge we have."[22]

Some have argued that Clark's report, prepared with Roger Wilkins's significant input, was sacrificed to John McCone's ego. The former CIA director "had thrown a fit when he heard . . . it would pre-empt the work of his commission. He would quit if we were published," Roger Wilkins remembered. Johnson had no wish for a public relations blowup, and although he had little political leverage over the powerful McCone, Ramsey Clark could easily be muzzled. The Justice Department's report was never released.[23] McCone's histrionics notwithstanding, Clark's findings were so uncompromising in appraising the extent of problems in Los Angeles—and, by extension, in other American cities—that the report might in any event have been deemed too politically sensitive by administration higher-ups and their political allies in southern California and thus it was shelved.

The McCone Commission's cautiously stated findings were published in November. According to an article in the New York Times, many commissioners "appeared to be losing patience with most of the panaceas offered them," and at least one member was troubled by the lack of any apparent regret for violence and property destruction on the part of the African Americans who appeared before the commission. The state-level commission documented organized and systematic looting and arson patterns by "skilled arsonists" but admitted there was "scant evidence the gangs or the many trained Communist agitators operating in Negro areas actually started the riots." Instead, Chief Parker's Los Angeles Police Department had played a catalytic role: "The riots seemed to stem from a sort of spontaneous combustion that followed specific police incidents."[24] The evocation of an uncontrollable and inexplicable natural phenomenon conveniently blurred the fact that a long history of police brutality had created a tinderbox in southern Los Angeles.

A rebuttal authored by the Southern California Advisory Commission to the United States Commission on Civil Rights almost immediately began to circulate within the Justice Department. Its verdict offered a scathing indictment: the McCone Report "prescribes aspirin where surgery is required." The advisory commission quoted the McCone Report's conjecture that "perhaps the people of Los Angeles should have seen trouble gathering under the surface calm." "This observation misses the point completely," McCone's critics noted angrily. "The officials of Los Angeles were expressly warned of the possibility of riots, failed to act, and instead chose to label those who cried out for reform as troublemakers or rabble-rousers." The advisory commission had absolutely no patience with McCone's assessment of "spontaneous combustion": "We conclude . . . that the McCone Commission deliberately whitewashed Chief Parker and the administration of the Police Department."[25]

For Ramsey Clark, the advisory commission's suppressed report was especially noteworthy for its effort "to bring the voice of the people in the ghetto to print. . . . And it's not a pleasant voice; they're very angry people." "It was a time of learning for us," the Justice Department official remembered. "It was a new world."[26]

Part of this learning focused on determining what was, or was not, happening in the nation's cities. Within days of the rioting in Los Angeles, George Reedy bemoaned the administration's lack of information on the leadership of the inner city, what he termed "the power structure of the slums." Reedy, who had resigned as White House press secretary only weeks earlier, called on Johnson to "establish—quietly—. . . a unit whose sole job should be to identify and catalogue the local leaders of Negro communities in every large city where there is a heavy Negro concentration."[27] These leaders should be selected "without regard to their reputability" but solely on their perceived ability to dissuade rioters in the event of urban violence.[28] The "ultimate objective," Reedy's memo continued, was an "intelligence center" within the executive branch with contacts in all the nation's large cities, which could function as an "'early warning' system" for predicting riots. Only through better information could the administration hope to weather the storm of unrest until the poverty program and other economic and civil rights reforms brought about a more "genuine solution."

Cold War military metaphors dominated private communications detailing the threat of rioting as the Containment Doctrine seeped into domestic discourse. Reedy's "'early warning' system" evoked the "distant early warning" strategy of an atomic era, and Clifford Alexander's similar suggestion of ghetto "listening posts" called to mind the "LPs" that were a tactical staple of the American counterinsurgency effort against communist guerrillas in Vietnam. Even if inner-city residents were not perceived as "the enemy," the choice of metaphors was extremely regrettable.[29]

Some of Johnson's most trusted advisers had warned that Watts, far from an anomaly, was a herald of things to come. With the eruption of additional violence in the summer of 1966, notably in Cleveland's Hough district and in

Chicago, Johnson and his top aides continued to be frustrated by the lack of what they deemed reliable and usable information on the nation's cities. They were reluctant to place faith in the FBI's secret files on the volatility of urban areas, files cross-referenced extensively with Hoover's incendiary—and now legendary—"Racial Matters" dossiers. The president was also extremely leery of the voluminous—and occasionally mind-numbing—statistic-driven reports percolating up the bureaucratic pipeline and, given the Kennedy legacy, perhaps even more ambivalent about the recommendations of outside "experts" in academia, foundations, and the like.[30]

Typically, Lyndon Johnson wanted firsthand information on the cities from those he most trusted, depending heavily on his aides' condensed one-page memos and verbal observations.[31] But with A. Philip Randolph in his seventies and Roy Wilkins in his sixties, some of the administration's closest civil rights allies were seen as "old school" by the "young militants," Harry McPherson reminded his chief. Martin Luther King Jr. and Whitney Young were significantly younger, McPherson argued, but they too had been on the scene for a long time. The new generation of angry blacks "will not always respond to advice from middle-aged and elderly men in their vested suits and regimental stripes. . . . Our lines of communication to the movement run generally (and from the White House, only) to the older Negro establishment." McPherson concluded, "We have very few contacts with younger Negro leaders. We *must* develop those contacts."[32]

In their lively exchange of memos preceding the 1966 November elections, Attorney General Nicholas Katzenbach strongly disagreed with what he felt was an internal inconsistency in McPherson's logic when Johnson's White House aide suggested that the president broaden his contacts with young and unfamiliar black leaders. If McPherson had already ruled CORE and SNCC outside the political pale, Katzenbach pointed out, what political advantage could accrue from directly involving similar—if perhaps organizationally unaffiliated—young leaders in a White House meeting? "We are not going to reach these [young] people except through results. And to the extent that we do reach them in the meantime is close to the same extent to which we corrupt them as leaders."[33]

Katzenbach also alluded to an idea circulating around the White House—particularly among McPherson's circle—of the more mainstream civil rights organizations forming an umbrella youth organization that would be "militant but peaceful." If Roy Wilkins could be persuaded to give it his blessing, and thus bring under its banner of "some of the Young Turks in the NAACP," this might ameliorate the image of Wilkins being out of touch with newer ideological and protest currents. Even if the White House had a vested political interest in the development of such an organization, Katzenbach stressed, the impetus had to come from beyond the administration: "To launch it at the White House would be to kill it before it was born."[34]

Instead of inviting militants to the White House, Katzenbach offered the novel suggestion that the government should go to the militants. He urged that "some of our younger people in the Government" visit cities with large black populations and there "meet with younger Negro leaders—not to organize or manipulate or steer, but solely out of alert curiosity—to gain a sense of their ideas, frustrations, and attitudes."[35] Deferring to Katzenbach's judgment, Johnson did not call young militants to a White House meeting in September 1966, but he did seem to be swayed by McPherson's suggestions about the value of broadening generational contacts with blacks, as well as by Katzenbach's emphasis on "alert curiosity" to learn more about nontraditional urban black leadership.

"How in the world does a fellow like myself, who's white, middle-class, and middle-western, go about living in the ghetto without getting his head cut off?" mused White House aide Sherwin Markman before his first visit to Chicago's South Side in late January 1967.[36] His unconventional business trip had its genesis in an otherwise normal staff meeting in the winter of 1966–67. Markman, a new White House aide at the time, remembered the president stating flatly: "I want to know what's happening in the ghettos. . . . If I could go, I'd go myself, but I can't. . . . The next best thing is, I'd like to have some of you fellows, if you would go out there, and live in the ghettos, and then report directly to me, and tell me what's happening, any observations or ideas you have."[37]

The response to Johnson's request was less than overwhelming. But Markman, a white lawyer, raised in Iowa, who had been serving on the White House staff for just under a year, was an early volunteer. His fears of urban decapitation notwithstanding, the midwesterner remembered seeing in Johnson's suggestion an "intriguing possibility." When others hesitated, the famous "Johnson treatment" eventually produced a string of ambivalent volunteers, lower-ranking staff assistants, among them at least two participants in the fledgling White House Fellows program. In the months leading up to the summer of 1967, members of Johnson's staff visited over a dozen cities, usually squeezing the trips into single weekends; following that season's urban violence, the visits were renewed.[38]

An obsession with secrecy underscored the importance of the visits to Johnson. The president insisted that the visits go unpublicized, reasoning that if powerful local mayors like Chicago's Richard Daley or Los Angeles's Sam Yorty were to find out about "someone from the White House moving around" in their bailiwick it would be "potentially embarrassing." White House secretary Marvin Watson and Sherwin Markman agonized over whether to tell Mayor Richard Daley about a visit to Chicago but ultimately opted to risk "keeping it quiet." All scouting efforts were to go unreported by the mainstream media, and Johnson's "volunteers" were to disavow—emphatically if necessary—any connection to the White House.

They adopted elaborate covers as reporters, private consultants hired by OEO to evaluate antipoverty programs, and lower-echelon government bureaucrats. Markman recalled: "As I told the Secret Service guys, after the fact, I just never made a very good undercover agent, because the whole business of having a false identity was very painful through all these experiences. Because people naturally are curious, and they ask you a question, and you're going to have to make up more as you go along and it's difficult."[39] One cannot help but wonder how many inner-city residents who encountered the scouts saw through the always-awkward, and often-clumsy, deceptions. The desire for a low profile can be seen at least in part as an effort at preemptive damage control, limiting the president's accountability for the riots that many of the scouts expected in the summers to come.[40]

Dubious about their ability to make meaningful contacts in inner-city black neighborhoods on their own, Markman and other administration representatives enlisted the help of local African American "guides," whom they trusted to go along with the "undercover" aspect of the scouting missions. Sherwin Markman remembered that prior to each scouting trip he first identified an African American man—and the gendered assumptions about who would serve in this role were quite evident—who "had fought his way out" of the inner city but who maintained contacts there and had firsthand experience with urban problems. A worker in the OEO's Chicago office helped the Iowan navigate Chicago's unfamiliar urban geography, and in Philadelphia Markman's former Yale Law School classmate, rising African American jurist Leon Higginbotham, served as his entrée and field guide. African American Louis Martin, at the Democratic National Committee Headquarters, furnished numerous contacts to White House "scouts," building on his extensive network of black newspaper publishers and reporters and personal contacts in African American communities.[41]

In the tow of these guides, Markman and other administration reconnoiterers visited still-segregated schools, antipoverty agencies and employment program offices, bars, restaurants, and church services—including one whose denominational affiliation a White House aide coyly labeled "Black Nationalist." In one city, a "Negro barber's wedding reception" was visited. In almost every instance, they toured what they described as "slum dwellings" in all-black areas, encircled by what White House aide Clifford Alexander called a "white noose" of suburbs.[42] The scouts expected to find run-down tenements infested with cockroaches and rats, and in many instances they did. Blasted landscapes fulfilled and exceeded their expectations. But they also encountered urban areas, like Watts, where even after the extensive damage resulting from the August 1965 riots, one-story homes, neatly kept yards, and ethnic diversity failed to match their preconceived notion of a "ghetto."[43] Indeed, the conflation of different urban geographies and ethnographies into one archetypal ghetto by most if not all of the White House scouts is noteworthy.

To a man—and the scouts were all men—what they found in America's cities stunned and profoundly moved the White House investigators. Sherwin Markman's reports eloquently capture the midwesterner's feeling of near-total displacement in an unfamiliar environment. "It was almost like visiting a foreign country," he wrote, "and the ghetto Negro tends to look on us and our government as foreign." His conclusions, like those of Ramsey Clark in the suppressed Watts report, were jarring. Markman spoke with embittered blacks who voiced a deep-seated alienation, a sense of being cut off from white, affluent America, of living in a world "severed from ours." He sought to reproduce the indignation of a self-proclaimed black "militant" in Chicago whose credo was later made famous by the boxer Cassius Clay/Muhammad Ali: "The Viet Cong never called me a nigger." We "cannot close our ears to what this man thinks," Markman urged the president, "for he is intelligent, energetic, *and listened to.*"[44]

Report after report spoke of blacks who had voiced their concerns that the legislatively mandated "maximum feasible participation" of the poor within antipoverty programs was being subverted. The catalog of villains varied city by city, from corrupt white-controlled political machines to networks of patronage dominated by middle-class blacks to "sociologists [who] came from under their rocks and got funded for their pet programs." A white minister working in black neighborhoods in Chicago put it simply: "The War on Poverty hasn't reached the street corner."[45]

McPherson, in the exchange of memos with Nicholas Katzenbach in September 1966, had concluded, "The question always comes back to who is a leader." The constituency supporting militants like Stokely Carmichael was vocal but not broad, he argued: "Surely the next generation of Negro leadership does not have to be dominated by Stokely Carmichael. . . . I would bet that the great majority of Negroes . . . has either never heard of him or doesn't want him as its 'leader.'" Instead, McPherson suggested "establish[ing] some kind of communication with people who might emerge as *responsible* leaders."[46]

So, along with attempting to identify what might be termed organic urban leadership, there clearly existed the temptation on the part of the White House in effect to *anoint* leaders. But in this period of growing ideological polarization it had become increasingly clear to civil rights leaders, and ultimately even to the president and his staff, that a White House blessing of a leader was tantamount to a curse. "We were poison to them; they were poison to us. . . . The hand of the Man's authority on their shoulders was damning to . . . the real militants."[47] This dilemma applied to the administration's moderate allies as well. As Harry McPherson reflected, "Johnson had enough acute political sense to understand that while he needed Young and Wilkins and Randolph . . . his embrace of them would endanger them after a time. . . . They would become 'Uncle Toms' and 'the white man's niggers.'"[48]

Struggles with evolving and expanding leadership in black communities troubled the "established" black civil rights organizations and "mainstream" leaders as well, as evidenced by the mixed success of SCLC's and Martin Luther King Jr.'s Chicago campaign.[49] "In terms . . . of the black ghetto, the deep ghetto," Ramsey Clark asserted, "the civil rights leadership itself doesn't have any communication."[50]

White House insiders were eager to emphasize to the president that many African American leaders, too, were encountering a black version of what one White House insider would term a "ghetto communications barrier." In the fall of 1965, Clifford Alexander wrote to Lee White of the pressing need to "get from Negro communities more expressions of what really is on their minds rather than statements from the Negro leadership or whites who think they know what is going on in the Negro community." Stan Ross visited Harlem nearly three years after the 1964 riots and concluded that "the fundamental interests of the Negro people are not well-represented by the Negro leadership. The leaders seem to have interests in terms of their own internal power groups and constituencies which may prevent them from taking responsibility for and truly helping the least advantaged."[51]

With segregation officially outlawed, the nightly drama of good versus evil that had marked the early days of the civil rights movement disappeared in the summer of 1966, replaced by equally dramatic but more troublesome images: black urban rioters in northern cities burning and looting and hooligans pelting Martin Luther King Jr. and his followers with rocks and bottles in a Chicago suburb. The struggle in the South had seemed relatively clear-cut to most whites outside the region. Once civil rights leaders turned their attention to national rather than regional problems, issues suddenly became far more complex. Neither television reporters nor the viewing public seemed interested in de facto employment and residential discrimination, poor housing, or police brutality. During the unrest of the 1950s and early 1960s, the black residents of northern ghettos were rightly described by one scholar as the "forgotten people of the Negro revolution." By 1966, civil rights issues were increasingly shaped by whites' fears of black criminality (which they often linked with street crime and the race riots) and their sense that the nation had done enough to help those who were racially and economically disadvantaged.[52]

Nowhere was the shift more apparent than among young people. One *New York Times* story described the dramatic decline in interest in civil rights among white college students in the North. An academic adviser to student groups at City College of New York tried to explain what had happened. It was easy to take a stand on civil rights in the South, he concluded. When students realized that attacks on housing and job discrimination in the North would directly affect them, however, many took a "vastly more critical attitude."[53]

As some white students turned away from the movement (also in part because of the insistence on separatism by Black Power advocates), activists within SNCC and CORE began to turn the spotlight of their growing radicalism on northern urban concerns—particularly the prevalence of police brutality. (James Baldwin noted that to many who lived in the ghetto a policeman was seen as "an occupying soldier in a bitterly hostile country.")

The Johnson administration could have responded to this changing political climate by better using the CRS, which had been created under the Civil Rights Act of 1964 to seek voluntary compliance with orders for desegregation in local communities. Lyndon Johnson and Ramsey Clark had talked about (and debated the desirability of) such an organization in the summer of 1963 against the backdrop of flaring civil rights protests in the South.[54] In fact, Senate Minority Leader Johnson had introduced a measure calling for just such an agency in the late 1950s.[55]

The role of the CRS has received little attention from historians, who seldom look beyond its role in "conciliation" efforts in the rural and small-town South or in key "settlements" like that brokered during the Selma crisis in 1965. But Title X of the 1964 Civil Rights Act gave the new agency a broad and even open-ended mandate to intervene in almost "any kind of racial dispute."[56] The legislative language emphasized that "conciliation assistance shall be conducted in confidence and without publicity" and was emphatic that no agency representatives should perform an investigatory role as a precursor to prosecution of local authorities. The law even mandated maximum fines and up to one year's imprisonment for violation of the confidentiality requirement.[57]

CRS had been originally placed in the Department of Commerce because of the belief that its services in mediation and conciliation would be sorely needed to facilitate the process of integration of public accommodations as mandated under the Civil Rights Act of 1964.[58] Although there were isolated cases of resistance and the unyielding force of custom and tradition meant that certain establishments remained "white only," in fact if not in name across the country, that process had proceeded far more smoothly than anticipated — particularly outside the heart of the Deep South. Under the reorganization plan crafted by Joseph Califano, Nicholas Katzenbach, and Lee White in the fall of 1965, many of the CRS's functions would be farmed out to different bureaucratic line agencies: problems in the area of employment would fall naturally under the purview of the Equal Employment Opportunity Commission; the ever-present problems arising from school desegregation would fall to the Commissioner of Education; and housing disputes would be left to the Department of Housing and Urban Development. What was left of the CRS, primarily its field operations and conciliation staff, would be moved to the Department of Justice once Congress approved the reorganization plan.[59]

LeRoy Collins, the former Florida governor (and southern "moderate") had directed the CRS from its inception and initially worked almost entirely in the South. Although the organization was supposed to operate behind the scenes, newsmen soon began referring to him as the "administration's civil rights spokesman." White House aide Lee White told a CRS staffer that "one day Lyndon Johnson picks up the *New York Times* and sees this picture [of Collins] and he pounds on his desk. . . . He's furious, [and] he says: 'Goddammit' . . . there's only one spokesman on civil rights for this Administration and it's me."[60] In early July 1965, Johnson named Collins undersecretary of Commerce; his assistant, Calvin Kytle, became the new acting director of the CRS.[61]

Kytle, a fellow southerner from Georgia, sensed that "everything was shifting from the South to the North." The CRS began to work in urban communities where racial tensions were on the rise, and its new acting director made a strong pitch to the Bureau of the Budget to increase the agency's stipend. Although Kytle had cleared his presentation with Joseph Califano, administration officials were annoyed at what they regarded as his aggressiveness. During the Watts riot, when Kytle gave an interview to *New York Times* reporter David Broder, he noted pointedly that Los Angeles was one of only two cities to refuse funding for "target cities"—cities prone to unrest that summer. "I'm pretty sure that Calvin signed his death warrant in the Johnson Administration with that interview," claimed his successor, Roger Wilkins.[62]

The ax came down when Kytle argued against a White House plan to shift the agency from the Department of Commerce to the Department of Justice. Kytle, like his predecessor LeRoy Collins, objected strongly to the shift, in part because civil rights organizations saw the Department of Justice as "poison" because of J. Edgar Hoover's long reign at the FBI. And the "FBI was the Justice Department as far as [many civil rights people] were concerned."[63] Likewise, the Justice Department was seen as poisonous to many southern whites, who decried its role in enforcing—however ineffectively—unpopular federal civil rights legislation.

"[Kytle] really thought they wanted his opinion rather than just rubber stamp the decision already made by Johnson," said fellow CRS staffer Max Secrest. "I heard that [Johnson] . . . said[,] 'well, who is that little shitass over there in the Community Relations Service [who] thinks he can tell us what to do? We want that moved over from Commerce to Justice, now do it! And get rid of that guy!'"[64] LeRoy Collins was baffled over what he felt was Johnson's unreasonable hostility, but twenty-four hours after he had criticized the transfer, Kytle reluctantly but graciously offered his resignation.[65]

Roger Wilkins was drafted as Kytle's replacement. After growing up in starkly different segregated urban landscapes in Missouri and New York, Wilkins had taken bachelor's and law degrees at the integrated University of Michigan before working as a welfare caseworker in Cleveland, Ohio. Amassing additional experience in a New York law firm and at the Agency for International Development in Washington, D.C., Wilkins came to CRS shortly after its inception in 1964. Joining Clifford Alexander, Louis Martin, Thurgood Marshall, and Robert Weaver, he became one of Johnson's highest-profile black appointments. As the nephew of the NAACP's Roy Wilkins, the dynamic young agency head was even more likely to have the president's ear.

Encounters with racial discrimination during his youth and his vivid memories of the challenges of social work in Cleveland's Hough district meant the thirty-three-year-old Wilkins felt a close connection to the hardest-hit black residents in the nation's cities. As one of the few blacks among the droves of white federal officials descending on Watts in the aftermath of the rioting in early August 1965, he quickly learned that a federal identification card guaranteed little immunity against initial judgments based solely on color. An LAPD cruiser pulled him over as he rode back to their hotel one night after unwinding over drinks with Commerce Department official John Perry, a white man, behind the wheel. Forcing the two men out of the car with shotguns at the ready, the policemen muscled Wilkins and Perry into spread-eagled positions against their car and then separated them for questioning. The officer interviewing Perry was "polite." Turning pale, he blurted, "Oh my God," when confronted with the evidence that his white suspect was a high-ranking federal official (his apprehension increased when he apparently misidentified Perry as a State Department, rather than a Commerce, official). From that point on, Perry noted, "the officer's whole attitude changed from one of politeness to obvious embarrassment and then to open friendliness."

Wilkins's interrogation did not go as well. He was "chop[ped] in the balls" in the initial search, Wilkins remembered, and the officer refused to recognize two different sets of federal credentials and demanded that Wilkins produce a driver's license. Increasingly irate, the CRS director refused, on the grounds that he had not been driving the car. Only then did the second policeman intervene, attempting to defuse the tense situation with forced jocularity: "Guess who it is we've got here."

The incident quickly came to a close, but the two lodged a private protest with embattled Los Angeles police chief William H. Parker, whose police force was under a national microscope and facing a rash of charges—many of them justified—of police brutality for behavior both before and during the riots. But given the clandestine nature of the initial federal presence in Los Angeles, Perry and Wilkins reluctantly decided not to publicize the indignity of the search, as it had, in Perry's opinion, "the makings of a sensational national story. . . . Our mission there was to seek peace rather than add to any ill feeling." For both men—and certainly for Wilkins—the experience was a far more effective lesson in the realities of a color-coded police response than anything they might have heard secondhand in Los Angeles. "If this kind of thing became a recurring fact in my life, it would not take me long to regard it as 'police brutality,'" Perry concluded. The two policemen's incident report hardly cast a positive light on the professionalism of the Los Angeles police; they insisted that the two well-dressed men driving in a federally rented sedan had exhibited the behavior of "likely robbery suspects."[66]

According to Calvin Kytle, Wilkins felt that the best way to prevent more riots was to direct more concentrated federal programs—and dollars—to cities at risk: "So what he was doing through the remnants of the Community Action division was working out a very imaginative liaison program with all the other agencies of government, any agency that had anything that could be brought to bear on the problem of race or poverty."[67]

It was not at all clear that this was what the White House had in mind. As late as December 1965—just days before Kytle's forced resignation—an internal memo posed the question that would dominate internal debates in CRS in the months to come. Put simply, would CRS only offer its conciliation and mediation services in areas where problems were fully evident or crises had emerged, or should it "seek to identify those communities in which race problems may erupt?"[68]

Early in January 1966, John Herbers, of the *New York Times*, interviewed the new CRS director, Roger Wilkins. Although Brooks Hays, former Arkansas congressman and newly installed associate director of CRS, would focus on the South and ongoing efforts to establish full compliance with civil rights legislation, said Wilkins, he planned "to concentrate on riot prevention in Northern ghettoes." The new mission of the CRS would be to "keep our fingers on the pulse of the ghettoes and transmit our findings to the people who have decision-making power."[69]

Like his predecessors, Wilkins managed to annoy Johnson even before he was sworn in because of his high public profile and his tactless decision to invite his home state senator, Robert Kennedy, to the swearing-in ceremony. (He repeatedly put Kennedy on his guest list only to receive word from the White House that his list was "too long." When he finally cut the New York senator, he received word that "the list was just fine.") But Wilkins, unlike Kytle, had a powerful constituency and powerful allies, and Johnson was hardly in a position to force him out. In fact, the agency's budget rose to $2 million, an increase of 50 percent, during the first year of Wilkins's tenure.[70]

Wilkins and Brooks Hays had inherited an organization with low morale; the CRS, despite Kytle's capable stewardship, had not received adequate support from the president. Wilkins and Hays gave a series of "pep talks" to their associates, promoting a broadened agenda for the agency.[71] And Wilkins quickly plunged into a number of tense urban situations, including a renewed flare-up in Watts in the spring of 1966.[72] The CRS, Wilkins believed, had the potential to identify local grassroots leaders and to help them obtain a hearing from established political elites in their urban communities. This might mean working with city governments to "put together local efforts to help the minority poor that they would never have considered without a riot." It also might mean the CRS would become a forceful advocate for the poor in dealing with local and national officials.[73]

As Martin Luther King Jr. began his demonstrations in Chicago in mid-July 1966, Wilkins was there. Although most of the people they met with on all sides of the political equation agreed with the desirability of opening more employment opportunities to blacks, "law and order" questions were never far from the surface. When Assistant Attorney General John Doar and Wilkins met with powerful Democratic mayor Richard Daley, they endured a lecture on the links between youth gangs and the potential for urban unrest, and Daley insisted on bringing them up to speed on his grave concerns over "the activities of some of Dr. King's assistants."[74] As tensions escalated in Chicago, Wilkins worked to calm the waters, but Ramsey Clark, who was also on site to monitor the crisis, informed Johnson that there was no role that the federal government could, or should, play in Mayor Daley's backyard.[75] In October 1966 Johnson offered little resistance when the Senate proposed cutting the budget appropriation for the CRS by $250,000, one-eighth of its proposed $2 million appropriation, funds intended to support the work of the CRS in northern urban areas.[76] Priorities within the Johnson administration had begun to shift away from the ambitious plans of the previous two years' agenda.

Within the CRS, previously South-centered internal debates had revolved around the merits and deficiencies of approaches grounded in "fire prevention" versus "fire-fighting." In the past experiences of the agency's perpetually overtaxed field staff, "fire prevention" had entailed efforts to promote racial amity and improve conditions — before a crisis atmosphere developed — through planning, careful cultivation of contacts, the establishment of authentic two-way communication between antagonistic parties, and ultimately "conciliation." "Fire-fighting," on the other hand, involved CRS efforts to contain and minimize any violence and to foster channels of communication and negotiation *after* a crisis had already "broken out." Both strategies had applications in the environments of the urban North and West.[77] The demand for the CRS to respond to rioting in the nation's cities hit the agency at an especially hard time, during its reorganization and transfer from the Department of Commerce to Justice, a move that some within CRS — especially veteran members — perceived as emasculating. One white southern conciliator voiced concern over whether the agency was now expected to serve as a "riot prevention squad."[78]

As their superiors argued over the relative merits of how best to contain urban "fires," CRS staffers at ground zero in the nation's cities were engaged in scouting efforts of their own. The advantages of a cover story and plausible deniability of any direct connection to the Johnson administration were readily apparent to two representatives of CRS who parachuted into tense urban situations in the midst of the "long, hot summer" of 1967. Willie Collier was one of a small number of representatives of the CRS who was shuttling between cities deemed volatile and penning weekly "field community tension factor reports."[79] The CRS had bestowed on him and his counterparts the awkward job title "community analyst."[80] Temporarily stationed in East Chicago, Indiana, Collier asked a young African American man what he thought about the antipoverty program and what advice he might have for the president. The man replied:

> President Johnson keeps getting these big-shot white folks to come and see how we niggers are getting along. The first thing the big-shot does is get him a comfortable suite at Howard Johnson's or the Holiday Inn. The second thing is to pick up the phone and call some of the black Uncle Toms in the local community who perhaps he met in Washington and invite him over to his suite. The Uncle Tom and his assistants then go prepared to give the information that the representative of Mr. Johnson is seeking. . . . I would tell Mr. Johnson to give me his most trusted and talented aide and instruct him to go home and live with me. I would vacate my bed and allow Mr. Johnson's aide to sleep, if he could, or lay awake and listen to the rats playing and running in the walls and overhead and now and then running across the covers over him.[81]

Many African Americans were keeping track of the growing disconnect between White House words and deeds. Johnson's strategy to combat racism and poverty, one black Mississippian said bitterly, was "like trying to cure tuberculosis with cough drops." Expressing their sense of having been cut adrift by the federal government and the promised and much-touted benefits of the antipoverty programs, blacks openly predicted more riots to come.[82]

Bill Graham, a perceptive White House intern, noted in 1967 how few of Sargent Shriver's ever-optimistic War on Poverty press releases pitched at the mainstream media were finding their way into the nation's hardest-hit urban areas. Graham suggested that in order to break through what he labeled the "ghetto communications barrier," "the poor who have not been reached should be told of the overall progress to date, the opportunities that presently exist, and made to understand that help is on the way." The very sincerity implicit in Graham's assurance—he clearly meant what he wrote—reflected the gulf in perceptions and the breakdown in communication.[83] However well-intentioned, such assurances easily could be perceived as patronizing and hollow by those they were meant to reassure.

Two federal employees found this out when they attempted to defuse tense urban situations in the summer of 1967. Roscoe Nix, another "community analyst" in the employ of the beleaguered CRS, described how a black man at a neighborhood meeting in Congress Heights, in Washington, D.C., "insulted" him when he spoke of the federal government's goal of aiding inner-city residents. Indignant, the young man confronted Nix: "You are taking notes and you are going to take those notes and put them in your brief case and then you are not going to do a damn thing. I have been to meetings like this before and every time I have seen men like you; I know you do not intend to do a damn thing but write something on that piece of paper and I am tired of this kind of stuff." The aggrieved government representative helpfully appended to his report the clarification: "My language is much cleaner than what he actually said."[84]

Repeated unpleasant encounters produced resentment on all sides. No doubt, many of these visitors elected to stay in the relative comfort afforded by Howard Johnson's motels on the periphery of the urban core—some of them were advised to opt for such lodging in less-depressed economic surroundings by their African American guides. Sherwin Markman recognized both the concrete and symbolic importance of not fleeing black neighborhoods with daylight's end and many times insisted on remaining overnight in the areas he visited. Still, when Markman contemplated spending the night with his guide in a dark apartment dwelling where two women and nine children resided, he rationalized: "We finally decided not to . . . not because of the filth, but because it was my judgment that a White House guy spending the night with just two women with kids, if it got out, could conceivably not look right." Local residents could not fail to observe that even the most well-intentioned visitors typically stayed in the area for no more than two days, hardly an immersion experience.[85]

But such an immersion was precisely what CRS director Roger Wilkins believed would be necessary. The "lesson" of the previous summer's rioting in Watts and elsewhere, he wrote in a memo penned in spring 1966, was that "riots happen in wildly unpredictable places." Ostrichlike behavior by city officials—the disturbingly prevalent pattern of urban mayors who insisted earnestly, "It can't happen here"—was especially dangerous in Wilkins's eyes. Blacks might respond to such sugar-coated assurances by thinking: "Only a Watts might jar this place into movement." The young CRS director stressed the importance of gathering "intelligence" on what was taking place in the nation's cities, not so much for the purposes of using that knowledge to suppress rioting as to aid in the process of "knowing, smelling, and feeling" the problems of the urban poor.[86] It was a call for empathy, and a difficult leap for many whites to make.

As the quiet weekend forays into America's poorest urban areas continued throughout the spring of 1967, White House representatives attempted to counterbalance their bleak appraisals of the potential for further rioting with praise for what was working in the cities. They lauded teachers who worked valiantly within struggling and underfunded schools and showcased antipoverty groups, like Chicago's Woodlawn Organization, that drew on and meaningfully involved the people they were committed to assisting. "All agreed that involved people do not riot," Markman wrote urgently to the president, in an implicit endorsement of the doctrine of "maximum feasible participation."[87]

In Philadelphia, black clergyman Leon Sullivan had devoted his ministry to creating jobs for the city's poorest residents. Markman was extremely impressed by Sullivan and commended his efforts to the president in terms sure to please a commander in chief beleaguered by the rising chorus of criticism of American involvement in Southeast Asia. Rev. Sullivan "is solely concerned with civil rights," Markman wrote, adding pointedly: "[He] does not become involved in Vietnam debates."[88] The timing of Markman's editorializing was significant. His report arrived on Johnson's desk just weeks after Martin Luther King Jr. had lambasted the United States as "the greatest purveyor of violence in the world today" for its conduct of the war in Vietnam.[89]

As Lyndon Johnson read through Markman's reports, the political horizon was darkening. The War on Poverty, suspect at the street corner, was under fire in Congress as well. With budget cutting becoming a veritable act of patriotism, congressional defenders of the antipoverty programs were few and far between.[90]

And as spring edged toward summer, the overwhelming tenor of the reports emerging from the visits to the cities was negative. Late in May 1967, White House fellow Thomas E. Cronin found little in West and East Baltimore that corresponded with the Chamber of Commerce's boast of equal opportunity in "the National Anthem City." He visited Baltimore's poorest black neighborhoods, noting in his report that "middle income Negroes bluntly refer to these sections of town as the 'jungles.'" The same areas had been the focus of a major urban campaign by CORE the previous summer, and a major outbreak of violence had narrowly been averted when working-class whites openly proclaiming "white supremacy" marched into African American districts.

At the conclusion of his report, Cronin drew from Lewis Carroll and wrote pessimistically of the need for the federal government to "run hard, like Alice, to stay in the same place." Baltimore's "star-spangled jungles" would be prone to unrest: "Baltimore summers are always hot; and life in the crowded 'jungles' will not stand still."[91] Staying in the same place would do little to forestall more "long, hot summers" to come.

Sherwin Markman made a similar prediction as he began to synthesize the accumulated insights of his own and others' initial visits to the cities for his April report, entitled "American Ghettoes: Our Challenge and Response": "I had the feeling that regardless of which ghetto was observed the countdown to trouble was proceeding; only the timing to zero was variable."[92] Markman

Lion In The Streets

LION IN THE STREETS. A 1967 *Herblock Cartoon, copyright by The Herb Block Foundation.*

clearly intended to raise the alarm, but his statement, like that of most contemporaries, conflated many cities into one predictive model. Both black and white observers usually viewed the nation's cities through similarly undifferentiated lenses—as *the* ghetto, just as many in and beyond Washington's Beltway had approached the Moynihan Report as though it were diagnosing all the ills of *the* black family, unitary in its pathology.[93]

All the visitors urged Johnson to "stay the course"—evoking Cronin's allusion to *Alice in Wonderland*—but Markman's report called on the president to consider broadening antipoverty efforts, as well as the overall federal commitment to the cities, with the long view in mind. But with warmer weather just around the corner, many expressed their concern that, in the interim, summer youth employment programs, recreation leagues, human relations committees, and antipoverty agencies were far from adequate as "riot insurance."

Both administration insiders and scathing public critics of the White House occasionally applied this cynical catchphrase to these programs.[94] The "scouting reports" agreed that the scale of federal assistance was too small and local government initiative too often lacking. Events seemed to be bearing out the grim prediction made a full year before by Johnson's high-profile director of CRS. Roger Wilkins had weighed the commitment of federal resources against the dimensions of the urban crisis and starkly determined: "We don't have the horses."[95]

Did the ghetto visits represent a genuine attempt on the part of the White House to recognize and respond to shifts in African American leadership? Lyndon Johnson had a long-standing pattern of meeting with a select group of civil rights leaders—typically the Big Six, although this 1960s version of a Rooseveltian Black Cabinet had shrunk steadily in and after 1965, with the attrition of CORE and SNCC in 1966 and increasing mutual estrangement between King and the White House. Conferring with this tiny group of African American civil rights leaders to craft national civil rights policy shaped the president's understanding of who "mattered" among blacks in the cities.

In all but a handful of cases, black women fell outside the White House's narrowly defined parameters of leadership, as did most working-class African Americans. Women often predominated in civil rights movements at the grass roots, but they seldom appeared on Johnson's radar screen until they became visible in a way the president deemed to be both familiar and politically "legitimate." Just as he welcomed the opportunity to engage black male politicians, like Cleveland's victorious mayoral candidate, Carl Stokes, he was perfectly at ease dealing with Barbara Jordan, victorious in her bid to gain a seat in the Texas statehouse. Johnson was also comfortable with women who had large middle-class constituencies, like Dorothy Height of the National Council of Negro Women.

But he had next to no patience for women who refused to play by the ground rules of political participation he expected others to observe, and for that reason he never forgave Mississippi's Fannie Lou Hamer for her fly-in-the-ointment disruption of "*his*" Democratic National Convention in 1964. Similar gender dynamics had probably made CDGM that much more expendable in the eyes of the White House, and perhaps those of Sargent Shriver and OEO as well. The great majority of the employees staffing CDGM centers, and many of its staff hierarchy, were women. That the MAP Board was virtually all male (Patt Derian was the lone exception) was perhaps not a coincidence.[96]

"Militants" in the nation's cities posed a special dilemma. Johnson's associates desperately wanted to cultivate political contacts in the inner city but invariably refused to deal directly or publicly with personalities they deemed too "radical"—the "bomb throwers." In later years, civil rights leader James Farmer sympathetically described the president's difficulties in connecting with a broader spectrum of black leaders: "[Johnson] was much better able to understand the black leaders whose orientation tended to be more . . . middle-class and . . . polite and courteous . . . white, in other words. . . . So he was talking to himself when he talked with some of them. He was much better able to understand that than he could understand the angry young blacks who would tell it like it is, and call him an MF."[97]

The "undercover" aspect of the "scouting" missions and the consequent absence of media attention at least hypothetically liberated Johnson and his associates from the political liability of being seen as "cuddling up" to those whom they often derided privately—and only half-jokingly—as "bomb throwers." "Maximum plausible deniability" replaced "maximum feasible participation" as the watchword of the day.

On a concrete level, the urban visits did contribute to more summer appropriations for cities and to introduction of an infamous "Rat Bill," aimed at more effective control of the runaway rodent population in poorer urban areas. The administration also used information gathered in the visits to support rent subsidy legislation and the perennial administration open-housing bill.[98] But despite its facile desire to move "ahead of the trends" and "leapfrog" the civil rights movement, the White House again found itself in all-too-familiar reactive mode with each summer's riots.

The "scouting" missions indicate ongoing attention to civil rights and issues of economic justice, which undercuts the "deliberate disengagement" thesis. But they also demonstrate that preoccupation does not always translate into policy. If the Johnson White House had once sought to ride "piggyback" on the cresting fortunes of the civil rights movement, the game of the moment appeared to be "duck and cover."

Sherwin Markman tried but failed to keep his initial report short—LBJ typically balked at reading memoranda much in excess of a single page—but instead of "catch[ing] all kinds of hell" from Johnson, as he expected, Markman found the president to be "enthralled . . . carrying it around and . . . reading it aloud in its entirety to various people who he'd trap into listening to it," including Lady Bird.[99] The lawyer from Iowa firmly believed that the reports motivated Johnson to step up his commitment to the nation's cities and that he gave far more credence to the observations of his trusted aides than to the far more numerous reports generated by faceless bureaucrats.

Markman also credited the visits with having brought into the president's circle Leon Higginbotham, whose counsel LBJ would value highly during the rioting following the assassination of Martin Luther King Jr. the next spring. Together, and over the strenuous objections of both the Secret Service and

White House secretary and "gatekeeper" Marvin Watson, Higginbotham and Markman were able to convince Johnson to visit one of Philadelphia's poorest black neighborhoods in the summer of 1967. The president briefly toured many of the same places his aides had scouted in preceding months. Due to elaborate and heightened security precautions, Johnson's visit remained a secret from virtually everyone in the city until hours before his arrival. Higginbotham recalled that when Philadelphia's mayor learned of the president's plan to visit the ghetto, he panicked and frantically "sent these street crews out to clean up the streets. And people in the area thought there had been a riot. Some people here said, 'My god, I saw all these trucks. The streets haven't been this clean since the last riot.'"[100]

As the term "long, hot summer" increasingly entered the parlance of everyday Americans, Johnson faced the dilemma of seeking somehow to move beyond dealing exclusively with the shrinking Big Six while avoiding becoming a "scapegoat" trapped between black militants on the one side and hostile white city governments and a perceived nationwide white backlash on the other. The nearly untenable situation demanded a delicate balancing act, for the greater the White House's public commitment to preventing urban disorder, the heavier the political consequences to be borne by the administration with each successive outbreak of rioting.[101]

Urban unrest has headlined the list of events offered by historians as contributing to a perceived disengagement of the Johnson White House from the civil rights agenda after passage of the Voting Rights Act in the summer of 1965. The existence of these scouting missions and the close attention they ultimately commanded from the president suggest the need for a careful reassessment of the Johnson administration's evolving response to the riots of the late 1960s.[102] Although the visits demonstrate conclusively that the linked issues of civil rights and economic justice were still firmly on the administration radar screen in the two-and-a-half years following Johnson's Howard University speech, they also reveal how difficult "getting ahead of the trends" could be in the case of urban unrest.

It may be possible to view the scouting missions of 1966 and 1967 as a barometer of the evolving relationships between the administration and the widening spectrum of civil rights movements in these years. Reports from the visits highlight the Johnson administration's misconceptions of the nation's inner cities, but these stereotyped ethnic notions echoed opinions held by a majority of white Americans, who were simultaneously intrigued and repulsed by their visions of "*the* ghetto." Itineraries also reveal White House staff's preconceptions of who were and who could be considered leaders among blacks, especially impoverished blacks, in the city. Who the administration and its representatives were willing to see and hear defined who they were prepared to acknowledge as leaders. Much of the policy drift that developed in this period can be attributed to Johnson's reluctance—one could argue failure—to acknowledge the cultural legitimacy of shifting currents in black leadership. He and most of his associates were alarmed by changes in both the substance of demands for reform by black activists and their ideological orientation and also, and not least, by what might be referred to as their "style."

Members of the Johnson administration agonized over how to shape "proactive" and consistent policy, as opposed to merely reacting in piecemeal fashion to each successive riot. The White House had consistently, from 1954 through 1965, ended up several steps behind in responding to civil rights crises in the South. The attempt to avoid having to play catch-up to developments at the grassroots level had clearly informed the "leapfrogging" strategy described by White House aides as one of the rationales for the Howard University speech in June 1965. But as the attention of many shifted from the grassroots struggles of African American civil rights activists in the Deep South, the administration found itself struggling to come to grips with new and challenging terrain.

Many African Americans viewed federal involvement in their communities with cynicism, or even outright hostility. The federal presence evoked possibilities of surveillance, control, and repression that mirrored residents' worst—and generally well-founded—opinions of local white law enforcement. During the period of the "scouting missions" to "the ghetto," when White House fellow Thomas Cronin appeared on the scene in one depressed neighborhood in Baltimore, black children accused him of being a "detective" who had come to take away a local female resident. As he attempted, unsuccessfully, to allay their suspicions, he quickly realized how little credibility they gave him. He was a white man in the ghetto—and, of course, he was a detective or some other representative of remote—and typically unfriendly—authority.[103]

Such suspicions were not without merit. Throughout the period from 1965 to 1968 the FBI was erecting an increasingly sophisticated urban surveillance and informant network. J. Edgar Hoover's agents relied on their own in-house "research" and paid informants in the cities, as well as regularly misappropriating the "field tension reports" generated by the well-intentioned "community analysts" of CRS. Hoover then often twisted this information for his own purposes in order to justify stepped-up surveillance of blacks and black-controlled institutions and protest organizations in American cities. COINTELPRO (counterintelligence program) reaped a bitter harvest.[104]

Unwillingly caught up in this web of intelligence gathering, CRS field personnel found themselves seeking to distinguish between their originally conceived role as "conciliators" and a new role as reluctant conduits in an information pipeline that sought to document the activities of certain urban leaders, who were regularly pilloried as "violent, lawless, subversive, and extremist . . . young hoodlums" in the FBI's internal and interagency memoranda.[105] Many CRS representatives, trained to cultivate trust with their urban contacts, found such a dual role incompatible and distasteful.

Examined in the context of these other clandestine efforts, the veil of secrecy over the White House's "scouting missions" to the cities also invites the dismissal of the administration's own quiet efforts as little more than attempts to establish an independent information-gathering network, with direct surveillance from the Oval Office differing from J. Edgar Hoover's intelligence apparatus only in proportion and not in intent. (Recent revelations that Johnson wiretapped his political rivals, even including Vice President Hubert Humphrey, would seem to bolster this case.) But such a dismissal is too easy.

The behind-the-scenes response to urban rioting reveals an administration clearly aware of the necessity of action yet paralyzed by fears of political liabilities that might result from any clear commitment in policy or of resources. Perhaps just as significant as Johnson's subsequent use of federal troops to quell rioters in Detroit in the summer of 1967, the scouting missions helped to generate the momentum for the establishment of the National Advisory Commission on Civil Disorders, more commonly known as the Kerner Commission.

Over and over again, White House insiders turned to the lessons of the Watts uprising of 1965 for guidance. In describing the challenges the federal government faced in responding to the newly apparent urban crisis, Johnson staffer Jack Rosenthal offered a specific critique of the squelched government report on the Watts riots: "I have too much the sensation," he wrote to Ramsey Clark, "that the [Watts] Task Force has a blind attraction for a federal Sir Galahad to ride in with the ideas, energy, and effort to solve the problems of Los Angeles—and . . . every other major city."[106]

Harry McPherson agreed that the confidential Watts report had indeed set forth an uncompromisingly bleak portrayal and indictment of urban leadership. But he offered another important reason that Ramsey Clark's analysis "was not surfaced and trumpeted by the Administration." The report had moved beyond diagnosis to prescription, calling for a major infusion of capital into areas hit by riots. "The President was quite dubious about the possibility of getting major social appropriations through in the aftermath of the riots," McPherson noted, and that reluctance to seek additional appropriations for social programs only grew as urban unrest escalated.[107]

Two years after Sherwin Markman's first visit to Southside Chicago, the National Advisory Commission on Civil Disorders released its report, which called for massive federal intervention in the nation's cities. Unlike the quiet and explicitly solicited observations of White House emissaries like Sherwin Markman or the Ramsey Clark report on Watts, the Kerner Commission Report arrived with huge media coverage and attendant political pressures. It cast a harsh spotlight on the national stage as its recommendations called for the administration to redouble its efforts in the battle for America's urban heartland. In essence, it would call for a federal champion to remount and rescue cities crying out in distress. But by that date, the scouting reports were in. The stakes had risen, and the summons would fall on an extremely reluctant Galahad.

CHAPTER EIGHT

Just File Them—or Get Rid of Them

LBJ and the Fate of the Kerner Commission Report

eRoy Collins, the affable former Florida governor and CRS director, delighted in regaling progressive interviewers and audiences with a modern-day fable that suggested how nothing was as it appeared to be in the Jim Crow South. Collins established the narrative mise-en-scène: Even amid the tumult of the civil rights era, a genteel group of white southerners sought to convey to the rest of the nation that most blacks "really loved their white masters, and actually wanted to continue their present ways of life," with the waters of segregation left untroubled by interference from without. In furtherance of the civic-minded paternalists' public relations effort, an elderly black man— "deeply rooted in the southern culture of his time"—kindly agreed to appear on a television broadcast to relate to a national audience his immense satisfaction with the racial status quo in the South. Collins would then settle into the rhythms of the narration: "The way they tell the story, the network cameramen all came down there, and insisted that it had to be spontaneous. The old black was sitting on his cabin porch in his rocking chair, tattered clothes, just sitting there. The cameras were set and the directors said, 'Now when we get ready we're going to give you the signal to go, and just start talking and tell the people in your own words just how you feel. . . . Now you be ready to go, and when I pull my hand down you start talking.'"

When the director motioned for the man to begin his monologue, there was a moment of silence. "Is it time to talk now?" the African American asked earnestly, quietly. The film crew whispered, "Yes, yes, go on, talk." The whites' designated spokesperson asked one more time for clarification: "Now I can say anything I want to?" "Yes, yes, go on," his sponsors insisted. The elderly black subject stared directly into the camera and shouted at the top of his lungs: "Help!"[1]

Collins's anecdote, amusing in its own right and straight out of the "trickster" tradition of African American folklore, highlights a pattern of miscommunication between the races that transcended region and often characterized the relationship between the Johnson administration and a wide assortment of African American leaders in the closing years of the Texan's presidency. The pattern applied equally well to garbled exchanges between whites and blacks outside the orbit of Washington policymaking, whether in the Jim Crow–haunted landscape of the South or in the de facto segregated landscape of the urban North, Midwest, and West.

LBJ's aide George Reedy had first sounded the alarm while Johnson was still vice president, in the summer of 1963. He noted how whites often responded with fear to the slogan "Freedom Now"—an expression heard as "militant" in the context of the times, three years before "Black Power" would recalibrate the semantics of radicalism. Reedy offered this observation: "The Negroes and the whites are talking about totally different things and are virtually using a different language."[2] Historian Steven F. Lawson offers the compelling observation that the president and the great majority of his associates did not "speak or comprehend the language of the militants . . . either in a literal or a symbolic sense." There can be little doubt that selective deafness greatly reduced Johnson's attempts to understand the resentment fueling urban unrest during his tenure in the White House.[3]

On March 2, 1967, nearly two years after his stirring June 1965 commencement address, Lyndon Johnson returned to Howard University. On very short notice, he made the decision to participate in a celebration of Howard's 100th anniversary. The president spoke of the university's founding as an attempt to "make the promise of the [Emancipation] Proclamation a fact of life." Quoting his own earlier remarks and reminding the audience of the "task" of giving blacks "the same chance as every other American," Johnson declared he had returned to the storied campus to "renew my commitment to that task, and to remind you . . . [that] so long as I live, in public or private life, I shall never retract or retreat or amend that commitment." Johnson lauded the achievements of the Great Society and their impact not just on blacks but on other disadvantaged groups, including the elderly. He detailed his active role in shaping four different civil rights bills, beginning with the admittedly "frail instrument" of the 1957 Civil Rights Act, which he had shepherded to passage as Senate majority leader after eight decades of congressional disengagement from the unfinished work of Reconstruction.

Reflecting on the past decade, Johnson sounded a plaintive note: "Because we have come so far, I know and you know that we have the power to go further; to make the past ten years only a prologue, and the next ten years the time when the Negro in America can say at last, 'I am a free man.' I believe it will be so. I shall bend my will to make it so."

The speech had its finer moments, but it lacked the thematic coherence of the 1965 Howard address. Johnson's speech clearly missed the talented ear and deft hand of speechwriter Richard Goodwin. In place of his earlier eloquence, the president now offered a droning catalog of his administration's black appointments, many of whom had Howard connections of one sort or another. (That it was an impressive list, dwarfing the African American appointments of all previous administrations, is indisputable, but it certainly made for less-than-riveting listening.) The president concluded by noting that the future would be filled with problems, but "tomorrow's problems . . . will not be divided into 'Negro problems' and 'white problems.' There will be only human problems, and more than enough to go around."[4]

Among the problems Johnson faced in the spring and early summer of 1967 were a logjam in Congress and a pessimistic sense that another "long, hot summer" was in the making. Southern congressmen had barely been able to restrain their glee as the "Negro problem" suddenly moved north of the Mason-Dixon Line during the "long, hot summers" of urban rioting from 1964 forward, pulling media coverage of American race relations in its wake. For white southerners of all political stripes, eager to see the "Yankees" squirm for a change, the riots, even more than white northerners' increasingly chilly response to additional civil rights legislation, offered compelling proof that Gunnar Myrdal and Lyndon Johnson had been right all along: race was an "American dilemma," not a regional embarrassment. Although black activists in the South could testify bitterly to the ongoing obstacles confronting them in the more familiar southern civil rights landscape, it was as though southern racism was "old news."

LBJ's fears of the wildcard of urban disorder and white backlash had been fueled by his aides' quiet forays conducted in the preceding months and the "scouting reports" they had produced. In June 1967, conservative congressmen began applying renewed pressure to secure "antiriot" legislation. Proponents of "law and order" demanded that their bills addressing urban unrest be linked to any prospective civil rights measure. Without the adoption of an antiriot bill, they promised to continue to block the administration's perennial open-housing proposal, its antidiscrimination measures for federal and state jury selection, and languishing legislation affording greater protection to civil rights workers exercising constitutionally protected rights.

Mississippi conservative Democratic congressman William Colmer and Florida Republican William C. Cramer were among those pushing most vocally for an antiriot bill, at one point maneuvering to have the legislation removed from New York Democratic congressman Emanuel Celler's Judiciary Committee. Given the popularity of the measure against the backdrop of national unease over urban unrest, Celler indicated he would consider such a linkage, provided the bill enhanced protection for those engaged in civil rights work. Colmer, an unapologetically unreconstructed southerner, angrily denounced Celler's proposal as a cynical ploy designed to curry favor with the steadily expanding black electorate. The southerner gave voice to the growing impatience of a number of congressional opponents of reform from both sections of the country when he publicly groused: "It's come to the point where we have to have a civil rights bill every year. We have to keep up. We have to keep vying for that black vote."

Any laws affording additional rights to African Americans, he implausibly argued, "would result in further tragic breakdown of good relations between the races" and would be perceived by blacks as a "license to go out in the streets and shoot people down and burn property to the ground." (The irony that virtually all of the shooting and burning in his own home state of Mississippi had been by whites against African Americans was evidently lost on him.) In his private correspondence, Colmer was even more candid about the "color-blind" sweep of his prejudices, noting on one occasion his diehard opposition to any legislation or taxation that would directly or indirectly "support rioters, hoodlums and lazy folk of any race."[5]

And, in the background, there was always the threat of additional urban riots. A staff member gathering information for CRS on conditions in Newark offered a bleak forecast. The increasingly militant SNCC had recently opened a chapter in the city, and elsewhere in Newark, LeRoi Jones (later Amiri Baraka) was rising in prominence as a proponent of African American cultural nationalism. Both blacks and whites in the New Jersey city were carefully attuned to reports of the potential for unrest circulating in the national media: SNCC's Stokely Carmichael and CORE's Floyd McKissick joined Martin Luther King Jr. in labeling Newark a "high riot potential city." In the estimation of the CRS representative, such statements were tantamount to predictions and had left "many Newarkers, including the police, quite jittery, causing over-reaction to minor incidents."[6]

In June, rioting shook the Roxbury district in Boston, and other disturbances erupted in Buffalo, Cincinnati, and Tampa (where the bitter news of violence accompanied the surprise that a phenomenon primarily associated with the urban North had visited the South). In Ohio, which had suffered through devastating riots in the Hough section of Cleveland in 1966, unrest boiled over in Cincinnati in mid-June and then in the first week of July. The "long, hot summer" of 1967 had begun, but few were prepared for the intensity of the conflagration to come.

After a week of relative quiet, Newark went up in flames between July 12 and July 15, leaving 26 dead, nearly 1,500 with injuries, almost as many arrests, and between $10 million and $15 million in property damage. Newark witnessed horrendous acts of violence directed against the city's black population by police and state troopers. Fears of black snipers—whose existence was never conclusively demonstrated—resulted in confusion, as poorly trained troops, including the National Guard, often opened fire on whole apartment buildings. In just one of several well-documented cases, National Guardsmen killed Eloise Spellman as she peered out of an apartment window from ten stories up. Tom Hayden's gripping narrative, *Rebellion in Newark*, documents numerous cases where bullet marks scarred buildings from the sixth floor to the tops of buildings, hardly indicative of disciplined gunfire.

At the time of the riot, New Jersey Democratic governor Richard Hughes condemned sniper attacks as "the last resort of the coward and murderer." Subsequent investigations suggested that most—if not all—of the "sniper" fire had come from different groups of uncoordinated law enforcement shooting in each other's general direction. Just months later, Newark's own police chief conceded: "I think a lot of the reports of snipers were due to the, I hate to use the word, trigger-happy guardsmen, who were firing at noises and firing indiscriminately."[7]

Not all fatalities were accidental. An eyewitness described how a policeman killed James Rutledge with a rifle from three-foot-range as the African American lay prone and unresisting after being apprehended in a tavern that had been looted. Law enforcement justified the initial shot by alleging that Rutledge had brandished a knife. Less conscionable was what happened next. After the first blast, the trooper continued to riddle Rutledge's body with bullets, according to one witness, shouting, "Die, you dirty bastard, die you dirty nigger, die, die." A medical examiner found over forty bullet holes in Rutledge's head and torso. A photographer for *Life* magazine captured the equally horrific image of troops shooting William Furr in the back as he walked down the street in the middle of the day carrying a six-pack of beer.

*Urban unrest in Newark in mid-July 1967, followed by rioting in Detroit,
leads to violence against large numbers of inner-city African Americans.
Courtesy of Don Hogan Charles/New York Times/Redux.*

The racial composition of the New Jersey National Guard (98.8 percent
white) and the State Police (99.6 percent white) did little to ease tensions
(5 black troopers out of 1,200 barely registered even as tokenism). To blacks—
who already viewed the police as an alien presence patrolling *against the entire* ghetto population, not just against criminal elements—the white armed
presence seemed to represent a veritable occupation. At the same time, the
smoke-filled streets of downtown Newark seemed terrifying in their unfamiliarity to the whites in the State Police and National Guard. Predictably—and
tragically—many of the young men responded with excessive violence directed
against blacks.[8]

Dismayed by the violence in New Jersey, A. Philip Randolph urged Johnson
to call together "a small group of responsible national leadership, including
civil rights leaders." Randolph suggested that the riots stemmed from a "gap
between progress and aspirations," which had grown dangerously wide. The
alternative to presidential action was further social chaos. The subtext of the
labor leader's letter to Johnson raised serious questions about what role so-
called responsible leaders could play, for Randolph conceded that each successive riot served to "increasingly separate the relevant Negro leadership from
the masses of unemployed and disinherited Negro people."[9]

With coverage of the Newark rioting still dominating the headlines, con-servatives on Capitol Hill moved swiftly to capitalize on a tailor-made political opportunity. On July 19, members of the House of Representatives sought by voice acclamation to pass legislation making it a federal crime to incite a riot (provided one crossed state lines at some point during the process). The follow-ing day, to what *Newsweek* described as "the giggly amusement of the *de facto* Republican-Dixiecrat coalition that once again rules the House," a Congress already notorious for its stinginess in the War on Poverty began to debate an additional funding package of $40 million for what became known as the "Rat Bill." As early as the summer of 1966, an increasing number of mayors from large metropolitan areas had begun applying for antipoverty funds to subsidize the extermination of rats. Houston's mayor sought a staggering $600,000 solely for this purpose. The mayors then proceeded to take credit for successful exter-mination efforts, glossing over the fact that such victories had only been made possible by the infusion of hefty sums and political capital from Washington. One White House aide privately voiced his concern that the need to control vermin certainly existed (Johnson aides had spent time "scouting" the poor tenements of the nation's cities and had heard firsthand tales of small children attacked by rats) but that he "personally hate[d] to see poverty funds used for this purpose."[10]

Legislative debate, accompanied by raucous laughter, made a mockery of this serious urban problem. A congressman from Florida coyly suggested a plan to have the federal government "buy some cats and turn them loose on the rats." While an Iowan congressman worried that legislation would not subsidize the extermination of "country rats," Virginia's Joel Broyhill proudly introduced a pun into the *Congressional Record*, as he called on his fellows with an exaggerated drawl to "vote down this rat bill '*rat*' now!" To "the stunned amazement of the Administration's lobbyists . . . who figured they were safe by at least fifteen votes," one reporter noted, the rat control bill went down to de-feat by a vote of 207 to 176, leaving conservatives in a self-congratulatory mood for their clever oratory.[11]

The initial fate of the "Rat Bill" was symptomatic of the yawning gulf in understanding between middle- and upper-income whites and those living in the hardest-hit sections of America's cities. In a moment of ill-advised candor, Hubert Humphrey had blurted, "If I had been raised in the slums, [and] found rats eating my children's feet, I'd riot too." Conservative congressmen seemed incapable of mustering similar empathy.[12]

Against the backdrop of a wave of urban disturbances in New Jersey and the callous attitudes of a majority in Congress, members of the Johnson administration turned to their imperfect information-gathering networks to gauge whether the summer's crisis was safely past. Despite the devastating toll of the rioting in Newark, from the White House perspective, the situation in New Jersey had been relatively positive, if only because Johnson had not been forced to dispatch federal troops to quell the burning and looting.[13] But any sense of complacency quickly evaporated in the closing days of July. Just days after firefighters in Newark had finally extinguished the worst of the flames from over 300 reported fires, Detroit exploded on July 23.

According to CRS, rioting began on a Sunday evening when police in Detroit raided an illegal drinking establishment—or "blind pig"—in a heavily black area of the city's downtown area. African Americans viewed the police presence as a provocation, part of a systematic attempt to intimidate the city's black community, and bottle throwing by bystanders quickly escalated into looting. As the situation deteriorated, rioting spread out into a sixteen-block area, and 150 fires quickly consumed a number of buildings. Firefighters left the area when local residents began pelting them with bottles, rocks, and bricks.

Michigan's governor, Republican George Romney, dispatched 8,000 National Guardsmen and several hundred state troopers to support the overwhelmed local police. After vacillating throughout the night, hoping against hope that the worst of the rioting was over, in the early morning hours of Monday, Romney reluctantly recommended that President Johnson dispatch federal troops. But he was loathe to admit that he had lost control of the situation and hesitated to make a formal request for the actual deployment of those troops in the city streets. Attorney General Ramsey Clark insisted that without such a formal request Johnson would not—and could not, under constitutional restrictions—act unilaterally.[14]

Those friendly to the White House quickly assumed that Romney was playing politics—he was widely regarded as a major contender for the 1968 Republican presidential nomination—and did not want to be perceived as weak or unable to defuse a disturbance in his urban backyard. Defending his own actions, the governor publicly stated that he was under the impression that he would have to declare that a state of insurrection existed in order to request troops formally. And such a declaration, he claimed, might void any insurance claims in the aftermath from the widespread urban devastation.[15] Republicans quickly leveled similar charges of politicizing the Detroit riots against President Johnson—that he had needlessly delayed dispatching federal troops in an attempt to embarrass the Republican governor.

The White House was the site of numerous meetings throughout Monday, July 24, the day after the riots broke out, as Johnson canvassed for options. As the day progressed, White House aides Harry McPherson, Douglass Cater, Clifford Alexander, and Ben Wattenberg engaged in a lively debate with CRS director Roger Wilkins and the Democratic National Committee's Louis Martin over whether the president should deliver a formal statement about the rioting in Detroit. Martin urged that no statement be made unless Johnson was prepared to "make some specific new proposals." He suggested that Johnson detail the secretary of defense to call together National Guard commanders and have them examine existing riot-control and riot-prevention procedures and propose more effective alternatives.

LBJ's lieutenants were justifiably concerned by a report in the *New York Times* focusing on the aftermath of the Newark riot, in which a National Guardsman pledged that when confronted with the next riot—such apparent certainty of future unrest was a telling indicator of the fatalistic mood in the summer of 1967—he would shoot to kill. McPherson sounded the cautionary note in a debate that was becoming more and more predictable. The White House aide warned Johnson that if he became too identified with the riots he ran the risk of "putting yourself in a spot where you have responsibility but no real power to deal with it."[16]

Metaphors of "Nero fiddling while Rome burned" were on the minds of many at the White House as Johnson sought to avoid committing federal troops, and both the president and Governor Romney were ultimately cast in the role of the Roman emperor before the Detroit crisis had ended. As pressure mounted for a White House decision, Roger Wilkins urged Johnson to wait until more accurate information was available rather than act precipitately. Heeding the advice of Wilkins and a handful of others, the president ordered Cyrus Vance (who had recently resigned as deputy secretary of defense due to a back injury) to lead a fact-finding team of civilians, including Warren Christopher, John Doar, and Roger Wilkins, to Detroit.

Johnson, Warren Christopher remembered, refused to "be stampeded into committing federal troops until he was satisfied that the situation was beyond the control of local resources."[17] If federal troops were to enter the city, LBJ wanted them to carry as little visible firepower as possible. In Wilkins's account, the president started to detail the worst-case scenario in typical Johnson fashion: "I don't want my troops shooting some ni—." Taking note of Wilkins's presence, the president left the epithet unfinished, awkwardly resuming with"—some pregnant woman." In contrast to Johnson's momentary embarrassment, Wilkins remembered being "amused, because I was sure it was one of the mainstay's of his uninhibited vocabulary."[18]

White House speechwriter Ben Wattenberg was in Canada when the

Newark riots broke out. He returned from a relative news blackout across the border to the huge coverage of the rioting in the U.S. media: "It suddenly seemed as if the whole country had come unglued. The talk of 'two Americas' and 'a Nation divided' leads me to think that *worse by far than the riots — is the reaction to the riots.*" Among the reportage that Wattenberg found most alarming were numerous accounts of white civilians in areas adjacent to black urban concentrated populations applying for gun permits and stockpiling weapons.[19]

Wattenberg felt passionately that Johnson should address the riots, but on his own terms and timing (the speechwriter clearly hoped for several days' delay to draft the most effective message). He predicted that, irrespective of anything the president did, "[George] Wallace for sure, and probably [Richard] Nixon and [Ronald] Reagan" would waste little time in attempting "to stick the blame [for the riots] on the president and the Democrats." Both Louis Martin and Wattenberg urged LBJ to launch a preemptive public relations strike. Johnson should remind the nation that "we have a program and a good one" and stress that elements of the program were currently bottled up in a hostile Congress. Such a "constructive program" was "something neither Wallace nor Reagan nor Nixon nor Black Powerites have," Wattenberg concluded, painting both ends of the political spectrum as reactive and opportunistic.[20]

Wattenberg got his wish for Johnson to address the nation, but when rioting escalated in Detroit the timing was out of his hands. As the evening wore on and the wire reports coming in from the Motor City were increasingly grim, Johnson summoned Secretary of Defense William McNamara, Attorney General Ramsey Clark, J. Edgar Hoover of the FBI, Press Secretary George Christian, and a handful of others to the Oval Office. Cyrus Vance, the administration's point man on the scene in Detroit, after a frantic flight from Washington, spoke with Johnson late that night and recommended that the president federalize the Michigan National Guard. Pentagon officials in Washington and in Detroit quickly made plans to divide the city between federalized National Guard troops and Regular Army troops should that become necessary.

Johnson offered the mordant observation: "Well, I guess it is just a matter of minutes before federal troops start shooting women and children." The president refused to be placated by the assurances of General John L. Throckmorton, the commanding officer in Detroit, that the army would "only shoot under the most severe provocations." LBJ offered a fascinating glimpse into his embattled psyche when he revealed to the war room–like gathering that he was "concerned about the charge that we cannot kill enough people in Vietnam, so we go out and shoot civilians in Detroit."

J. Edgar Hoover helped Johnson make the ultimate decision to commit troops. "They have lost all control in Detroit," the FBI director declared. "Harlem will break loose within thirty minutes. They plan to tear it to pieces." Hoover's attitudes toward blacks and riotous "hoodlums" were well known to most of the men in the room, and the director's use of "they" therefore needed little clarification. In the hour leading to midnight, Johnson signed the necessary paperwork giving the go-ahead to the army units and prepared to deliver a hastily written ten-minute address to the nation as the cameras were readied.[21]

Carried live on all three networks, the president's speech drew criticism on a number of fronts, from unflattering lighting to Johnson's decision to be flanked on either side by the attorney general and the secretary of defense (even a friendly critic observed that the two officials "look[ed] like props").[22] But the president's overly legalistic tone and his repeated attempts to suggest that Michigan's Republican chief executive had lost control caused the greatest concern. Governor Romney and the Detroit mayor, Jerome Cavanagh, watched the address together in the Motor City's downtown police station. Cavanagh remembered the governor "getting furious," "just mad as hell," as Johnson "whacked the hell out of Romney, mentioning him ten or fifteen times, really the traditional Johnsonian overkill."[23]

"Law enforcement is a local matter," the president began. "The fact of the matter, however, is that law and order have broken down in Detroit, Michigan." Following the suggestions of aides who insisted a strong condemnation of those involved in the disturbance was necessary in order to reassure the rest of the public, Johnson castigated the rioters: "Pillage, looting, murder and arson have nothing to do with civil rights. They are criminal conduct. . . . We will not tolerate lawlessness. We will not endure violence. It matters not by whom it is done or under what slogan or banner. It will not be tolerated. This nation will do whatever is necessary to do to suppress and to punish those who engage in it."

LBJ punctuated the speech on numerous occasions with the phrase "law and order" and an indictment of lawlessness. Once order had been restored, he suggested vaguely, "attention can immediately be turned to the great and urgent problems of repairing the damage that has been done." The phrase could be read by conservative critics as giving political recognition to the act of rioting, but it would require semantic contortions. And those seeking some evidence that the president was willing to acknowledge publicly the devastating conditions and police provocations that laid the groundwork for urban unrest could draw little comfort from the address.[24]

As Johnson spoke, close to 5,000 U.S. Army paratroopers were taking up positions and patrolling the streets of Detroit. Along with National Guardsmen and the State Police, 13,000 fully armed troops soon patrolled the city streets. The statistics in the aftermath of the Detroit riots were even more grim than those from Newark: 44 deaths, 351 serious injuries, and over 4,000 arrests.[25] According to most evidence, U.S. Army troops behaved with admirable restraint and professionalism. The same could not be said for the poorly trained and often openly hostile Michigan troops. Three black men were killed and seven other black men and two white women were savagely beaten, by a combined force of Detroit police, state troopers, and National Guardsmen, who responded to a report of sniper fire near the downtown Algiers Motel on July 26, 1967, and discovered a mixed-race gathering. As writer John Hersey convincingly argued, age-old taboos about interracial sex fueled the white authorities' murderous rampage. Despite claims of widespread snipers, law enforcement officials in Michigan—and in New Jersey—were never able to document their existence.[26]

White House and Justice Department officials initially denied that there was any political dimension to Johnson's response to the Michigan governor's muddled requests, although they were more candid later. In the opinion of Harry McPherson, the president delayed authorizing the deployment of federal troops largely due to constitutional concerns, but, in addition, he may have had "gigging Romney in mind."[27] And it is clear that Johnson was gravely concerned about the potential for negative political fallout if regular U.S. troops wounded or killed civilians. In the ensuing weeks, the White House caught plenty of flak for its indecisiveness during the Newark and Detroit riots. But Johnson continued to trumpet privately the fact that no regular U.S. troops had been shot and none had been conclusively proven to have killed a citizen. By assigning the blame to the National Guard and other local law enforcement officials, he escaped some of the onus of the dozens of lives lost that summer.

Even before he addressed the nation late on Monday evening, July 24, the political maneuvering in Washington and on Capitol Hill had begun. Johnson met briefly with Democratic congressional leaders and expressed his concern over a UPI wire item carrying a statement from the Republican Coordinating Committee. The committee collectively accused Johnson of having "totally failed to recognize the problem" of a nation sliding toward "a state of anarchy." Its statement, signed by former president Eisenhower, Senate minority leader Everett Dirksen, and other prominent Republicans, also gave credence to evidence that recent outbreaks of urban unrest "may be the result of organized planning and execution on a national scale."[28]

Publicly, Johnson refused to endorse the widespread rumors of a black radical conspiracy; privately, he was far more receptive. At one point, he directed Attorney General Ramsey Clark to have the FBI use the "maximum available resources, investigative and intelligence, to collect and report all facts bearing upon the question as to whether there has been or is a scheme or conspiracy by any group of whatever size, effectiveness or affiliation, to plan, promote or aggravate riot activity." Hoover obliged by providing summaries, which never explicitly described such a conspiracy but blamed "outside agitators."[29]

Although members of each party sought political advantage in the heated lead-up to the 1968 elections, the Republican Coordinating Committee called for a joint House and Senate committee to examine the disorders and propose measures to end urban unrest. According to Republican leaders, "The most basic of civil rights is being denied to the American people," that of protection "on the streets . . . from riots and violence."[30] Connecting the discourse on civil rights to the rhetoric of "law and order" and white backlash was an astute political move; that it rankled liberal observers was another bonus. Michigan Republican Gerald Ford introduced a concurrent resolution on Tuesday, July 25, providing for a twelve-member body with full subpoena power to investigate the riots, search for evidence of conspiracy, and make recommendations for action. The resolution was referred to the House Rules Committee, giving the administration some breathing room, but it placed even more pressure on Johnson to respond concretely to the riots.[31]

The choreography grew in complexity as the day wore on. Later in the afternoon, Democratic senator Fred Harris from Oklahoma introduced a joint resolution in the Senate, cosponsored by Minnesota senator Walter Mondale. The Democrats, clearly in reactive mode, called for the creation of a "Special Commission on Civil Strife," whose members would be appointed by the president. (The Republican resolution would have mandated that service on the investigatory joint committee be determined by Congress, with heavy involvement of the Republican minority leaders.) In a letter sent to Johnson early in the evening, Senator Harris suggested that Johnson "go ahead . . . and *by Executive Order* appoint such a Commission and set it to work," in essence rendering both congressional joint resolutions moot. The proposed commission would be composed of nine members, ideally representing all three branches of the federal government, city and state officials, and "informed citizens . . . [with] consideration to appropriate representation from racial groups and political parties." Its life span would be six months.[32] Fred Harris had basically described the Kerner Commission, which the president would soon appoint.

The public's responses to the riots in July revealed increased polarization. Letters coming into the White House mail room were decidedly more negative than positive. Ann Norman, of Riverside, California, captured the dominant tenor: "I never thought I would write such a letter to a President of my country," she wrote on the morning following Johnson's address to the nation justifying his decision to send troops to Michigan. "But after watching you on TV last night, carefully covering all the political bases while Detroit burns, I was disgusted. Nero fingered the fiddle and you finger the polls." The president had tacitly encouraged the chaos unfolding in the nation's cities, she continued: "You declared War on Poverty, got the votes of the poor, and now our entire country pays the price of your demagogy."[33] White backlash was in full swing.[34]

As Johnson struggled to ride out the currents of public opinion, civil rights leaders sought a balance between condemnation and moral urgency in their response to the riots. In a show of solidarity, on July 26, Martin Luther King Jr., A. Philip Randolph, Roy Wilkins, and Whitney Young signed a joint statement speaking out strongly against the violence and arguing that the primary victims of the rioting were blacks themselves, making the riots that much more senseless. Simultaneously, they called for "a redoubling of efforts" to redress inequalities and took Congress to task for the cruel mockery that had accompanied its defeat of the rat control legislation.[35]

The riots of 1967, even more than those of the preceding three summers, had forced the Johnson White House back to a position of reacting to events. The proponents of "law and order" shared the momentum with the spokesmen of militancy in the streets: Ronald Reagan, George Wallace, and Richard Nixon competed for headlines with Stokely Carmichael and H. Rap Brown. (Brown was assured extensive media coverage when he proclaimed in the midst of the summer's disorders: "Violence is necessary; violence is a part of America's culture; violence is as American as cherry pie.")

As White House aide Hobart Taylor considered the challenges posed by the latest wave of riots, he advised the president of the necessity of "turning this thing around, bring[ing] peace, and show[ing] our ability to control this situation." Taylor noted that the joint statement by the remnants of the Big Six only revealed the precarious position of established African American leaders: "Civil rights leaders cannot handle this situation and it is a clear rejection of their approach as too slow and too limited. At the same time the riot does not substitute anything workable in place of the present civil rights package, so the true initiative remains with us—free to be used unless we wait so long that . . . a counterforce of white fear and resentment destroys our options."[36]

Whether or not the approach of the major civil rights leaders was "too slow and too limited" is of course debatable. One wonders, however, if Hobart Taylor ever got the chance to read the telegram Martin Luther King Jr. had penned to the president just one day earlier. In the midst of the Detroit rioting, King called on Johnson to launch a massive program of job creation, coordinated through a "national agency." What was needed, the SCLC leader pointed out, was "not some cheap way out. Not some frugal device to maintain a balanced budget within an unbalanced society." What was needed, King clearly implied, was a withdrawal of American forces from Vietnam. Such a course of action would, of course, have achieved a "double victory" of sorts, in King's eyes: the abandonment of a foreign policy abroad that the clergyman viewed as racist and immoral, and the freeing up of huge amounts of fiscal resources to address the persistence of racial and economic inequality at home.[37]

Reeling from the negative response to his national address justifying troops for Detroit, and seeking to regain the initiative, Lyndon Johnson appeared to take the advice of Hobart Taylor to heart. A major presidential address on July 27, 1967, called for the creation of a National Advisory Commission on Civil Disorders, to be chaired by Illinois Democratic governor Otto Kerner, with Republican New York City mayor John Lindsay serving as vice chairman. David Ginsburg would be named as executive director shortly thereafter.[38] After announcing the new Kerner Commission's members in the opening moments of the address, the president appeared to be rehashing his "law and order" stance from the rushed address delivered just three nights before. "First, let there be no mistake about it," Johnson admonished. "The looting, arson, plunder and pillage which have occurred are not part of a civil rights protest. That is crime—and crime must be dealt with forcefully, swiftly, and certainly under law."[39]

The president then outlined plans to provide training for National Guard units in "riot control procedures," to ensure that "the violence . . . be stopped: quickly, finally, and permanently." Presumably, everyone in his audience could find something in this goal to applaud. Conservatives heard the message as more "law and order." Those who deplored the loss of innocent lives in Newark and Detroit hoped additional drills—in nonlethal means of crowd dispersion and control—might help to prevent a repeat of the generally miserable performance of the poorly trained, terrified, and trigger-happy National Guardsmen in those two cities.

The tone of Johnson's message then changed abruptly. "Garrison state" was a phrase that appeared with increasing frequency in internal White House and Justice Department memoranda, and the charged term had clearly struck a nerve: "It would compound the tragedy," the president insisted, "if we should settle for order imposed by the muzzle of a gun."

> In America, we seek more than the uneasy calm of martial law. We seek peace based on one man's respect for another man—and upon mutual respect for law. We seek a public order that is built on steady progress in meeting the needs of all of our people. Not even the sternest police action, nor the most effective Federal Troops, can create lasting peace in our cities. The only genuine, long-range solution for what has happened lies in an attack mounted at every level upon the conditions that breed despair and violence. All of us know what those conditions are: ignorance, discrimination, slums, poverty, disease, joblessness. We should attack these conditions—not because we are frightened by conflict, but because we are fired by conscience. We should attack them because there is simply no other way to achieve a decent and orderly society in America.[40]

Somewhat defensively, Johnson offered a detailed list of progressive legislation passed under his watch, a "roll call of laws," including two civil rights acts, Medicare and Medicaid, Model Cities, Head Start and other antipoverty programs, and rent supplements. But evoking the theme of Howard, he suggested that a still-greater battle lay ahead: "Our work has just begun."

Johnson chided those "who feel that even this beginning is too much," singling out those in Congress who had voted down the administration's $40 million appropriation request "to fight a pestilence of rats—rats which prowl in dark alleys and tenements, and attack thousands of city children." Setting the hook, Johnson turned deadly serious: "A strong government that has spent millions to protect baby calves from worms could surely afford to show as much concern for baby boys and girls." Although forceful, the president's language was toned down substantially from what Ben Wattenberg had suggested just three weeks earlier: LBJ should consider a "get tough" approach and chastise Congress for its negative vote on rat-control funding with the zinger and double entendre: "The rats won in Congress."[41]

Johnson ended his message with a plea for national calm: "This is not a time for angry reaction. It is a time for action." A retreat into "hatred . . . insecurity . . . fear . . . [and] heated words" would do nothing to heal the wounds. It was imperative to "condemn the violent few," but all Americans must "remember that it is law-abiding Negro families who have suffered most at the hands of the rioters." Concluding with a call for a day of prayer "for order and reconciliation among men," the president challenged his listeners to work to build a better future, "*one Nation* under God—with liberty and justice for all."[42]

Illinois Democratic governor Otto Kerner, flanked by the NAACP's Roy Wilkins and the president, discusses the charge of the newly created National Advisory Commission on Civil Disorders in a White House meeting. Courtesy of the LBJ Library.

Once again, listeners' reactions varied wildly. The responses were, on balance, far more favorable than they had been to the address Johnson had delivered three nights earlier, but the hostile messages were every bit as intense. A terse, unsigned communication (its staccato punctuated only by the telegram "stops") arrived at the White House at 5:42 A.M., just hours after Johnson's speech: "I want to burn the house down. I have Moltov [*sic*] cocktail. Will government give me a new house? Heard your speech tonight. Got ill. [Signed,] Ex Democrat."[43]

In the first meeting of the National Advisory Commission on Civil Disorders, in the White House, which followed shortly upon the heels of his speech announcing the formation of the Kerner Commission, Johnson asked the new appointees three primary questions about the recent riots in a deceptively simple charge: "What happened? Why did it happen? What can be done to prevent it from happening again and again?" In addition, the president asked the new commissioners to provide profiles of the rioters and their victims as they simultaneously examined a myriad of other issues, including the volatile issue of whether a conspiracy lay behind the riots and whether media coverage had an effect on the spread of the riots.[44]

Johnson was explicit in his insistence that the Kerner Commission should remain above politics. He assured the newly appointed members that he did not expect a "stamp of approval on what the Administration already believed." Instead, Otto Kerner and his ten associates were "to guide the country through a thicket of tension, conflicting evidence and extreme opinion," in search of an answer to explain the unrest. LBJ implored each member to take the work of the commission seriously; only with such a commitment "can America have the kind of report it needs and will take to its heart."

The list of questions and suggestions for study was as dizzying as the geographic and circumstantial diversity of the riots themselves. Attorney General Ramsey Clark later reflected on what an "impossible assignment" the commission had been given, noting sympathetically: "It's just as big as all out-of-doors."[45] After the press had snapped the obligatory pictures of the newly recruited commissioners, a dazed-looking Illinois governor, Otto Kerner—still absorbing the president's ambitious charge—voiced his concern about public expectations of the commission being so high as to be virtually "impossible" to meet: "we will not be able to deliver all."[46]

The composition of the commission—heavily stacked with racial "moderates"—opened up Johnson to charges of having left out representation of the voice of the "militants." But the president may have followed the same line of reasoning he had articulated two years before, when he had believed that placing conservative John McCone in charge of the California commission examining the Watts riots in 1965 would lend greater weight and legitimacy to its findings and preemptively forestall criticism from the conservative end of the political spectrum. (When the Kerner Commission Report summarized the results of the investigation, journalist Tom Wicker would argue that the "moderate" political complexion of the panel was precisely why the group's findings in the early months of 1968 had to be taken seriously.)

At the time of the Kerner Commission's formation, however, even some within the administration fretted over the absence of at least a token "militant" voice. Visiting Harlem just two weeks after the president's announcement of the commission, Harry McPherson informally polled residents and reported back with discouragement that many dismissed the commission's two African American appointees—Massachusetts senator Edward Brooke and NAACP leader Roy Wilkins—as "'office' leaders . . . [with] no following on the streets." The miscommunication ran in both directions, respondents told McPherson: Such leaders "neither understand nor are understood by people on the streets."[47]

While the commission began its investigations, White House aides resumed their efforts to better understand the conditions that "bred" riots. As Johnson continued to express interest in finding out whether there was a conspiracy behind the rioting, his aides and representatives from the bureaucratic line agencies once again mounted a series of low-profile fact-finding missions to the nation's cities. Clifford Alexander, Louis Martin, and Harry McPherson devoted a weekend to gaining a sense of the problems experienced by the poorest black residents in Harlem and Bedford-Stuyvesant in New York, and Roger Wilkins and three other representatives of CRS spent three days "looking around in Northeast Washington." McPherson announced plans to dispatch additional representatives to riot-prone areas the following weekend.[48]

From the time the first major riots broke out during the summer of 1964 through the devastating wave of disorders that followed the assassination of Martin Luther King Jr., in April 1968, Johnson was never able to reconcile conflicting feelings about whether there was some sinister force behind the outbreaks of violence in the nation's cities. There was plenty of figurative smoke that seemed to suggest there might be an organized attempt to incite rioters, but conclusively proving such charges led to endless frustration. Ramsey Clark, Nicholas Katzenbach's successor at the helm of the Justice Department, was surprisingly restrained; the new attorney general resisted substantial pressure from the White House, Congress, and public opinion to mount a case against Stokely Carmichael, H. Rap Brown, and other militant voices. He did not doubt that they were capitalizing on urban disorder to enhance their own stature, but proving that this exploitation constituted criminal behavior was another matter. Moreover, placing the most visible spokesmen of Black Power behind bars would in all likelihood only add to their stature and radical cachet.

Billy Graham, unabashedly applying his expertise as a revivalist to the nation's urban crisis, spoke out in the immediate aftermath of the Watts riot to warn that the flames in Los Angeles were "only a dress rehearsal of what is to come," for "a hard core is at work to destroy our country."[49] A handful of angry ideologues stood ready to confirm Graham's apocalyptic predictions. Just weeks after Watts, the White House staff circulated a telegram sent by Gus Hall, head of the American Communist Party, to the president. Arguing that "every slum and every ghetto of every city of America . . . is like a smoldering volcano," Hall's rhetoric paralleled Billy Graham's, as he suggested that the riots of 1964 and 1965 were "only forerunners of even graver things to come."

Where Billy Graham imagined a "hard core," Gus Hall saw the urban disturbances through the lens of the masses: Watts had been "a pent-up people's explosion." Upon reviewing the telegram's blistering critique of Johnson's social policies, Lee White, Marvin Watson, and McGeorge Bundy—all of whom took a clear interest in Hall's incendiary rhetoric—archly suggested that J. Edgar Hoover "might want a copy."[50]

A deluge of information from the FBI, at least in part, prompted the president repeatedly to voice his conviction that the riots of the "long-hot summers" were tied together by a conspiracy. In the memory of Harry McPherson, Hoover "served up a lot of raw evidence" suggesting there was a conspiracy, and Johnson was predisposed to believe that where there was so much smoke assuredly there must be a fire.[51] In a sense, it was easier to subscribe to Hoover's wild-eyed suspicions than to accept the frustrating reality of the urban disorders: that they were largely unpredictable and "essentially uncontrollable." Johnson was not alone in his desire to believe there were more sinister forces at work behind the ghetto riots. The growing "law and order" movement, spearheaded by California's Richard Nixon, Alabama's George Wallace, and North Carolina's Sam Ervin, among many others, championed the idea that the riots could be brought under control if the loudest of the "agitators" who cried "burn, baby, burn" were placed behind bars. Harry McPherson satirically simplified the belief that undergirded such logic: "Good Negroes simply don't go around shooting the people unless they're inspired by bad Negroes or bad white people . . . Communists."[52]

Others attempted to steer Johnson away from his intermittent paranoia. Less than twenty-four hours after the president's speech creating the Kerner Commission, Douglass Cater urged that the new investigation become a high-profile vehicle to disprove, conclusively, allegations of systematic conspiracy behind the riots: "This should serve to remove that issue from partisan conflict," Cater urged.[53] (Early the next year the Kerner Commission issued its verdict on the question of whether a conspiracy—communist-directed or otherwise—existed. Although there were numerous cases of "incitement"— and commission members betrayed not a trace of hesitation in deploring such instances—there was next to no evidence to support theories of widespread planning and conspiracy.[54])

Four days after the president announced the establishment of the Kerner Commission, reporters slammed Johnson with a barrage of questions in a White House press conference. Why were there not more "representatives of the more militant Negro point of view?" journalists demanded. The president dodged that pointed question and attempted to outline the various components of the administration's overall response to urban unrest. A reporter then bluntly asked: "Mr. President, do you recognize the problem of accelerating aid to the cities in a manner that does not seem to reward the rioters?" LBJ answered simply, "Yes." And the press conference ended.[55] Even as Johnson spoke, a riot was raging in Milwaukee, Wisconsin, which ultimately claimed the lives of four people, the last riot-related fatalities of the summer of 1967, bringing that season's death toll to approximately seventy-five.[56]

Warren Christopher later recalled, "We were always walking a difficult line of wanting to assist the cities in their relief and rehabilitation, but at the same time not wishing to have the occasion of a riot made the reason for a city to get preferential treatment on its normal programs."[57] White House aide and Johnson confidant Harry McPherson remembered a similar dilemma. With each new outbreak of urban unrest, the administration agonized over whether acceleration of federal aid to ghettos would be perceived as "rewarding the rioters." "There was almost a standard conversation after the riots that began by saying that the country wouldn't tolerate rewarding the rioters," McPherson related. "And it would end by the development of substantial programs to rush into the area . . . knowing that we were doing precisely what we said we were not doing." The degree of White House involvement in response to urban rioting sparked lengthy debates, but little emerged in the way of consensus. McPherson offered the frank admission that "this was nowhere near clear to any of us."[58]

The role of the media only added to the pressures facing Johnson and his cohorts. Over the course of his tenure in office, the president became more sensitive to the impact of the media in defining how events played with the public, but he remained surprisingly resistant to micromanagement of his own image.[59] The White House went back and forth on this issue. One week, White House aides urged Johnson to pay more attention to matters of image; the next, they found salient a criticism from Walter Ridder that "the President was giving the impression of trying too hard to get public support."[60] Such vacillation left Johnson impatient with the unpredictable calculus of media relations. But his impatience paled when compared to the rage he felt when he suspected administration insiders and members of the "permanent government" of engineering press leaks to feather their own nests, or worse yet, to attempt to circumscribe his freedom of action.

Scholars still need to explore more fully the impact of media depictions of urban unrest. Historian Hugh Davis Graham offers a promising point of departure, suggesting that civil rights and antipoverty reforms after 1965 "harbored a vulnerability in the mercurial image of [their] chief clientele." "During 1965–1966 the Negro image in America was sharply transformed, although probably in opposite directions for whites and blacks," Graham suggests. "In the spring of 1965 the dominant symbol was a petitioning black voter being brutalized by Sheriff Jim Clark in Selma. By 1966 this had been countered, *if not displaced* in the volatile world of *Time* and *Newsweek*, by the rampaging ghetto rioter in Watts, or the black racist harangues of an H. Rap Brown."[61]

Even more than weekly news magazines, television played a critical role in that displacement. What might be labeled the politics of gesture, wielded so skillfully by Stokely Carmichael during the Meredith March of 1966 and subsequently by groups like the Black Panther Party for Self Defense, might have served as a potent means of communicating new ideas and ideology. But with the medium of television, image often swamped idea. This was both the promise and the trap of militancy.

Media coverage of the urban riots also had a voyeuristic quality, giving an immediacy to the images that emerged, in contrast to earlier coverage of white repression in the South. Juxtaposed against the public's abhorrence of the violence represented by the riots of the years 1964 to 1968 was a fascination with the condition of the nation's inner cities, a desire on the part of many Americans to peer behind the tenement curtain to see how "reality" comported with their stereotyped visions of blighted urban lives and landscapes. The relatively recent advent of live television feeds and the saturation coverage of urban unrest went a long way toward satisfying this voyeurism, even as it fueled a backlash against the civil rights agenda the Johnson administration professed to be dedicated to fulfilling.

Last, the riots represented a political bonanza for hard-line conservatives. In California, television ads opposing the state's fair-housing laws depicted anarchist rioters and burning cities while a former actor whose political star was on the rise narrated a harrowing future. "Every day the jungle draws a little closer," intoned Ronald Reagan. "Our city streets are jungle paths after dark."[62] And feisty Alabama governor George Wallace made civil unrest a key plank in what would become his third party run in 1968, as he blamed the "guerrilla bands that burn and loot and riot" on Lyndon Johnson's "bearded beatnik bureaucrats" who had laid the ground for the riots by "contributing leadership and in some instances, public funds to help finance organized discord."[63]

If the Johnson White House had once sought to ride "piggyback" on the cresting fortunes of the civil rights movement, the game of the moment in the early spring of 1968 appeared to be "duck and cover." Across the country, the discourses of domestic policy and foreign policy clashed in ever-more-dramatic fashion, just as they had during the ghetto visits in the preceding months. Following the devastating Newark riots of July 1967, a National Guard officer blamed "indecisive civilian authority" for guardsmen "having to operate 'with one hand tied behind their backs' in riot areas. . . . Greater commitment of force," including "recommended use of heavy weapons including hand grenades, recoilless rifles, and bazookas" "might have prevented rioting."[64] (At least napalm is missing from his Newark qua Da Nang weaponry wish list.)

New Jersey Democratic governor Richard Hughes's initial public response to the riots in his state picked up the refrain of the evolving "law and order" rhetoric, and, like Ronald Reagan, he seemed more attuned to African rhythms in his none-too-subtle negrophobic comments than to Southeast Asian strains. In a grandstanding appearance on television in the midst of the July 1967 riot, Hughes declared: "The line between the jungle and law and order might as well be drawn here as any place in America." Activist Tom Hayden offered an international parallel of his own but inverted the rhetoric of the "Dark Continent" into a decidedly anticolonial vein: Hughes's "words sounded more like those of a Rhodesian military governor than a liberal Democratic politician."[65]

Against this increasing polarization and upheaval, the newly created Kerner Commission began to conduct its investigation into urban unrest in the late summer and early fall of 1967. Ramsey Clark later marveled at how quickly the commission had been thrown together. "We got this thing up in less than forty-eight hours." In that frantic interval, Clark and other Justice Department officials had lobbied hard for the inclusion of Otto Kerner and John Lindsay, believing that both men had demonstrated sound leadership when faced with racial disturbances in their home states.[66]

Attempting to guess what the Kerner Commission might emphasize after conducting its investigations was an exercise akin to political astrology. Douglass Cater expressed his hope that the commission's hearings might "provide general endorsement for keeping the heat on Congress not to run away from [Johnson's] programs." But he offered a salient warning: "There will be a danger [that the commission] may try to brainstorm big new programs of its own."[67]

The group's eleven members and large professional staff repeatedly behaved unpredictably, and the labels "liberal," "moderate," and "conservative," applied to individual commissioners, often failed to predict shifting coalitions or the remarkable unity of accord that ultimately developed.[68] Detroit mayor Jerome Cavanagh, who was convinced that testimony about his city's devastating 1967 riot helped to sway the thinking of more conservative members of the commission, believed that in the early stages of the investigation "fragmentation" characterized the commissioners' outlook on the riots. "I don't think they had any idea of where they were going or what kind of report they'd come out with. . . . I don't think they had any real understanding of what it was all about."[69] They soon proved to be apt pupils.

Testifying before the Kerner Commission, CRS director Roger Wilkins offered some of the most uncompromising evidence of the extent of city problems and racial unrest from his vantage point as insider in a branch of the federal bureaucracy that actually had a fair amount of face-to-face contact with the constituencies it served. He spotlighted "the failure of the system . . . to serve the needs of poor black people." Dismissing the mounting suspicion that the riots were somehow being manipulated by subversives and ideological firebrands, he insisted that the disorders were "not about outside agitators . . . not centrally about conspiracies . . . not about interstate travel or even about a couple of obstreperous fellows in their mid-20's"—presumably a reference to Stokely Carmichael and H. Rap Brown.

Wilkins's concluding remarks focused on the same divergent outlooks among black and white Americans that so many of the White House ghetto visits had documented in the preceding months: "There is a great gulf between the visions of America that these [white and black] groups of Americans hold." The riots were black people's way of dramatizing that gap in perceptions and economic results, and the first step toward addressing the urban crisis was to "close the gap of perception, to close the gap of understandings."[70]

Gerald W. Christenson, executive director of the President's Council on Youth Opportunity, chaired by Hubert Humphrey, bemoaned "minimal communication" between urban politicians and civic leaders—"the establishment"—and their poor minority constituents. Although the former group "felt they were doing everything possible to deal meaningfully with the needs of ghetto youth . . . spokesmen for ghetto groups felt little of consequence was being done." Representatives of the poor felt like "maximum feasible participation" had fallen by the wayside and identified the outlook of white politicians as "a desire to neutralize the militants with handout programs and to keep a lid on the summer."[71]

Even before its first official meeting—at which Johnson signed the executive order bringing the Kerner Commission formally into existence—the administration had considered ways to politicize the advisory body and to steer its conclusions or, if necessary, to exercise damage control. Johnson's White House remarks encouraging the commission to avoid the temptation to serve as a "rubber-stamp" made for good copy and evidently convinced several of the commissioners that they had been uttered in good faith. But the president's statement was disingenuous. He certainly had no wish for the commission to turn against its creator. (Califano supplied the literary allusion to Mary Shelley, likening the Kerner Commission to a "political Frankenstein's monster."[72])

Less than half an hour before Johnson went on television to announce the formation of the Kerner Commission, he telephoned Oklahoma senator Fred Harris to say that he was "gonna put you on the damn thing." Harris feigned surprise. "I never expected it," he responded, "but I'll do the best I can."

And "another thing," the president added pointedly, "I want you to remember you're a Johnson man."

"I'm your friend, Mr. President," responded Harris, "and I won't forget it."

"If you do," warned Johnson, "I'll take out my pocketknife and cut your peter off."[73]

Administration officials kept close tabs on the commissioners' deliberations.[74] And Johnson wielded a blunt budgetary club throughout the brief life span of the commission, enjoining executive branch Bureau of the Budget director Charles Schultze to withhold funding, justifying the tightening of the purse strings as part of a larger pattern of fiscal retrenchment in the winter of 1967–68 but clearly in this case acting with a different motive, as the White House grew leery of what the commission might ultimately recommend. (Schultze, according to some reports, used creative budgetary sleight of hand to restore some of this funding.)[75] But, once the appointments had been made, Johnson's leverage over the committee members was significantly diminished.

Late in January 1968, Otto Kerner and commission executive director David Ginsburg requested $162,000 more to fund a skeleton staff to oversee publication of the upcoming report and to cover printing and production costs, to field correspondence and respond to congressional and media inquiries, and, in various other ways, to relate the findings of the commission to the public. For his part, Charles Schultze was of two minds on the subject of diverting supplemental funds to Kerner's staff. He noted to the president that it would be "useful" to have commission staff around should the nation experience additional episodes of urban unrest in the summer of 1968. But knowing LBJ's predilection, he was reluctant to retain a professional staff, "if their report urges large, new programs which we cannot handle at the present time." The more ambitious the proposals, the more Schultze professed to be uninterested in those ideas having advocates on the federal payroll: "Having a staff around promoting such projects could give us trouble."[76]

Two weeks earlier, on January 10, Kerner and Lindsay had conducted a joint press briefing to announce that the report of the National Advisory Commission on Civil Disorders would be released in early March. The members of the Kerner Commission had conducted hearings from August 1 to November 7, 1967, and had taken testimony from over 130 witnesses. Devoting most of their answers to slowing down the hyperactive rumor mill, Kerner and Lindsay attempted to telegraph some of the commission's anticipated conclusions: "It will . . . be a report that we believe is going to be uncomfortable for the people of the United States." Asked specifically if the White House would find the conclusions uncomfortable, Kerner stated elliptically: "I don't think it will be comfortable for anybody." The Illinois governor steadfastly denied press rumors of "pressure from the White House to tone the report back" and was at pains to discount leaks by staffers displaced from the commission due to cutbacks in funding who were predicting that "the report was going to be the biggest sanitary job on earth."

Kerner refused to "put a price tag" on the recommendations of the commission, saying that some might even come free of charge, such as "the measures that would do away with racism. . . . Let's not sweep [racism] under the rug . . . and if we can change people's attitudes, this will not cost a penny." Kerner was at pains to assure reporters that the commission would not extend its life beyond one year from the initial appointment. Aside from routine "housekeeping work," tasks related to wrapping up and distributing the report, the commission's work was essentially done.[77]

In February, commission members met in the Indian Treaty Room of the Executive Office Building. All sections of the report had gained approval on a piecemeal basis, including the introduction and summary, and most members assumed there would be a final ceremonial vote on the full report, a few official photographs, and then adjournment. As Kerner called the meeting to order, however, Charles "Tex" Thornton—one of the most conservative members of the commission, announced: "Mr. Chairman, I have a minority report that I would like to have appended to the majority report."

"John Lindsay and I exploded," recalled Oklahoma senator Fred Harris. Several times during the deliberations, said Harris, he and Lindsay had wanted to include more hard-hitting recommendations. Lindsay had spoken with particular passion on the need to end the war in Vietnam so that the "peace dividend" could be directed toward addressing America's domestic problems. But Lindsay, like other members, was committed to obtaining a unanimous report and had accepted defeat. Faced with Thornton's threat, however, Harris and Lindsay, the two most liberal members of the commission, warned that they were prepared to present their own—more hard-hitting—recommendations. Other members joined in, and suddenly it seemed that everyone was going to have a minority report reflecting their personal views. In less than twenty minutes, recalled Harris, "it looked like the whole son of a bitch was going to fall apart." At that point, said Harris, Thornton withdrew his motion and the committee—perhaps fearful of another uproar—quickly voted unanimously to approve the report as it was written.[78]

"Our nation is moving toward two societies, one black, one white—separate and unequal."

So ran the conclusion of the introductory summary to one of the most-quoted reports in the long history of government commissions. "Two societies" and "two nations" were rhetorical themes familiar to most Americans, from Lincoln's Civil War–era metaphor of a "house divided" to John Dos Passos's response to the trial and execution of Sacco and Vanzetti in the 1920s. Lyndon Johnson had himself tested their variants on numerous occasions.

But, as Illinois governor Kerner had warned in the January press conference, the report would directly confront racism in American history and in contemporary society, and it would not be swept under the rug: "What white Americans have never fully understood—but what the Negro can never forget," read the report's summary, "is that white society is deeply implicated in the ghetto. White institutions created it, white institutions maintain it, and white society condones it." Drafters of the report devoted eight additional pages of prefatory material setting up the language that would instantly be seized upon by the media and hostile and sympathetic observers alike. In responding to Johnson's charge to answer the question, "why did [the riots] happen?" the report's authors averred: "The most fundamental [factor] is the racial attitude and behavior of white Americans toward black Americans. Race prejudice has shaped our history decisively; it now threatens to affect our future. *White racism* is essentially responsible for the explosive mixture which has been accumulating in our cities since the end of World War II."[79]

How should the Johnson administration respond? The White House had received reliable intelligence about the basic contours of the report, and Johnson aides repeatedly assured their chief that the report generally depicted an administration that was "heading in the right direction," in the summation of Joseph Califano, but "moving too slowly, devoting insufficient resources to make a dramatic difference and organizationally scattering its shots."[80] Johnson seemed deaf to the praise as he obsessed over the implicit critique of *his* generalship, *his* War on Poverty, *his* beloved Great Society.

In the last week of February, as the Kerner Commission geared up for a public release of its entire report over the weekend, the White House wrestled with its options. That Johnson would not ceremonially accept the report was a near certainty. Califano wrote: "I have assumed you would not want to receive the Report personally." Califano thought that LBJ was making a mistake in this symbolic rejection of the commission's findings, but he correctly gauged the intransigence of his chief. Califano and Johnson were on the same page on another matter, however. The White House aide cautioned against directly seeking the input of the commission on how best to bring some of the report's proposals to fruition: "I fear many members (led by [John] Lindsay) would get into Viet Nam and some members would recommend that we pull out of Viet Nam to pay for their programs." Such an approach was obviously politically unpalatable to Johnson.[81]

Timing called for David Ginsburg to release the report to the newspapers on Friday, March 1, with a moratorium on publication before the Sunday papers on March 3, which would presumably devote extensive coverage to the commission's findings. Califano and other White House insiders predicted that the initial media responses would be focused less on the question of implementing its suggestions for national action—"What can be done?"—than on the findings about what had led to the current crisis—"What happened?"[82] *New York Times* journalist Tom Wicker, who penned the introduction to the publication of the Kerner Commission's findings in a paperback format geared at a mass audience, equated the report with an "indictment" and noted how remarkable were its conclusions, given the relatively "moderate" credentials of those who had served on the commission.[83]

Ben Bradlee, editor at the *Washington Post*, made plans to publish a story on Friday, March 1, in violation of the press embargo. He insisted that the *Post* had received a copy of the report that was missing the all-important cover page, which detailed the embargo against using the information prematurely. Despite a dressing-down by Califano, Bradlee made clear his intention to run with the story. Anxious to deny the *Post* an exclusive, LBJ, through Califano, authorized commission director David Ginsburg to inform the *New York Times* and other major dailies that they could offer initial coverage of the report before the anticipated in-depth stories in the Sunday editions.[84] Johnson was so angry about the "leak" that he refused even to accept the report from David Ginsburg in private, much less with the expected and choreographed media fanfare and photo ops, which typically accompanied the conclusion of work by presidentially appointed commissions.

Johnson, Califano wrote later, suspected all along that certain commission members—he was particularly suspicious of the handsome Republican mayor of New York, John Lindsay—would attempt to use the riot investigation to "box him in." Johnson was well aware that Lindsay had tried, unsuccessfully, to get his fellow commissioners to link racial and economic issues with the war

New York's Republican mayor John Lindsay, a prominent member of the Kerner Commission, activates the political fears of an increasingly besieged Johnson White House. Courtesy of LBJ Library.

in Vietnam. And even though the commission members fully supported the far-reaching conclusions of the report, it was Lindsay—or actually two of his aides—who drafted much of the hard-hitting sections of the introduction and summary.[85]

As early as October 1967, the president and Califano felt that "Lindsay had pursued his own political agenda," after the New York mayor indicated to reporters that he planned to release an "interim report" so that the commissioners' early thinking concerning programs would be available to influence budgetary planning in the White House. LBJ had exploded, telling Califano: "That's bullshit. And you tell Lindsay that there's something I've learned from a long life in politics: It's a darn sight easier to slip on bullshit than it is to slip on gravel. If he doesn't stop the bullshit he's gonna slip and break his ass."[86]

If the initial public response from the White House to the release of the Kerner Commission Report was muted—or virtually absent—others were quick to offer their opinions. Unrepentant segregationist Georgia governor Lester Maddox, the pick handle–wielding poster child for massive resistance, asserted that the report's authors had either not done their "homework or they are not telling the truth." Either way, they did not "have the guts to say [that the cause of the riots is] communism. . . . They are trying to bribe people into being good citizens." The government should herald success stories of those who had risen out of poverty and "quit making bums out of people." Georgia's Grand Dragon in the United Klans of America explored a similar theme: "The report is pure political blackmail . . . [telling] the American people that they must furnish more billions of dollars or their stores will be looted and their cities burned."[87]

Atlanta's mayor, Ivan Allen, and the city's police chief, Herbert Jenkins, praised the report. Jenkins called his appointment to the commission the "greatest honor and the greatest challenge" of his career and defended the effort: "I'll buy it, I stand with it, I fall with it."[88] Martin Luther King Jr. called the commission's findings of white racism "an important confession of a harsh truth. . . . The lives, the incomes, the well-being of poor people everywhere in America are plundered by our economic system." The Kerner Commission seemed to reinforce the need for King's planned Poor People's Campaign, tentatively scheduled for later in the spring of 1968.[89]

Analyzing media coverage, historian Michael P. Flamm demonstrates that liberals *outside* the administration generally praised the report and conservatives for the most part condemned it. North Carolina senator Sam Ervin followed the lead of the Georgia Klansman in likening the report's expansive recommendations for social reform to "ransom legislation." Radicals found the document benign but evasive in its approach to the most fundamental questions. Journalist Andrew Kopkind, for example, took commissioners to task for failing to adequately address deeply embedded "structural flaws" in America's economy and polity.[90]

Public opinion was sharply divided, with polling data gathered by the Harris Survey indicating a notable gap in perceptions of the Kerner Commission findings by race. White respondents rejected the claim that "white racism" was the primary cause of the rioting, 53 to 35 percent. Blacks, on the other hand, supported that finding by a margin of greater than three to one. In an ominous sign for an administration concerned about both fiscal conservatism and a perceived growing white backlash, whites, by a bare margin of 45 to 43 percent, were in favor of providing money to the cities "to rehabilitate their slums" but were opposed, by a margin of 63 to 23 percent, to a hike in taxes to bankroll such an effort. African Americans, by a three to one ratio, expressed a willingness to pay higher taxes.[91] And it is worth noting that many blacks, following the dictates of realpolitik, thought that the recommendations for new programs outweighed in significance the diagnosis of white racism. Bayard Rustin's response to the Kerner Commission Report, when asked by a reporter, was that he "would rather have a job program for blacks than a psychoanalysis of whites."[92]

White House speechwriter Ben Wattenberg described what he saw as one of the fundamental ironies of the Kerner Commission Report and the ambivalence of its reception. The media, Wattenberg later reflected, had greeted Johnson's appointment of the commission derisively in the summer of 1967 with the journalistic equivalent of: "Great Christ, here are all of these cities burning down," and this is the best the president has to offer. "What a jerk he is." Reporters for the same "liberal press" labeled the commission's report in the spring of 1968 as "God's gift to America." "[The commissioners] really saw the truth of American society, and God, what great recommendations they put out!" Wattenberg dripped acid: "As if this was some instrumentality of government that created itself! This was Johnson's commission! These were his guys he put on it."[93]

Whitney Young, of the National Urban League, offered a variation on Wattenberg's theme when he insisted that Johnson "couldn't have disagreed with the findings because in his own speeches many, many times he has pointed out that the real agitators are not Communist-trained infiltrators, but they are rats and poverty. . . . He had said most of the things that are in that report."[94] The flaw in Young's analysis was that it demanded both political consistency and emotional rationality from Johnson. By 1968, the president's reserves in both areas were perilously low.

While Kerner and other commission members steadfastly resisted the temptation to quote budget figures, the White House was busy running projected numbers. Joseph Califano reported to the president that initial Budget Bureau estimates indicated that fulfilling the report's ambitious agenda would require tens of billions of dollars, with measures for full employment, more generous welfare, additional assistance to schools, and federally funded housing starts devouring the lion's share of the imaginary funds.[95]

For President Johnson, the Kerner Commission Report could not have arrived at a less auspicious moment. Stymied in his attempts to win passage of a tax bill, increasingly worried by the threat of runaway inflation, and as always distracted by the morass of Vietnam, LBJ felt like even the preservation of existing Great Society programs would be an uphill battle. From the perspective of the Oval Office, the report seemed to ignore fiscal and political realities. Ramsey Clark recalled the mood at the time: "And here this report came and said, 'But we've got to do many, many times more than what we're doing. We've got to spend billions.'"[96]

New York Times journalist Tom Wicker concluded his introduction to the report of the Kerner Commission with the admission that "reading it is an ugly experience." But confronting the findings of the commission and grappling with the dimensions of the problems that so desperately needed addressing brought "something like the relief of beginning. What had to be said has been said at last."[97] As he confronted the report, however, LBJ dwelt on all of the "ugliness" and felt little or none of the "relief" that Wicker had promised. In his presidential memoir, *The Vantage Point*, Johnson's discussion of the Kerner Commission episode is terse but relatively generous compared to his private responses. He stressed the "extremely close agreement between the commission's proposals and the Administration's program" but concluded with the obvious: "The major difference lay in the scale of effort recommended."

The problem, said Johnson was simple: "money." In November 1967, the House of Representatives had cut nearly $500 million from a $2 billion antipoverty appropriation sought by the White House. "At the moment I received the report," he recalled, "I was having one of the toughest fights of my life, trying to persuade the Congress to pass the 10 per cent tax surcharge without imposing deep cuts in our most critical Great Society programs. I will never understand how the commission expected me to get this same Congress to turn 180 degrees overnight and appropriate an additional $30 billion for the same programs that it was demanding I cut by $6 billion. This would have required a miracle."[98]

In the days before publication of the report, Johnson had demanded that Califano call David Ginsburg and request that "some suggestion must be in [the] Report on how to pay [for it]." "Anyone can recommend spending, but preparing methods to fund the costs of new programs takes more ability."[99]

The Kerner Commission Report's authors never shied away from the fact that none of the solutions would be easy or free. They called for "a commitment to national action—compassionate, massive and sustained, backed by the resources of the most powerful nation on this earth." Over and over again, the Kerner Commission emphasized that what was necessary to arrest the drift toward "two nations" was "new will," undergirded by "new attitudes" and "new understanding."[100] Without such "will," debates about the budget were an academic exercise, nothing more. On this, assuredly, the commissioners and the president could agree.

Increasingly annoyed that he was hearing about the report through back channels and press leaks before receiving his own copy from the commission, Johnson insisted that the commissioners "be as imaginative on taxing as on spending."[101] "I have been seeing on the wire and hearing on the radio all day long what the Commission on Civil Disorders is going to report to me," Johnson darkly informed Califano. "As you know, I would prefer to receive the Report before I hear about it from news media." He asked Califano "to tell Ginsburg that the report was 'destroying the president's interest in things like this.'"[102]

Attorney General Ramsey Clark suggested that Johnson appoint a task force "to analyze the report" and to study the most effective means to put its recommendations into practice, to prioritize federal approaches, to see about overlap with preexisting programs, and, if necessary, to draft legislation. Clark urged the president to walk a delicate line. He could "praise the work and dedication of the Commission members but you need not embrace all of its findings or recommendations." Clark made a subtle but very important point in his conclusion. If Johnson appointed such a task force, he would "show decisive action without subscribing to everything the report says *and encourage governors and mayors to act.*" He left unstated the obvious. If the president ignored the report's findings, why should local or state officials treat it seriously? Since so many of the commission's findings were even more applicable at local or state levels than the federal one—those findings indicting police brutality and the conduct of state police and the National Guard, for example—for mayors and governors to follow the president's lead in discounting the Kerner Commission Report's recommendations would be tragic indeed.[103]

Califano voiced similar concerns about the dangers of "ignoring" the report, and McPherson chimed in to the debate: "The more I think about it, the more I fear that a cold reception to the Kerner Report is bad policy for us." McPherson urged Johnson to give less attention to how the extremes of "bomb-throwing liberals, *New York Times* editorial writers . . . or militant Negroes" would respond. Instead, the administration should attempt to reach "ordinary moderate people," those whose support for civil rights seemed to be on the wane in recent polling and those "concerned about finding some way out of the tragic tailspin we are in."[104]

Grudgingly responding to repeated urging from trusted advisers, including an impassioned plea from Louis Martin not to neglect core Democratic constituencies, President Johnson did belatedly commend the report to the attention of a group of elite savings and loan bank officials gathered at the White House on March 6, urging them to study the Kerner Commission's findings and offering cautious praise for its members: "It is a very distinguished group and a lot of talent went into that report after hearing witness after witness. . . . I won't ask you to embrace every recommendation they make, but I hope you can help us all that you can in good conscience." But the president could not resist a subtle sideswipe at the commission for having spent "an unprecedented amount of money—millions of dollars in the period of several months" to fund its investigations and pay its staff. He nonetheless recommended the report for study as "one of the most thorough and exhaustive studies ever made."[105] But the setting was hardly calculated to maximize media exposure of this tentative endorsement, and LBJ's larger silence spoke volumes compared to these few words of faint praise.

Largely at the behest of Louis Martin, on March 15 Johnson met with "Negro editors and publishers" in the White House Cabinet Room and labeled the commission's findings "the most important report made to me since I have been President." His verdict in this company was that "the report was more good than bad."[106] The problem, he told the newspapermen and women, as he would stress in his presidential memoirs later, was "money." "First thing we have got to do is find the money," a problem the commission members "didn't touch upon. . . . It's like saying we need sirloin steaks three nights a week, but only have the money to pay for two steaks." He suggested that a tax bill would be vital if even a tiny fraction of the commission's sweeping policy recommendations were to be put into place.[107]

One week later, in a press conference on March 22, Johnson and Califano "planted" a question at a press conference asking for the president's feeling about the commission's findings three weeks after its release to the public. Johnson, again deferring reluctantly to the judgment of his political advisers, spoke guardedly of the report as "very thorough . . . very comprehensive." The commissioners "made many good recommendations," which would now be thoroughly reviewed by the cabinet: "We did not agree with all of the recommendations, as certain statements have indicated."[108] The lukewarm endorsement was as close to a public thank-you as LBJ ever came.

So what conclusions can be drawn from an examination of Johnson's non-response to the Kerner Commission's grim warning of "white racism" driving a wedge between "two societies . . . separate and unequal"? In Ben Wattenberg's memory, the political damage incurred by Johnson's faltering response to the Kerner Commission was largely self-inflicted. The president "could have been very gracious about it all," the speechwriter insisted. Johnson could have praised the efforts of the commissioners, while distancing himself from their conclusions and recommendations. "Instead he chose to smolder in silence for awhile."[109]

Always eager to view the world through an intensely personal filter, the president found it hard not to interpret the commission's report as a 500-page personal insult, a failure to register proper recognition of his efforts in launching "his" Great Society programs and winning civil rights legislation. He had similarly equated the Watts riot with an act of political "betrayal."

"On reflection," wrote Joseph Califano, "I believe the President refused at first even to acknowledge the report because he was hurt. He shared most of the commission's goals. But he felt let down by Kerner and Ginsburg for not adequately recognizing what he had already done and for failing to point out sharply that Congress would not let him do more. When the report surfaced prematurely, he immediately suspected it had been leaked by someone on the commission to box him in. For Lyndon Johnson, that settled it."[110]

Among the "Confidential Files" in the Lyndon Baines Johnson Presidential Library is a small collection of materials related to the Kerner Commission. In the box is an otherwise nondescript file-sized envelope related to the Kerner Commission. On the outside of the large envelope is written "DO NOT RELEASE TO ANYONE—DO NOT OPEN," underlined three times in bold red. Inside the envelope is a stack of unremarkable, personally addressed but otherwise identical form letters, expressing the president's "deep appreciation" to each of the Kerner Commission members in sterile prose for their "valuable service" to the country and for the "exhaustive study" informing their "historic report."

"Through your efforts," read the letters, "local, State and Federal officials will be better able to prevent violence and disorder. More importantly, you have documented the need to build something much more lasting: a better America for all Americans. I hope that your message will reach into the hearts and minds of all our citizens, and inspire each of them to join in this vital work."[111]

Each letter concludes, "You have the gratitude of your President and your Nation," followed by the word "Sincerely" and then a blank space awaiting Johnson's signature.

Harry McPherson and Joseph Califano had carefully edited the text (the initial draft was the work of White House aide James Gaither). When McPherson forwarded the thank-yous to Johnson for his signature on March 13, less than two weeks after the Kerner Commission Report's release, the aide stressed that the letters "make no reference to the specific proposals which the Commission made. They are similar to the letters of thanks which you have sent members of Task Forces and other Commissions."

But Johnson was unconvinced. A slip attached to the envelope of letters, dated March 13, 1968, documents a phone conversation between Lyndon Johnson and inner-circle confidant Harry McPherson. "I just can't sign this group of letters, [Harry]," the president said. "I'd be a hypocrite. And I don't even want it let known that [the letters] got this far . . . otherwise somebody will leak that I wouldn't sign them. Just file them—or get rid of them."[112]

In an oral history, NAACP head and Kerner Commission member Roy Wilkins, one of LBJ's few intimate African American acquaintances and one of the president's staunchest defenders, remarked on Johnson's failure to follow protocol in thanking commission members for their report: "I think probably, maybe the word racism, white racism [in the Kerner Commission Report's summary], frightened him. He didn't want to go down in history as the president who had pointed his finger at his own people. This I think is understandable."[113]

Tom Wicker could argue, as he did in his introduction to the mass paperback publication of the report, that its authors were all "moderates," and as such they had to be taken more seriously than if the report had been generated by extreme liberal whites and militant blacks. But when Roy Wilkins argued that "the language was too hard" for Johnson to accept, he introduced the larger corollary. In many ways, LBJ exemplified millions of white Americans who were manifestly uncomfortable with the findings of the report: "They couldn't accept the report; they thought things were just fine with the colored: there we were over in our end of town, with our churches, and wasn't a colored boy captain of the basketball team? What were we yelling about?"[114]

Wilkins was normally a defender of Johnson, but he had a hard time forgiving the president for not thanking the commission members and for snubbing them by refusing to receive them in person to deliver the report to the White House. "He's a very courteous person and a very close observer of official protocol," the NAACP leader noted, "so that his thanks would not necessarily convey . . . approval of the entire report."[115]

In Roy Wilkins's mind, drafting the report of the National Advisory Commission on Civil Disorders was like being the bearer of "bad news." Sharing it was not a pleasant task, but it "had to be delivered. You had to be honest." White House aide Harry McPherson was not sure whether such honesty helped anyone in the long term. Like many others seeking to make sense of Johnson's shoddy treatment of the commissioners in refusing to thank them, even privately, Harry McPherson attributed at least part of Johnson's unceremonious behavior and "extremely negative" response to the Kerner Commission Report to it having "hurt his pride. There wasn't enough said about what had been done in the last few years."[116]

Without an explicit and public profession of gratitude from the commissioners in their report, Johnson may well have seen himself engaged in an act of spiteful reciprocity when he refused to sign the letters thanking them for their service. "Just file them—or get rid of them," LBJ had directed. "I don't even want it let known that they got this far." As Richard Nixon entered the White

House, the letters left it, unsigned and unsent, bound for archival processing and deposit in Johnson's planned presidential library in Austin, Texas. They remain there today among the volumes of other materials once designated "Confidential Files," now open to public scrutiny, another posthumous insult to a wounded and bitter man.

Harry McPherson argued in retrospect that the Kerner Commission struck at the core of the Roosevelt coalition; it "scared the be-Jesus out of a lot of [white] members of this coalition," appearing to telegraph a signal "that nobody really gave a damn about their concern—that the city was going to be burned down; that you couldn't walk in it at night anymore, and all the rest. . . . Programs were being shaped to take care of Negro needs and not to meet any of the needs of the other members of the coalition." Given the demographic realities of the electoral coalition that had helped to bring about Johnson's 1964 landslide, these were not unimportant concerns. Journalist John Herbers's dry wit seemed apt: "The Kerner Report was hardly a document that an incumbent president would use as a platform for re-election."[117]

Many of the low-profile scouts, like Sherwin Markman, had anticipated the recommendations of the Kerner Commission, even as they echoed those of the earlier quashed Ramsey Clark report for the task force on Watts. These multiple sources of "quiet" intelligence presumably should have served as a documentary vaccine, inoculating the president against an overreaction to the findings of the Kerner Commission. But Ramsey Clark's task force and the scouting missions had been in-house affairs. Johnson, while appearing genuinely receptive to this firsthand, authenticated, "primary news," was also at complete liberty to sit on it and not act. With the Kerner Commission, both partisan politics and the harsh glare of the media lights had entered the equation. Each variable restricted the president's maneuvering room in an already-tense election year, and by the spring of 1968 he showed few signs of wanting to embark on another major domestic policy crusade.

But Lyndon Johnson still held one dramatic announcement up his sleeve.

Two Nations

The Scars of Centuries

L
ess than three weeks after refusing to sign the letters thanking the members of the Kerner Commission, the president declared a unilateral bombing halt in Vietnam in a nationally televised prime time address, on March 31, 1968. At the end of one of the most important foreign policy speeches he had ever delivered, Johnson paused, appearing to hesitate one final time before plunging ahead, bound by the words appearing on the teleprompter. "There is division in the American house," he said, a close echo of the Kerner Commission Report, but also an admission of the stark differences of opinion separating Americans over the prosecution of the war in Vietnam.

> With America's sons in the fields far away, with America's future under challenge right here at home, with our hopes and the world's hopes in the balance every day, I do not believe that I should devote an hour or a day of my time to any personal partisan causes or to any duties other than the awesome duties of this office — the Presidency of your country.
>
> Accordingly, I shall not seek, and I will not accept the nomination of my party for another term as your President.[1]

Johnson's remarkable decision came just over two weeks after Democratic challenger Eugene McCarthy won 40 percent of the vote in the New Hampshire presidential primary, an electoral bellwether. The peace candidate's political stock had risen sharply following the brutal Tet offensive early in the new year, with "Lyndon's War" looking ever more unwinnable in the court of public opinion. Emboldened by the upstart McCarthy's strong showing against the incumbent president, Robert F. Kennedy threw his hat into the ring four days later. LBJ's paranoid fixation on the "Bobby factor" entered the realm of electoral realities, a calculus the president had mastered over the course of his

Lyndon Johnson addresses the nation on March 31, 1968. Courtesy of LBJ Library.

remarkable political career. This was one vote Johnson didn't think he could win.

LBJ did achieve one more legislative triumph, but it was a bittersweet victory and at least partially won on the back of tragedy. Less than one hundred hours after Johnson's withdrawal from the presidential race, with the chorus of long-absent praise that greeted the Texan's announcement still gathering intensity, James Earl Ray fired the bullet that snuffed out the life of Martin Luther King Jr. as he stood on the balcony of the Lorraine Motel in Memphis, Tennessee. It was April 4, 1968, exactly one year since King had broken with the administration so dramatically in his "Beyond Vietnam" speech at Riverside Church. Johnson took to the airwaves once more to decry the violence and signaled his intention to deliver a speech before a Joint Session of Congress in the days to follow.

But it was his nemesis, Robert Kennedy, who stole LBJ's thunder as he delivered the news of King's assassination to a crowd gathered for a rally in Indianapolis. Speaking without notes to a shocked audience, his quiet eloquence seemed to spring from the painful memories of his brother's death. He spoke of Martin Luther King Jr.'s lifelong struggle to create an America of "love and wisdom, and compassion toward one another, and a feeling of justice toward those who still suffer within our country." He acknowledged the instinctive reaction to seek revenge, but, in the spirit of the slain King, he called upon his listen-

The president studies the extent of rioting in Washington, D.C., with White House adviser Joseph Califano on April 5, 1968, following the assassination of Martin Luther King Jr. in Memphis. Courtesy of LBJ Library.

ers to reject violence and retaliation. Instead, he concluded, "let us dedicate ourselves to what the Greeks wrote so many years ago, to tame the savageness of man and make gentle the life of this world. Let us dedicate ourselves to that, and say a prayer for our country and for our people."[2]

As Kennedy had feared, however, within hours of the news of King's death, riots erupted in over one hundred cities. In the next two days the wave of violence claimed the lives of thirty-nine Americans, the overwhelming majority of them black. It was as though the preceding four long, hot summers had rolled into one boiling forty-eight-hour period, a nightmare in spring, as columns of smoke rose miles above the Capitol and tens of thousands of National Guardsmen and Regular Army troops—even U.S. Marines—poured into urban blocks around the nation. By the time the flames had been brought under control, Johnson had no stomach left for an address to Congress. When Joseph Califano gently reminded the president on April 10 that he had virtually promised to speak to a Joint Session, LBJ angrily scrawled across his aide's memo, "Forget it. . . . I promised nothing. I stated my intentions only. Since changed by riots!"[3]

And yet, on the very same day that the president dismissed Califano's memo, Congress passed the Fair Housing Act of 1968. After three years of legislative battles, weariness, and stalemate, Senate supporters of the measure had finally mustered the votes to achieve cloture after Republican Everett Dirksen prevailed upon the administration to compromise on the bill's coverage, in the process diluting the law. In the aftermath of the King assassination and against the backdrop of the wave of rioting, the House ultimately agreed to accept the Senate version of the bill, avoiding a conference committee in which the enforcement provisions of the legislation might have been further diluted. Dismissed by some critics as an empty gesture, the passage of a law prohibiting discrimination in home sales and rentals represented an important symbolic victory, even though the comfortably lopsided margins of the final votes in the two chambers was a telltale sign of how few teeth the bill had in terms of federal enforcement powers.[4]

It was the last civil rights bill that Johnson would sign, and it attracted little fanfare in the wake of the King assassination. With successive challengers— George W. Romney, Nelson Rockefeller, and finally Ronald Reagan—unable to derail Richard Nixon's momentum as he moved toward cinching the Republican nomination, McCarthy, Kennedy, and Hubert Humphrey waged a spirited battle to become the Democratic standard-bearer. The vice president entered the race in the imposing shadow of Johnson and with the millstone of Vietnam around his neck, and Democrats and Republicans alike looked ahead with dread to another summer of urban violence.

Kerner Commission executive director David Ginsburg wrote Johnson in early May 1968 to announce that he had completed all his duties; aside from the publication of a handful of statistical compendia, the work of the commission was done. "I have understood the anguish you must have suffered during these past months and have shared it. I would have given a great deal to be able to hand you a Report which would have brought you joy and satisfaction."[5]

There had been little of either in the spring of 1968. As one historian has astutely observed of the denouement of the Kerner Commission episode, "Johnson found himself in the end . . . in the worst of all possible political worlds, absorbing blame from foes for proposing the commission and from friends for not endorsing its conclusions."[6] For a politician addicted to consensus, the fallout from the Kerner Commission Report was one more example of how that common sense of purpose in the summer of 1965 had all but evaporated by the spring of 1968. The Kerner Commission's reluctance to lavish praise on the president left LBJ feeling even more besieged in a year that had begun with television anchorman Walter Cronkite editorializing against the Vietnam War and fuming off the air against the backdrop of the Tet offensive: "What the hell is going on? . . . I thought we were *winning* this war!"[7]

In the grim aftermath of King's death—and soon thereafter a second Kennedy assassination—the lame-duck president's tenure as master of the legislative process was effectively at an end, as the chaos of the election year continued to mount. There would be no more talk of "leapfrogging the movement" or getting "ahead of the trends." The quintessential political player had taken himself out of the game.

In Mississippi, there had been multiple tremors, but had the iceberg of race relations really cracked open? In late June 1967, more than a year after Aubrey James Norvell had blasted him with a shotgun, James Meredith had set out to retrace much of the route of the preceding summer's "March against Fear." "I want to show Mississippi Negroes that fear can be eliminated," he said, in explaining his action. Governor Paul Johnson, nearing the end of his tenure in office, was anxious to avoid any incident, given Meredith's notoriety. The Mississippi State Highway Patrol and the omnipresent but typically ineffectual FBI monitored the eccentric activist's progress accordingly. But aside from small groups of curious onlookers—some whites jokingly requested Meredith's autograph and some blacks were less than warm in their welcome—the man who a half-decade earlier had broken the color bar at Ole Miss proceeded unmolested.

Eleven days and 162 miles later, he concluded his largely solitary pilgrimage in Canton, scene of the brutal attacks by Mississippi lawmen the preceding summer. "We made it," he said, as he rested on the Madison County courthouse lawn and then briefly addressed a crowd of about fifty: "The last 11 days have shown . . . that the state and the local police officers, if they choose to, can afford protection to Negroes." Writing in the New York Times, Walter Rugaber offered a different explanation for Meredith's safe passage through the state, suggesting "that most white segregationists had simply lost interest."[8]

The willingness of some white Mississippians to police the color line with deadly force, however, was far from exhausted in 1967. Wharlest Jackson, of Natchez, Mississippi, was not as lucky as James Meredith. On February 27, four months before Meredith set out on his second march, Jackson—an African American Korean War veteran, veteran NAACP activist, husband, and father of five—had pulled his pickup truck out of a space in the parking lot of the Armstrong Tire and Rubber Company where he worked. He had recently been promoted at the Natchez tire plant to a job that no nonwhite had ever before held, and if the New York Times had not taken notice of this small story hinting at a new fluidity in the Deep South's economic order, somebody else had.

As he drove away, a powerful bomb detonated in the truck engine, tearing the vehicle apart in a spectacular explosion and killing him instantly. Among the pallbearers carrying Wharlest Jackson's flag-draped coffin was George Metcalfe, president of the local NAACP, who had been severely wounded in a similar car bombing attack in the late summer of 1965.[9] NAACP executive director Roy Wilkins quickly traveled to Natchez, met with local white officials, and praised them publicly for keeping local African Americans apprised of the status of the murder investigation. "Things have changed in Natchez and throughout the state of Mississippi," he proclaimed, arguing that moderation and progress were "becoming noticeable in the rural areas of Mississippi." "These killings are the tail end, we believe," the increasingly isolated acts of "diehards."[10]

Mississippi governor Paul Johnson sang in the same key. The politician who had once smirked and winked in commenting three years earlier on the disappearance of the "Mississippi Three" during Freedom Summer labeled the 1967 murder of Wharlest Jackson an "act of savagery which stains the honor of our state." "Americans have a particular loathing for assassins," he averred, and "Mississippians look with scorn and contempt and disgust upon the repulsive deeds of cowards who hide in darkness to violate the law of God and of all decent men."[11]

The world was changing—for the white men who had killed black Mississippians like Emmett Till, Herbert Lee, Medgar Evers, Lewis Allen, James Chaney, and Wharlest Jackson, and for the many more whites who had allowed those martyrs to go to their graves unmourned. Paul Johnson's rhetoric in condemning Wharlest Jackson's killers seems a watershed when measured against the tragic baseline of Mississippi's race relations. Like many white politicians across the South in a period where the most naked rhetorical forms of race-baiting were increasingly viewed as beyond the pale, he had his finger in the political wind and was modulating his responses accordingly, at least when they were captured for television. Beyond the camera's eye, he showed little evidence of contrition for his state's violent past. Repentance, too often, was for public consumption only.[12]

The mercurial gauge of Mississippi change came in 1968 at the tumultuous Democratic National Convention in Chicago. Black Mississippians and their white allies—including a growing group of white moderates from the Magnolia State—renewed the battle begun four years earlier in Atlantic City. This time the credentials committee and Democratic presidential nominee Hubert Humphrey offered "half a loaf," agreeing to divide the state delegation's seating allotment evenly between lily-white "Regulars" (widely predicted to favor

Richard Nixon in the fall election) and the integrated delegation billing itself as "Loyalist" Democrats.

Not able to reach Charles Evers and Fannie Lou Hamer in Mississippi, Loyalists Aaron "Doc" Henry—the perennial NAACP activist—and newly elected black state representative Robert Clark conferred over whether to accept the compromise offer. Many veterans of the Mississippi struggle felt that it failed to live up to commitments the national party had made in 1964 in promising to bar segregated southern delegations from future conventions. "Aaron, I've played some big ballgames," Clark remembered saying. "I've lost some and I've won some. . . . This is a big one. Now let's go for all of it."

As a frustrated Humphrey and a succession of high-ranking Democratic officials, including the governor of Iowa, who served as Credentials Committee chairman, berated Henry for his obstinacy in rejecting the compromise, the venerable civil rights activist stuck to his nonaccommodationist position. "And then we sat there in the room and we waited. And directly Millie Jeffrey came back shouting and ran in the door and jumped and hugged us and said we had won it," Henry recalled, chuckling. "And we had [all] been seated."[13] Inside the convention hall, Mississippians claimed their seats, "black and white together," their leap of faith in democracy seemingly rewarded. But outside the convention hall, democracy was in full retreat. "The whole world [was] watching" as Mayor Daley's "police riot" raged unchecked against impassioned antiwar protesters.

For those black and white Mississippians aligning themselves with the new Democratic coalition—even as many more defiant white erstwhile Democrats began their flight into the Republican Party—the outcome in Chicago was sweet vindication. The "whole ballgame" of Robert Clark and Aaron Henry was indeed a dramatic improvement over the two-seat offer MFDP delegates had rejected as a betrayal of government promises amid much rancor in Atlantic City four years before.

Chicago's 1968 sequel to that earlier, and better-known, battle between rival Mississippi delegations was in fact more problematic than Aaron Henry's euphoric victory narrative would indicate. The Loyalists in Chicago seemed to be a direct answer to Bayard Rustin's 1965 call for blacks to move "from protest to politics" by entering coalitions with liberal-minded whites. But many longtime MFDP activists saw Henry's NAACP-dominated "Loyalists" as very similar to the largely middle-class biracial MAP coalition that had largely supplanted CDGM in the struggle for control of Head Start funding in 1966 and 1967.

Many MFDP veterans still seeking to fulfill an undiluted vision of grassroots political empowerment for African American Mississippians sensed correctly that they would not be equal partners in the new coalition alliance. Their time on the stage of Mississippi politics had been steadily running out, and mainstream American politics had never been willing to accord them a seat at the table. Following their rejection of the 1964 Atlantic City "back of the bus" offer, MFDP activists had sought to unseat the segregationist state congressional delegation in Washington, D.C., the following year. Although they were not without allies on Capitol Hill, MFDP had lost its bid. Congress had joined ranks in support of tradition and incumbency, rejecting the MFDP's challenge by a vote of 228 to 143. When reporters sought a response from a weeping Fannie Lou Hamer, she had answered: "I'm not crying for myself alone. . . . I'm crying for America. Because it's later than you think."[14]

Looking back on the violent chronology of the period from 1965 to 1968—the assassinations, the murders, the riots, the political betrayals, the unfinished revolution of economic opportunity—in Washington, D.C., in Mississippi, in hundreds of cities across America, it is tempting to take up the tragic narrative once again, to fall back upon clichés of history repeating itself. Few captured the feeling of bitter déjà vu more elegiacally than Kenneth B. Clark. In his testimony before the National Advisory Commission on Civil Disorders, later reproduced in the concluding passages of the Kerner Commission Report, Clark offered a history lesson to the American public, having revisited the reports of earlier "riot commissions":

> I read that report . . . of the 1919 riot in Chicago, and it is as if I were reading the report of the investigating committee on the Harlem riot of '35, the report of the investigating committee on the Harlem riot of '43, the report of the McCone Commission on the Watts riot.
>
> I must again in candor say to you members of this Commission—it is a kind of Alice in Wonderland—with the same picture re-shown over and over again, the same analysis, the same recommendations, and the same inaction.[15]

But to suggest that the actors of the period from 1965 to 1968 were mere participants, witting or not, in a tragedy worthy of Sophocles or Shakespeare or in an absurdist universe as imagined by Lewis Carroll—moving inexorably toward a bleak final act or trapped in a surreal journey "through the looking glass"—is to discount the experiences and perspectives of both local people and often well-intentioned members of the executive branch. Such a narrative diminishes the importance of the choices these women and men made and the enormous risks they took.

The years 1965 to 1968 illuminate both abortive advances and disorganized retreats in the "next and more profound stage of the battle for civil rights" declared by Johnson at Howard University. Historians examining the civil rights era from the vantage point of the nation's center have properly emphasized the tremendous power the federal government could wield, for good or ill, in the ongoing struggle for racial equality. But that perspective often fails to account for the growing impact of grassroots mobilization by those lobbying for civil rights reforms and a greater measure of economic equality in these years.

Social historians examining the civil rights movement—or, as is now generally recognized, movements—at the local and state levels have documented their great diversity, occasional fragmentation, and multifaceted nature, reshaping our understandings of grassroots social protest. More recent studies have shown how local civil rights coalitions could be fractured from within by ideological, class, and occasionally gender-driven tensions, even as these protest movements faced external harassment by local, state, and federal authorities who seldom hesitated to exploit such divisions. If they were sometimes divided, civil rights activists nevertheless made a place for themselves within the political landscape of the 1960s.

Many historians have failed to recognize the same plurality of actors and motivations in their treatment of "the state." The federal government in particular often seems a monolith carved in bas-relief against the complex landscape of civil rights groups. White House debates in the years between 1965 and 1968 clearly show that similar fractures divided federal interests. And the irregular pattern of interactions between civil rights movements and the federal government did not abruptly lose its intricacy as the decade reached what many have viewed as its turning point in 1965. If anything, the relationships became even more complex in the chaotic interval until Johnson's decision not to seek reelection in the spring of 1968.

In the long-reigning periodization of 1954 to 1965, what might be termed the civil rights "metanarrative," some of the most insightful work is beginning to synthesize top-down and bottom-up perspectives on the same issues and events. At the same time, recent scholars have challenged that periodization itself in seeking the roots and origins of the modern civil rights movement in black and white activism in the decades preceding the Supreme Court's 1954 *Brown v. Board of Education* school desegregation decision.[16] The ongoing process of interaction in the turbulent period immediately following passage of the Voting Rights Act in 1965, what might be called the neglected years of the civil rights era, has attracted far less historical scrutiny.

Between the summer of 1965 and the early spring of 1968, policymakers within the Johnson administration struggled to reach a consensus on how best to be proactive in waging the "next and more profound battle for civil rights" and economic results, announced in the Howard speech. The result was a period of policy drift, with the White House and officials in the civil rights–related bureaucratic line agencies often operating in reactive mode, even as policymakers spoke of the desirability of "leapfrogging" the movement and setting the civil rights agenda.

During the same years, both established civil rights leaders and an increasingly diverse pool of African American grassroots community activists heatedly debated which strategies, tactics, and ideological moorings would best serve black Americans in the aftermath of hard-fought civil rights and voting rights victories. They too were struggling to forge a consensus, and they too fell short of that goal.

Although grassroots politics and "high politics" remained organically interrelated in this period, the administration was extremely reluctant to respond to the ongoing dramatic evolution and expansion of civil rights leadership. Consistent patterns of misperception, miscommunication, and mutual distrust short-circuited potential relationships between the Johnson administration and unfamiliar civil rights advocates.

Members of the Johnson administration were grappling with the possibility of a larger, and from their perspective unconventional, pool of black leaders, even as they consistently failed to take the political risks of reaching out and initiating a dialogue: meaningful, authentic two-way communication. In some ways like awkward high school teenagers, White House emissaries could be seen as tentatively sizing up the prospects of new dance partners, all the while dreading the consequences of asking them to dance.

As the opportunity for authentic two-way communication fell by the wayside, policy drift threatened to become policy paralysis, and concrete White House initiatives dwindled. Although advocates for civil rights and economic justice within the federal government continued to push for change, in the absence of strong executive backing and in an increasingly polarized legislative environment their task was far more daunting.

In part, Johnson's political dilemma grew out of his attempt to mobilize public support for his ambitious civil rights and antipoverty programs. There had always been a vibrant and influential black middle class, albeit a small one. It served as the filter through which the White House defined acceptable black leadership and the basis for the president's African American appointments. And even though change came at glacial speed, the black middle class grew steadily through the 1960s and seemed poised to grow far more rapidly in the future. Such exponential growth would in large part come as the result of black activism, which had pressured the federal government to usher in the civil rights reforms of the decade, with the expansion of affirmative action policies paving the way for additional political and economic gains.[17]

But even the most transcendent of those gains were hard fought and often bypassed millions of black Americans still trapped in poverty and isolation. For all the progress, forty years after Lyndon Johnson's War on Poverty, African Americans were still twice as likely to live in poverty as whites. In any case, emphasizing that improvement in the fortunes of the African American middle class in the closing years of the Johnson administration would hardly have strengthened LBJ's case for dramatic action on behalf of those left behind.

As the Moynihan Report, the Kerner Commission, and a long history of studies done by white-dominated investigatory bodies had shown, it was easy to point to the damage done to black families by bleak economic and social conditions linked to the nation's long history of white supremacy. In calling attention to the adverse circumstances faced by the most truly disadvantaged members of "another nation," however, Johnson ran the risk of strengthening age-old pathological stereotypes about African Americans harbored by whites, both hostile and sympathetic. After 1965, many white Americans came to see the rights revolution as having been completed. For them, hearing LBJ's and others' accounts of drug-infested slums and rampant poverty reinforced their alienation from the black inner-city poor even as it angered many African Americans who resented being subjected to the diagnostic scrutiny of white "experts."

In examining the Johnson administration's attempts to generate proactive policy after the summer of 1965, one essential irony is unavoidable: successive riots dampened the possibilities for fundamental, structural economic reforms, even as they dramatized how vitally necessary such a stepped-up policy crusade was. Along with intelligence gathering, concrete plans for containment of riots that broke out (in the sense of working to minimize loss of life and property destruction), and a patchwork of politically dictated responses like summer employment programs for youth, the administration had begun to appreciate the scale and dimension of the urban crisis *before* the establishment of the Kerner Commission. White House responses to urban crises—even, in some cases, deliberate decisions not to respond—indicate ongoing engagement with civil rights and issues of economic justice.

With every riot, the logic of the Howard University address stressing the desirability of equal results seemed all the more imperative. And yet, with every riot, the range of political possibility seemed to contract. Moreover, with every

Johnson finds himself embattled and paranoid in his closing months in office. © R. Cobb 1967. All rights reserved. Courtesy of Ron Cobb.

troop transport plane that carried anxious soldiers to Vietnam, Lyndon Johnson grew progressively more distracted from the domestic agenda, more embattled overall, and more and more suspicious of criticism, to a degree that bordered on paranoia.

Evaluating the administration's halting responses to five consecutive years of urban unrest—from the Harlem riot of 1964 to the dizzying array of disturbances following the King assassination in the spring of 1968—it is hard to avoid concluding that a "credibility gap" in domestic policy emerged in counterpoint to the yawning distance between rhetoric and reality that characterized the administration's pronouncements on Vietnam over the same interval. Just as many Americans came to view with suspicion the surreal Pentagon mantra of "light at the end of the tunnel" in Southeast Asia and an increasingly skeptical international press corps in Saigon came to ridicule military briefings on enemy kills and body counts as the "5 o'clock follies," black activists and their white allies increasingly perceived a "Great Society" and a "War on Poverty" that "never lived up to [their] promises." Many erstwhile supporters of the president's agenda were keeping track of the growing disconnect between White House words and deeds, and liberal discontents penned an epitaph for the War on Poverty: "Declared but never fought."

Wilbur J. Cohen, assistant secretary of the Department of Health, Education, and Welfare, later warned of the consequences of overselling Johnson's domestic programs and accomplishments, particularly the War on Poverty. Shriver's OEO "tried to do too much at one time," Cohen reasoned. Historian James T. Patterson has argued that this "contrast between promise and performance infuriated some of the poor." As one government official explained sympathetically: "There was the assumption of regularly increased funding. Promises were made that way . . . the result was a trail of broken promises. No wonder everybody got mad and rioted."[18]

White House aides and bureaucrats charged with civil rights duties often operated in an atmosphere of policy confusion, attempting to stay attuned to an increasingly discordant political and ideological soundscape dominated by clashing themes, polarization, and reaction: "Law and order," white backlash, black separatism and cultural nationalism, and competing interpretations of Black Power were only some of the dissonances. The White House's attempts to call the tune inevitably sounded off-key and contrived and its representatives' efforts to dictate meter overbearing.

Striving to maintain consensus, Johnson and other representatives of the federal government might have fared better had they opened themselves up to the rich unpredictability of polyphony. Increasingly, attempts to isolate different elements of the cacophony seemed to administration officials as agonizingly perplexing as how to control the spiraling escalation of the Vietnam War. But, like Ramsey Clark in the long hours of a community meeting with embittered residents of Watts in August 1965, some within the administration were still insistent on *listening*. However timid their efforts at ongoing engagement may appear by our lights, given the political realities of the hour they are worth remembering.

And what of Johnson himself?

The Kerner Commission's verdict of "white racism" had driven a sharp wedge even deeper into the fragile and embattled consensus Johnson had struggled to preserve, with many whites opting for a measure of political revenge for what they perceived as their abandonment by the Democratic Party. George Wallace and Richard Nixon had reaped the political windfall of this growing disaffection.

White House aide Clifford Alexander saw Johnson's pique at the Kerner Commission Report as part of a larger trend in the closing years of his presidency:

As the movement moved on and as the self-esteem of blacks became of greater significance, blacks were not turning around every ten seconds and saying, "Thank you, Mr. President." . . . They were saying, "This is as it ought to be." And I think President Johnson perhaps misinterpreted this as a slap in his face. I think that toward the end of his administration he felt a little put upon by some blacks. He felt, "Since I've done so much!" There's no question in my mind that he did ten times as much as any other president has ever done as far as blacks are concerned. [But I think he felt] that he wasn't getting enough "Thank yous" for it.[19]

Johnson's most ardent supporters were nearly unanimous in their critique of his handling of the National Advisory Commission on Civil Disorders, even as they offered compelling rationalizations for his rebuff of the Kerner Commission Report, rooted in both his pique at not being adequately appreciated and his sense that the report's findings were a fantastic departure from fiscal possibilities and hard political realities.

But in the months and years following Johnson's withdrawal from the political stage, as those who had known him, worked with him, and occasionally fought him sought to make sense of his place in the history of the civil rights era, the verdict of many from across the political and ideological spectrum was surprisingly clear. Roy Wilkins stressed the paradoxical nature of LBJ's relationship to black America in a conversation with Jack Valenti. "It's very strange, isn't it," he told Valenti, "that the bravest and strongest and most compassionate man that the Negro has ever had in this country is Lyndon Johnson? God does move in wondrous ways."[20]

And in the harsh light of Richard Nixon's presidency, the estrangement between civil rights activists and the ex-president further softened. In mid-December 1972, the LBJ Library hosted a symposium that brought together many of the men (and a few women) linked to the civil rights struggles of the 1960s: senior figures like Roy Wilkins, Hubert Humphrey, and Earl Warren, as well as younger individuals—Julian Bond, Barbara Jordan, Vernon E. Jordan, Roy Innes, and Henry Gonzales. In the opening session of the conference, Bond, the former SNCC secretary who had been expelled from the Georgia legislature for his opposition to the Vietnam War, spoke passionately of his admiration for the former president. When the "forces demanded and the mood permitted, for once an activist, human-hearted man had his hands on the levers of power and a vision beyond the next election." Johnson was there when the nation needed him most, said Bond, "and oh, my God, do I wish he was there now."[21]

On the closing night of the two-day symposium, against the advice of his doctor, an ailing Lyndon Johnson traveled the seventy miles from his ranch over icy roads to make one of his last public appearances. As he slowly walked to the podium, it was obvious to everyone in the audience that he was in failing health.

"Of all the records that are housed in this Library," he began, the record of the civil rights struggle "holds for me the most intimate meanings." He readily admitted that his understanding of the special plight of African Americans had changed from the time he began his political career nearly a half-century earlier. And, he confessed, "I'm kind of ashamed of myself that I had six years and couldn't do more."

At one point, in obvious discomfort, he stopped to take one of his nitroglycerine pills, and then he continued. The work was far from done, he told his listeners. "To be black, I believe, to one who is black or brown, is to be proud, is to be worthy, is to be honorable. But to be black in a white society is not to stand on level and equal ground. While the races may stand side by side, whites stand on history's mountain and blacks stand in history's hollow. We must overcome unequal history before we overcome unequal opportunity."[22]

It was an eloquent restatement of the themes he had laid out on a June day at Howard University when history waited and anything seemed possible. As he stepped into the audience, brown, black, and white surrounded him. In the emotional warmth of that December evening, Johnson and his audience embraced their common struggle and put aside their past grievances over political betrayals and the war that had so bitterly divided them.

But those segregated memories too were part of a shared history.

Nothing is inevitable until it happens.

As the Kerner Commission Report had emphasized, "two societies . . . separate and unequal" was a verdict that might yet be appealed. "This deepening racial division is not inevitable. The movement apart can be reversed. Choice is still possible. Our principal task is to define that choice and to press for a national resolution."[23]

Occasionally, in an older public building in the South, one can still see the discoloration on the wooden doors and paneled walls above restrooms and water fountains where the signage of segregation has been removed but the image remains, like a scar. Similarly, Detroit's urban landscape still features physical reminders of the 1967 riot over three decades later, with still-empty lots and burned-out and abandoned buildings marking the urban geography as latter-day ruins.[24]

Looking back at the crowded metaphorical palette of Lyndon Johnson's 1965 Howard University speech, images of violence and disfigurement, echoes of slavery and lynchings, stand out most vividly: Johnson had spoken of "open wounds," of the "scars of centuries." Like the remnants of the signage of segregation, like the abandoned ruins of urban unrest, scar tissue may be the most appropriate metaphor to capture the lingering impact of the misunderstandings that came to fester in the chaotic period from 1965 to 1968.

Those scars are at times livid and angry, at other times cosmetically, clumsily, concealed. Our deepest national wounds may no longer be so fresh, but our segregated memories too often divide us into "two nations," and the scars are still with us. If the "gates of opportunity" appear to be open wider today than ever before in our past, we are nonetheless far from assuring that "all our citizens . . . have the ability to walk through those gates." Even in the midst of profound changes, what Lyndon Johnson hailed as "the next and . . . more profound stage of the battle for civil rights" has yet to be fully joined. But if a "Second Reconstruction" failed to topple the barriers to racial and economic equality in the United States, the unfinished music of the movement still lingers in our collective memory to inspire the efforts of a new generation in a third symphony of reconstruction.

"The nation was watching its two Gemini astronauts whirl through space Friday and thus did not pay much attention to President Johnson's Howard University address on the American Negro problem." So began Douglas Kiker in a piece that appeared in the *New York Herald Tribune* on June 7, 1965, three days after LBJ's Howard address. "But it may be that history will remember that speech as the more important of the two events," the journalist continued, for Howard "marks an important historical turning point in this nation's agonizing attempt to adjust national principles with national realities."[25]

The Gemini module derived its name from the myth of the Dioscuri, the unequal twins who never attempted to outshine each other in leadership. Inseparable, Castor and Pollux have served for ages as an emblem of fraternal affection.[26] In one version of that myth, Zeus places the twins in the sky as a reward for their brotherly love. There they form the constellation Gemini, the morning and evening star.

The Gemini 4 module splashed down safely in the Atlantic Ocean on June 7, 1965, three days after Lyndon Johnson received his honorary degree from Howard University. Today it sits grounded on the lobby floor of the Smithsonian National Air and Space Museum on the Mall in Washington, D.C. Its heat-battered hull is sheathed within a thick layer of Plexiglas to protect it from the curious hands of children—hands of all colors. The stubby capsule holds their attention a brief moment, if at all. They quickly move on, eyes drawn upward by the sleeker shapes of the craft that hang far overhead, pinioned in mid-flight.

Notes

Abbreviations

CRDJA   Steven F. Lawson, ed. *Civil Rights during the Johnson Administration, 1963–1969*, LBJL (microfilm)

LBJ   Lyndon Baines Johnson

LBJL   Lyndon Baines Johnson Presidential Library, Austin, Tex.

MHS   Minnesota Historical Society

Moynihan Report   U.S. Department of Labor, Office of Policy Planning and Research. *The Negro Family: The Case for National Action*. Washington, D.C.: Government Printing Office, 1965.

MSUSC   Mississippi State University Special Collections Department, Mitchell Memorial Library, Starkville

SovCom   Online records of the Mississippi State Sovereignty Commission, Mississippi Department of Archives and History, Jackson

TCSC   Tougaloo College, Lillian Pierce Renbow Room of Special Collections, Zenobia Coleman Library Archives, Jackson, Miss.

USMSC   University of Southern Mississippi, Special Collections, McCain Library and Archives, Hattiesburg

WHCF   White House Central Files

Preface

1. Special Message to the Congress: The American Promise, March 15, 1965, *Public Papers of the Presidents of the United States: Lyndon B. Johnson*, 1:281–87.

2. In retrospect, urban unrest in Harlem and Rochester, New York, in the summer of 1964 sounded the tocsin for the "long, hot summers to come." But few Americans, outside of those in the areas immediately affected, astute media observers, and a small number of local, state, and federal officials with an eye on the difficult conditions faced by African Americans in urban areas, seemed unduly alarmed by urban unrest that summer. See, for example, Norrell, *House I Live In*, 219.

3. Hall, "The Long Civil Rights Movement and the Political Uses of the Past," 1233–63. Three important works establishing the deep roots of the "long civil rights movement" are Egerton, *Speak Now against the Day*; Gilmore, *Defying Dixie*; and Sullivan, *Days of Hope*. For an exceptionally helpful road map of recent historiography challenging the traditional periodization of the civil rights movement, see also Minchin, "Making Best Use of the New

Laws," 669–702. For one of the most eloquent accounts of the post-1965 civil rights era, see Tyson, *Blood Done Sign My Name*.

4. See, for example, Lawson, *Running for Freedom*, xi–xiii; and Lawson's rich collection of essays organized around this theme, *Civil Rights Crossroads*.

5. Susan Youngblood Ashmore's *Carry It On* similarly helps to transform our understanding of the legacy of the linked struggles for civil rights and economic justice in Alabama. Both she and Frye Gaillard, in *Cradle of Freedom*, extend the timeline of movement activity in that state beyond the familiar battles of Montgomery, Birmingham, and Selma as they craft riveting narratives encompassing the post-1965 Alabama chronology.

6. *Report of the National Advisory Commission on Civil Disorders* (Kerner Commission), 1.

Chapter One

1. See *New York Times*, June 3 and 4, 1965; and *Ebony*, June 1965. In the article in *Ebony*, a Pentagon source confirmed that Dwight had lost any realistic chance of promotion in the astronaut training program when he "bucked the system" by complaining.

2. *Washington Post*, June 4, 1965; *Ebony*, September 1965; Fairclough, *Race and Democracy*, 364–69.

3. *Time*, June 11, 1965; *Newsweek*, June 14, 1965; *Washington Post*, June 7, 1965; *New York Times*, June 4, 1965.

4. On June 3, Johnson pledged the withdrawal of all remaining U.S. Marines from the Dominican Republic. *New York Times*, June 4, 1965; *Washington Post*, June 2, 1965; Dallek, *Flawed Giant*, 262–68.

5. Branch, *At Canaan's Edge*, 230–31.

6. Journalists' estimates of the crowd size varied widely, from the *New York Times*' 5,000 to the *Washington Post*'s 10,000, to the *New York Herald Tribune*'s 14,000. Most sources place the size of the audience at 10,000 or higher.

7. *Public Papers of the Presidents of the United States: Lyndon B. Johnson*, 2:635–40. All subsequent quotes from the Howard speech are from the *Public Papers*. See also Lyndon Baines Johnson, *Vantage Point*, 166. The Howard University speech is discussed or at least briefly mentioned in virtually all the major biographies of Lyndon Johnson, in the memoirs of other political actors and activists during the period, and in dozens of monographic works on the civil rights era. See, for example, Califano, *Triumph and Tragedy*, 56–57; Dallek, *Flawed Giant*, 221–22; Hamilton and Hamilton, *Dual Agenda*, 137; Herbers, *Lost Priority*, 42–45; Walter A. Jackson, *Gunnar Myrdal and America's Conscience*, 297; Lawson, *In Pursuit of Power*, 24; Lemann, *Promised Land*, 171; Moynihan, *Miles to Go*, 186; Scott, "Politics of Pathology," 81–105; and Southern, *Gunnar Myrdal and Black-White Relations*, 258. Several works offer more in-depth treatment, including Branch, *At Canaan's Edge*, 230–34; Gareth Davies, *From Opportunity to Entitlement*, 62–74; Goodwin, *Remembering America*, 342–48; Hugh Davis Graham, *Civil Rights Era*, 174, 511; Moynihan, "The President and the Negro," 31–45; and Rainwater and Yancey, *Moynihan Report and the Politics of Controversy*, 1–7, 32 (the entire Moynihan Report is reprinted here).

8. Poinsett, *Walking with Presidents*, 152.

9. Harry McPherson interview, March 24, 1969, by Thomas H. Baker, tape 2, 7, LBJL; Lawson, *In Pursuit of Power*, 24.

10. The metaphor of the "seamless web," actually an editorial change suggested by White House aide Horace Busby from an earlier Goodwin draft's "senseless web," echoed Daniel Patrick Moynihan's discussion of a "tangle of pathologies." That charged phrase, often quoted out of context, stirred significant controversy in later months, after the release of the Moynihan Report.

11. Harry McPherson interview, March 24, 1969, by Thomas H. Baker, tape 1, 9, LBJL; Goodwin, *Remembering America*, 343. See also Lawson, "Civil Rights," 110; and Lawson, *In Pursuit of Power*, 24.

12. Tom Wicker, "News Analysis," *New York Times*, June 7, 1965; Goodwin, *Remembering America*, 346–47; *New York Times*, June 5, 1965.

13. It appears that Goodwin derived the metaphor of "another nation" from Benjamin Disraeli, who had posed the dilemma of "two nations" in describing the class divide in Britain in the mid-nineteenth-century political novel *Sybil, or the Two Nations*. Novelist John Dos Passos had also bitterly pronounced, "We are two nations," after the persecution and ultimate executions of the immigrants Sacco and Vanzetti in the 1920s.

14. Taylor Branch offers a moving antiphonal narrative of Kennedy's speech and the Medgar Evers assassination, in Branch, *Parting the Waters*, 823–25.

15. See John 1:5, King James Version Bible. One of Lady Bird Johnson's favorite sayings was, "It is better to light a candle than to curse the darkness," an adage favored by Eleanor Roosevelt as well. See Richard and Betty Hughes interview, 47, LBJL.

16. The Howard speech effectively blindsided many within the executive branch's cabinet-level agencies as well. Most bureaucrats expressed enthusiastic support for the Howard speech, but some privately harbored parochial concerns about what impact this next "battle" might have on their bureaucratic "turf" and felt piqued at not having been given advance warning. Johnson had tackled the shortcomings of "equal opportunity" before. In September of 1962, as vice president, he had delivered a speech in Washington to a meeting of the Commission on the Status of Women and reflected: "The slogan 'Equality of Opportunity' can no longer—and will no longer—serve as a mask for social injustice. We are past that stage of history." Catalog of Johnson quotes related to race prejudice and civil rights legislation, Selected Civil Rights Files of George Reedy, *CRDJA*, Part I, Reel 12, 0308–15.

17. It should be noted that Hugh Davis Graham and, more recently, Gareth Davies have argued that some within the bureaucratic line agencies, or "permanent government," did in effect launch a policy revolution that bore fruit in the Nixon years. Graham, *Civil Rights Era*; Davies, *From Opportunity to Entitlement*.

18. Liberals and their opponents both inside and outside of government conducted heated debates on these questions as early as the Kennedy years, and the vocabulary of policy was dominated by the charged lexicon of "quotas." Hugh Davis Graham, *Civil Rights Era*, 159–61; Hamilton and Hamilton, *Dual Agenda*.

19. Moynihan, *Miles to Go*, 181.

20. Gareth Davies, *From Opportunity to Entitlement*, 55.

21. Dallek, *Flawed Giant*, 190.

22. Hamilton and Hamilton, *Dual Agenda*.

23. Pfeffer, *A. Philip Randolph*, 245–67.

24. Sitkoff, *Struggle for Black Equality*, 92. For an extremely useful statistical compendium and an approach to the terminology of a "politics of rights" and a "politics of resources," see Jaynes and Williams, *A Common Destiny*, 3–32.

25. Rustin, "From Protest to Politics," 263. For the definitive biographical treatment of Rustin, see D'Emilio, *Lost Prophet*. See also Harold A. Nelson, "Whither the Civil Rights Struggle?" *Crisis*, November 1965, 556–57.

26. Rustin, "From Protest to Politics," 270, 268 (emphasis in original).

27. Moynihan Report, 3.

28. Marshall, *Federalism and Civil Rights*.

29. *Public Papers of the Presidents: Lyndon B. Johnson*, 1:281–87.

30. See, for example, Radosh, "From Protest to Black Power," 278–93.

31. Goodwin, *Remembering America*, 334. See also Louis Martin to Marvin Watson, March 16, 1965, WHCF, Louis Martin Name File, box 127, LBJL.

32. Lawson, *Running for Freedom*, x–xii.

33. Speech at Howard Commencement, June 9, 1961, in Statements of LBJ, box 55, LBJL. Kennedy speechwriter Richard Goodwin also played a role in this 1961 speech.

34. Marvin Watson to the President, April 30, 1965, Handwriting File, box 7, LBJL; April–June 1965, Handwriting File, box 7, LBJL.

35. Goodwin, *Remembering America*, 329. See also McPherson, *Political Education*, 139–40, for discussion of how the Cotulla narrative was regularly "summoned up." Johnson's other pat—if no less powerful—story on the harmful effects of prejudice dealt with how Jim Crow customs forced the members of the family of his black cook Zephyr Wright to relieve themselves on the side of the road when traveling between Washington and Texas during Johnson's tenure as vice president because filling station restrooms would not admit them. "The cook of the Vice President of the United States would squat in the road to pee. . . . That's wrong. And there ought to be something to change that." See Dallek, *Flawed Giant*, 113. Historian Randall Woods is particularly insightful in describing the importance of Johnson's early life experiences in shaping his later political commitments. Woods, *LBJ*, 1–69.

36. Goodwin, *Remembering America*, 342–43. A friend of the president told *U.S. News and World Report*: "Lyndon likes to talk out a speech. He likes to have the writer at his elbow at the start. The writer is expected to be within earshot of the President most of the time. The speechwriter will eat and sleep that speech." "Who's Writing LBJ's Speeches," *U.S. News and World Report*, June 28, 1965, 57.

37. In the immediate context of the Howard speech, Goodwin's memoir mentions Moynihan only in passing: "I informed Johnson that I had shown drafts of the speech to Jack Valenti, Bill Moyers, and 'Pat Moynihan of Labor.'" Goodwin, *Remembering America*, 343. Most commentators on the Howard University speech recognize the critical role Moynihan's report played in furnishing statistical evidence and analytical nuance and even in supplying early draft writing. See Lemann, *Promised Land*, 173–74, 382; McPherson, *Political Education*, 339; Morris Abram interview, March 20, 1984, 10–11, LBJL; and Jack Valenti interview,

March 3, 1971, by Joe B. Frantz, 31, LBJL. One compelling explanation for Goodwin's reluctance to recognize Moynihan's role in the origins of the Howard address—aside from the speechwriter's natural proprietary interest as Johnson's "regular alter ego"—is his desire to have Johnson's eloquent statement remain free of the subsequent Moynihan Report controversy.

38. See Rainwater and Yancey, *Moynihan Report and the Politics of Controversy*, 14; Goodwin, *Remembering America*, 258, 343–44; and Herbers, *Lost Priority*, 57.

39. Goodwin, *Remembering America*, 344; Ben Wattenberg interview, November 23, 1968, 14–15, LBJL.

40. Goodwin, *Remembering America*, 258, 344. See also Herbers, *Lost Priority*, 55–56; and Roy Wilkins, *Standing Fast*, 311. Writing from the vantage point of the mid-1980s, Goodwin appended to his account of the phone calls to "check [the speech] out" with civil rights leaders the parenthetic: "Stokely Carmichael, Rap Brown, and Malcolm X were not on my calling list; the establishment hadn't come that far." Goodwin had badly muddled the chronology of the mid-1960s: Malcolm X had been assassinated over three months before the Howard speech, and it seems unlikely that Carmichael and Brown would have shown up on the White House mental map of civil rights leadership as early as the summer of 1965. Goodwin's remark about a White House having a "calling list" is revealing though, and it is probably significant that the list evidently did not include James Farmer of CORE or John Lewis and James Forman of SNCC. See Lawson, "Mixing Moderation with Militancy," 82–116; and Hugh Davis Graham, *Civil Rights Era*, 511.

41. Goodwin, *Remembering America*, 343–44; "Who's Writing LBJ's Speeches," *U.S. News and World Report*, June 28, 1965, 57; Dallek, *Flawed Giant*, 218–19; Rainwater and Yancey, *Moynihan Report and the Politics of Controversy*, 4.

42. Dallek, *Flawed Giant*, ix. Interestingly, the Department of Justice, where so much of civil rights energy had its locus during the Kennedy period and in the transition to Johnson, appears to have been removed from the vetting process for the Howard address. See *New York Amsterdam News*, June 5, 1965.

43. *Newsweek*, June 14, 1965. Friday was generally considered a "slow" news day in Washington; moreover, news generated at the end of the week interfered with preplanned weekend layouts and afforded journalists little time to produce analysis for their newspapers' weekend editions.

Douglas Kiker explicitly noted the nation's preoccupation with the space race in his piece entitled "Johnson Spoke for History," *New York Herald Tribune*, June 6, 1965. Building on this theme of national inattentiveness, historian David W. Southern probably goes too far in his suggestion that "the nation turned a deaf ear to the president's plea at Howard University." Southern, *Gunnar Myrdal and Black-White Relations*, 258. Many commentators "rediscovered" the speech when they began to view it against the context of later events like the Watts riot and the Moynihan Report.

44. Marquis Childs, "Two Nations," *Washington Post*, June 9, 1965. See also Kearns, *Lyndon Johnson and the American Dream*. For a sampling of both original reporting and variations in wire coverage of the speech, see *Atlanta Constitution, Baltimore Afro-American, Carolina (Durham, N.C.) Times, Chicago Tribune, Christian Science Monitor, Columbia*

(S.C.) *State, Times* (London), *Memphis Commercial Appeal, New Orleans Times-Picayune, New York Amsterdam News, New York Herald Tribune, New York Times, Le Monde* (Paris), *Washington Post, Washington Star, Wall Street Journal, America, Crisis, Ebony, Economist, Nation, National Review, Newsweek, Time,* and *U.S. News and World Report.*

45. Tom Wicker, "News Analysis," *New York Times,* June 5 and 7, 1965; Hamilton and Hamilton, *Dual Agenda,* 135.

46. *New York Times,* June 6, 1965.

47. *New York Herald Tribune,* June 5, 1965; Kiker, "Johnson Spoke for History," *New York Herald Tribune,* June 6, 1965.

48. In the week following the Howard speech, Johnson received only 139 letters, 4 cards, and 5 telegrams deemed related to civil rights by the White House mail staff; by contrast, in the same week he received approximately 500 letters on the Dominican crisis, approximately 1,000 pieces of mail on Vietnam, and more than 1,000 letters opposing legislation regulating firearms, the product of a letter-writing campaign. January 1965–August 1965, Mail Summaries, LBJL.

49. Mrs. Oscar D. Stern to the President, June 4, 1965, WHCF, Gen SP 3–93, box 172, LBJL. See, especially, Lee White to Roy Wilkins, June 7, 1965, WHCF, Roy Wilkins Name File, box 312, LBJL; Martin Luther King Jr., Telegram to the President, June 7, 1965, WHCF, Martin Luther King Jr. Name File, box 144, LBJL; A. Philip Randolph Telegram to the President, June 8, 1965, WHCF, Gen SP 3–93, box 172, LBJL; Dorothy Height to the President, June 10, 1965, WHCF, Ex HU2–ST24, box 27, LBJL; Lyndon Johnson to Roy Wilkins, June 28, 1965, WHCF, Ex HU2, box 3, LBJL; and Lyndon Johnson to James Farmer, "night letter," June 29, 1965, WHCF, Ex HU2, box 3, LBJL.

50. Charlotte Webb to the President, June 24, 1965, WHCF, Gen SP 3–93, box 172, LBJL.

51. J. J. McGowan to the President, June 9, 1965, WHCF, Gen SP 3–93, box 172, LBJL; Ernest C. Arnold to the President, June 12, 1965, WHCF, Gen SP 3–93, box 172, LBJL (original spelling retained).

52. Kenneth McFarland to the President, June 5, 1965, Gen SP 3–93, box 172, LBJL. Such concerns, while common among conservative intellectuals, were shared by liberals, including Daniel Bell and Kyle Haselden, managing editor of *Christian Century.* Writing in the *New York Times Magazine* in the fall of 1963, just weeks after the famous March on Washington for Jobs and Freedom, Haselden had argued that "compensation for Negroes is a subtle but pernicious form of racism. It requires that men be dealt with by society on the basis of race and color rather than on the basis of their humanity." Hamilton and Hamilton, *Dual Agenda,* 132.

53. David Lawrence, "President Johnson's Pro-Negro Speech," *New York Herald Tribune,* June 7, 1965.

54. The African American *Carolina (Durham, N.C.) Times,* on June 12, 1965, was one of the few papers that did take note: "It is significant that Vice President Humphrey in a commencement address at the University of Maryland, only a few miles away, was also calling for equal rights and opportunities for all Americans."

55. Herbers, *Lost Priority,* xiv–xvi. For one of the more detailed and well-crafted narratives

in this tradition, see Matusow, *Unraveling of America*. Daryl Michael Scott has written, "In less than six months [following the Howard speech], Johnson's initiative was all but dead." Scott, "Politics of Pathology," 81. For similar analyses, see Moynihan, "The President and the Negro," 31–45; and Moynihan, *Miles to Go*, 186–88.

56. Goodwin, *Remembering America*, 343–44, 336. The President's Howard "summons . . . was doomed by the actions of the very man who had issued it," Goodwin concluded. See also Eric Sevareid script, March 12, 1965, Legislative Background, Voting Rights Act of 1965, Drafting of Voting Rights Message/Activities in Alabama, box 1, LBJL.

57. Matusow, *Unraveling of America*, 196.

58. Lemann, *Promised Land*, 171–72. Journalist John Herbers described "many events coming at once, like scores of streams converging to form a mighty flood." Herbers, *Lost Priority*, 48. In his memoir, *Remembering America*, having finished his treatment of the Howard speech, Richard Goodwin, with virtually no transition, launched into his account of Johnson's "digging the ditch" in Vietnam. Goodwin saw 1965 as the "stress point" that neatly split the president from his beloved Great Society: "For in the single year of 1965—exactly one hundred years after Appomattox—Lyndon Johnson reached the height of his leadership and set in motion the process of decline." Goodwin, *Remembering America*, 343, 349. It is worth noting that some of the best biographies of major actors in this period manage to break out of the flattened chronological restraints of the tragic narrative approach, as do a number of state and local case studies. Important examples include Ashmore, *Carry It On*; Dan T. Carter, *The Politics of Rage*; Chafe, *Civilities and Civil Rights*; Crespino, *In Search of Another Country*; Crosby, *A Little Taste of Freedom*; Dittmer, *Local People*; Fairclough, *Race and Democracy*; Frederick, *Stand Up for Alabama*; Gaillard, *Cradle of Freedom*; Jackson, *From Civil Rights to Human Rights*; Lee, *For Freedom's Sake*; Moye, *Let the People Decide*; Payne, *I've Got the Light of Freedom*; and Tyson, *Radio Free Dixie*.

59. Robert J. Norrell, "One Thing We Did Right: Reflections on the Movement," in Robinson and Sullivan, *New Directions in Civil Rights Studies*, 72–73. See also Roberts and Klibanoff, *The Race Beat*.

60. Gareth Davies, *From Opportunity to Entitlement*, 72–73.

61. Fairclough, *Race and Democracy*, 364–69; *Ebony*, September 1965; *Economist*, June 12, 1965. See also Tyson, "Robert F. Williams, 'Black Power,' and the Roots of the African American Freedom Struggle," 540–71; Tyson, *Radio Free Dixie*; Wendt, *Spirit and the Shotgun*; and Hill, *Deacons for Defense*. Nicholas Lemann and John Herbers have demonstrated that even as an increasingly fractured civil rights coalition worked to preserve a public display of unity in the Selma to Montgomery March, major civil rights leaders were widely discussing the necessity of "moving North." Lemann has also perceptively noted that with the Howard speech in June 1965 "Johnson moved rhetorically North." Lemann, *Promised Land*, 171; Herbers, *Lost Priority*, 14–15.

62. Goodwin, *Remembering America*, 345; *Baltimore Afro-American*, June 12, 1965; *Washington Post*, June 5, 1965; *New York Herald Tribune*, June 6, 1965.

63. Herbers, *Lost Priority*, 15. The Lincoln imagery also made its way into two letters sent to Johnson soon after Howard. Letter writer Dave Herring remarked that "your actions and words have put you, in my opinion, above the plane enjoyed by Abraham Lincoln when he

made his second inaugural address." At the opposite pole, J. J. McGowan warned Johnson, "You are not making yourself into another Lincoln. You are simply being used." Dave Herring to the President, June 22, 1965, WHCF, Gen SP 3–93, box 172, LBJL; J. J. McGowan to the President, June 9, 1965, WHCF, Gen SP 3–93, box 172, LBJL. Joseph Califano also makes the Lincoln comparison in describing the subsequent signing ceremony of the Voting Rights Act on August 6, 1965. Califano, *Triumph and Tragedy*, 57–58.

64. *Washington Post*, June 5, 1965.

Chapter Two

1. Portions of this chapter appeared in David C. Carter, "Romper Lobbies and Coloring Lessons."

2. OEO Department of Public Affairs Press Release, February 14, 1965, WHCF, Gen WE9-1, November 22, 1963–July 16, 1965, box 46, LBJL; Vinovskis, *Origins of Head Start*.

3. Lemann, *Promised Land*, 323; interview excerpt with unnamed mother of CDGM preschoolers, in Coles, "Rural Upheaval," 113 (emphasis in original).

4. Dittmer, *Local People*, 368; Lawrence Guyot interview, tape recording; Daniel Perlstein, "Minds Stayed on Freedom," 249–77; Daniel Perlstein, "Teaching Freedom," 297–324.

5. Charlie Cobb, a Howard University student who played a central role in envisioning the Freedom Schools, quoted in Payne, *I've Got the Light of Freedom*, 302.

6. Ibid., 303.

7. Marvin Hoffman and John Mudd, "The New Plantations," *Nation*, October 24, 1966, 413; Lawrence Guyot interview, tape recording.

8. *The Movement* 2, no. 3 (March 1966): 7, in Carson, *The Movement: 1964–1970*.

9. Mary Holmes Junior College, which had fewer than 500 students, was almost 200 miles from the site of most of the CDGM centers. Accordingly, the planners of the summer Head Start program used the abandoned Mt. Beulah College campus as the central headquarters for the new antipoverty agency. CDGM sympathizer Kenneth Dean described the use of third-party granting agencies such as Mary Holmes as "a loophole and a way to . . . circumvent the governor's office or legislature." Kenneth Dean interview, June 9, 1992, by Betsy Nash, 11, MSUSC.

John Dittmer's *Local People* describes Brown University president Barnaby Keeney's complicated and often secretive role in connecting Tougaloo with lucrative sources of foundation support and also demonstrates that the price of playing little brother to an elite institutional heavyweight like Brown was a reduction in Tougaloo's autonomy. Along with the short-circuiting of the relationship with CDGM and a move away from affiliating with civil rights activist Bob Moses's Delta literacy project, Keeney was instrumental in the ouster of the college's white president, Daniel Beittel, under whose leadership many Tougaloo students like Anne Moody had felt emboldened to play leading roles in Jackson's and the state's civil rights struggle. See Dittmer, *Local People*, 234–36.

10. Polly Greenberg, *Devil Has Slippery Shoes*, 65.

11. Interview excerpt with "Mr. Peter," in Coles, "Rural Upheaval," 108; Kenneth Dean interview, May 21, 2008, by author, author's notes; Lawrence Guyot interview, tape recording.

12. *New York Times*, January 22, 1964.

13. Cagin and Dray, *We Are Not Afraid*, 356–57.

14. Dittmer, *Local People*, 382–84. See also *The Movement* 3, no. 9 (September 1967): 9, in Carson, *The Movement: 1964–1970*, for another version of Paul Johnson's quote.

15. Governor Paul Johnson to Sargent Shriver, June 29, 1965, WHCF, Gen WE9-1, November 22, 1963–July 16, 1965, box 46, LBJL.

16. Jeff Woods, *Black Struggle, Red Scare*, 85–111. As Yasuhiro Katagiri notes in his history of the commission, from its earliest founding it sought to achieve respectability by emphasizing race-neutral language of "sovereignty" and states' rights. Nowhere in the establishing legislation were the words "segregation" or "integration" used. Katagiri, *Mississippi State Sovereignty Commission*, 6.

17. SovCom document 2-21-2-7-1-1-1.

18. Paul Hendrickson, "Unsealing Mississippi's Past," *Washington Post Magazine*, May 9, 1999, W-8. The files themselves are now available at the Mississippi Department of Archives and History and online through the MDAH Digital Collection.

19. Erle Johnston Jr. to Herman Glazier, July 12, 1965, SovCom document 6-45-1-14-1-1-1; Crespino, *In Search of Another Country*, 134; Dittmer, *Local People*, 371. The Mississippi State Sovereignty Commission had a history of using informants to spy on civil rights activities dating back to its formation in 1956, an effort that was increased in the mid-1960s. Katagiri, *Mississippi State Sovereignty Commission*, 36–63, 140–75.

20. Christopher Jencks, "Accommodating Whites: A New Look at Mississippi," *New Republic*, April 16, 1966, 19; William Spell interview, 38, MSUSC.

21. Kenneth Dean interview, June 9, 1992, by Betsy Nash, 15–16, MSUSC.

22. Ibid., 17; Kenneth Dean interview, May 21, 2008, by author, author's notes; Lawrence Guyot interview, tape recording; Newman, *Divine Agitators*; Findlay, *Church People in the Struggle*; Findlay, "Mainline Churches and Head Start in Mississippi," 237–50; Carson, *In Struggle*, 172–73.

23. SovCom document 2-152-0-18-3-1-1; *Jackson Daily News* editorial, quoted in Dittmer, *Local People*, 370–71.

24. Andrew Kopkind, "Bureaucracy's Long Arm: Too Heady a Start in Mississippi?" *New Republic*, August 21, 1965, 21.

25. Schulman, *From Cotton Belt to Sunbelt*, 189–90; Lemann, *Promised Land*, 326. See also R. A. Coulter to Bill Moyers, February 18, 1966, WHCF, Gen WE9-1, box 46, LBJL; and Polly Greenberg, *Devil Has Slippery Shoes*, 623.

26. Crespino, *In Search of Another Country*, 102–3.

27. Polly Greenberg, *Devil Has Slippery Shoes*, 266 (emphasis in original); Dittmer, *Local People*, 371–73; Kenneth Dean interview, May 21, 2008, by author, author's notes; Lawrence Guyot interview, tape recording.

28. Cobb, *Most Southern Place on Earth*, 253–76; Lawrence Guyot interview, tape recording.

29. Kenneth Dean interview, June 9, 1992, by Betsy Nash, 25–26, MSUSC; Andrew Kopkind, "Bureaucracy's Long Arm: Too Heady a Start in Mississippi?" *New Republic*, August 21, 1965, 20–21; "Given a Chance," episode 2 of *America's War on Poverty*, produced and directed

by Dante J. James, Blackside Productions, 1995, videocassette; Citizens' Board of Inquiry, "Final Report on the Child Development Group of Mississippi," submitted to the Executive Committee of the Citizens' Crusade against Poverty," 15, WHCF, Gen WE9, October 14, 1966–November 1, 1966, box 41, LBJL.

30. O'Reilly, *Racial Matters*, 178, 247.

31. Cobb, *Most Southern Place on Earth*, 217.

32. Ibid., 270–71.

33. Rev. M. L. Young, president, Mutual Association of Colored People, "Letter to the Editor," unidentified clipping attached to Paul Johnson to Sargent Shriver, June 29, 1965, WHCF, Gen WE9-1, November 22, 1963–July 16, 1965, box 46, LBJL.

34. Payne, *I've Got the Light of Freedom*, 342–43; Matusow, *Unraveling of America*, 253.

35. Erle Johnston Jr., Memorandum for File, September 23, 1965, in Paul Johnson Family Papers, Folder 2, Sovereignty Commission, September 1965, box 138, USMSC.

36. Kenneth Dean interview, June 9, 1992, by Betsy Nash, 9, MSUSC; Kenneth Dean interview, May 21, 2008, by author, author's notes.

37. Patricia Derian interview, MSUSC; Erle Johnston interview, July 30, 1980, by Orley B. Caudill, 95–96, USMSC; Johnston, *Mississippi's Defiant Years*, 178–83.

38. Erle Johnston Jr., File Memorandum, July 1, 1965, SovCom document 6-45-1-9-1-1-1; O'Reilly, *Nixon's Piano*, 267; Lemann, *Promised Land*, 325.

39. "Mississippi Counterattacks the War on Poverty," in *The Movement* 1, no. 10 (October 1965): 6, in Carson, *The Movement: 1964–1970*; Larold K. Schulz, "The CDGM Story," *Christianity and Crisis* 26 (January 23, 1967): 317.

40. For a detailed list of OEO criticisms of these alleged "irregularities" and "deficiencies," see "CDGM Situation Report," September 27, 1966, attached to George D. McCarthy to Edwin C. Kruse, November 9, 1966, WHCF, Gen WE9-1, box 47, LBJL.

41. Andrew Kopkind, "Bureaucracy's Long Arm: Too Heady a Start in Mississippi?" *New Republic*, August 21, 1965, 22; Patricia Derian interview, 17–18, MSUSC; Dittmer, *Local People*, 374; Lawrence Guyot interview, tape recording.

42. Dittmer, *Local People*, 374; William F. Haddad, "Mr. Shriver and the Savage Politics of Poverty," *Harper's Magazine*, December 1965, 49.

43. "Given a Chance," episode 2 of *America's War on Poverty*, Blackside Productions; Marvin Hoffman and John Mudd, "The New Plantations," *Nation*, October 24, 1966, 414.

44. Lawrence Guyot interview, tape recording. The Justice Department did undertake prosecutions in several instances, but the amount of legal legwork in bringing such a case to trial and the improbability of securing a guilty verdict militated against most of these attempts. And black Mississippians remained unconvinced of the utility of this ex post facto "protection" from white violence. Navasky, *Kennedy Justice*, 108–275; Lawson, *In Pursuit of Power*; Powledge, *Free at Last*, 294–305.

45. For riveting accounts of how the MFDP challenge to the Mississippi regulars at the Atlantic City convention upset Johnson's planned "coronation," see Dittmer, *Local People*, 272–302; Lewis, *Walking with the Wind*, 274–84; and Lawson, *Black Ballots*, 302–6. For use of the phrase "trickle-down democracy," see Chester Bowles speech at Lincoln University, February 15, 1963, Selected Civil Rights Files of George Reedy, *CRDJA*, Part I, Reel 12, 0298–307.

46. Lawrence Guyot interview, tape recording.

47. Powledge, *Free at Last*, 601. James Farmer interview, July 20, 1971, by Paige E. Mulhollan, 5–7, LBJL.

48. Pat Watters, "Mississippi: Children and Politics," *Dissent* 14 (May–June 1967): 294.

49. *New York Times*, February 12, 1966; Polly Greenberg, *Devil Has Slippery Shoes*, 445–51; Dittmer, *Local People*, 374–75; Payne, *I've Got the Light of Freedom*, 346.

50. Larold K. Schulz, "The CDGM Story," *Christianity and Crisis* 26 (January 23, 1967): 318. For insightful analysis of popular support for the War on Poverty policies and the political opposition tactic of emphasizing accounts of fiscal "mismanagement," a tactic usually championed by congressional Republicans and southern Democrats, see Sundquist, *Politics and Policy*, 150.

51. Polly Greenberg, *Devil Has Slippery Shoes*, 267.

52. Interview excerpt with unnamed mother of CDGM preschoolers, in Coles, "Rural Upheaval," 113 (emphasis in original).

53. Lawrence Guyot interview, tape recording.

Chapter Three

1. In 1965 and 1966 White House aides used the shorthand of "social dynamite" to allude to issues that might fuel black restiveness. Louis Martin to Joseph Califano, September 24, 1965, WHCF, Gen Ex HU2, August 19, 1965–September 24, 1965, box 13, LBJL. The Moynihan Report and the phrase "social dynamite" often turned up in the same sentence in internal White House conversations.

2. John Kenneth Galbraith to the President, June 7, 1965, WHCF, Ex SP 3–93, Pro-Con/A–Z (Howard), box 172, LBJL. Carl Rowan and the U.S. Information Agency arranged for copies to be distributed to African chiefs of state and chiefs of mission in residence in the nation's capital. See WHCF, Confidential File SP 302, box 89, LBJL. Although Galbraith's linking of international Cold War politics with domestic civil rights was explicit, he had the good sense to give the geography of Southeast Asia a wide berth, limiting his analysis to the South American and African continents and not triggering Johnson's neurosis about criticism of his war policies.

3. Jack Valenti to the President, June 21, 1965, WHCF, Ex SP 3–93, Howard University Commencement, June 4, 1965, box 172, LBJL.

4. "The Road to Justice: Three Major Statements on Civil Rights by President Lyndon B. Johnson," Selected Civil Rights Files of Harry McPherson, *CRDJA*, Part I, Reel 11, 0448–75. Calvin Kytle, a white southerner from Georgia who was then serving as acting director of CRS, also urged a formal publication and widespread distribution of the Howard speech. Calvin and Elizabeth Kytle interviews, July 11, July 29, 1997, tape recording. See chapter 7 for additional discussion of Kytle and the CRS.

5. Lyndon Johnson to the Southern Christian Leadership Conference Convention, August 3, 1965, Martin Luther King Jr. Name File, 1965, box 144, LBJL.

6. The language of the Howard speech had read: "Thus it is not enough just to open the gates of opportunity. All our citizens must have the ability to walk through those gates."

7. *Public Papers of the Presidents of the United States: Lyndon B. Johnson*, 2:843.

8. Farmer, *Lay Bare the Heart,* 298–300; Lawson, "Mixing Moderation with Militancy," 86–88, 108–9. Johnson's power to shape Farmer's fortune was further revealed when he worked to sabotage an ambitious literacy program Farmer was spearheading (see chapter 6). James Farmer interview, July 20, 1971, by Paige E. Mulhollan, 4–5, LBJL. See also Miroff, "Presidential Leverage over Social Movements," 12–14.

9. See chapter 1; and Califano, *Triumph and Tragedy,* 58.

10. Louis Martin memo, *CRDJA,* Part I, Ex HU2/MC, Reel 5, 0544–45. Several weeks later, Humphrey proposed a similar solution, calling for a conference of "working delegates" in mid-November to be followed by a one-day conference one to two months later. Humphrey was quite clear about the rationale for the second larger conference; as he envisioned it, it would "involve a broader spectrum of persons, to fill a number of political requests for involvement in the conference." Hubert Humphrey to the President, September 1, 1965, *CRDJA,* Part I, Ex HU2/MC, Reel 5, 0551.

11. Harry McPherson interview, March 24, 1969, by Thomas H. Baker, tape 2, 17, LBJL; Lawson, "Mixing Moderation with Militancy," 83. As other members of the Big Six were cut off from the White House — or chose to cut themselves off — Roy Wilkins's political stock continued to rise. Harry McPherson to the President, May 12, 1966, Selected Civil Rights Files of Harry McPherson, *CRDJA,* Part I, Reel 11, 0034.

12. For references to the "Big Six," see, for example, Lee White to the President, November 16, 1964, Whitney Young Name File, box 41, LBJL; "News Conference, March 18, 1966," Appointment File (Diary Backup), box 31, LBJL. For public relations purposes, Bill Moyers and other administration spokespeople often referred to the Civil Rights Leadership Conference as made up of seven members: Martin Luther King Jr., Roy Wilkins, Whitney M. Young Jr., Floyd McKissick (earlier James Farmer), John Lewis, Dorothy Height, and A. Philip Randolph.

13. Special Message to the Congress: The American Promise, March 15, 1965, *Public Papers of the Presidents of the United States: Lyndon B. Johnson,* 1:281–87.

14. Dallek, *Flawed Giant,* 222–24; Horne, *Fire This Time,* 3. Of the thirty-four deaths, thirty-one were shooting deaths, and police and soldiers of the National Guard shot twenty-three of the thirty-one victims. Gerald Horne lists property damages as nearing the $200 million mark, evidently relying on figures from Sears and McConahay, *Politics of Violence.* Most other contemporary and historical sources place the damage estimate at approximately $35 million. See, for example, *Report of the National Advisory Commission on Civil Disorders* (Kerner Commission).

15. Califano, *Triumph and Tragedy,* 59–64; Randall B. Woods, *LBJ,* 590–91; Kearns, *Lyndon Johnson and the American Dream,* 305.

16. Goodwin, *Remembering America,* 456–57; Califano, *Triumph and Tragedy,* 59–63. See also Dallek, *Flawed Giant,* 223.

17. Between Johnson's historical vision of this period and that of his predecessor, John F. Kennedy, there was a remarkable degree of overlap; both appear to have uncritically accepted the William A. Dunning school of Reconstruction history as a "carnival of Radical misrule," and for both of them the "lessons" of Reconstruction sharply delimited their understandings of the limits of federalism.

18. Califano, *Triumph and Tragedy*, 59–64. A variation on this quote, which was also attributed to Johnson, where the explosive nexus of sex and race in southern history was even more explicit, ran: "Remember the Negroes in Reconstruction who got elected to Congress and then ran into the chamber with bare feet and white women. They were simply not prepared for their responsibility. And we weren't just enough or kind enough to help them prepare. . . . We'll never know how high a price we paid for the unkindness and injustice we've inflicted on people." Kearns, *Lyndon Johnson and the American Dream*, 305. See also O'Reilly, *Nixon's Piano*, 275.

19. Lee White to the President, May 5, 1965, Ex Handwriting File, Folder May 1–15, 1965 (2 of 2), box 7, LBJL.

20. Presumably the very language and overriding focus of the Howard speech on the travails facing another "nation" should have inoculated the president against misunderstanding the "message of Watts," but he was still tempted to personalize the unrest in Los Angeles, viewing it through the lens of loyalty and implicit disloyalty or "betrayal."

21. Quote in Robert Moskin, "The Attorney General of the United States, Nicholas deB[elleville] Katzenbach, Talks about Crime in Our Streets, Racial Violence This Summer, Business and Trust-Busting, Children and Punishment," *Look*, June 1, 1965, 30. See also *New York Amsterdam News*, June 5, 1965.

22. It was a phrase White House staffers appear to have lifted directly from the pages of the nation's major newspapers. For use of the phrase "long, hot summer" before the Watts riot, see, for example, *Christian Science Monitor*, June 8, 1965; *New York Times*, June 5 and 13, 1965; *New York Amsterdam News*, June 5, 1965; and *New York Herald Tribune*, June 5, 1965.

23. O'Reilly, *Racial Matters*, 231.

24. FBI report, September 18, 1964, Office Files of the White House Aides, Bill Moyers, Crime/Delinquency, box 39, LBJL. Two additional disturbances in Seaside, Oregon, and Hampton Beach, New Hampshire, over the Labor Day weekend in early September involved mainly white juveniles.

25. *New York Times*, June 13, 1965.

26. See Roger Wilkins, *A Man's Life*, 163–64. The list of "target cities" reads like a roll call of urban centers that experienced civil disorders in 1964, 1966, 1967, and 1968 and includes New York, Philadelphia, Oakland, Detroit, Cleveland, Gary, Boston, Newark, and Rochester. See John T. Connor, Secretary of Commerce, Memorandum for the President, Commerce Department Progress under the Civil Rights Act of 1964, Ex HU2, April 21, 1965–July 16, 1965, box 3, LBJL. (Chicago experienced a minor riot in the weeks after Watts.) LeRoy Collins stressed the fact that it was in Los Angeles and Chicago—the cities that elected not to participate—"where the most serious trouble of all developed." LeRoy Collins interview, 41, LBJL.

27. Califano, *Triumph and Tragedy*, 64–65. Califano argues compellingly that Johnson had felt "humiliated" as vice president, but that after a honeymoon period, when Johnson treated Humphrey with a degree of sensitivity—his own recent slights at the hands of the Kennedy brothers fresh in his mind—LBJ began to visit similar and even worse indignities on his understudy, forcing the Minnesotan to clear all travel plans ahead of time and virtually every conceivable vice presidential expense through the White House.

28. Statement by the President to the Cabinet, Youth Opportunity Campaign, May 13, 1965, Cabinet Papers, box 3, LBJL; Hubert Humphrey to the President, May 19, 1965, Vice Presidential Files, 1964–68, box 824, Hubert Humphrey Papers, MHS. For a recent biography of Humphrey that emphasizes the vice president's role as head of the Youth Opportunity Campaign, see Thurber, *Politics of Equality*. All items from the Humphrey Papers were generously shared with me by Thurber.

"Employers are being harried night and day by that happy harrier, the Vice President," wrote an editorialist in the *Economist* in mid-June as preface to a more pessimistic assessment: "But this is only a poultice for a wound which will not be healed without determination and realism on the part of both races." *Economist*, June 12, 1965.

29. Less than three weeks after his appointment to chair the PCEO, Humphrey was calling on government officials to address the "summer problems" of youth unemployment and underemployment in the nation's cities. Hubert Humphrey to John Stewart, February 25, 1965, William Connell Papers, box 1, MHS; Hubert Humphrey to the President, Ex FG 440, box 346, LBJL.

Some urban mayors, including powerful Democrat Richard Daley of Chicago, feared they were being set up to take the fall if violence did break out in their urban backyards. Such fears were not totally off the mark, as Hubert Humphrey stressed in a memo to the president that, in meeting with mayors, task force members gave notice of the "heavy responsibility which the mayor and his administration bear in the effort to prevent riots this summer." Hubert Humphrey to the President, June 10, 1965, and LeRoy Collins to the President, April 12, 1965, *CRDJA*, Part I, both in WHCF, Ex FG 155–18, Folders 18 and 18A, box 229, Reel 1, 0277, 0257, LBJL.

30. Sargent Shriver to the President, with attached news clippings, July 20, 1965, WHCF, Ex WE9, June 15, 1965–July 31, 1965, box 26, LBJL.

31. Representatives of the administration and spokespeople for the major civil rights organizations engaged in mutual recriminations after Watts, each claiming that the other party was more at a loss on how to proceed. Although few of these accusations made their way into media coverage during that summer, they suggested a growing gap in perception and increasingly strained communication between the federal government and civil rights activists. David Garrow describes King's sense of dislocation as he visited the scenes of rioting in Harlem in 1964 and Watts in 1965, in *Bearing the Cross*, 342–44, 439–40.

32. Rainwater and Yancey, *Moynihan Report and the Politics of Controversy*, 192.

33. George Reedy to Lyndon Baines Johnson, August 23, 1965. Joseph Califano, Harry McPherson, and Lee White all read the Reedy memo before passing it on to Johnson nearly six months later. Reel 11, *CRDJA*, Part I, Reel 11, 0499–502.

34. Quotes in Rainwater and Yancey, *Moynihan Report and the Politics of Controversy*, 193. In Bayard Rustin's *Commentary* piece, written in February 1965, he wrote of lessons to be derived from "last summer's race riots." Rustin, "From Protest to Politics," 265.

35. Califano, *Triumph and Tragedy*, 63.

36. Rainwater and Yancey, *Moynihan Report and the Politics of Controversy*, 192.

37. "Report of the President's Task Force on the Los Angeles Riots, August 11–15, 1965," September 10, 1965, Ramsey Clark Papers, Los Angeles (2 of 2), box 71, LBJL.

38. Robert Weaver memo, August 22, 1965, WHCF, Confidential File HU2/ST#, Equality of the Races, box 56, LBJL.

39. C. Harrison Mann to the President, June 8, 1965, and C. Harrison Mann to Bill Moyers, August 17, 1965, both in WHCF, Gen SP 3–93, Pro-Con/A–Z (Howard), box 172, LBJL. See also *New York Times*, August 17, 1965.

40. Califano, *Triumph and Tragedy*, 59.

41. See Lyndon Johnson to Richard Goodwin, September 10, 1965, Richard N. Goodwin Name File, box 198, LBJL. Goodwin occasionally offered his speechwriting services in the first half of 1966. Despite Goodwin's reorientation toward Kennedy, the president and Goodwin remained on at least cosmetically good terms through at least the end of 1966; after that point, their relationship became more distant as Johnson's resentments toward Kennedy increased.

42. Joseph Califano, "Notes for Meeting with Wiley Branton," attached to Joseph Califano to the President, September 24, 1965, WHCF, Ex HU Human Rights, box 1, LBJL.

43. Hubert Humphrey to the President, May 25, 1965, Vice Presidential Files, box 825, Humphrey Papers, MHS. The rioting in Los Angeles provoked many within the executive branch to ask hard questions about the current division of responsibilities in the arena of civil rights. Berl Bernhard, for example, viewed Watts as a signal that the CRS should be merged with the Civil Rights Commission, referring to a "shot-gun marriage" of the two "statutory creatures." Berl Bernhard to Bill Moyers, Lee White, and Harry McPherson, August 24, 1965, WHCF, Confidential File HU2/ST#, Equality of the Races, box 56, LBJL.

44. Collins argued that during his tenure as head of the CRS he had come to believe that "much more significant mergers are not only in order but badly needed." Based on his direct experience in the conciliation and mediation efforts led by the CRS—including during the Selma crisis in March of 1965 and in the immediate aftermath of the Watts riot—he had come to the conclusion that "having several civil rights agencies poking around in the same troubled community" left local whites and blacks bewildered as to who represented the federal government's interests, provoked interagency conflict among the government representatives themselves, and ultimately ran the risk of further "exacerbating" the situation. LeRoy Collins, Undersecretary, Department of Commerce, "Analysis of Civil Rights Functions of the Federal Government and Recommendations for Their Consolidation in a Single Agency," September 20, 1965, WHCF, Confidential File HU2, Equality of the Races, 1964–66, box 56, LBJL. Calvin Kytle, who moved up to serve as acting director of the CRS when Collins left to take a post as undersecretary of commerce, felt that the former Florida governor had ambitions to head the proposed Agency for Civil Rights and that he accordingly custom-designed the blueprint for the organization to suit his own strengths.

45. The *Honey Fitz*, named by John Kennedy for his maternal grandfather, was the smaller of the presidential yachts, generally—but not exclusively—preferred by Johnson over the larger and more lavishly furnished *Sequoia*.

46. Rainwater and Yancey, *Moynihan Report and the Politics of Controversy*, 195–96; Califano, *Triumph and Tragedy*, 60–69.

47. Hugh Davis Graham, *Civil Rights Era*, 184–86.

48. Calvin and Elizabeth Kytle interview, July 11, July 29, 1997, tape recording.

49. Califano, *Triumph and Tragedy*, 66–67 (emphasis in original). In his oral history, Harry McPherson agreed with Califano's and Ramsey Clark's accounts in stressing that the civil rights reorganization plan "originated in the White House." McPherson credited Califano with much of the fine print, dubbing him "the reorganization man." Harry McPherson interview, April 9, 1969, by Thomas H. Baker, tape 1, 6, LBJL; Ramsey Clark interview, March 21, 1969, 10, LBJL.

50. Harry McPherson interview, April 9, 1969, by Thomas H. Baker, tape 1, 10, LBJL.

51. Memorandum for the President from the Vice President on Recommended Reassignment of Civil Rights Functions, September 24, 1965, Selected Civil Rights Files of Harry McPherson, *CRDJA*, Part I, Reel 11, 0339–42. Plans for such a reshuffling were clearly under way as early as late August, when McPherson, in a memo to Califano, cryptically referred to "certain consolidations and other action . . . which will rather change the picture." Humphrey's fall was anticipated, but the timing was indeterminate, with McPherson concerned about the appearances of a major reorganization and how it might be perceived as an attempt to downplay the centrality of civil rights in the president's agenda: "I wouldn't demolish the VP's Council until the [White House] Conference in November," McPherson urged. Johnson ultimately went against the advice. Harry McPherson to Joseph Califano, August 20, 1965, Selected Civil Rights Files of Harry McPherson, *CRDJA*, Part I, Reel 11, 0424.

52. Farmer's remarks offered a witty update on Gertrude's profession in *Hamlet*. James Farmer interview, July 20, 1971, by Paige E. Mulhollan, 21, LBJL. See Lawson, "Civil Rights," 112, for speculations about the implications of the reorganization "at a time when Johnson and the civil rights movement had reached a crossroads."

53. Joseph Califano, "Notes for Meeting with Wiley Branton," attached to Joseph Califano to the President, September 24, 1965, WHCF, Ex HU Human Rights, box 1, LBJL. Califano's cover memo detailing the choreography of Humphrey's downgrading and the briefing notes for the meeting with Wiley Branton were wrapped up at 1:20 A.M., giving an indication of the high priority Johnson placed on a "damage control" approach to the civil rights reorganization.

54. As Calvin Kytle remembered—he succeeded LeRoy Collins as director of the CRS—Branton was effectively "pigeon-holed" at the Department of Justice after the PCEO "went down the toilet." Calvin and Elizabeth Kytle interview, July 29, 1997, tape recording.

55. In his memoirs, Humphrey blamed Califano for his demotion. Although Humphrey biographer Timothy Thurber concludes that Califano persistently undercut the vice president, he and Johnson biographer Robert Dallek agree that the president made the decision to demote Humphrey. Dallek suggests that the Watts rioting compelled Johnson "to mute his public commitment to black rights and opportunities. While he wished to sustain the fight for legal and de facto equality he had spoken of so warmly in his Howard University speech, he now wanted to give it less notoriety." In reining in Humphrey as "point man," Dallek reasons, the president "signaled his sensitivity to the changing political mood in the country on aid to African Americans." Dallek, *Flawed Giant*, 224–25; Hugh Davis Graham, *Civil Rights Era*, 175–77. See also Califano, *Triumph and Tragedy*, 68–69. As Harry McPherson noted in his memoirs, Califano was often saddled with the chore of delivering strong messages: "Do this, stop doing that. . . . [Although] they came from the President, whatever offense they gave

was attributed to Califano. That was part of the job—getting the President's message across while exposing him to as little personal and political cost as possible." McPherson, *Political Education*, 254–55.

56. Hugh Davis Graham, *Civil Rights Era*, 175.

57. A 1966 memo referred to the demolition of Humphrey's PCEEO as the removal of a "straining or filtering mechanism." "Observations on the Proposed Transfer of Community Relations Service to the Justice Department," *CRDJA*, Part I, Ex FG 155–18, Reel 1, 0336–37.

58. McPherson, *Political Education*, 334–36.

59. The controversy that ultimately surrounded Elkins's thesis had not fully developed even as late as 1964; in hindsight, Moynihan might have been tempted to draw parallels between the criticism his work received and that faced by Elkins once an avalanche of scholarship began to emerge challenging Elkins's claims and often accusing the scholar of racism and worse. Nicholas Lemann describes the Moynihan Report as "probably the most refuted document in American history . . . though of course its dire predictions about the poor black family all came true." Elkins was surely a close rival in terms of a virtual crusade of scholarly refutation, and in some respects it can be argued that Elkins has begun to benefit from a similar scholarly rehabilitation. See Lemann, *Promised Land*, 177.

60. Ibid., 174.

61. Quote in ibid., 173–74.

62. Quote from Moynihan Report, in Remarks of the President at Commencement Exercises at Howard University: "To Fulfill These Rights," June 4, 1965, Statements of LBJ, box 149, LBJL. Nicholas Lemann offers a hard-hitting account of the genesis and reception of the Moynihan Report and concludes that the end result of the blow up over the report was that it banished from the realm of "the mainstream liberal circles" all discussions of black family composition and the "culture of poverty." See Lemann, *Promised Land*, 171–78. Presumably after 1965 such discussions would largely be the purview of the Far Right, a point that Daryl Michael Scott also stresses in his article and book. Scott, "Politics of Pathology," 81–105. See also Matusow, *Unraveling of America*, 197.

63. Moynihan Report, especially 5–14 and 29–45. See Lemann, *Promised Land*, 174.

64. Quote from Moynihan Report, front material.

65. Moynihan had coauthored, with Nathan Glazer, a book by this same name in 1963 examining the question of the extent of assimilation by different immigrant groups in New York City. Glazer and Moynihan, *Beyond the Melting Pot*.

66. Wiley Branton, head of the PCEO before its dismantling, was evidently among those troubled by use of the article "the," remarking that "it struck me in a psychologically bad way." Rainwater and Yancey, *Moynihan Report and the Politics of Controversy*, 7, 189.

67. Ibid., 93–94 (emphasis added).

68. Ibid., 26.

69. In the report, Moynihan's data were usually presented in tabular or graphic form, with "white" and "nonwhite" statistics juxtaposed with little socioeconomic specificity. Large titles headed the graphic depictions; see, for example, page 9, where a table carries the bold title: "The Nonwhite Illegitimacy Ratio Is 8 Times the White Ratio." Moynihan Report, 9.

70. James Farmer, "The Controversial Moynihan Report," "The Core of It," December 18, 1965, reprinted in Rainwater and Yancey, *Moynihan Report and the Politics of Controversy*, 410.

71. Moynihan later came to believe that his report had been leaked due to pressure on the part of the media and press to have the Watts riot somehow "explained." Nicholas Lemann, however, argues that Moynihan, in his opinion a shameless self-promoter, engineered a series of leaks, wanting to be sure that no one at the White House stole his intellectual thunder. Secretary of Labor Willard Wirtz, alternately accused of leaking and "suppressing" the report, in retrospect fingers Moynihan as having had a hand in the timing of the report's first, unofficial release. See Lemann, *Promised Land*, 174–75. For internal debates at the Labor Department and White House over the pros and cons of releasing the Moynihan Report, see Bill Moyers to Joseph Califano, July 30, 1965, with attached memo from John W. Leslie to Frank Erwin, WHCF, Ex SP 3–93, Howard University Commencement, June 4, 1965, box 172, LBJL.

72. Rainwater and Yancey, *Moynihan Report and the Politics of Controversy*, 136–39.

73. See Herbers, *Lost Priority*, 58–65.

74. Rainwater and Yancey, *Moynihan Report and the Politics of Controversy*, 133. For a brief discussion of this linkage, see Branch, *At Canaan's Edge*, 370–72.

75. Rainwater and Yancey, *Moynihan Report and the Politics of Controversy*, 192.

76. See Daniel Patrick Moynihan to Harry McPherson, September 22, 1966, WHCF, Ex WE, August 23, 1966–February 15, 1967, box 1, LBJL.

77. *Economist*, June 12, 1965.

78. Mary McGrory, "President Talks Frankly to Negroes," *Washington Star*, June 6, 1965; Rainwater and Yancey, *Moynihan Report and the Politics of Controversy*, 135.

79. Aminda Wilkins to the President, July 31, 1965, WHCF, Ex SP 3–93, Pro-Con/A–Z, box 172, LBJL.

80. Whitney M. Young Jr., "Agenda for the Future," Address at 55th Annual Urban League Conference, Miami Beach, Florida, August 1, 1965, WHCF, Gen HU2, July 22, 1965–August 18, 1965, box 13, LBJL.

81. Lee White to the President, Notes for Meeting with Roy Wilkins, August 3, 1965, Appointment File (Diary Backup), box 20, LBJL.

82. McPherson, *Political Education*, 340.

83. Rowland Evans and Robert Novak, "Inside Report: The Moynihan Report," *Washington Post*, August 18, 1965.

84. Walter A. Jackson, *Gunnar Myrdal and America's Conscience*, 305. For probing analysis of the Moynihan Report and its impact on policy debates and among social activists, see also Rainwater and Yancey, *Moynihan Report and the Politics of Controversy*; Scott, "Politics of Pathology," 81–105; Scott, *Contempt and Pity*, 150–56; and Hamilton and Hamilton, *Dual Agenda*, 137–40.

85. The president had used the phrase "the scars of centuries" in the Howard University speech.

86. Clearly, two prodigious egos were at work. According to Moynihan, Goodwin did little more than edit the speech: "*I had written the first draft of the Howard address*, the whole

enterprise being carried off in a matter of days." Moynihan, *Miles to Go*, 186 (emphasis added). Harry McPherson's oral history makes it clear that, in his mind at least, the Moynihan Report was the motivating force behind the Howard speech. In McPherson's memory, Bayard Rustin was among a handful of early critics who warned the administration that the focus on the black family might prove politically hazardous. Such a focus, Rustin predicted, would cause "a lot of trouble," and some of Rustin's contacts in the broad spectrum of civil rights leadership "thought this was a bum place to go." Harry McPherson interview, March 24, 1969, by Thomas H. Baker, tape 1, 4, tape 2, 10, and April 9, 1969, by Thomas H. Baker, tape 3, 6, LBJL.

87. Rainwater and Yancey, *Moynihan Report and the Politics of Controversy*, 31, 3; see also Moynihan, *Miles to Go*, 188.

88. Some of Moynihan's fiercest critics in the months following the release of the Moynihan Report had been among those who praised Johnson's Howard speech most effusively in the days immediately following the speech. As rancorous as the Moynihan controversy became, some in the White House must have felt like they had come close to dodging a bullet when so much more of the hostility revolved around Moynihan than it did around Johnson.

89. Metaphors of stagecraft or manipulation predominate in virtually every lengthy description of the White House Conference on Civil Rights and were evident in the contemporary news coverage as well. See, for example, an Associated Press story by Joseph E. Mohbat that appeared in the *Jackson Daily News*, on June 2, 1966, which relates how the conference "opened under a cloud of charges that the White House has rigged its outcome" and quotes CORE's national director Floyd McKissick to that effect. Rowland Evans and Robert Novak's column developed this theme at length. See also Morris Abram interview, March 20, 1984, 15, LBJL. Steven F. Lawson uses the verbs "staged," "managed," and "orchestrated" at various points in his treatment of the White House Conference on Civil Rights and establishes a level of dramatic momentum and graceful metaphoric continuity that then propels his narrative— "when the show [in Washington] closed"—to James Meredith's march in Mississippi, the activist's "own production." Lawson, *In Pursuit of Power*, 44–48. See chapter 5 for discussion of the Meredith March.

Chapter Four

1. Califano, *Triumph and Tragedy*, 58–59 (emphasis in original).

2. Morris Abram interview, March 20, 1984, 9, LBJL (emphasis added).

3. Moving ahead on the White House Conference on Civil Rights, Califano insisted, would "confirm" the promise of the Howard University speech to strengthen civil rights. Joseph Califano to the President, September 25, 1965, WHCF, Ex HU2/MC, November 22, 1963–November 15, 1965, box 22, LBJL.

4. McPherson, *Political Education*, 344–45.

5. Lee White to the President, August 10, 1965, Appointment File (Diary Backup), August 11, 1965, box 20, LBJL.

6. Calvin and Elizabeth Kytle interviews, July 11, July 29, 1997, tape recording. Randolph,

head of the Brotherhood of Sleeping Car Porters and the guiding hand behind the 1963 March on Washington, was a longtime member of the "Big Six" civil rights leaders. Randolph, Roy Wilkins, and Whitney Young undoubtedly topped the list of civil rights leaders with whom Johnson felt the greatest degree of comfort. Jack Valenti, in a memo to the president late in the spring of 1966, described Wilkins and Randolph as "the two [civil rights] leaders who are closest to you." Jack Valenti to the President, May 19, 1966, WHCF, Roy Wilkins Name File, (NAACP), box 312, LBJL.

7. Rainwater and Yancey, *Moynihan Report and the Politics of Controversy*, 202–3.

8. Lee White to the President, November 2, 1965, Ex HU2/MC, *CRDJA*, Part I, Reel 5, 0587.

9. Calvin Kytle, while serving as acting director of the CRS, grew alarmed by the volume of FBI reports crossing the desks of various agencies that contained unsubstantiated background information on individuals of interest to J. Edgar Hoover, many of whom were African Americans the director was tracking in his "Racial Matters" files. Dubious about the veracity of much of the material included in the dossiers, Kytle approached Ramsey Clark in the Justice Department and asked whether it might not be possible to have their circulation restricted. An agitated Clark responded with a warning: "Calvin, *just don't make any noise.* If you raise this as a question, I promise you that one thing will happen. You will be under FBI surveillance the rest of your life." Calvin and Elizabeth Kytle interview, July 11, 1997, tape recording.

10. For an examination of how Rustin's sexual and political identities overlapped and drew unwelcome attention, see D'Emilio, "Homophobia and the Trajectory of Postwar American Radicalism," 80–103.

11. White did acknowledge Rustin's strong reputation among civil rights leaders as a "creative intellectual leader": "Despite his *personal problems,* [Rustin] enjoys a very good press." And White stressed to Marvin Watson that Rustin's "morals" record had not been subjected to significant media scrutiny during his prominent role organizing the 1963 March on Washington. Lee White Secure Wire to Marvin Watson, WHCF, Confidential File HU2, Equality of Races, 1964–66, box 56, LBJL (emphasis added).

12. Morris Abram interview, March 20, 1984, 10, LBJL. "[King] was so mad with LBJ about Vietnam," remembered Abram. See chapter 6 for a discussion of the Vietnam War and Johnson's relationship to the spectrum of civil rights leadership.

13. Kevin Yuill has a detailed account of the planning conference and the final conference in his article, "The 1996 White House Conference on Civil Rights," 259–82. See also Lawson, *In Pursuit of Power*, 24–29.

14. Johnson appears to have been at best lukewarm about Moynihan even before the controversy over the Moynihan Report, in large part because of a controversy over the Job Corps within the Labor Department that had led Labor Secretary Willard Wirtz to criticize Moynihan to Johnson. Job Corps was a darling of the Great Society, and the president, in Nicholas Lemann's account, was "predictably furious." See Lemann, *Promised Land*, 173. Part of Johnson's animosity toward Moynihan also stemmed from his conviction that he was allied with Robert Kennedy.

15. Rainwater and Yancey, *Moynihan Report and the Politics of Controversy*, 247.

16. Morris Abram interview, March 20, 1984, 11, LBJL (emphasis added). See below for discussion of the reception of Moynihan and his ideas at the June 1966 full conference.

17. Rainwater and Yancey, *Moynihan Report and the Politics of Controversy*, 4–5.

18. Johnson indicated that the legislation would go to Capitol Hill in January 1966, but the president ultimately did not deliver the White House civil rights message to Congress until the last days of April 1966.

19. Clifford Alexander to the President, June 22, 1966, WHCF, Confidential File HU2/MC, White House Conference on Civil Rights, box 56, LBJL.

20. The carefully worded distinction between these two forms of "extreme" violence, one as ignorant, the other as despairing, is significant; the latter adjective arguably conveys a softer touch on the issue of urban unrest. "Remarks of the President at the Civil Rights Reception," November 16, 1965, Legislative Background — Voting Rights Act of 1965, January 1964–August 1966 Voting Rights Legislation, Legislative Background and Domestic Crises File, box 1, LBJL.

21. Rainwater and Yancey, *Moynihan Report and the Politics of Controversy*, 248; Harry McPherson interview, March 24, 1969, by Thomas H. Baker, tape 2, 15, LBJL. See also Moynihan, *Miles to Go*, 188, where Moynihan describes Bernhard's remarks as having been made "in serious fun, as you might say."

22. Ben Heineman insisted that "there was not any pressure" from Johnson to squelch any discussion of the Moynihan Report. "The decision was made . . . largely or exclusively by the planning group." Ben Heineman interview, 18, LBJL.

23. Morris Abram interview, March 20, 1984, 11–12, LBJL; Rainwater and Yancey, *Moynihan Report and the Politics of Controversy*, 252–54, 261. See also Frazier, *Negro Family in the United States*. In 1964, Charles Silberman had equated "the problem of the black family" with "the absence of strong black males" and offered as his prescription "jobs for black males." Silberman, *Crisis in Black and White*. Kenneth Clark was also playing with the "dynamite" of black family "pathology," in *Dark Ghetto*, published earlier, in 1965. See also Scott, "Politics of Pathology," 95.

24. Rainwater and Yancey, *Moynihan Report and the Politics of Controversy*, 193. Rainwater and Yancey note that Carter's statement might have been equally applicable to the black response to the rioting in Watts.

25. Daniel Patrick Moynihan to the President, July 18, 1965, WHCF, Daniel Patrick Moynihan Name File, box 617, LBJL. The president's belated acknowledgment of Moynihan's departure, most certainly ghostwritten by a White House staff aide, betrayed no hint of the ongoing controversy over the Moynihan Report. See Lyndon Johnson to Daniel Patrick Moynihan, October 7, 1965, WHCF, Daniel Patrick Moynihan Name File, box 617, LBJL.

26. See Daniel Patrick Moynihan to Harry McPherson, September 22, 1966, WHCF, Ex WE, August 23, 1966–February 15, 1967, box 1, LBJL.

27. For discussion of the impact of A. Philip Randolph's and Bayard Rustin's call for a Freedom Budget with a price tag of $100 billion, see Morris Abram interview, March 20, 1984, 11–12, LBJL. Whitney Young, of the Urban League, had spoken of a domestic Marshall Plan shortly after taking the helm of the organization in 1961, and CORE's James Farmer had endorsed the idea in 1963. See Scott, "Politics of Pathology," 93–94. In the week before the

White House Conference on Civil Rights, Martin Luther King Jr. also used the rounded-off number of $100 billion to describe the scale of the commitment needed to ease the problems facing poor Americans. King envisioned a hefty portion of the funds going toward a "guaranteed annual income." See Garrow, *Bearing the Cross*, 472.

28. Martin Luther King Jr. would later compare Vietnam's ability to drain both soldiers and dollars to a "demoniacal suction tube."

29. McPherson, *Political Education*, 345; Harry McPherson interview, June 12, 1973, by Robert Hawkinson, 14, LBJL.

30. When another attendee confidently predicted to McKissick that "when you get the [voter registration] problem solved, you won't have a civil rights movement," the CORE leader replied: "That would be nice, but I just don't foresee it any time soon. I wish it were like that. My wife would be quite happy." "Planning Session papers, November 18, 1965, Panel III, Voting," 225–26, in *CRDJA*, Part IV, Reel 7, 0227–28.

31. Ibid., 208–9, in ibid., 0209–11. Moore argued, for example, that federal registrars ought to be canvassing for black registrants in the "safe" territory of black churches rather than requiring African Americans to go to unfamiliar (and thus potentially intimidating) "neutral" locations: "I just can't see why on Saturday and Sunday . . . those registrars could not speak in [black] churches. Because the people react differently when they know that the registrar has come here like the politicians do, in a different sense, and that the registrars will not shoot me. You see, I am a Negro, and when I go to another Negro and say, 'Let's go down the street and register,' he says, 'you are still sending me to a white man.' And the fact about the matter is that he does not understand the difference between state and Federal Government in those terms, as we try to explain it."

Mississippi civil rights leader Aaron Henry argued in a similar vein that Department of Justice equivocation resulted in situations where "you have used up so much of your energy in trying to get the job done that when they finally decide to send one [a federal registrar] in here you are pooped. You have spent your energy in trying to get it done. And as Guyot says, nothing succeeds like success. And nothing destroys your ability to move like defeat. And when you have carried these people down [to register] time and time again, and they have been denied the right to register, the more times you get them down and they are denied the less likely you are to get them back again, although it appears now [since passage of the Voting Rights Act] that the thing has been opened up, because they think you are selling them another boondoggle to get them down there one more time to get them embarrassed and chagrined because of their ignorance. . . . If we could get it done a little sooner, if we could get the affirmative response out of the Justice Department, say, in a tenth of the time that it takes, maybe we could still have a little steam left when they get to that."

32. Lemann, *Promised Land*, 182. In their interviews with Nicholas Lemann, Bill Moyers and other White House aides suggested that Johnson never read the Moynihan Report. This assertion seems unlikely, if not implausible, given Johnson's penchant for micromanagement, the relative brevity of the report, and the vitriolic debate that raged around the report's findings. But it is true that Johnson demanded distilled memos from his aides, preferably of one page or less. Perhaps one of his assistants summarized Moynihan's findings. On Johnson's desire for abbreviated reports, see Sherwin Markman's observations in chapter 7.

33. McPherson, *Political Education*, 346. See also Miroff, "Presidential Leverage over Social Movements," 16; and Lawson, *In Pursuit of Power*, 44–47.

34. Morris Abram interviews, May 3, 1984, 5, and March 20, 1984, 14, LBJL.

35. Joseph Califano to Harry McPherson, April 25, 1966, WHCF, Louis Martin Name File, box 127, LBJL. In late April, Johnson let it be known that he wanted both Martin and Weaver to attend all civil rights meetings linked to the upcoming White House Conference on Civil Rights.

36. Although the steady antiwar heckling that Johnson would endure for the last years of his presidency, increasingly confining his speech-making to "controlled" venues, was not yet in high gear, the president was still uniquely attuned to the possibilities of disruption. In mid-April 1966, six weeks before the White House Conference on Civil Rights convened, delegates at a meeting of the Citizens' Crusade against Poverty had heckled War on Poverty czar Sargent Shriver relentlessly, ultimately causing him to abandon the podium. The possibilities of Johnson or other high-ranking administration officials receiving similar treatment weighed heavily on planners' minds. Johnson appears to have removed from the list of potential conference invitees some of the most vociferous critics of the War on Poverty, among them many notable academics. See *New Republic*, April 30, 1966, 5–6; and "Hooting of Shriver, Pacifism of King," *Herald Tribune*, April 18, 1966. Yuill stresses the notable absence of liberal academics from the list of invitees. For a useful discussion of the composition of participants in the conference and how Johnson engineered a disappearing act that effectively removed from the 1966 conference invitation list most academicians critical of administration policies, see Yuill, "The 1966 White House Conference on Civil Rights," especially 81–84.

37. Nicholas von Hoffman, "A 'Come-On,' Said Bogalusa Man," *Washington Post*, June 3, 1966, in clipping file in *CRDJA*, Part IV, "General Area—Press Clippings," Reel 20, 0161.

38. Lawson, *In Pursuit of Power*, 45. Ramsey Clark interview, March 21, 1969, 18–19, LBJL. The breakdown of those invited to represent civil rights groups was revealing as well, with the Urban League and the NAACP each slated to be represented by forty-five delegates, a full 50 percent more than CORE, SNCC, and SCLC delegations, who were to send thirty delegates each. (SNCC's allocation ultimately didn't matter because the organization withdrew from the conference.) The National Council of Negro Women (NCNW) received only twenty-five delegate slots. Historian Allen J. Matusow argues that the sheer scale of the invitation list threatened to dilute dissent; the assembled, he wrote archly, "represent[ed] every point except the Ku Klux Klan and the Black Muslims." Matusow, *Unraveling of America*, 198.

39. Robert Kintner to the President, May 25, 1966, WHCF, Confidential File HU/2 MC, White House Conference on Civil Rights, box 56, LBJL.

40. White House Conference Executive Council, *Council's Report and Recommendations to the Conference*. Receiving far less attention than concerns about militants, the squelching of discussion of the Vietnam War, and the ongoing repartee about Moynihan and his controversial report, the council's report, which formed the point of departure for the conference, also boldly laid out the principles of what it labeled "affirmative actions." As the report read, "Employers need to look, think, and act beyond simple nondiscrimination and *pro forma* or passive equal employment opportunity programs." It called for "ac-

tive and deliberate efforts to increase and improve jobs for Negroes." The language of the report still paid heavy lip service to the defense of "equal opportunity," but the beginnings of preferential hiring are clearly visible, as when one suggestion spoke of companies devoting "particular effort . . . to locat[ing] Negroes in responsible management and policy positions as a visible example of policy." Suggested job postings meeting these criteria were supervisors and personnel officers. For an interesting account of a White House aide who insisted that the genesis of the phrase "affirmative action" should be properly attributed to him, see Hobart Taylor interview, January 6, 1969, 12–13, LBJL.

41. Rainwater and Yancey, *Moynihan Report and the Politics of Controversy*, 275–76.

42. Having said this, it is worthwhile to note that a memo circulated for "limited official use" by administration personnel on the eve of the fall planning conference called on those in attendance representing the government to highlight favorable aspects of Johnson's record "without appearing to boast," while simultaneously endorsing the ongoing War on Poverty. The memo was intended to shape the message conveyed by administration representatives in all their dealings with representatives of the media. Limited Official Use memoranda, White House Civil Rights Conference, "To Fulfill These Rights"—November 17–18, 1965, CRDJA, Part I, Ex HU2/MC, box 22, Reel 5, 0638.

43. Harry McPherson interview, March 24, 1969, by Thomas H. Baker, tape 2, 15–16, LBJL; Lawson, *In Pursuit of Power*, 44–45.

44. Carson, *In Struggle*, 192–206; Lawson, *In Pursuit of Power*, 51.

45. Lewis, *Walking with the Wind*, 368.

46. Others, including white leftist and SNCC staffer Jack Minnis, were leery of Lewis's robust ties to the SCLC, and some felt that Lewis's strong Christianity and his unwavering commitment to nonviolence were out of step with "what the times required." Lewis, *Walking with the Wind*, 362; Carson, *In Struggle*, 202–3.

47. Harry McPherson interview, March 24, 1969, by Thomas H. Baker, tape 1, 7, LBJL. See also Lawson, "Mixing Moderation with Militancy," 92–94, for an excellent summary of the deterioration in the relationship between the Johnson White House and SNCC over time.

48. Lawson, *In Pursuit of Power*, 45.

49. Louis Martin, Deputy Chairman, Democratic National Committee, to Marvin Watson, May 20, 1966, Selected Civil Rights Files of Marvin Watson, CRDJA, Part I, Reel 12, 0406. Berl Bernhard went so far as to suggest that the principal purpose of the White House Conference on Civil Rights had become less a chance for discussions of programmatic advances on the civil rights agenda than a means "to prevent 'rioting' in major metropolitan cities . . . to let the participants freely 'sound off' and to let off steam." O'Reilly, *Racial Matters*, 238.

50. McPherson, *Political Education*, 346–47.

51. Robert Kintner to the President, May 31, 1966, WHCF, Confidential File SP, Remarks at White House Conference on Civil Rights, box 89, LBJL.

52. *Washington Post*, April 15, 1966; *New York Times*, April 15, 1966. Organizers of the "Poor People's Convention" apologized to Shriver the next day and emphasized that the demonstrators represented only a handful of the 1,000 delegates, but—although the heckling

received front page coverage—the *New York Times* only briefly mentioned the apology in a follow-up story that was buried on page 12. *New York Times*, April 16, 1966.

53. Robert Kintner to the President, June 1, 1966, WHCF, Confidential File HU2/MC, White House Conference on Civil Rights, box 56, LBJL. Johnson followed a similar logic when he indicated in a televised address following Martin Luther King Jr.'s assassination in April 1968 that he would address a Joint Session of Congress; but after rioting swept the nation, he refused to follow through with the planned speech, angrily telling an aide that he had "promised nothing."

54. LBJ phone call with Benjamin Heineman, 8:59 A.M., June 1, 1966, Cit. 10201, Audio-tape WH6606.01, LBJL.

55. Dallek, *Flawed Giant*, 441.

56. The phraseology evoked both "No, We'll Never Turn Back" and "Ain't Gonna Let Nobody Turn Me 'Round." Remarks of the president at the White House Conference on Civil Rights at the Sheraton Park Hotel, Washington, D.C., June 1, 1966, Selected Civil Rights Files of Harry McPherson, *CRDJA*, Part I, Reel 12, 0036–39. Attorney General Nicholas Katzenbach sounded many of the same themes at a commencement address at Seton Hall University on June 4, 1966, just two days after the White House Conference on Civil Rights adjourned and on the first anniversary of the Howard commencement speech. The attorney general called on "the meshing of public and private actions" to bridge the opportunity gap. He too sought to deflect expectations away from federal activism, insisting that "no statute alone can trumpet down the ghetto walls." Nicholas Katzenbach, Address to Commencement at Seton Hall University, June 4, 1966, Selected Civil Rights Files of Harry McPherson, *CRDJA*, Part I, Reel 11, 0879–86.

57. McPherson, *Political Education*, 346–47; Harry McPherson interview, June 12, 1973, by Robert Hawkinson, 16–19, LBJL.

58. McPherson, *Political Education*, 349. No longer on the inside, Richard Goodwin later described a conference that had "collapsed in rancorous fruitless dispute over sociological abstractions, a debate that only masked awareness that Lyndon Johnson's 'To Fulfill These Rights' was not to be answered, *was doomed by the actions of the very man who had issued it.*" Goodwin, *Remembering America*, 457. McPherson's and Goodwin's remarks are in a similar vein to those discussed in chapter 1 and offer additional evidence of a tragic narrative approach to the history of the years 1965 to 1968 put forward by historical participants, journalists, and historians alike.

59. For Whitney Young's assessment of the significance of Johnson's speech, see Joseph Califano to the President, June 4, 1966, WHCF, Whitney M. Young Jr. Name File, box 41, LBJL.

60. Evans and Novak, "Inside Report: Rights Conference Avoids Explosion," in *Jackson (Miss.) Clarion-Ledger*, June 9, 1966; Ben Heineman interview, 15–16, LBJL; Garrow, *Bearing the Cross*, 473.

61. As historian Allen J. Matusow has noted, one of the few concrete actions taken by the conference was the voting down of CORE-sponsored resolutions opposed to America's involvement in Southeast Asia. Matusow, *Unraveling of America*, 198. See *Philadelphia Inquirer*, June 5, 1966, in clipping file in *CRDJA*, Part IV, "General Area—Press Clippings,"

Reel 20, 0008; William R. MacKave, "Rights Parley Representation Protested by Some Churchmen," *Washington Post*, June 5, 1966, in ibid., 0094; "Civil Rights Conference Ends with Johnson in Command: Delegates Apparently Happy," *Detroit News*, June 3, 1966, in ibid., 0146. Labor leader Walter Reuther displayed little patience for discussion of Vietnam at a civil rights parley: "If people want to debate foreign policy . . . they should have a White House Conference on Foreign Policy." *New York Times*, June 3, 1966, in ibid., 0158.

62. "Important Issues Raised at White House Conference," *Washington Afro-American*, June 7, 1966, in *CRDJA*, Part IV, "General Area—Press Clippings," Reel 20, 0008, 0087–88. Clarence Mitchell, NAACP chief lobbyist, had made the point even more starkly at the November 1965 White House Planning Conference, linking the foreign policy parallel to an implicit warning about the rising current of militancy and armed self-defense among many blacks. Arguing that the Department of Justice had failed to use its full power to enforce voting rights for blacks, Mitchell maintained that the federal government ultimately bore the burden of choosing "whether each [black] man is going to be his own private army or whether the Government of the United States is going to give people in Mississippi the same protection it would give them if they were on a foreign shore." Jerome S. Cahill, "U.S. Refusal to Protect Negroes Assailed at White House Session," *Philadelphia Inquirer*, November 19, 1965, in clipping file in *CRDJA*, Part IV, "Planning Session—Press Coverage," Reel 19, 0003.

63. Yuill, "The 1966 White House Conference on Civil Rights," 89. See below for discussion of domestic parallels with Vietnam.

64. In the aftermath of the conference, the president drafted an affectionate "Dear Louie" thank-you to Louis Martin, praising him for his role in staging the White House Conference. The consensus among Johnson's closest advisers in the White House, the president reported, was that "'we don't know what we would have done without Louie Martin.' I share in that consensus, as I always have." Lyndon Johnson to Louis Martin, June 7, 1966, WHCF, Louis Martin Name File, box 127, LBJL.

65. "Civil Rights: Moderate vs. Militant," *Newsweek*, June 13, 1966, in clipping file in *CRDJA*, Part IV, "General Area—Press Clippings," Reel 20, 0083.

66. Lawson, *In Pursuit of Power*, 47.

67. McPherson, *Political Education*, 352.

68. Rainwater and Yancey, *Moynihan Report and the Politics of Controversy*, 279–81. A black man from Thomasville, Georgia, lambasted the Georgia administrator of the Farm Home Administration for his clearly stated position of being "not in sympathy" with the FHA program geared at improving rural housing for impoverished rural residents, many of them black. See William Chapman, "Civil Rights Forces Direct Wrath at U.S. Agent," *Washington Post*, June 5, 1966, Part IV, "General Area—Press Clippings," Reel 20, 0036.

69. James K. Batten, "Negro Says Klan Threats Halting N.C. Integration," *Charlotte (N.C.) Observer*, June 2, 1966, in clipping file in *CRDJA*, Part IV, "General Area—Press Clippings," Reel 20, 0205.

70. "White House Conference—Committee Hearings, Committee II—Virginia Suite, June 2, 1966, Administration of Justice and Other," 48–50, in *CRDJA*, Part IV, Reel 9, 0811–12 (emphasis added). An administrator in the Department of Health, Education, and Welfare

pointed out this dynamic when he described how he had relied on the recommendations of local whites in a southern town to bring about the integration of a local hospital board. "What Washington didn't know and couldn't know . . . was that it [local whites] had managed to find the only three John Birch–type Negroes in the state and to give them positions of power." Richard H. Rovere, "Letter from Washington," *New Yorker*, June 18, 1966, in clipping file in *CRDJA*, Part IV, "General Area—Press Clippings," Reel 20, 1069.

71. Peter Lisagor, "But Who Is Oppressed?" column from News World Service reprinted in *Charlotte (N.C.) News*, June 4, 1966, in clipping file in *CRDJA*, Part IV, "General Area—Press Clippings," Reel 20, 0275–77. Voicing a similar critique was Albert Turner, a civil rights activist from Marion, Alabama (where white state troopers had killed Jimmie Lee Jackson, helping to spur the Selma to Montgomery March in the spring of 1965). Turner heard a catalog of programs designed to improve education in black "slums" and declared: "All these programs you're discussing, we've just heard of them. . . . If you're going to make this conference a reality, we've got to get these programs [in the South], too."

72. Robert Cahn, "Delegates Pool 'Rights' Experiences," *Christian Science Monitor*, June 7, 1966, in *CRDJA*, Part IV, "General Area—Press Clippings," Reel 20, 0032.

73. It bears mentioning that this animus directed against federal authorities transcended sectional lines; representatives of the urban poor in the North repeatedly raised similar concerns. William Chapman, "Civil Rights Forces Direct Wrath at U.S. Agent," *Washington Post*, June 5, 1966, in *CRDJA*, Part IV, "General Area—Press Clippings," Reel 20, 0036.

74. *Washington Afro-American*, n.d., in *CRDJA*, Part IV, "General Area—Press Clippings," Reel 20, 0118–19.

75. Don Irwin, "Southern No, Northern Woe?" *Los Angeles Times*, June 7, 1966, in *CRDJA*, Part IV, "General Area—Press Clippings," Reel 20, 0359–60 (emphasis added). In some ways the existing historiography for the War on Poverty and post-1965 civil rights era replicates the trend that so troubled Albert Turner, although one could certainly point to recent work on southern states and locales by Susan Youngblood Ashmore, John Dittmer, Adam Fairclough, Kent Germany, Steven F. Lawson, Chana Kai Lee, Charles Payne, and others as exceptions to this tendency.

76. Andrew Kopkind, "No Fire This Time," *New Republic*, June 18, 1966, 15–16. See also Lawson, *In Pursuit of Power*, 47.

77. Quote in Nicholas Von Hoffman, "A 'Come-on,' Said Bogalusa Man," *Washington Post*, June 3, 1966.

78. Ben Heineman interview, 13–14, LBJL.

79. Saul Friedman, "'Nice Tea Party': Negroes Disappointed in White House Meet," *Charlotte (N.C.) Observer*, June 2, 1966, in *CRDJA*, Part IV, "General Area—Press Clippings," Reel 20, 0209. On Andrew Young's skepticism about the utility of the conference, see Andrew Young interview, LBJL, 21–22. See also Yuill, "The 1966 White House Conference on Civil Rights," 90–91; and Fairclough, *To Redeem the Soul of America*, 293.

80. Mary McGrory, "A 'Real Peaceful' Session," *Evening Star* (Washington, D.C.), June 3, 1966, in *CRDJA*, Part IV, "General Area—Press Clippings," Reel 20, 0056. McGrory was more cynical, arguing that some delegates, rather than pushing for concrete results, seemed "content to reminisce about the bad old days and Southern sheriffs they had known."

81. "Civil Rights: Moderate vs. Militant," *Newsweek*, June 13, 1966, in *CRDJA*, Part IV, "General Area—Press Clippings," Reel 20, 0083. Roy Wilkins, in the peroration of his closing address to the conference on June 2, followed up on this theme with a detour into what critics of the conference would certainly have seen as hyperbole: "It has been held in some quarters that conferences such as this are nothing but talk. . . . The answer is that in an honest and accurate sense they *are* talk. But so, too, was the Sermon on the Mount. . . . So too were the Lincoln-Douglas debates. . . . What were the lamentations of the ancient Hebrews but talk to revive their people and to restore their relationship to God and to hope? What, indeed, were the spirituals of the slaves of our own South but talk set to the chants for a new day of freedom and dignity?" Wilkins speech, quoted in Richard H. Rovere, "Letter from Washington," *New Yorker*, June 18, 1966, in *CRDJA*, Part IV, "General Area—Press Clippings," Reel 20, 1066.

82. Aaron Henry interview, September 12, 1970, by Thomas H. Baker, 12, LBJL.

83. See Clifton Carter to the President, June 3, 1966, Selected Civil Rights Files of Marvin Watson, *CRDJA*, Part I, Reel 12, 0391. Carter penned a sycophantic memo that struck all the right chords with Johnson, meticulously counting the number of interruptions to Johnson's speech due to applause and standing ovations. See also Lawson, *In Pursuit of Power*, 47.

84. Lemann, *Promised Land*, 181. Lemann colorfully writes that the public image of Moynihan sank at one point to where he was seen "in effect, [as] the Sheriff Clark of the North." See also Daniel Patrick Moynihan to Harry McPherson, September 22, 1966, WHCF, Ex WE, August 23, 1966–February 15, 1967, box 1, LBJL.

85. Harry McPherson to the President, June 10, 1966, attached to Clifford Alexander to the President, June 22, 1966, WHCF, Confidential File HU2/MC, White House Conference on Civil Rights, box 56, LBJL.

86. McPherson, *Political Education*, 351. See also Lyndon Johnson to Harry McPherson, WHCF, Confidential File HU2, Equality of the Races (1964–66), box 56, LBJL. Clifford Alexander reflected on how the White House Conference on Civil Rights followed a general pattern for White House–sponsored meetings: "Like all conferences . . . too many of those reports are on somebody's desk and filed away some place. And too little is done to bring them off." Clifford Alexander interview, February 17, 1972, 29, LBJL.

87. Harry McPherson to the President, June 10, 1966, attached to Clifford Alexander to the President, June 22, 1966, WHCF, Confidential File HU2/MC, White House Conference on Civil Rights, box 56, LBJL.

88. Notes from August 25, 1966, Cabinet Meeting, attached to Robert Kintner to Harry McPherson, August 23, 1966, Appointment File (Diary Backup), box 43, LBJL; Rainwater and Yancey, *Moynihan Report and the Politics of Controversy*, 283–84.

89. "A 'Freedom Budget' for All Americans," Fourth Draft, July 1966, Selected Civil Rights Files of Harry McPherson, *CRDJA*, Part I, Reel 11, 0759–820.

90. See Clifford Alexander to Harry McPherson, October 3, 1966, Selected Civil Rights Files of Harry McPherson, *CRDJA*, Part I, Reel 11, 0820.

91. Bayard Rustin, Executive Director of A. Philip Randolph Institute, to "Friends," November 1, 1966, WHCF, A. Philip Randolph Name File, box 33, LBJL.

92. Morris Abram interview, March 20, 1984, 15, LBJL. Regarding the outcome of the conference, McPherson drew virtually identical conclusions: "The best thing that can be said about it is that we got away with a conference without violence." Harry McPherson interview, March 24, 1969, by Thomas H. Baker, tape 1, 16, LBJL.

93. Morris Abram interview, May 3, 1984, 4, LBJL.

94. Evans and Novak, "Inside Report: Rights Conference Avoids Explosion," in *Jackson (Miss.) Clarion-Ledger*, June 9, 1966.

95. *Scranton (Ill.) Tribune*, June 1, 1966; Herbers, *Lost Priority*, 64.

96. Herbers, *Lost Priority*, 64.

97. Morris Abram interview, May 3, 1984, 4, LBJL.

Chapter Five

1. Matusow, *Unraveling of America*, 198; Rainwater and Yancey, *Moynihan Report and the Politics of Controversy*. See Moynihan, "The President and the Negro," 39–41; and Lawrence Guyot interview, tape recording.

2. *New York Times*, January 13, 1966.

3. James H. Meredith, "My Long Road to Freedom," *Saturday Evening Post*, August 13, 1966, clipping in Edwin King Papers, box 4, TCSC. For vivid accounts of Meredith's wounding and the subsequent Meredith March, see Lawson, *In Pursuit of Power*, 49–62; Dittmer, *Local People*, 389–407; Fairclough, *To Redeem the Soul of America*, 309–20; and Sellers, *River of No Return*, 160–69.

4. John Stennis telegram to the President, June 7, 1966, WHCF, Ex HU2–ST4, February 15, 1966–, box 27, LBJL; Jack Rosenthal, Special Assistant to the Attorney General, to Bill Moyers, June 8, 1966, WHCF, Confidential File HU2/ST#, Equality of Races, box 56, LBJL; Branch, *At Canaan's Edge*, 475–76.

5. Governor Paul B. Johnson, Press Release, June 7, 1966, Paul Johnson Family Papers, Folder 2, Sovereignty Commission: September 1965, box 138, USMSC.

6. Lewis, *Walking with the Wind*, 370–71. As *New York Times* reporter Gene Roberts would note, the debate over "Black Power" may have been formally unveiled in the Meredith March, but it "grew out of six years of cumulative anger on the part of student committee members." *New York Times*, July 3, 1966.

7. Martin Luther King Jr., *Where Do We Go from Here*, 25–26; Branch, *At Canaan's Edge*, 476–77. Historian David Goldfield describes how some among SNCC's and CORE's field staffs had begun to spread the lyrics: "Too much love/Too much love/Nothing kills a nigger like/Too much love." See Goldfield, *Black, White, and Southern*, 222–24.

8. Branch, *At Canaan's Edge*, 476–79.

9. Carson, *In Struggle*, 207; Payne, *I've Got the Light of Freedom*, 376–79; Garrow, *Bearing the Cross*, 476–78; Branch, *At Canaan's Edge*, 476–79.

10. Dittmer, in *Local People*, 391–95, describes the role of the Deacons for Defense and SNCC's shrewdness in recognizing the importance of keeping King affiliated with the Mississippi March as a public relations ploy. See also Hill, *Deacons for Defense*; and Viorst, *Fire in the Streets*, 372.

11. *Eyes on the Prize*, "The Time Has Come," 1964–66; transcript at <http://www.pbs.org/wgbh/amex/eyesontheprize/about/pt_201.html> (January 7, 2008); Dittmer, *Local People*, 395–96.

12. Garrow, *Bearing the Cross*, 478–79; Dittmer, *Local People*, 402.

13. Dittmer, *Local People*, 396.

14. Garrow, *Bearing the Cross*, 481.

15. Lawson, *In Pursuit of Power*, 56–57.

16. Paul Good, "The Meredith March," in Carson et al., comp., *Reporting Civil Rights*, 500.

17. Lawson, *In Pursuit of Power*, 57; Fairclough, *To Redeem the Soul of America*, 316–19.

18. Garrow, *Bearing the Cross*, 483; Fairclough, *To Redeem the Soul of America*, 317; Dittmer, *Local People*, 398. Dittmer's equally harrowing account tells of a man in the crowd yelling out, "They're right behind you!" and a crowd of whites cheering appreciatively.

19. *New York Times*, June 24, 1966; Dittmer, *Local People*, 399–400; Garrow, *Bearing the Cross*, 485–86.

20. Governor Paul B. Johnson, Press Release, June 24, 1966, Paul Johnson Family Papers, Folder 15, Press Releases: June 1966, box 104, USMSC. The ubiquity of the phrase "so-called" stands out conspicuously as an all-purpose arrow in the rhetorical quiver of anticommunism and massive resistance in the 1950s and 1960s. One veteran of decades of activism on behalf of "so-called" "leftist" causes, a self-professed "fellow traveler" and aficionado of "front" organizations, remembered overhearing a comment from a rabid anticommunist and race-baiter disparaging the "so-called Southern Conference on Human Welfare," active in the late 1930s and early 1940s. "The so-called Southern Conference on Human Welfare," the activist replied with mock earnestness, "*is* so-called *because* it *is* so called." Anecdote related at the Popham Seminar, of veteran journalists who covered the civil rights movement, Athens, Georgia, 1998.

21. Carson, *In Struggle*, 210–11; Dittmer, *Local People*, 401–2.

22. Lawson, *In Pursuit of Power*, 54, 58–59, 61; Garrow, *Bearing the Cross*, 485–86; Floyd McKissick, National Director, CORE, to the President, June 20, 1966, Governor Paul B. Johnson Name File, box 128, LBJL.

23. Branch, *At Canaan's Edge*, 495. Dittmer highlights the profound difference between the Johnson administration's tepid response to Canton and its far more assertive response to events in Alabama fifteen months earlier. Dittmer, *Local People*, 400–401. See Martin Luther King Jr., Telegram to the President, June 22, 1966, and Harry McPherson to the President, with attached draft of press release from Attorney General Nicholas Katzenbach, Selected Civil Rights Files of Harry McPherson, *CRDJA*, Part I, Reel 11, 0895–96; and Lyndon Johnson to Martin Luther King Jr., June 23, 1966, Martin Luther King Jr. Name File, 166, box 144, LBJL. Doar's presence, along with that of other federal officials, seemed only to reinforce a well-established pattern of federal involvement in Mississippi, according to which white representatives from Washington or regional FBI offices would document police brutality and extralegal violence but refuse to stop it, justifying their passivity as being required by federalism. Both Steven F. Lawson and Charles Payne have noted that the Vernon Dahmer murder six months before the Meredith March helped to dramatize the issue of inadequate federal

protection for the exercise of constitutionally guaranteed rights. See Lawson, *In Pursuit of Power*, 58–59, and Payne, "The View from the Trenches," in Lawson and Payne, *Debating the Civil Rights Movement*, 127.

24. Branch, *At Canaan's Edge*, 495–96.

25. Dittmer, *Local People*, 401; Carson, *In Struggle*, 210; Garrow, *Bearing the Cross*, 481.

26. Harry McPherson, Memo, Possible Questions (and Answers) at a Press Conference, June 1966, Selected Civil Rights Files of Harry McPherson, *CRDJA*, Part I, Reel 12, 0040–44.

27. Martin Luther King Jr., *Where Do We Go from Here*, 32.

28. Carson, *In Struggle*, 210.

29. I am indebted to Timothy Tyson, whose discussions of Black Power have influenced my own thinking about the tension between the emergence of the "Black Power" slogan in the summer of 1966 and the much deeper "roots" of black protest. Tyson, "Robert F. Williams, 'Black Power,' and the Roots of the African American Freedom Struggle," 540–71; Tyson, *Radio Free Dixie*.

30. Payne, "Debating the Civil Rights Movement: The View from the Trenches," in Lawson and Payne, *Debating the Civil Rights Movement*, 113.

31. Moskin, "The Attorney General of the United States, Nicholas deB[elleville] Katzenbach, Talks about Crime in Our Streets, Racial Violence This Summer, Business and Trust-Busting, Children and Punishment," *Look*, June 1, 1965, 28–33. See also *New York Amsterdam News*, June 5, 1965.

32. Meredith, "My Long Road to Freedom," 24, 27.

33. Statement by Paul B. Johnson, submitted to Senate Judiciary Committee, Subcommittee on Constitutional Rights, in opposition to Senate 3296, 89th Congress (undated, Fall 1966), Paul Johnson Family Papers, Folder 10, Civil Rights Bill (1966), box 110, USMSC; *Washington Post*, July 7, 1966; *Time*, July 8, 1966, 23; Marvin Hoffman and John Mudd, "The New Plantations," *Nation*, October 24, 1966, 414.

34. George Reedy to Vice President Lyndon Johnson, July 3, 1963, Selected Civil Rights Files of George Reedy, *CRDJA*, Part I, Reel 12, 0251–53.

35. Fairclough, *To Redeem the Soul of America*, 319, 311–22; Payne, *I've Got the Light of Freedom*, 376–79.

36. In addition to his illuminating discussion of SNCC leaders' "testing" of the slogan "Black Power," historian Clayborne Carson demonstrates how that phrase or variants of it had been used throughout the 1950s, well before white media and white viewers and readers suddenly seized on it with a mixture of consternation and fascination. Carson, *In Struggle*, 207–11. For a discussion of CORE director Floyd McKissick's claims to have used the phrase "Black Power" before Carmichael, see Dooley, *Robert Kennedy*, 37. Malcolm X had spoken the words earlier, and Richard Wright had entitled a book *Black Power*, based on observations he had made while traveling in Ghana in 1953.

37. Garrow, *Bearing the Cross*, 489.

38. Roy Wilkins, *Standing Fast*, 316, 319; Fairclough, *To Redeem the Soul of America*, 314–15, 320. Roger Wilkins claims that he urged his uncle "to tone down a lot of his rhetoric," including the explosive phrase "Black Power means black death." He believed that the offending remark had been stricken from Wilkins's speech and was dismayed when his uncle

restored it: "I knew he had lost the youth [but] Roy knew how to grab a headline and he got it across the nation." Roger Wilkins, *A Man's Life*, 184–85.

39. "State CDG Gave Food to Marchers," *Jackson (Miss.) Clarion-Ledger*, August 24, 1966, and CDGM Press Release, n.d., clipping and press release both attached to John Maguire to Douglass Cater, September 29, 1966, WHCF, Gen WE9-1, box 46, LBJL; Lawrence Guyot interview, tape recording.

40. Dittmer, *Local People*, 366.

41. Governor Paul Johnson telegram to the President, February 23, 1966, WHCF, Gen WE9-1, box 46, LBJL.

42. Bandy, "Eastland Joins Headstart Attack," news clipping, n.p., n.d., ca. February 1966, James F. McRee Papers, box 4, TCSC.

43. *The Movement* 2, no. 4 (June 1966): 7, in Carson, *The Movement: 1964–1970*.

44. McPherson, *Political Education*, 353–55.

45. Sargent Shriver, address to the General Assembly of the United Presbyterian Church, May 25, 1965, quoted in Larold K. Schulz, "The CDGM Story," *Christianity and Crisis* 26 (January 23, 1967): 315 (emphasis in original).

46. McPherson, *Political Education*, 353–55; Kearns, *Lyndon Johnson and the American Dream*, 290–91.

47. Vinovskis, *Origins of Head Start*, 97–98; *Washington Post*, December 2, 2006.

48. Lemann, *Promised Land*, 326; McPherson, *Political Education*, 353–54. See also Califano, *Triumph and Tragedy*, 78–80.

49. Dittmer, *Local People*, 377; Lemann, *Promised Land*, 325.

50. McPherson, *Political Education*, 353–54.

51. Dittmer, *Local People*, 377–78; Lawson, *In Pursuit of Power*, 92–98.

52. Kenneth Dean, executive director of the Mississippi Council on Human Relations— who began working in Mississippi in early 1965—would later assert that the NACCP funneled negative intelligence on CDGM to the OEO, as did Stennis. Kenneth Dean interview, June 9, 1992, by Betsy Nash, 20, MSUSC. *Jackson (Miss.) Clarion-Ledger*, October 9, 1966; Kenneth Dean interview, May 21, 2008, by author, author's notes; Lawrence Guyot interview, tape recording.

53. Aaron Henry interview, May 1, 1972, by Neil McMillen and George Burson, 79–80, USMSC. In Kenneth Dean's estimation, one grounded in similar realpolitik, CDGM had been about far more than its avowed altruistic purpose—"to serve the children and to support civil rights groups." "It was a mechanism for overcoming and tearing down the state's opposition to Federal programs and to cooperation with the Federal government." If this latter motive were the primary desideratum, MAP could just as easily have stood in as a similar "mechanism" and been all the more effective because it stood a greater chance of slipping under segregationists' radar screens. Kenneth Dean interview, June 9, 1992, by Betsy Nash, 18, MSUSC; Kenneth Dean interview, May 21, 2008, by author, author's notes; Lawrence Guyot interview, tape recording.

54. Dittmer, *Local People*, 379.

55. Ibid., 378. Republican critics of MAP were quick to highlight the fact that several members of MAP's board of directors were major Democratic boosters; at least two of them

were members of President Johnson's exclusive "$1,000 a head President's Club." "Children and Politics," *Nation*, November 14, 1966, 501; Cobb, "Somebody Done Nailed Us on the Cross," 912–36.

56. Dittmer, *Local People*, 379.

57. Although Harry McPherson and other Johnson aides professed ignorance, the emphasis from Stennis and Eastland that their "assurances" about CDGM's fiscal fate emanated *"from the administration"* suggest the likelihood of at least some White House involvement rather than a decision originating with the OEO alone. Given the president's reputation for micromanagement, it seems unlikely that the maneuvering behind MAP's formation did not have at least his or his closest advisers' tacit blessing. *Jackson (Miss.) Daily News*, September 30, 1966 (emphasis in original); *National Observer*, October 10, 1966; Kenneth Dean interview, June 9, 1992, by Betsy Nash, 30–31, MSUSC; Kenneth Dean interview, May 21, 2008, by author, author's notes; Lawrence Guyot interview, tape recording; Lemann, *Promised Land*, 326–27.

58. Office of Economic Opportunity Press Release, October 11, 1966, attached to Routing Slip, Herb Kramer to Douglass Cater, October 15, 1966, WHCF, Gen WE9, box 46, LBJL; Citizens' Board of Inquiry, "Final Report on the Child Development Group of Mississippi," submitted to the Executive Committee of the Citizens' Crusade against Poverty, copy in WHCF, Gen WE9, October 14, 1966–November 1, 1966, box 41, LBJL. Rust College had previously submitted antipoverty grant applications to the OEO and had been refused; see also Press Releases, Office of Economic Opportunity, October 7 and 11, 1966, attached to George D. McCarthy to Edwin C. Kruse, November 9, 1966, WHCF, Gen WE9-1, box 47, LBJL, which contains the announcement of the Rust grant.

59. Lemann, *Promised Land*, 326; Polly Greenberg, *Devil Has Slippery Shoes*, 603.

60. Tom Etheridge, "Mississippi Notebook: Small Talk over the Coffee Cups," *Jackson (Miss.) Daily News*, October 7, 1966.

61. "Bring Some Clean Drawers," Winson Hudson interview, in Henry, *Aaron Henry*, 237.

62. Polly Greenberg, *Devil Has Slippery Shoes*, xv (dialect reproduced as in original).

63. Dittmer, *Local People*, 378–79; Lemann, *Promised Land*, 326–27.

64. *Jackson (Miss.) Clarion-Ledger*, October 9, 1966; Hamer quote in Cobb, *Most Southern Place on Earth*, 271. For a nuanced view of the controversy between CDGM and MAP, see Crespino, "Strategic Accommodation," 2003.

65. Marvin Hoffman and John Mudd, "The New Plantations," *Nation*, October 24, 1966, 415. Playing out the Reconstruction parallels, Hoffman and Mudd implicitly compared the origins of this "New Plantation" to the advent of sharecropping as a system of economic and social control in the aftermath of emancipation. "What is M.A.P.?" Edwin King Papers, Folder 147, CDGM v. MAP, September 1966, box 4, TCSC (emphasis in original).

66. Payne, *I've Got the Light of Freedom*, 345; Dittmer, *Local People*, 378–81. Journalists were quick to note local African American Mississippians' preferences for CDGM over its rival MAP upstart. According to the *New Republic*, which had given consistent coverage to the controversy at each stage, "in Mississippi, the people voted . . . with their feet," and blacks decisively chose CDGM. "Shriver Comes Across," *New Republic*, January 7, 1967.

67. Patricia Derian interview, 22, MSUSC.

68. Citizens' Board of Inquiry, "Final Report on the Child Development Group of Mississippi," submitted to the Executive Committee of the Citizens' Crusade against Poverty, copy in WHCF, Gen WE9, October 14, 1966–November 1, 1966, box 41, LBJL.

69. Reflecting on the impact of liberal advocacy on the original Head Start program in Mississippi, Kenneth Dean argued: "I think that OEO and Shriver . . . were embarrassed into a position [of] continuing to fund CDGM." Kenneth Dean interview, June 9, 1992, by Betsy Nash, 30, MSUSC; Kenneth Dean interview, May 21, 2008, by author, author's notes; John David Maguire, editor's introduction to Larold K. Schulz, "The CDGM Story," *Christianity and Crisis* 26 (January 23, 1967): 315; Pat Watters, "Mississippi: Children and Politics," *Dissent* 14 (May–June 1967): 303; Jule Sugarman interview, in Gillette, *Launching the War on Poverty*, 279–90; Jule Sugarman interview, 27–38, LBJL.

In addition to the convoluted CDGM/MAP controversy, the War on Poverty in the Magnolia State was unfolding in an increasingly unpredictable manner. As historians John Dittmer and James Cobb have shown convincingly, Mississippi's white political establishment ultimately sought to contain and control the War on Poverty by seeking to take it over at the state level (George Wallace's political machine was following a similar battle plan in neighboring Alabama). Led by Governor Paul Johnson, whites began to form CAPs with handpicked boards, often dominated by staunch segregationists. See, for example, Dittmer, *Local People*, 375–76; and Cobb, "'Somebody Done Nailed Us on the Cross," 912–36.

70. Harry S. Ashmore, *Civil Rights and Wrongs*, 184–85 (emphasis in original).

71. Matusow, *Unraveling of America*, 217–71; Moynihan, *Maximum Feasible Misunderstanding*; Donovan, *Politics of Poverty*.

72. The riveting and provocative documentary film, *The Intolerable Burden*, from 2003, examines the process of segregation, desegregation, and "resegregation" in the small community of Drew, Mississippi, in the Delta's Sunflower County. For discussion of the eventual process of public school desegregation in Mississippi and white flight into private academies, see Bolton, "The Last Stand of Massive Resistance," 329–50; Callejo-Pérez, *Southern Hospitality*; Cleary, "Gubernatorial Leadership and State Policy on Desegregation," 165–70; Curry, *Silver Rights*; Dittmer, *Local People*; Fuquay, "Civil Rights and the Private School Movement in Mississippi," 159–80; Hudson and Curry, *Mississippi Harmony*; and Sheffield and Stewart, "Fiscal Neglect as a Response to School Desegregation," 192–204.

73. Payne, *I've Got the Light of Freedom*, 347; Lawrence Guyot interview, tape recording.

74. Editor's introduction to Larold K. Schulz, "The CDGM Story," *Christianity and Crisis* 26 (January 23, 1967): 315.

75. William C. Harris, *The Day of the Carpetbagger*, 668.

76. For a summary of this shift, see Erskine, "The Polls: Demonstrations and Race Riots," 655–77; and Erskine, "The Polls: Speed of Racial Integration," 513–24.

77. *The Movement*, 2, no. 4 (June, 1966): 7, in Carson, *The Movement: 1964–1970*.

78. Payne, *I've Got the Light of Freedom*, 347–48.

79. McFeely, *Sapelo's People*, 125–26.

Chapter Six

1. Randall B. Woods, *LBJ*, 597.

2. LBJ phone call with Martin Luther King Jr., 8:05 P.M., July 7, 1965, Cit. 8311, Audiotape WH6507.02, LBJL.

3. Randall B. Woods, *LBJ*, 605.

4. *New York Times*, June 6, 1965.

5. Walter Heller to the President, December 21, 1965, WHCF, Confidential File WE9, Poverty Program (Great Society) (1964–66), box 98, LBJL. Heller also suggested that if cuts were necessary to continue to balance both "guns and butter," Johnson should "cut things, not people." Heller targeted one area that he felt was ripe for reductions in the nation's space program: "A Headstart for poor children is more vital than a headstart to Mars."

6. See Clifford Alexander to Lee White, January 5, 1966, WHCF, Ex SP/HU, box 46, LBJL; and Joseph Califano to the President, December 23, 1965, WHCF, Ex FI4, Budget Appropriations, November 23, 1965–January 18, 1966, box 22, LBJL; see also numerous other items in this folder.

7. During the process of drafting Johnson's 1966 State of the Union address, Bill Moyers had contacted White House aide and speechwriter Douglass Cater with his concerns that members of Congress felt "that we are talking too much about 'the poor.'" Bill Moyers to Douglass Cater, January 4, 1966, WHCF Ex WE9, December 18, 1965–March 11, 1966, box 26, LBJL.

8. Garrow, *Bearing the Cross*, 429–30, 437–39. Despite his growing misgivings about Vietnam, King muted his criticisms in two July conversations with the president and assured him he did not doubt his commitment to a diplomatic solution to the war. LBJ phone call with Martin Luther King Jr., 8:05 P.M., July 7, 1965, Cit. 8311, Audiotape WH6507.02, LBJL.

9. Bill Moyers to the President, August 30, 1965, Roy Wilkins Name File (NAACP), box 312, LBJL.

10. Perry Barber to Jack Valenti, August 31, 1965, Louis Martin Name File, box 127, LBJL.

11. Poinsett, *Walking with Presidents*, 31–32.

12. Ibid.

13. LBJ phone call with John McCone, 12:10 P.M., August 18, 1965, Cit. 8550, Audiotape WH6508.05, LBJL.

14. Daniel Patrick Moynihan to Harry McPherson, "The Under Representation of Negroes in the Armed Forces," July 16, 1965, Selected Civil Rights Files of Harry McPherson, *CRDJA*, Part I, Reel 11, 0391–95.

15. See undated memo, "With Regard to Negro Casualties in Vietnam for 1961–1965," Selected Civil Rights Files of Harry McPherson, *CRDJA*, Part I, Reel 11, box 22, 0912–13. African Americans also volunteered at far higher rates for the hazardous army airborne units, which in Vietnam often bore a disproportionate risk due to airborne infantry insertion tactics.

16. Associated Press wire report and Pentagon data forwarded by Larry Levinson to Harry McPherson, March 9, 1966, Selected Civil Rights Files of Harry McPherson, *CRDJA*, Part I, Reel 11, 0528.

17. One level of the sensitivity of African Americans on this subject may be seen in the demands of Mississippi's NAACP leadership that Johnson work to have blacks added to draft

boards throughout the Magnolia State. Aaron E. Henry, President, and Charles Evers, Field Director, NAACP Mississippi State Conference, telegram to the President, undated, Fall 1966, Charles Evers Name File (Jackson, Miss.), box 138, LBJL.

18. William Taylor, staff director of U.S. Commission on Civil Rights, memorandum on proposed 1966 civil rights legislation, December 8, 1965, Selected Civil Rights Files of Harry McPherson, *CRDJA*, Part I, Reel 11, 0353–55; Westheider, *African American Experience in Vietnam*, 23–24.

19. Nicholas Katzenbach interview, November 23, 1968, 1, LBJL.

20. William E. Leuchtenburg to Joseph Califano, July 6, 1966, WHCF, Ex WE9, June 10, 1966–August 1, 1966, box 27, LBJL. See also Lemann, *Promised Land*, 186–87.

21. Herbers, *Lost Priority*, 191–92.

22. *New York Times*, January 7, 1966. See also Hogan, *Many Minds, One Heart*, 233–34, 251–52, 291–93, 391.

23. The high profile accorded his case also cast the harsh glare of the national media spotlight on SNCC's antiwar position. For an illuminating discussion of the impact of these events, see Grady-Willis, *Challenging U.S. Apartheid*, 79–82.

24. "News Conference, March 18, 1966," Appointment File (Diary Backup), box 31, LBJL.

25. As early as July 1965, Lee White was looking into the possibility of meeting with Martin Luther King Jr. around August 5: "It is rumored that Dr. King will have a rally in Lafayette Park to denounce your foreign policy either on August 5 or 6." See attached memo from Marvin Watson, July 23, 1965, Handwriting File, July 20–July 31, 1965 (1 of 2), box 7, LBJL.

26. James Farmer interview, July 20, 1970, by Paige E. Mulhollan, tape 2, 10, LBJL.

27. For background on the maneuvering that led to the collapse of Farmer's proposal and the critical role played by Adam Clayton Powell, see James Farmer telegram to Sargent Shriver, copy to the President, July 3, 1966, James Farmer Name File, box 23, LBJL; Loftus, "Doomed Literacy Drive: Powell's Pressure on Poverty Office to Withhold Funds Believed Decisive," *New York Times*, July 6, 1966; Dallek, *Flawed Giant*, 332; and James Farmer interview, July 20, 1970, by Paige E. Mulhollan, 12–13, LBJL.

28. Robert Kintner confidential memo to the President, July 7, 1966, WHCF, Confidential File FA, Federal Aid, box 14, LBJL.

29. Dallek, *Flawed Giant*, 331–32.

30. Robert E. Kintner to the President, October 13, 1966, WHCF, Ex WE9, September 1, 1966–October 14, 1966, box 28, LBJL. Secretary of Heath, Education, and Welfare Wilbur J. Cohen recalled that Johnson was obsessed by his belief that "the people in OEO were disloyal to him." On several occasions, Cohen vividly remembered Johnson blocking an appointment on the basis of a prospective nominee's connection to the OEO: "I don't want to appoint that fellow. He's from OEO. He's disloyal to me. He's a troublemaker." Wilbur J. Cohen interview, December 8, 1968, 10, LBJL.

31. Johnson message to SCLC Convention, August 7, 1966, Martin Luther King Jr. Name File, 1966, box 144, LBJL.

32. See, for example, Norbert A. Schlei, Assistant Attorney General, to Joseph Califano, December 18, 1965, WHCF, Ex WE9, December 18, 1965–March 11, 1966, box 26, LBJL.

33. "Memorandum for Honorable Bill Moyers," attached to Bill Moyers to Joseph Califano, August 5, 1966, WHCF, Ex WE9 August 3, 1966–August 31, 1966, box 27, LBJL.

34. Ticker Report, August 18, 1966, attached to Henry H. Wilson Jr. to the President, September 26, 1966, WHCF, Ex WE9, September 1, 1966–October 14, 1966, box 28, LBJL.

35. Charles L. Schultze, Director, Bureau of the Budget, to the President, November 6, 1965, WHCF, Ex WE9, October 24, 1965–December 17, 1965, box 26, LBJL.

36. Ibid., Memo on "Poverty Program: Opposition from the Mayors," September 18, 1965, WHCF, Ex WE9, August 1, 1965–September 21, 1965, box 26, LBJL. Even in the heady early days of the War on Poverty, the administration saw maximum feasible participation as a method by which — in Robert Kennedy's words — the various antipoverty programs could include "real representation for the poor . . . giving them a real voice in their institutions." The key words were "representation" and "voice," not control. Schlesinger, *Robert Kennedy and His Times*, 640.

37. Columnist Ted Lewis, writing in the *New York News*, characterized the OEO director as "easily the Administration's glibbest exponent of the Madison Avenue selling techniques" and perceptively noted that Shriver's "masterful job in selling the Peace Corps to a skeptical Congress" uniquely prepared him for the challenges of securing congressional appropriations for the War on Poverty. Lewis, "Capitol Stuff," *New York News*, November 25, 1965.

38. Bill Crook to Bill Moyers, "Progress Report," May 3, 1966, WHCF, Ex WE9, March 12, 1966–May 10, 1966, box 27, LBJL (emphasis in original).

39. Sargent Shriver to the President, June 22, 1966, WHCF, Ex WE9, June 10, 1966–August 1, 1966, box 27, LBJL.

40. "War on Poverty: 'Present Danger,'" *Newsweek*, August 6, 1966, clipping in Bertrand M. Harding Personal Papers, Conference File: Washington, D.C., Urban Affairs Conference re Ribicoff Hearings on Urban Affairs, August 12, 1966, box 41, LBJL.

41. Vice President Hubert Humphrey to the President, December 2, 1965, WHCF, Ex WE9, October 24, 1965–December 17, 1965, box 26, LBJL.

42. Testimony of Sargent Shriver before Senate Subcommittee on Executive Reorganization, August 16 and 19, 1966, Bertrand M. Harding Papers, Office of Economic Opportunity, 1966–68, Conference File: Washington, D.C., Urban Affairs Conference re Ribicoff Hearings on Urban Affairs, August 12, 1966, box 41, LBJL.

43. On January 3, a Tuskegee, Alabama, gas station attendant murdered SNCC organizer Sammy Younge Jr. for using the white-only public toilet. A week later, Klansmen firebombed the home of Dahmer, a black Hattiesburg, Mississippi, businessman and voting rights activist the day after he announced that his black neighbors could pay their poll tax at his general store.

44. Lawson, *In Pursuit of Power*, 65. After more than four decades, in 2007 the African American district attorney in Marion County, Alabama, obtained an indictment against James Fowler, the state trooper who had killed Jimmie Lee Jackson in 1965.

45. For a wide-ranging discussion of the evolution of the 1966 civil rights legislative package, see Lawson, *In Pursuit of Power*, 64–77. See also Belknap, *Federal Law and Southern Order*, 205–28.

46. The invitation list included Dorothy Height; Martin Luther King Jr.; John Lewis;

CORE's new director, Floyd McKissick; A. Philip Randolph; Roy Wilkins; and a handful of other civil rights allies, including NAACP lobbyist Clarence Mitchell and Louis Martin from the Democratic National Committee.

47. Nicholas Katzenbach Briefing Memo for the President for Meeting with Civil Rights Leaders on March 18, 1966, March 17, 1966, Selected Civil Rights Files of Harry McPherson, *CRDJA*, Part I, Reel 11, 0538–40. Two days earlier, Katzenbach had played out an intriguing scenario in which the failure of civil rights legislation would redound to the administration's benefit if Republicans joined with white southern Democrats in killing Johnson's bill: "I can see worse fates than saddling the Republicans with our failure—if it is failure—to secure enactment." Attorney General Nicholas Katzenbach to Henry H. Wilson, March 15, 1966, Handwriting File, March 1966 (2 of 4), box 13, LBJL.

48. Katzenbach, Joseph Califano, and a chorus of others from inside and outside of the administration urged Johnson to move on introducing the bill. See Joseph Califano to the President, April 13, 1966, Handwriting File, April 1966 (2 of 2), box 14, LBJL.

49. Joseph Califano to the President, April 23, 1966, filed with April 28, 1966, Appointment File (Diary Backup), box 33, LBJL.

50. Among its other impacts, the jury laws, if passed, would have voided state legislation in Alabama, Mississippi, and Louisiana, where women were completely excluded by law from jury service.

51. Campbell, *Senator Sam Ervin*, 153.

52. William Colmer (D.-Miss.) *Congressional Record—House*, August 3, 1966, 18110–11.

53. After talking with a number of Democratic congressmen on Capitol Hill in early September, Nicholas Katzenbach warned Joe Califano that the bill was in trouble because the housing provision, as the "first attempt to secure legislation on a civil rights problem that exists in serious form in the north," was the most "controversial and explosive of all civil rights issues." Campbell, *Senator Sam Ervin*, 153.

54. Branch, *At Canaan's Edge*, 522; Lawson, *In Pursuit of Power*, 72–74. Young and King quotes in Ralph, *Northern Protest*, 123. Ralph offers the most authoritative treatment of King and the SCLC's Chicago campaign.

55. Sam Ervin (D.-N.C.) and Allen J. Ellender (D.-La.), *Congressional Record—Senate*, September 16, 1966, 22806. Ellender was pleased to report to the Senate that he was hearing reliable reports that white contributions to the civil rights coffers of SNCC and SCLC were drying up. In the case of SNCC in particular, "many of the Jews of our country who formerly furnished money to this organization are beginning to see the light."

56. Governor Paul Johnson, Press Release, September 18, 1966, Paul Johnson Family Papers, Folder 18, Press Releases: September 1966, box 104, USMSC. On the white attacks in Grenada, see Branch, *At Canaan's Edge*, 527–29.

57. Lawson, *In Pursuit of Power*, 76–77.

58. Lawson's chapter, "The Land of the Tree and the Home of the Grave," offers a compelling history of civil rights legislative efforts in 1966, 1967, and 1968. Lawson, *In Pursuit of Power*, 43–88.

59. Harry McPherson to Nicholas Katzenbach, September 20, 1966, Selected Civil Rights Files of Harry McPherson, *CRDJA*, Part I, Reel 11, 0643–52.

60. Harris Survey, by Louis Harris, release date of August 15, 1966, Selected Civil Rights Files of Harry McPherson, *CRDJA*, Part I, Reel 11, 0701–4; Gallup Poll, release date of July 20, 1966, ibid., 0705–6. The Johnson administration gained regular access to polling data before it was released to the public. Lou Harris asked that the White House keep confidential the fact that the administration was learning what the polls said before the public did, and occasionally newspaper editors at the *Washington Post* grew apoplectic when they learned of the White House's "early warning system" for polling data. See, for example, Fred Panzer, confidential memo to the President, December 28, 1967, WHCF, Confidential File HU2-2, Freedoms, box 57, LBJL.

61. Harry McPherson to the President, September 12, 1966, Selected Civil Rights Files of Harry McPherson, *CRDJA*, Part I, Reel 11, 0650–53 (emphasis in original). For a useful discussion of this exchange of memos among McPherson, Nicholas Katzenbach, and the president, see Miroff, "Presidential Leverage over Social Movements," 19–20.

62. LBJ phone call with Richard Daley, 7:10 P.M., July 19, 1966, Cit. 10414, Audiotape WH6607.02, LBJL.

63. Louis Martin interview, 31, LBJL; Note from the President, March 24, 1967, WHCF, Louis Martin Name File, box 127, LBJL. See also Clifford Alexander interview, June 4, 1973, 31, LBJL.

64. Harry McPherson to the President, September 12, 1966, Selected Civil Rights Files of Harry McPherson, *CRDJA*, Part I, Reel 11, 0650–53.

65. McPherson's self-assurance in identifying the aspirations of "*the* Negro community" comes across strikingly in this memorandum and highlights the importance of perception as a central component in shaping the dynamics of interaction between the White House and black Americans. Implicitly, those African Americans who *did* choose to dance to the tune of "extremists" did not merit inclusion in this unitary definition of black community; and presumably those who fell outside of the spectrum of "Negro moderation" in McPherson's estimation represented a "problem," an intriguing update on the classic age-old articulation of the "Negro problem."

66. As a corollary, which reflected the growing apprehensions about white "backlash" in the White House inner circle and the feeling of being besieged from two directions at once, McPherson suggested that Johnson would be "damned" by many whites no matter what he did: "[They] will still identify you as the Negroes' protector."

67. Nicholas Katzenbach to Harry McPherson, September 17, 1966, Selected Civil Rights Files of Harry McPherson, *CRDJA*, Part I, Reel 11, 0646–48.

68. Miroff, "Presidential Leverage over Social Movements," 15; Harry McPherson to Nicholas Katzenbach, September 20, 1966, Selected Civil Rights Files of Harry McPherson, *CRDJA*, Part I, Reel 11, 0643–45.

69. Gerson, *Neoconservative Vision*. After the mid-1970s, Wattenberg proudly described himself as a neoconservative, but he continued to defend LBJ's antipoverty policies as something quite different from the "turbulence" that followed Johnson's administration. Wattenberg, "The Great Society's Bum Rap," in Cowger and Markman, *Lyndon Johnson Remembered*, 166.

70. In one draft of the speech, the item "family problems" is crossed off of the list, clear

evidence that one year after the Moynihan controversy first erupted the administration still felt that mention of Moynihan's "tangle of pathology," in virtually any context, would be deemed politically radioactive. "Negro Speech" drafts, n.d. (ca. September 1966), Selected Civil Rights Files of Marvin Watson, *CRDJA*, Part I, Reel 12, 0407–43.

71. Harry McPherson interview, March 24, 1969, by Thomas H. Baker, 9, LBJL; Ben Wattenberg interview, November 23, 1968, 27–31, LBJL. See also Lawson, *In Pursuit of Power*, 24.

72. *New York Times*, October 14, 1966. The advertisement contained an embedded endorsement of the right of any individual — white or black — to exercise force in the cause of self-defense but warned against the doctrine of armed self-defense being "perverted into a cover for aggressive violence," a trend many of the signers felt was already under way.

73. *New York Times*, October 14, 1966; Martin Luther King Jr., "I Have a Dream," in Mullane, *Crossing the Danger Water*, 647.

74. Solicitor General Thurgood Marshall to the President, January 14, 1966, "Remarks of the President at the Civil Rights Reception," November 16, 1965, Voting Rights — State of the Union, Legislative Background and Domestic Crises File, box 2, LBJL.

75. Mary McGrory, *Evening Star* (Washington), August 5, 1966, in Sundquist, *Politics and Policy*, 279. Over a year earlier, on the day after Johnson's Howard University speech, the African American–published *New York Amsterdam News* quoted Attorney General Katzenbach's critique of northern clergymen "who rush to join Southern freedom marchers but do little for Negroes in their own home parishes. . . . 'These ministers who are quick to fly to Selma are less quick to see the problem back home. They had better do something about it. If they don't, the problems are going to get worse.'" *New York Amsterdam News*, June 5, 1965. The insinuation of northern white hypocrisy was a time-tested theme in white southern opposition to the involvement of white northerners — seen as "outside agitators" and "neo-abolitionists" in a latter-day sectional conflict. See, for example, David C. Carter, "Williamston Freedom Movement," 1–42.

76. Dallek, *Flawed Giant*, 339.

77. *New York Times*, November 12, 1966.

78. Ibid., November 23, 1966.

79. For those who wanted to view the survey through rose-tinted glasses, two statistical measures offered some measure of solace. Although whites remained unconvinced that antipoverty programs could reduce the volatility so apparent in the nation's cities, fully two-thirds of all Americans felt that "it is both desirable and possible to develop a program of federal aid for those at the bottom of the economic scale," this despite "the prevailing view that the war on poverty has been fouled up."

80. *Washington Post*, December 19, 1966. Rauh actually played the "riot card," raising the possibility of urban unrest as reporters dutifully recorded him saying: "If there is any trouble in this city . . . they who held back a few dollars will know who is responsible for it."

81. Robert E. Kintner to Marvin Watson, December 20, 1966, WHCF, Confidential File WE9, Poverty Program (Great Society), 1964–66, box 98, LBJL.

82. The President, Greetings to the Urban League, November 10, 1966, Whitney M. Young Jr. Name File, box 41, LBJL.

83. Dallek, *Flawed Giant*, 331–33; Patterson, *America's Struggle against Poverty*, 143.

84. Bill Moyers to the President, December 19, 1966, Sargent Shriver Name File, box 279, LBJL. Sensitive to the matter of appearances, Shriver was anxious for Johnson to receive his resignation before new budget figures were announced so that "the President will know that the budget has nothing whatsoever to do with my resignation." Moyers concluded his memo with a wink at Shriver's desire to remain near the levers of political power: "It was clear to me that Shriver is serious about this, but was also apparent that he is more anxious to turn the War on Poverty over to someone else than he is to leave the government."

85. Dallek, *Flawed Giant*, 332–33. See also Califano, *Triumph and Tragedy*, 80. Shriver ultimately remained at the helm of the OEO until spring 1968, when he accepted a short-lived appointment as U.S. ambassador to France, one interrupted by Nixon's ascension to the White House following the election of 1968.

86. The degree of turnover in personnel at the OEO rose sharply from later in 1965 to 1966. As the OEO came under a barrage of renewed attacks in spring 1967, there was growing concern by liberal supporters that the agency would be dismembered or defunded into oblivion. See, for example, Walter P. Reuther, Chairman, Citizens' Crusade against Poverty, to the President, April 13, 1967, WHCF, Ex WE9, April 8, 1967–April 19, 1967, box 29, LBJL.

87. McPherson to the President, December 19, 1966, Selected Civil Rights Files of Harry McPherson, *CRDJA*, Part I, Reel 11, 0663–66.

88. Donald H. Radler to Marvin Watson, January 6, 1966, WHCF, Confidential File FG 11–15, box 21, LBJL.

89. See Harry McPherson to the President, "En Route to Ranch," December 30, 1966, Selected Civil Rights Files of Harry McPherson, *CRDJA*, Part I, Reel 11, 0695–97.

90. Grant, *Black Protest*, 396–400; Garrow, *Bearing the Cross*, 550–53. Thomas F. Jackson's discussion of King's opposition to the Vietnam War is especially instructive. See Jackson, *From Civil Rights to Human Rights*, 308–28.

91. In Roche's view, King was in part joining the peace movement because of the increasingly dire fiscal straits facing many civil rights organizations. Members of the "Communist-oriented" peace movement would provide "money to keep up his standard of living" and guarantee him "a crowd to applaud." John P. Roche, "Eyes Only" Memorandum for the President, April 5, 1967, WHCF, Confidential File HU2, Equality of the Races, 1967, box 56, LBJL (emphasis added). For a detailed breakdown of the positive and negative media coverage that greeted King's Riverside Church speech—more of the latter than the former—see Garrow, *Bearing the Cross*, 553–56. *Life* magazine offered scathing commentary, describing King's text—much of it improvised—as "demagogic slander that sounded like a script for Radio Hanoi."

92. Fairclough, *Martin Luther King, Jr.*, 114.

93. Branch, *At Canaan's Edge*, 659–60. The fund-raising solicitation clearly irked Johnson and his advisers, and it was widely circulated through the White House. Joseph Califano passed on the SCLC fund-raising appeal to White House secretary Marvin Watson and snidely remarked: "I am a little pressed because of Christmas buying, but I thought you might like to contribute." Martin Luther King Jr., "Dear Friend," November 1967, attached

to Joseph Califano to Marvin Watson, November 24, 1967, WHCF, Martin Luther King Jr. Name File (1967), box 144, LBJL.

94. George Christian to the President, April 8, 1967, Martin Luther King Jr. Name File, 1967, box 144, LBJL.

95. Garrow, *Bearing the Cross*, 554–55. Both Carl Rowan and Hoover were obsessed by the alleged "communistic" influence of King adviser Stanley Levinson.

96. Clifford Alexander to the President, Notes for Meeting with Roy Wilkins, April 18, 1967, WHCF, Ex Appointment File (Diary Backup), LBJL.

97. Louis Martin to John Criswell, forwarded to White House Secretary Marvin Watson, August 28, 1967, WHCF, Ex WE9, August 16, 1977–September 12, 1967, box 30, LBJL. As historian Steven F. Lawson has perceptively noted, "Vietnam and the riots isolated the President from black radicals, but drew him closer to such moderates as Wilkins and Young." Lawson, "Civil Rights," 108.

98. Garrow, *Bearing the Cross*, 556. Malcolm X had drawn the same connections in the months before his assassination.

Chapter Seven

1. Martin Luther King Jr., "Where Do We Go from Here?" Annual Report Delivered at the 11th Convention of the Southern Christian Leadership Conference. Full citation from <http://www.stanford.edu/group/King/publications/speeches/Where_do_we_go_from_here. html> (January 6, 2008).

2. Billy Graham to the President, July 6, 1964, WHCF, Ex FG 155–18, *CRDJA*, Part I, Reel 1, 0194. Graham agreed to serve as an ordinary member of the committee.

3. Douglass Cater to the President, June 23, 1964, WHCF, Ex FG 155–18, *CRDJA*, Part I, Reel 1, 0219.

4. Califano, *Triumph and Tragedy*, 61–62.

5. Morris Abram interview, March 20, 1984, 13–14, 16, LBJL.

6. *New York Times*, November 7, 1965.

7. Bill Graham to the President, May 18, 1967, WHCF, Ex WE9, May 11, 1967–June 14, 1967, box 29, LBJL. See also Rainwater and Yancey, *Moynihan Report and the Politics of Controversy*, 214–16.

8. Morris Abram interview, March 20, 1984, 17, LBJL.

9. Harry McPherson to the President, September 7, 1966, Selected Civil Rights Files of Harry McPherson, *CRDJA*, Part I, Reel 11, 0728.

10. For more detailed discussion of the role and impact of the media in shaping public perceptions of the riots, see chapter 8.

11. Thomas E. Cronin to the President, May 31, 1967, WHCF, Ex WE9, box 29, LBJL.

12. O'Reilly, *Racial Matters*, 231.

13. *Ebony*, the nation's leading black magazine, unsuccessfully tried to reframe the issue by publishing an entire issue in August 1965 entitled "The WHITE Problem in America." "For more than a decade through books, magazines, newspapers, TV and radio, the white man has been trying to solve the race problem through studying the Negro," wrote *Ebony*'s

editor. "We feel that the answer lies in a more thorough study of the man who created the problem."

14. Kearns, *Lyndon Johnson and the American Dream*, 340.

15. In 1938's *The Anatomy of Revolution*, author Crane Brinton first developed the notion of a "revolution of rising expectations," a concept that would be widely used by social scientists in the 1960s and 1970s to explain the rise of urban unrest even as progress was being made.

16. "Although my fingers are still crossed," Taylor ended his memo, "I believe that we are safe through the next three weeks [until Election Day]." Hobart Taylor to the President, October 13, 1964, WHCF, Ex FG 155–18, box 229, LBJL. Michael Flamm discusses how the "law and order" campaign theme that would prove to be so successful for Richard Nixon and George Wallace in the presidential campaign of 1968—and arguably during the 1966 congressional elections as well—made its first appearance during the Goldwater campaign of 1964. See Flamm, *Law and Order*, 31–50. For mention of the 1964 riots as "Goldwater rallies," see chapter 1; and Dan T. Carter, *Politics of Rage*, 222.

17. Guthman and Shulman, *Robert Kennedy*, 66.

18. Califano, *Triumph and Tragedy*, 63; LBJ phone call with Nicholas Katzenbach, 11:55 A.M., August 17, 1965, Cit. 8544, Audiotape WH6508.05, LBJL.

19. LBJ phone call with John McCone, 12:10 P.M., August 18, 1965, Cit. 8550, Audiotape WH6508.05, LBJL.

20. Roger Wilkins, *A Man's Life*, 71–73. See Ramsey Clark interviews, February 11, 1969, 22–23, and March 21, 1969, 1, LBJL.

21. "Report of the President's Task Force on the Los Angeles Riots, August 11–15, 1965," September 10, 1965, Ramsey Clark Papers, Los Angeles (2 of 2), 46–48, box 71, LBJL.

22. Ramsey Clark Papers (1 of 2), box 71, LBJL . See also Roger Wilkins to Ramsey Clark, November 11, 1966, ibid.

23. Horne, *Fire This Time*, 286; Roger Wilkins, *A Man's Life*, 173.

24. *New York Times*, October 31, 1965.

25. Southern California Advisory Commission to the Civil Rights Commission on the McCone Report, attached to Roger Wilkins to Ramsey Clark, January 11, 1966, Ramsey Clark Papers, Los Angeles (1 of 2), box 71, LBJL.

26. Ramsey Clark interview, March 21, 1969, 7, LBJL.

27. Interestingly, Reedy suggested that the intelligence-gathering unit be placed within the CRS. George Reedy to the President, August 22, 1965, Selected Civil Rights Files of Harry McPherson, *CRDJA*, Part I, Reel 11, 0499–502. For a similar suggestion, see Wilbur J. Cohen, Department of Health, Education, and Welfare Undersecretary to Joseph Califano, August 23, 1965, WHCF, Confidential File HU2/ST#, box 56, LBJL.

28. George Reedy to the President, August 22, 1965, Selected Civil Rights Files of Harry McPherson, *CRDJA*, Part I, Reel 11, 0499–502. Reedy and many others within the Johnson administration appear to have seen the "slum"—or "ghetto," the term most frequently used to describe urban concentrations of poverty—in monochromatic terms. The crisis in the nation's cities was seen as essentially a black crisis, in the same way as what Gunnar Myrdal had identified and universalized as the "American dilemma" of deprivation of civil rights

had far more typically been cast as a "Negro problem." See Southern, *Gunnar Myrdal and Black-White Relations*, 261–92; and Walter A. Jackson, *Gunnar Myrdal and America's Conscience*.

29. George Reedy to the President, August 22, 1965, Selected Civil Rights Files of Harry McPherson, *CRDJA*, Part I, Reel 11, 0499–502; Clifford Alexander to Lee White, September 27, 1965, WHCF, Ex HU2, box 56, LBJL. For an insightful discussion of the rhetorical and ideological overlap between the discourse of "law and order" and containment of communism in the jungles of Vietnam, see Flamm, *Law and Order*, 111–23. See, for example, Fred Panzer to the President, December 7, 1967, WHCF, John V. Lindsay Name File, box 214, LBJL.

30. When it came to the question of "usable" information on the conditions of inner cities, the president made clear his disdain for the contents of "all these reports from the bureaucracy and the experts." Sherwin Markman interview, 24, LBJL.

31. Sherwin Markman interview, 27–28, LBJL.

32. Harry McPherson to the President, September 12, 1966, Selected Civil Rights Files of Harry McPherson, *CRDJA*, Part I, Reel 11, 0650–53 (emphasis in original).

33. Nicholas Katzenbach to Harry McPherson, September 17, 1966, Selected Civil Rights Files of Harry McPherson, *CRDJA*, Part I, Reel 11, 0646–48.

34. Nicholas Katzenbach to Harry McPherson, September 17, 1966, Selected Civil Rights Files of Harry McPherson, *CRDJA*, Part I, Reel 11, 0646–48. Dwight Ink, a high-ranking administrator in the newly created Department of Housing and Urban Development, discussed with Joseph Califano a similar program of outreach. Dwight A. Ink to Joseph Califano, August 15, 1966, WHCF, Ex WE9, August 3, 1966–August 31, 1966, box 27, LBJL.

35. Nicholas Katzenbach to Harry McPherson, September 17, 1966, Selected Civil Rights Files of Harry McPherson, *CRDJA*, Part I, Reel 11, 0646–48.

36. Sherwin Markman interview, 25, LBJL.

37. Ibid., 24–25, LBJL. I am indebted to the work of Steven F. Lawson, whose article on Johnson's relationships with the broad spectrum of black leadership first alerted me to the phenomenon of the "ghetto visits." See Lawson, "Mixing Moderation with Militancy," 97–100. For accounts of how the low-profile visits to the cities originated, see also Clifford Alexander interview, February 17, 1972, 3, LBJL; and A. Leon Higginbotham Jr. interview, 22–24, LBJL. There is some evidence that Johnson was considering the possibility of going into "poverty areas" in the summer of 1966. See Sargent Shriver to Bill Moyers, July 1, 1966, WHCF, Ex WE9, June 10, 1966–August 1, 1966, box 27, LBJL.

38. In typical White House accounting sleight of hand, the money to cover expenses incurred during the visits by Johnson's staff usually came from funds earmarked for various presidential task forces, typically operating out of the Labor Department. Joseph Califano to the President, May 6, 1967, WHCF, Ex WE9, box 29, LBJL.

39. Sherwin Markman interview, 26–27, LBJL. A. Leon Higginbotham Jr. interview, 23, LBJL. In Philadelphia, Higginbotham and Markman posed as reporters for the *Philadelphia Tribune*.

40. Sherwin Markman interview, 27, LBJL.

41. Ibid., 1–2; A. Leon Higginbotham Jr. interview, 21–22, LBJL. Louis Martin had long

played such a role, often working closely with other high-ranking administration officials to arrange meetings with local black officials and community activists. See Clifford Alexander to the President, February 1, 1967, Louis Martin Name File, box 127, LBJL. Lyndon Johnson Remarks to Negro Officials, n.d., 1966, Selected Civil Rights Files of Harry McPherson, *CRDJA*, Part I, Reel 11, 0910–11; "Contacts with Civil Rights Leaders, 1963–1968," Legislative Background and Domestic Crises File, Voting Rights Act of 1965, box 1, LBJL.

42. Clifford Alexander to Harry McPherson, November 22, 1966, Office Files of the White House Aides, Harry McPherson, box 22, LBJL; James C. Gaither to the President, May 9, 1967, WHCF, Ex WE9, April 20, 1967–May 10, 1967, box 29, LBJL.

43. The process by which White House scouts readily conflated different urban geographies and ethnographies into one archetypal "ghetto" merits further inquiry.

44. Sherwin Markman to the President, "American Ghettos: Our Challenge and Response," April 5, 1967, WHCF, Ex WE9, box 31, LBJL (emphasis added). See also Lewis, *Walking with the Wind*, 356, for a discussion of how as early as 1965 SNCC workers hung a sign on the wall of their Atlanta headquarters reading: "NO VIETNAMESE EVER CALLED ME NIGGER." Historian Steven F. Lawson notes that much of the established middle-class black civil rights leadership navigated a similar divide in perception and understanding; the experiences of the young and poor in the nation's cities "remained foreign both to white liberals and their older, middle-class black allies." Lawson, "Mixing Moderation with Militancy," 97.

45. Bill Graham to the President, May 18, 1967, WHCF, Ex WE9, box 29, LBJL. (The White House staffer shared a name with the more famous evangelist.) For a similar argument, see the confidential memo of Bernard L. Boutin, Deputy Director to Joseph Califano, April 6, 1966, WHCF, Confidential File HU/ST#, Equality of the Races, box 56, LBJL.

46. Harry McPherson to Nicholas Katzenbach, September 20, 1966, Selected Civil Rights Files of Harry McPherson, *CRDJA*, Part I, Reel 11, 0650–53 (emphasis added).

47. Harry McPherson interview, April 9, 1969, by Thomas H. Baker, tape 1, 12, LBJL. Variations on the theme of "the touch of the administration hand is death" were often heard in the White House in the last three years of the Johnson administration, but McPherson argued that, given Johnson's generally favorable rating among most blacks, White House recognition would not taint leaders irreparably. See Harry McPherson to Nicholas Katzenbach, September 20, 1966, and Nicholas Katzenbach to Harry McPherson, September 17, 1966, Office Files of the White House Aides, Harry McPherson, box 22, LBJL; Lawson, *In Pursuit of Power*, 9–10; Lawson, "Mixing Moderation with Militancy," 97; and Miroff, "Presidential Leverage over Social Movements," 11. Miroff categorizes White House attempts to "call the shots" for moderate civil rights as "managerial efforts," and he rightly notes that the White House was aware of the dangers of such an approach.

48. Harry McPherson interview, April 9, 1969, by Thomas H. Baker, tape 1, 12, LBJL.

49. See Lawson, "Mixing Moderation with Militancy." For a detailed treatment of the Chicago campaign, see Ralph, *Northern Protest*.

50. Ramsey Clark interview, March 21, 1969, 16, LBJL.

51. See Douglass Cater to the President, July 23, 1964, Ex FG 155–18, box 229, LBJL; Clifford Alexander to Lee White, September 27, 1965, Ex HU2, box 56, LBJL; and Stanford G. Ross to the President, May 9, 1967, Ex WE9, box 29, LBJL.

52. Although the term "white backlash" was in use by this time, it was only in the aftermath of the 1966 and (even more so) the 1968 elections that the full extent of the growing opposition to civil rights became apparent to many observers.

53. *New York Times*, October 24, 1966.

54. Ramsey Clark in 1963 was assistant attorney general in the Department of Justice's Lands Division. See Ramsey Clark to George Reedy, June 6, 1963, and George Reedy to Vice President Lyndon Johnson, June 7, 1963, Selected Civil Rights Files of George Reedy, *CRDJA*, Part I, Reel 12, 0256–62.

55. According to Harry McPherson, liberals opposed it because they believed it would become nothing more than "an attempt to ameliorate away Negro rights." Harry McPherson interview, April 9, 1969, by Thomas H. Baker, tape 1, 6, LBJL. See also Lawson, "Civil Rights," 111.

56. Calvin and Elizabeth Kytle interview, July 11, 1997, tape recording. A recent exception to the general neglect of CRS is Levine's *Resolving Racial Conflict*.

57. As Ramsey Clark noted in an interview about the benefits of confidentiality, "If [CRS representatives are] performing as they should, they're invisible." He agreed with interviewer Thomas H. Baker's assessment: "Their success is marked in what doesn't happen." Ramsey Clark interview, March 21, 1969, 15–16, LBJL.

58. It should be noted that the CRS was never granted any enforcement authority. It depended on suasion and was premised on the belief that controversies could best be defused behind closed doors, out of the media spotlight, which tended to harden positions on all sides.

59. "Memorandum for the President from the Vice President on Recommended Reassignment of Civil Rights Functions," September 24, 1965, Selected Civil Rights Files of Harry McPherson, *CRDJA*, Part I, Reel 11, 0339–42. This was the memo prepared by Califano, White, and Katzenbach, on which Humphrey bestowed a reluctant blessing and a claim of authorship when pressured by Johnson, losing much of his authority over civil rights in the process.

60. Calvin and Elizabeth Kytle interview, July 11, 1997, tape recording.

61. Calvin Kytle Letter of Resignation to John T. Connor, Secretary of Commerce, December 14, 1965, copy of letter in author's possession, courtesy of Calvin Kytle.

62. Roger Wilkins, *A Man's Life*, 163–64.

63. Calvin and Elizabeth Kytle interview, July 11, 1997, tape recording.

64. Andrew "Mac" Secrest interview, tape recording. Collins's interviewer expressed surprise that Johnson would "reach down that far" to derail Kytle, someone "beneath his notice." "No, no," the former Florida governor replied: "He was the kind of president that reached down that far." LeRoy Collins interview, 36, 39, LBJL.

65. Calvin Kytle Letter of Resignation to John T. Connor, Secretary of Commerce, December 14, 1965, copy of letter in author's possession, courtesy of Calvin Kytle; *New York Times*, December 15, 1965.

66. LeRoy Collins to John McCone, November 22, 1965, Roger Wilkins to Ernest Friesen, November 22 and 23, 1965, John Perry, "Response to Mr. McCone's Communication about the Encounter of Members of Your Staff with the Police in Los Angeles," all in Ramsey

Clark Papers, Los Angeles (1 of 2), box 71, LBJL; Roger Wilkins, *A Man's Life*, 166–68; Harry McPherson interview, April 9, 1969, by Thomas H. Baker, tape 1, 5, LBJL.

67. Calvin and Elizabeth Kytle interview, July 29, 1997, tape recording.

68. Unsigned Memo, "Questions Regarding the Responsibilities of the Department of Justice in the Field of Civil Rights," December 9, 1965, Selected Civil Rights Files of Harry McPherson, *CRDJA*, Part I, Reel 11, 0388–90.

69. *New York Times*, January 10, 1966. Some observers were stunned to see the youthful Roger Wilkins elevated to a position of authority over Brooks Hays; in one blow, the White House upended both generational and racial hierarchies. For his part, Hays claimed, "it didn't bother me a bit in the world. . . . My sensibilities were not shocked at all." Brooks Hays interview, October 5, 1971, 17, LBJL.

70. Ramsey Clark interview, March 21, 1969, 13, LBJL; Harry McPherson interview, April 9, 1969, by Thomas H. Baker, 12, LBJL. See Roger Wilkins, *A Man's Life*, especially 171–72, for Wilkins's early impressions of Clark.

71. Brooks Hays to Bill Moyers, December 20, 1965, Roger W. Wilkins Name File, box 312, LBJL.

72. Bill Moyers to the President, March 16, 1966, Roger W. Wilkins Name File, box 312, LBJL.

73. Roger Wilkins, *A Man's Life*, 182.

74. Roger Wilkins to Harry McPherson, "Chicago Employment Project," July 27, 1966, Selected Civil Rights Files of Harry McPherson, *CRDJA*, Part I, Reel 11, 0726–27.

75. See Harry McPherson to the President, August 5 and 12, 1966, Selected Civil Rights Files of Harry McPherson, *CRDJA*, Part I, Reel 11, 0724–25. McPherson praised Wilkins's activities in Chicago and helped to raise the profile of CRS efforts in Johnson's eyes by making sure Wilkins's CRS reports made it through the restrictive documentary gauntlet to the president's "night reading" and Oval Office desk.

76. See Clifford Alexander to the President, October 14, 1966, WHCF, Ex FG 155–18, Community Relations Service, February 11, 1966–, box 229, LBJL.

77. Andrew "Mac" Secrest interview, tape recording. Gerald Horne describes the CRS's Roger Wilkins as "rapidly becoming the firefighter of choice for urban areas." Horne, *Fire This Time*, 287. See also Lawson, "Mixing Moderation with Militancy," 113 n. 76.

78. Andrew M. Secrest to George W. Culberson, April 6, 1966, Community Relations Service internal memorandum, in author's possession, courtesy of Andrew M. Secrest; Andrew "Mac" Secrest interview, tape recording. Although Calvin Kytle's perspective was no doubt affected by his unceremonious ouster at the behest of Lyndon Johnson, he concluded that the CRS had became a secretive "information-gathering unit of the Justice Department. Its function as a conciliation unit continued . . . but my impression from what my friends who stayed on told me, it was told simply to collect information for the Department of Justice." Calvin and Elizabeth Kytle interview, July 11, 1997, tape recording.

79. During LeRoy Collins's tenure as director of the CRS, agency officials developed a system to measure levels of antagonism among whites and blacks. The "tension quotient," originally designed to take the pulse of conflicts in southern communities, was soon applied to the volatile landscape of the urban North. LeRoy Collins interview, 32, LBJL. See also

CRS Field Community Tension Factors Report guidelines, March 25, 1967, Ramsey Clark Papers, box 63, LBJL.

80. Perhaps there was some tongue in cheek at play by the CRS planner, given the otherwise tedious duty of assigning titles to personnel under the government's ubiquitous bureaucratic "organizational flow charts."

81. Willie Collier, Community Tension Factor Report, East Chicago, Indiana, August 7–13, 1967, Ramsey Clark Papers, box 63, LBJL.

82. Sherwin Markman to the President, May 9, 1967, WHCF, Ex WE9, box 29, LBJL; Bill Graham to the President, May 18, 1967, WHCF, Ex WE9, box 29, LBJL.

83. Louis Martin had called for a similar public relations initiative during the preceding summer of 1966, in the weeks following the full meeting of the White House Conference on Civil Rights. And Sherwin Markman emphatically agreed with Bill Graham. "We are not communicating with the Negro ghetto. They are basically a nonreading public and they have little or no awareness of what the federal government is doing to help. Traditional modes of communication have not penetrated and new techniques must be developed." Bill Graham to the President, April 18, 1967, WHCF, Ex WE9, box 29, LBJL; Louis Martin to Harry McPherson, July 12, 1966, Selected Civil Rights Files of Marvin Watson, CRDJA, Part I, Reel 12, 0393; Sherwin Markman to the President, February 1, 1967, WHCF, Ex WE9, box 28, LBJL.

84. Roscoe R. Nix to Ramsey Clark, Weekly Report to the Attorney General on Washington, D.C., July 17–23, 1967, Ramsey Clark Papers, box 65, LBJL. In a memo to Joseph Califano, Dwight A. Ink, an assistant secretary in the Department of Housing and Urban Development and a veteran of "undercover" visits to Watts, Harlem, and Bedford-Stuyvesant, described the cynicism with which most inner-city residents regarded visits by government officials, who were often accompanied by reporters, cameramen, and official escorts. Dwight Ink to Joseph Califano, August 15, 1966, WHCF, Ex WE9, box 27, LBJL.

85. Sherwin Markman interview, 29–30, LBJL.

86. Roger Wilkins to Clifford Alexander, March 23, 1966, Selected Civil Rights Files of Harry McPherson, CRDJA, Part I, Reel 11, 0548–56.

87. Sherwin Markman to the President, May 9, 1967, WHCF, Ex WE9, box 29, LBJL; Bill Graham to the President, May 18, 1967, WHCF, Ex WE9, box 29, LBJL.

88. Sherwin Markman to the President, May 9, 1967, WHCF, Ex WE9, box 29, LBJL. For an in-depth discussion of Leon Sullivan's activism in Philadelphia, see Countryman, Up South.

89. See also Sherwin Markman to the President, "American Ghettos: Our Challenge and Response," April 5, 1967, WHCF, Ex WE9, March 12, 1968–April 30, 1968, box 31, LBJL.

90. Congressman Joe Resnick referred to himself during this period as "the loneliest man on the Hill," because in his own mind he was defending the antipoverty program against the Republican-wielded budgetary ax, while other liberal Democrats were less vocal in their objections. See Larry Levinson to the President, April 19, 1967, WHCF, Ex WE9, April 8, 1967–April 19, 1967, box 29, LBJL.

91. Thomas E. Cronin to the President, May 31, 1967, WHCF, Ex WE9, box 29, LBJL. Although the "jungle" metaphor reflects embedded assumptions worthy of analysis, it should

be noted that numerous "ghetto" areas were described as "jungles" in popular discourse during this time period by both blacks and whites. It was a phrase drawn from many sources, notably *The Blackboard Jungle*, a popular 1955 movie starring Glenn Ford and featuring a young Sidney Poitier. Johnson himself (or rather his ghostwriters) periodically used the word "jungle" to refer to the most depressed ghetto areas. In his 1965 introduction to a special issue of *Daedalus* (ghostwritten by Daniel Patrick Moynihan), Johnson argued that it would "not be enough to open up job opportunities, if the Negro must remain trapped in a *jungle* of tenements and shanties." Quote in Moynihan, *Miles to Go*, 187 (emphasis added).

92. Sherwin Markman to the President, "American Ghettos: Our Challenge and Response," April 5, 1967, WHCF, Ex WE9, March 12, 1968–April 30, 1968, box 31, LBJL. An Inspection Report from OEO employees just over a year earlier had made similarly dire predictions about the possibility of a recurrence of violence in Watts: "Watts could happen all over again at any time. We are bombarded with this viewpoint everywhere in Los Angeles, and we see nothing to discredit it." Dick Fullmer to Edgar May, February 5, 1966, attached to Marvin Watson to Bill Moyers, February 22, 1966, WHCF, Confidential File HU2/ST#, Equality of Races, box 56, LBJL.

93. As Steven F. Lawson has observed, from a purely pragmatic standpoint there is next to no evidence that the visits served a concrete predictive function. Visitors "to Detroit in May 1967 did not turn up a clue that a disastrous riot would break out only two months later," he notes, "nor did travelers to Oakland in March mention the Black Panther party." Lawson, "Mixing Moderation with Militancy," 99.

94. Hubert Humphrey presented this viewpoint himself a full two months before the Watts riot, when the vice president wrote to Johnson: "The problems of the urban slums are so large and so profound, and the anger, alienation, frustration and despair of the Negroes who live in them are so great, that crash programs cannot be viewed as any dependable *insurance* against disorder." Hubert Humphrey to the President, "Task Force on Urban Problems," June 10, 1965, WHCF, Ex HU2, box 3, LBJL (emphasis added).

95. Roger Wilkins to John G. Stewart, March 15, 1966, Harry McPherson Files, box 21, LBJL. "A lot of this is essentially uncontrollable," another White House aide was forced to concede, referring to the growing urban crisis: "It will happen no matter what the federal government does." See Lawson, "Mixing Moderation with Militancy," 97; and Lawson and Payne, *Debating the Civil Rights Movement*, 36.

96. For a nuanced discussion of how all but a handful of women fell outside the model of "interest-group politics" most familiar to the president, see Lawson, "Mixing Moderation with Militancy," 96–97.

97. James Farmer interview, July 20, 1971, by Paige E. Mulhollan, 27, LBJL.

98. Clifford Alexander interview, November 1, 1971, 13–14, LBJL; Sherwin Markman interview, 28–31, LBJL; James R. Jones to Joseph Califano, February 4, 1967, WHCF, FG 11–8–1, box 20, LBJL. For detailed treatment of the "Rat Bill" controversy, see chapter 8.

99. Sherwin Markman interview, 28, LBJL.

100. See A. Leon Higginbotham Jr. interview, LBJL.

101. In the summer of 1966, for example, with tensions rising in Chicago as a result of the SCLC's campaign there, Joseph Califano wrote the president: "I think we should do

everything we can in the nature of Federal programs to avoid being accused of not doing all we can. At the same time I think we should stay out of the situation in terms of sending a Presidential representative, or your involvement in it." Joseph Califano to the President, July 15, 1966, WHCF, HU 2/ST 13, box 26, LBJL.

102. Other federal initiatives, such as Model Cities, youth employment, and the Task Force on Summer Domestic Programs, are largely beyond the immediate scope of this chapter, but for trenchant analysis of those issues, see, for example, Countryman, *Up South*.

103. Thomas E. Cronin to the President, May 31, 1967, WHCF, Ex WE9, May 11, 1967–June 14, 1967, box 29, LBJL.

104. On still another front in the federal response to the threat of riots, Pentagon experts on urban warfare and counterinsurgency were drawing up remarkably detailed contingency plans for rapid mobilization and deployment of regular army troops in response to disturbances. Such contingency planning went into even higher gear following the devastating Newark and Detroit riots of 1967.

105. See, for example, FBI memo, May 29, 1967, "Prevention and Control of Major Disturbances," reproduced in Belknap, *Urban Race Riots*, 23.

106. Jack Rosenthal to Ramsey Clark, September 14, 1965, Ramsey Clark Papers, box 32, LBJL.

107. Harry McPherson interview, April 9, 1969, by Thomas H. Baker, 5–7, LBJL.

Chapter Eight

1. LeRoy Collins interview, 47–48, LBJL.

2. Unless that communications gap could somehow be bridged, Reedy had warned, many whites would conclude that they had little choice but "to repress the aspirations of the Negro." Conversely, "the Negro will become more and more convinced that he has no future unless he can somehow smash the white." George Reedy to Vice President Lyndon Johnson, July 3, 1963, Selected Civil Rights Files of George Reedy, *CRDJA*, Part I, Reel 12, 0251–53.

3. Lawson, "Mixing Moderation with Militancy," 104, 97–100.

4. Remarks of the President at a Ceremony Marking the 100th Anniversary of Howard University, March 2, 1967, WHCF, Ex SP, box 230, LBJL.

5. "Package of Civil Rights, Anti-Riot Bills Is Urged," *Washington Post*, June 20, 1967, A3; News Release, August 16 and 17, 1967, William M. Colmer Papers, Speeches, News Releases, Tearsheets, box 49, USMSC; William M. Colmer to Warden Downs, August 1, 1967, William M. Colmer Papers, Legislation, L–R, 1967, box 84, USMSC.

6. April 1967: Field Community Tension Factors Report, Newark, Ramsey Clark Papers, CRS Field Community Tension Factor Reports (Milwaukee-Paterson), box 64, LBJL. See also Woodard, *Nation within a Nation*, 74–84.

7. Statement by Governor Richard J. Hughes, July 28, 1967, Ramsey Clark Personal Papers, Newark—Riot—July 1967, LBJL; "trigger-happy guardsmen," in Hayden, *Reunion*, 155.

8. Hayden, *Rebellion in Newark*, 151–58. See also Woodard, *Nation within a Nation*, 80–84.

9. A. Philip Randolph to the President, July 18, 1967, Ramsey Clark Papers, Milwaukee, Miami, and Miscellaneous Riots, box 72, LBJL.

10. Bill Crook to Bill Moyers, August 12, 1966, WHCF, Ex WE9, August 3, 1966–August 31, 1966, box 27, LBJL.

11. "You Can't Run Away," *Newsweek*, July 31, 1967, 17. See also Matusow, *Unraveling of America*, 215.

12. Harry McPherson interview, March 24, 1969, by Thomas H. Baker, 22, LBJL. As historian Allen J. Matusow notes, the House ultimately "reversed itself" several months later in 1967 "and passed a modified rat bill." Matusow, *Unraveling of America*, 482.

13. White House aide Harry McPherson was apologetic for having drawn this conclusion, "in the light of the suffering of Newark, but I tell it because that's what I know about it." Harry McPherson interview, April 9, 1969, by Thomas H. Baker, tape 1, 19, LBJL; Richard and Betty Hughes interview, tape 1, 82–87, LBJL.

14. Statement by Attorney General Ramsey Clark, September 12, 1967, Warren Christopher Papers, Detroit File, box 15, LBJL; Ramsey Clark interview, April 16, 1969, 7–8, LBJL.

15. In a later oral interview, Warren Christopher, who as deputy attorney general had served as part of a presidential fact-finding group, tactfully dismissed Romney's expressed concern as "something that I didn't understand at the time and thought somewhat short-sighted and I still don't understand it." Warren M. Christopher interview, November 18, 1968, 14, LBJL.

16. Ben Wattenberg to the President, July 24, 1967, WHCF, Ex SP 3–194, Remarks on Detroit Riots, box 188, LBJL; *New York Times*, July 22, 1967, clipping attached to this memo.

17. Warren M. Christopher interview, November 18, 1968, 9, LBJL; Cyrus Vance interview, 30–31, LBJL.

18. Roger Wilkins, *A Man's Life*, 195–96. See also Warren M. Christopher interview, November 18, 1968, 10–11, LBJL.

19. Ben Wattenberg to the President, July 24, 1967, WHCF, Ex SP 3–194, Remarks on Detroit Riots, box 188, LBJL (emphasis in original). The language Wattenberg referred to foreshadowed the verdict of the Kerner Commission Report.

20. Wattenberg broke down the administration's program in the following legislative short-hand: "Safe streets, Rats, Model Cities, Rent Supplements, OEO, job training, playgrounds, 12–month school programs." Ben Wattenberg to the President, July 24, 1967, WHCF, Ex SP 3–194, Remarks on Detroit Riots, box 188, LBJL.

21. Tom Johnson Meeting Notes, July 24, 1967, Detroit Riots, box 1, LBJL. Throughout the evening, Johnson carried around a bound volume containing *New York Times* coverage of the Detroit race riot of 1943, evidently intent on comparing his handling of the crisis with his political forebear, Franklin Delano Roosevelt. In an Oval Office interview with Ray Scherer of NBC, Frank Reynolds of ABC, and Dan Rather of CBS, conducted nearly five months later, Johnson compared the Detroit riot of 1967 and his response to it to Roosevelt's handling of the 1943 Detroit race riot. Interview with the President, December 18, 1967,

Appointment File (Diary Backup), box 85, LBJL. During three days of rioting in June 1943, there were nearly 700 serious injuries and 34 fatalities (9 whites and 25 blacks, 17 of the latter shot by police). Sugrue, *Origins of the Urban Crisis*, 29. See also Fine, *Violence in the Model City*.

22. Joseph Califano to the President, July 25, 1967, WHCF, Ex SP 3–194, Remarks on Detroit Riots, box 188, LBJL.

23. Jerome P. Cavanagh interview, 49–50, LBJL.

24. Statement by the President, WHCF, Ex SP 3–194, Remarks to the Nation on Detroit Riots and Participation by Federal Troops, July 24, 1967, box 188, LBJL.

25. Riot Toll in Cities with Major Incidents, 1964–67, August 11, 1967, Warren Christopher Papers, Civil Disturbances 1967 #1, box 10, LBJL.

26. Hersey, *Algiers Motel Incident*. See also Hayden, *Reunion*, 156.

27. Harry McPherson interview, April 9, 1969, by Thomas H. Baker, tape 1, 21–22, LBJL.

28. Ramsey Clark, Memorandum for the Director, Federal Bureau of Investigation, September 14, 1967, Warren Christopher Papers, Civil Disturbances 1967 #1, box 10, LBJL.

29. Ibid.; Fred R. Harris, *Does People Do It*, 110–11; Fred Harris interview, tape recording.

30. Notes from the President's Meeting with the Congressional Leadership, July 24, 1967, Tom Johnson Meeting Notes, box 1, LBJL.

31. Concurrent Resolution, H. Con. Res. 425, sponsored by Gerald Ford and others, July 25, 1967, Ramsey Clark Papers, Milwaukee, Miami, and Miscellaneous Riots, box 72, LBJL.

32. Senator Fred R. Harris to the President, July 25, 1967, attached to Douglass Cater to the President, July 25, 1967, WHCF, Ex JL, December 12, 1963–July 31, 1967, box 1, LBJL (emphasis added); Fred R. Harris, *Does People Do It*.

33. Ann Norman to the President, July 25, 1967, WHCF, Gen SP 3–194, Con/A–Z, box 188, LBJL. See also WHCF, Gen SP 3–194, Remarks to the Nation on Detroit Riots and Participation by Federal Troops, July 24, 1967, box 188, LBJL. Dozens of constituents criticized the president for "ducking" his responsibilities. An administration that had consistently come under fire for having hidden behind federalism as a means of avoiding intervening in local civil rights crises was being criticized for not intervening in local affairs. Lawson, "Civil Rights," 93–125.

34. The critical role of the riots in laying the foundations for the rise of Richard Nixon and the long-term success of American conservatism is a central theme of Rick Perlstein, *Nixonland*.

35. Negro Leaders Statement, attached to Don Slaiman, Director, Department of Civil Rights, American Federation of Labor and Congress of Industrial Organizations, "Dear Friend" informational letter, July 27, 1967, WHCF, Gen HU2, July 19, 1967–July 27, 1967, box 15, LBJL.

36. Hobart Taylor to the President, July 26, 1967, WHCF, Confidential File HU2, Equality of Races, 1967, box 56, LBJL.

37. Martin Luther King Jr. telegram to the President, July 25, 1967, Martin Luther King Jr. Name File, 1967, box 144, LBJL.

38. The other nine commissioners were (in alphabetical order): I. W. Abel, president,

United Steelworkers of America; Edward R. Brooke, U.S. senator from Massachusetts; James C. Corman, U.S. representative from Ohio; Fred R. Harris, U.S. senator from Oklahoma; Herbert Jenkins, chief of police, Atlanta; William M. McCulloch, U.S. representative from Ohio; Katherine Graham Peden, commissioner of commerce, State of Kentucky (1963–67); Charles B. "Tex" Thornton, chairman of the board and CEO, Litton Industries; and Roy Wilkins, executive director, NAACP. Victor Palmieri served as deputy executive director, working closely—although occasionally at cross-purposes—with executive director David Ginsburg.

39. President's Address to the Nation on Civil Disorders, July 27, 1967, WHCF, Ex SP 3–195, Civil Disorders, box 188, LBJL.

40. Historian Steven F. Lawson notes that such a bifurcated message was "characteristic" of Johnson's "moderate course in dealing with . . . urban rebellions. He moved between denouncing the rioters and expressing concern for the continuing plight of Blacks." Lawson and Payne, *Debating the Civil Rights Movement*, 36.

41. Ben Wattenberg to the President, July 24, 1967, WHCF, Ex SP 3–194, Remarks on Detroit Riots, box 188, LBJL. Frustrated aides struggled to mobilize a political response by emphasizing the role of conservative Republicans in cutting Great Society programs, but they were well aware that their arguments had little resonance with many angry white voters. Roche, "The Death of a Thousand Cuts," "Eyes Only" memo to Joseph Califano, Harry McPherson, Larry O'Brien, and Marvin Watson, July 5, 1967, WHCF, Confidential File PL2, Elections-Campaigns (1967), box 77, LBJL (emphasis in original); Roche, "Eyes Only" memo to the President, July 6, 1967, WHCF, Confidential File PL5, Platforms, box 77, LBJL. See also proposed speech drafts, in Leadership, July 24 and 27, 1967: President's Address to Nation on Civil Disorders, Statements of LBJ, July 6–19, 1967, box 243, LBJL.

42. Emphasis added. The Kerner Commission would take Johnson's aspiration of "one nation" and warn how elusive that goal remained.

43. Unsigned telegram to the President, July 28, 1967, WHCF, Ex SP 3–195, President's Address to the Nation on Civil Disorders, July 27, 1967, box 188, LBJL. For more correspondence in a similarly angry vein, see, for example, G. H. Dooley to the President, July 31, 1967, WHCF, McKir– Name File, box 299, LBJL. For an overall breakdown on the volume of positive and negative mail, see Whitney Shoemaker to the President, August 4, 1967, Mail Summaries, August 1967—Mail, LBJL.

44. "Talking Points to the Commission on Civil Disorders," WHCF, Ex FG 690, November 23, 1963–September 30, 1967, box 386, LBJL. See also President's Meeting with the National Advisory Commission on Civil Disorders, July 29, 1967, Tom Johnson Meeting Notes, box 1, LBJL.

45. Ramsey Clark interview, April 16, 1969, 15, LBJL.

46. President's Meeting with the National Advisory Commission on Civil Disorders, July 29, 1967, Tom Johnson Meeting Notes, box 1, LBJL.

47. Lawson, "Mixing Moderation with Militancy," 100.

48. Harry McPherson to the President, August 11, 1967, WHCF, Roger Wilkins Name File, box 312, LBJL. For McPherson's polished account of his own ghetto visits, see McPherson, *Political Education*, 359–61, 370–76.

49. Quotes in *Los Angeles Times*, August 16 and 17, 1965.

50. Gus Hall, Communist Party, U.S.A., to the President, September 7, 1965, WHCF, Ex PR14, February 1, 1965–October 14, 1966, box 290, LBJL.

51. In the president's earliest meeting with Kerner Commission executive director–designate David Ginsburg, LBJ expressed his belief that the riots were tied together at least to some extent by a conspiracy. Flamm, "Law and Order," 336.

52. Harry McPherson interview, April 9, 1969, by Thomas H. Baker, tape 1, 6, LBJL.

53. Douglass Cater to the President, July 28, 1967, WHCF, Ex FG 690, National Advisory Commission on Civil Disorders, November 23, 1967–September 30, 1967, box 386, LBJL.

54. See Tom Wicker, "Introduction," in *Report of the National Advisory Commission on Civil Disorders* (Kerner Commission), ix–x; Fred Harris interview, tape recording. Although Hoover's fantasies of a domestic communist conspiracy were far-fetched, there is little question that communist governments abroad found the riots made for effective propaganda, just as earlier civil rights disturbances from the 1950s on had. See Jeff Woods, *Black Struggle, Red Scare*; and Dudziak, *Cold War Civil Rights*, 242–48.

55. Lyndon Johnson Press Conference, July 31, 1967, Ramsey Clark Papers, Detroit—President's Statements, box 66, LBJL. The president's awareness of this dilemma became evident in the week preceding the Detroit riots when the White House pressured Sargent Shriver to cancel a scheduled trip to Newark, no doubt because of the appearance it would give of the highest-ranking antipoverty representative descending on a city before the figurative and literal ashes had had a chance to settle. Warren Christopher phone message, dictated for Attorney General Ramsey Clark, July 22, 1967, Ramsey Clark Papers, Milwaukee, Miami, and Miscellaneous Riots, box 72, LBJL.

56. Riot Toll in Cities with Major Incidents, 1964–67, August 11, 1967, Warren Christopher Papers, Civil Disturbances 1967 #1, box 10, LBJL.

57. Warren M. Christopher interview, November 18, 1968, 2, LBJL. See also Lawson, "Civil Rights," 106–8.

58. Harry McPherson interview, April 9, 1969, by Thomas H. Baker, 4–5, 3, LBJL.

59. See, for example, a fascinating memo from Robert Kintner to Johnson in the summer of 1966 calling for a more tightly focused "information campaign over a period of time . . . [of] intelligently planned news" related both to the prosecution of the war in Vietnam and to the War on Poverty. Johnson authorized Kintner and Moyers to develop such a concerted effort to improve media relations, but, as a revealing gauge of his interest in the politics of image management, he urged them to "keep the ball out of my court as much as possible." Kintner to the President, June 14, 1966, WHCF, Confidential File FG1, President of the United States, 1966, box 16, LBJL. In contrast, Johnson was obsessed with matters of image and appearance when it involved comparison with his predecessor, John F. Kennedy, at one point ordering a systematic comparison between his pronouncements on poverty and those of his predecessor. Telephone request from the President, November 25, 1966; Charles Maguire memo to Robert Kintner, November 25, 1966; and Fred Panzer to Jake Jacobsen, November 26, 1966; all in Ex WE9, October 15, 1966–December 31, 1966, box 28, LBJL.

60. Robert Kintner to the President, June 21, 1966, WHCF, Confidential File, FG1, President of the United States, 1966, box 16, LBJL. In a separate memo on the same day, Kintner

relayed to the president the advice of one constituent that he learn to master the medium of television and "compete with such professionals as [Ronald] Reagan." Kintner to the President, June 21, 1966, WHCF, Confidential File WE9, Poverty Program (Great Society) (1964–66), box 98, LBJL.

61. Hugh Davis Graham, *Civil Rights Era*, 234. In their recent Pulitzer Prize–winning account, *The Race Beat*, veteran journalists Gene Roberts and Hank Klibanoff quote storied civil rights activist John Lewis's eloquent assertion that "if it hadn't been for the media—the print media and television—the civil rights movement would have been like a bird without wings, a choir without a song." Roberts and Klibanoff, *The Race Beat*, 407. But although the authors devote twenty-two chapters and nearly four hundred pages to the relationship between the mass media and the struggle for black equality from World War II through the passage of the Voting Rights Act of 1965, they allocate only twelve pages to their coverage of the period from 1965 to 1968 in a chapter entitled simply, "Beyond." Writing elsewhere, both Julian Bond and Jenny Walker are more proportional in their treatment of the evolution of media coverage of the movement during the period after 1964–1965, but their thoughtful essays in Brian Ward's edited collection *Media, Culture, and the Modern African American Freedom Struggle* are in many respects exceptions that prove a larger rule: the role of media receives fairly systematic and nuanced attention in the early sections of the civil rights timeline but gets very little sustained analysis during the post-1965 era. See Bond, "The Media and the Movement: Looking Back from the Southern Front," 16–40, and Walker, "A Media-Made Movement? Black Violence and Nonviolence in the Historiography of the Civil Rights Movement," 41–66, both in Ward, *Media, Culture, and the Modern African American Freedom Struggle*.

62. Branch, *At Canaan's Edge*, 544. See also McGirr, *Suburban Warriors*, 203–6.

63. Dan T. Carter, *Politics of Rage*, 305.

64. Hayden, *Rebellion in Newark*, 59–67. Harry McPherson thought the extreme "law and order" approach had little to recommend it, raising the explosive but increasingly commonplace comparison to a two-front war. "If Vietnam has proved one thing, it is that heavy weapons cannot easily subdue an upheaval based even in part on social unrest." Harry McPherson to the President, March 1, 1968, attached to Joseph Califano to the President, March 2, 1968, WHCF, Confidential File FG690, National Advisory Commission on Civil Disorders, box 39, LBJL.

65. Statement by Governor Richard J. Hughes, July 28, 1967, Ramsey Clark Papers, Newark—Riot—July 1967, LBJL; Hayden, *Reunion*, 156. Miami's police chief seemed to take his cue from the Newark National Guardsman, instituting a "stop and frisk" policy, increasing police patrols in black neighborhoods, and announcing publicly: "We don't mind being accused of police brutality. They haven't seen anything yet. . . . Felons will learn that they can't be bonded out from the morgue." Newsclipping in Ramsey Clark Papers, CRS Field Community Tension Factor Reports, box 63, LBJL.

66. Ramsey Clark interview, April 16, 1969, 14–15, LBJL.

67. Douglass Cater to the President, July 28, 1967, WHCF, Ex FG 690, National Advisory Commission on Civil Disorders, November 23, 1967–September 30, 1967, box 386, LBJL. On August 3, former White House aide George Reedy similarly called attention to the fact

that the Kerner Commission "could easily wind up creating almost as many problems as the riots themselves." George Reedy to the President, August 3, 1967, WHCF, Ex FG 690, National Advisory Commission on Civil Disorders, November 23, 1963–September 30, 1967, box 386, LBJL.

68. Many, for example, thought that Atlanta police chief Herbert Jenkins would be among the more conservative voices on the commission. But Jenkins, like other commission members, was evidently deeply moved by the evidence in the testimony. Dan T. Carter interview, March 25, 2001, by author, notes; Herbert Jenkins interview, 29, LBJL. See also Fred R. Harris, *Does People Do It*, 172; and Ramsey Clark interview, April 16, 1969, 15, LBJL.

69. Jerome P. Cavanagh interview, 64, LBJL. Cavanagh was convinced that of all the suggestions he and other Detroit representatives presented in a hearing, "practically all of them wound up as recommendations of the Kerner Commission. You could almost take our presentation and change the title on it and you'd think it was the Kerner Commission Report."

70. Statement of Roger W. Wilkins, Director, CRS, Department of Justice, to the Kerner Commission, Warren Christopher Papers, National Advisory Commission on Civil Disorders #2, box 13, LBJL.

71. Gerald W. Christenson, Executive Director, President's Council on Youth Opportunity, Statement before the National Advisory Commission on Civil Disorders, November 3, 1967, Hubert Humphrey Vice Presidential Files, box 1204, Humphrey Papers, MHS.

72. Califano, *Triumph and Tragedy*, 219, 260. The tragic narrative impinges once more, with Califano writing that "it was almost inevitable that Lyndon Johnson would sour on his hasty creation." Johnson's aide later describes the Kerner Commission's attempt "to nip its creator's hand."

73. Fred R. Harris, *Does People Do It*, 108.

74. "These commissions don't work in a vacuum," Attorney General Ramsey Clark later averred. Justice Department officials "saw drafts as they progressed and even the plans." In Clark's memory, it was Joseph Califano and Harry McPherson who invested the most energy in monitoring the progress of the commission's investigation, always alert to the possibility of negative political repercussions. David Ginsburg and Otto Kerner were two of the most reliable sources of political intelligence for the White House and Justice Department. Ramsey Clark interview, April 16, 1969, 16–17, LBJL.

75. Lemann, *Promised Land*, 190; Charles L. Schultze, Confidential, to the President, September 7, 1967, CF FG690, National Advisory Commission on Civil Disorders, box 39, LBJL.

76. Charles L. Schultze to the President, January 25, 1968, Handwriting File, January 1968 (2 of 2), box 27, LBJL.

77. Otto Kerner and John Lindsay, Press Briefing, January 10, 1968, WHCF, Ex FG 690, National Advisory Commission on Civil Disorders, January 1, 1968–January 25, 1968, box 386, LBJL.

78. Fred Harris interview, tape recording.

79. *Report of the National Advisory Commission on Civil Disorders* (Kerner Commission), 2, 10 (emphasis added).

80. Joseph Califano to the President, February 27, 1968, WHCF, Ex FG 690, February 28, 1968–March 13, 1968, box 387, LBJL.

81. Joseph Califano, handwritten note to the President, February 28, 1968, WHCF, Ex FG 690, February 28, 1968–March 13, 1968, box 387, LBJL.

82. See Gareth Davies, *From Opportunity to Entitlement*, 204.

83. Tom Wicker, "Introduction," in *Report of the National Advisory Commission on Civil Disorders* (Kerner Commission), viii–xi. Califano used the same language of an "indictment" of white America in his initial memo to Johnson and later spoke of the report as "a blistering indictment of white racism" in his political memoir. See Joseph Califano to the President, February 28, 1968, WHCF, Ex FG 690, February 28, 1968–March 13, 1968, box 387, LBJL; and Califano, *Triumph and Tragedy*, 260. Whitney M. Young also opted for the word "indictment." Whitney M. Young Jr. interview, 12, LBJL. As noted below, Martin Luther King Jr. would opt for the religious idiom, comparing it to a "confession."

84. Califano, *Triumph and Tragedy*, 261–62. After reading the entire report, Califano had encouraged Johnson to consider strategic White House leaks in an attempt to soften the impact of the report in the days preceding its official release.

Otto Kerner remembered that he and David Ginsburg pleaded with Bradlee, asking him "please not to do it." The *Post*'s refusal to reconsider "upset all of us." Otto Kerner interview, 22, LBJL.

85. Fred R. Harris, *Does People Do It*, 110; Cannato, *Ungovernable City*, 205–7.

86. Califano, *Triumph and Tragedy*, 260.

87. Lester Maddox quote in Steve Ball Jr., "Riot Report Just a Bribe, Governor Says," *Atlanta Journal*, March 2, 1965, clipping and quote from Klansman and Grand Dragon Calvin F. Craig in Field Community Tension Factor Report, Atlanta, Georgia, February 19, 1968–March 3, 1968, Ramsey Clark Papers, CRS Field Community Tension Factor Reports, LBJL.

88. Herbert Jenkins quoted in Orville Gaines, "Chief Jenkins Firmly Backs Proposals to Remedy Riots," *Atlanta Journal*, March 2, 1968. See also Junie Brown, "Antiriot Report Wins [Mayor Ivan] Allen Praise," *Atlanta Journal*, March 2, 1968.

89. Garrow, *Bearing the Cross*, 599–600. Along with the theological metaphor of the confessional, King also opted for the prescriptive: The report was "a physician's warning of approaching death [of American society] with a prescription to life." Quote in O'Reilly, *Racial Matters*, 250.

90. Quotes in Flamm, "Law and Order," 342. For an illuminating discussion of King's responses, see Jackson, *From Civil Rights to Human Rights*, 332–40.

91. Fred Panzer to Jim Jones, for the President, April 19, 1968, WHCF, Ex FG 690, March 14, 1968–June 15, 1968, box 387, LBJL.

92. Quote in McPherson, *Political Education*, 376. See also Harry McPherson interview, March 24, 1969, by Thomas H. Baker, tape 2, 22, LBJL.

93. Ben Wattenberg interview, November 23, 1968, 32–33, LBJL.

94. Whitney M. Young Jr. interview, 12, LBJL.

95. Joseph Califano to the President, February 28, 1968, WHCF, Ex FG 690, February 28, 1968–March 13, 1968, box 387, LBJL.

96. Ramsey Clark interview, April 16, 1969, 16, LBJL.

97. Wicker, "Introduction," in *Report of the National Advisory Commission on Civil Disorders* (Kerner Commission), xi.

98. Lyndon Baines Johnson, *Vantage Point*, 172–73. The 10 percent tax hike was necessary to offset some of the huge expenditures going toward the Vietnam War and stem the tendency toward increased deficit spending. See Joseph W. Sullivan, "House GOP 'Activism' Takes a Drubbing," *Wall Street Journal*, November 17, 1967, clipping in WHCF, Ex WE9, November 16, 1967–November 21, 1967, box 30, LBJL.

99. Dallek, *Flawed Giant*, 516.

100. *Report of the National Advisory Commission on Civil Disorders* (Kerner Commission), 1–2.

101. See penciled notes, on Larry Temple to the President (two memoranda), February 26, 1968, and Lyndon Johnson to Joseph Califano, February 26, 1968, both in WHCF, Ex FG 690, National Advisory Commission on Civil Disorders, February 26, 1968–February 27, 1968, box 387, LBJL.

102. Califano, *Triumph and Tragedy*, 260–62. "What [Johnson] didn't like" about the Kerner Commission Report, Clifford Alexander remembered, "was certain ways that it was presented and reading the headlines before he had a chance to come to his own views." Clifford Alexander interview, November 1, 1971, 30, LBJL.

103. Ramsey Clark to the President, March 2, 1968, WHCF, Ex FG 690, February 2, 1968–March 13, 1968, box 387, LBJL (emphasis added).

104. Harry McPherson to Joseph Califano, March 1, 1968, attached to Joseph Califano to the President, March 2, 1968, WHCF, Confidential File FG690, National Advisory Commission on Civil Disorders, box 39, LBJL.

105. Remarks of the President at the Meeting with the Joint Committee on Urban Problems of the Savings Bank and Loan Industries, March 6, 1968, WHCF, Ex SP, Speeches, March 1, 1968–April 11, 1968, box 5, LBJL.

106. Clifford Alexander interview, November 1, 1971, 30, LBJL. Alexander felt that "the 'alleged' informed white media" had overlooked the generally positive coverage of the president's response to the Kerner Commission that appeared in black newspapers. Although Ben Wattenberg chided Johnson for his delay— "by then . . . it wasn't news any more"—he had a similar response, faulting the media for failing to cover the president's remarks to the black media representatives because the news would have reflected favorably on the administration: "When you say something is good, you don't get any coverage, or you get coverage that says either the figures are inaccurate or the president is blowing his own horn. . . . When you say something is bad or when somebody else says something is bad, that seeps into the national consciousness and it's just regarded as absolute fact." Ben Wattenberg interview, November 23, 1968, 34, LBJL.

107. Notes on the President's Meeting with Negro Editors and Publishers, March 15, 1968, WHCF, Ex FG 690, National Advisory Commission on Civil Disorders, March 14, 1968–June 15, 1968, box 387, LBJL.

108. Califano, *Triumph and Tragedy*, 262.

109. Ben Wattenberg interview, November 23, 1968, 33, LBJL.

110. Califano, *Triumph and Tragedy*, 260–62. See also Lawson, *Debating the Civil Rights Movement*, 37, where Lawson suggests that in ignoring the Kerner Commission's findings, "Johnson's response betrayed more than a bit of personal pique. The miffed president believed that Blacks had not shown him proper gratitude for all he had done to combat racism." Robert Dallek argues that the Kerner Commission Report "incensed" Johnson. His nonresponse derived from "a combination of personal pique and political realism. . . . But his response . . . was more ambivalent than simply hostile." Dallek, *Flawed Giant*, 516.

111. See Telephone Message, March 13, 1968, attached to Harry McPherson to the President, March 13, 1968, and manila envelope with unsigned "thank-you" letters to Kerner Commission members, all in WHCF, Confidential File FG690, National Advisory Commission on Civil Disorders, box 39, LBJL.

112. See Telephone Message, March 13, 1968, attached to Harry McPherson to the President, March 13, 1968, WHCF, Confidential File FG690, National Advisory Commission on Civil Disorders, box 39, LBJL. For brief discussions of various dimensions of this "letters never sent" episode, see O'Reilly, *Nixon's Piano*, 264–65; Lemann, *Promised Land*, 191; Gareth Davies, *From Opportunity to Entitlement*, 207; and Flamm, *Law and Order*, 104–7. See also Roy Wilkins, *Standing Fast*, 328–29; and Roy Wilkins interview, 17–20, LBJL.

113. Roy Wilkins interview, 17–20, LBJL. Ramsey Clark, on the other hand, resisted the notion that LBJ had been "irritated by the white racism concept." "I never saw any evidence of that at all." For Clark, Johnson's response—or lack thereof—was dictated by pragmatic political and economic considerations: "I was fairly close to him through all considerations on the Kerner Commission Report and I just think that he felt that it would be impossible for him to speak in terms of spending these billions when he couldn't ask the country to do it for fear of the economic consequences." Ramsey Clark interview, April 16, 1969, 17–18, LBJL.

114. Roy Wilkins, *Standing Fast*, 328.

115. Roy Wilkins interview, 18, LBJL. Wilkins suggested that LBJ misconstrued the report as a slap in his face. To the NAACP leader, the verdict of "white racism" was an indictment of the very forces Johnson had worked mightily to undermine. Johnson's failure to make this all-important distinction, in Wilkins's mind, was "one of [the President's] rare mistakes in his estimation of public opinion and in his courageous, daring outlook . . . on the whole racial situation."

116. Harry McPherson interview, March 24, 1969, by Thomas H. Baker, tape 2, 20, LBJL.

117. Herbers, *Lost Priority*, 180.

Epilogue

1. Bernstein, *Guns or Butter*, 491.

2. Gottheimer, *Ripples of Hope*, 318–19.

3. Joseph Califano to the President, April 10, 1968, WHCF, Confidential File HU2, 1964–66, box 56, LBJL. See also Califano, *Triumph and Tragedy*, 282–83.

4. Bernstein, *Guns or Butter*, 497–99.

5. David Ginsburg to the President, May 8, 1968, WHCF, Ex FG 690, National Advi-

sory Commission on Civil Disorders, March 14, 1968–June 15, 1968, box 386, LBJL. Two weeks earlier, on April 24, Otto Kerner had reported to the press that "I can see no further work for this particular Commission" and privately relayed to Joseph Califano his belief that there existed "an obvious effort to use the Commission for political purposes." Somewhat defensively, Kerner insisted that he had "tried, and I think successfully, to prevent the Commission from being used for any political purposes during its hearings, and the report itself." Califano was astute enough to realize that what his chief wanted more than any defensive assurances or Monday morning quarterbacking from Otto Kerner was simply an endpoint to what a self-pitying Johnson already felt was a public relations debacle. Accordingly, Califano relayed the Illinois governor's statement on to Johnson with a simple cover note, albeit one pregnant with meaning: "I hope the attached closes out the Kerner Commission problem." Otto Kerner to Joseph Califano, April 25, 1968, and Otto Kerner Press Release, April 24, 1968, both attached to Joseph Califano to the President, April 30, 1968, WHCF, Ex FG 690, National Advisory Commission on Civil Disorders, March 14, 1968–June 15, 1968, box 387, LBJL.

6. Flamm, "Law and Order," 343. For a description of the "siege" mentality under which Johnson increasingly operated, see Lawson, "Mixing Moderation with Militancy," 102.

7. Streitmatter, *Mightier Than the Sword*, 198.

8. Lawson, *In Pursuit of Power*, 80; *New York Times*, June 25, July 2, 5, 1967.

9. "Bomb Murderers Can Be Punished If 1967 Civil Rights Bill Is Enacted," Roy Wilkins message in NAACP pamphlet, "Public Order Based on Equal Justice," attached to Joseph Califano memo for the President, May 10, 1967, WHCF, Ex SP 2–3/1967/HU2, Message on Equal Justice, February 15, 1967, box 89, LBJL; Roy Wilkins, *Standing Fast*, 324. Wilkins recalled, "I felt that murder [of Wharlest Jackson] more deeply than anything since Medgar Evers's assassination." Dittmer, *Local People*, 417.

10. *New York Times*, March 6, 1967.

11. Governor Paul B. Johnson, Press Release, February 28, 1967, Paul Johnson Family Papers, Folder 23, Press Releases: February 1967, box 104, USMSC.

12. Johnson's condemnation of the "loathsome," "cowardly" "assassins" in 1967 begs for historical contextualization. In June 1964, Klansmen in rural Mississippi's Neshoba County brutally murdered James Chaney, Andrew Goodman, and Michael Schwerner. The murders rank among the most well-known events in the martyrology of the southern-based civil rights movement. But despite this familiarity, Mississippi governor Paul B. Johnson Jr. was not above an attempt to reshape popular memory of the three civil rights workers' deaths. In his surreal account, in an oral history conducted in 1970—six years after Freedom Summer—by researchers at the Lyndon Johnson Presidential Library, the former governor insisted that the murderers "did not actually intend to kill these people. . . . What they were going to do, they were going to hang these three persons up in a big cotton sack and leave them hanging in the tree for about a day or a day and a half, then come out there at night and turn them loose. They thought that they'd more or less scare them off." The wheels came off their plans when James Chaney, "the Negro boy from over at Meridian"—the "ringleader"—"was acting kind of smart aleck and talking pretty big." An enraged Klansman hit him with a trace chain harder than he intended to. It "killed him as dead as a nit," the Mississippi governor

concluded cheerily. History meets white supremacy. It bears repeating that Johnson gave his eerily unapologetic account of the notorious 1964 murders in Neshoba County in an oral history he granted in 1970, confirming that whatever he said publicly to condemn the racially motivated killing of Wharlest Jackson in 1967 more likely expressed a shift in tactics than a change of heart. Paul B. Johnson Jr. interview, 32–33, LBJL.

13. Robert G. Clark interview, 20–22, MSUSC. Although the decision to award credentials to Henry and Clark and their allies in 1968 represented a victory of sorts for Mississippi's black activists, it is worth noting that over the period from 1964 to 1968 Johnson's attempts to favor interracial "Loyalist" Democrats over the more grassroots MFDP were ultimately successful.

14. Lewis, *Walking with the Wind*, 351–52.

15. *Report of the National Advisory Commission on Civil Disorders* (Kerner Commission), 483.

16. Examples of this literature include Dittmer, *Local People*; Egerton, *Speak Now against the Day*; Fairclough, *Race and Democracy*; Gilmore, *Defying Dixie*; Sullivan, *Days of Hope*; and Tyson, *Radio Free Dixie*.

17. Historian Timothy Minchin describes some of the struggles for economic justice in the southern United States in his recent collection of essays, *From Rights to Economics*.

18. Patterson, *America's Struggle against Poverty*, 152. Steven F. Lawson refers to the impact of this domestic "credibility gap" on the relationship between the Johnson administration and "disgruntled African Americans," in Lawson, "Mixing Moderation with Militancy," 99. See also Rainwater and Yancey, *Moynihan Report and the Politics of Controversy*, 136; and Herbers, *Lost Priority*; and Matusow, *Unraveling of America*.

19. Clifford Alexander interview, November 1, 1971, 13, LBJL.

20. Jack Valenti interview, October 18, 1969, by Joe B. Frantz, 35, LBJL.

21. *New York Times*, December 1, 1972; Rooney, *Equal Opportunity in the United States*, 128.

22. LBJ Speech, December 12, 1972, Reference File: Post-Presidential: Civil Rights Symposium, LBJL; Dallek, *Flawed Giant*, 621–22.

23. *Report of the National Advisory Commission on Civil Disorders* (Kerner Commission), 1. "The alternative [to ongoing polarization] is not blind repression or capitulation to lawlessness," wrote the commissioners. "It is the realization of common opportunities for all within a single society."

24. Sugrue, *Origins of the Urban Crisis*, 259.

25. Kiker, *New York Herald Tribune*, June 7, 1965.

26. Sometimes Polydeuces.

Bibliography

Archival Collections

Hodding and Betty Werlein Carter Papers. Special Collections Department. Mitchell Memorial Library. Mississippi State University, Starkville.

Ramsey Clark Papers. Lyndon Baines Johnson Presidential Library. Austin, Tex.

William M. Colmer Papers. McCain Library and Archives. University of Southern Mississippi, Hattiesburg.

Hubert Humphrey Papers. Vice-Presidential Files, 1964–1968. Minnesota Historical Society. St. Paul.

Lyndon Baines Johnson Presidential and Vice-Presidential Papers. Lyndon Baines Johnson Presidential Library. Austin, Tex.

Johnson (Paul B.) Family Papers, 1917–70. Papers of Gov. Paul Johnson Jr., including materials generated by the State Sovereignty Commission and forwarded to the governor. McCain Library and Archives. University of Southern Mississippi, Hattiesburg.

Edwin King Papers. L. Lillian Pierce Renbow Room of Special Collections. Zenobia Coleman Library Archives. Tougaloo College, Jackson, Miss.

Harry C. McPherson Jr. Papers. Lyndon Baines Johnson Presidential Library. Austin, Tex.

James F. McRee Papers. L. Lillian Pierce Renbow Room of Special Collections. Zenobia Coleman Library Archives. Tougaloo College, Jackson, Miss.

National Archives and Records Administration, College Park, Md.

Lee H. Reiff Papers. Special Collections Department. Mitchell Memorial Library. Mississippi State University, Starkville.

State Sovereignty Commission Papers. Mississippi Department of Archives and History, Jackson.

White House Conference on Civil Rights Papers. Lyndon Baines Johnson Presidential Library. Austin, Tex.

Lee C. White Papers. Lyndon Baines Johnson Presidential Library. Austin, Tex.

Commercial Microfilm

Lawson, Steven F., ed. *Civil Rights during the Johnson Administration, 1963–1969*, Parts I–III. Lyndon Baines Johnson Library, Austin, Tex.; Frederick, Md.: University Publications of America, 1984. Microfilm.

——, ed. *Civil Rights during the Johnson Administration, 1963–1969*, Part IV. Lyndon Baines Johnson Library, Austin, Tex.; Frederick, Md.: University Publications of America, 1985. Microfilm.

——, ed. *Civil Rights during the Johnson Administration, 1963–1969*, Part V. Lyndon
Baines Johnson Library, Austin, Tex.; Frederick, Md.: University Publications of
America, 1987. Microfilm.

Oral Histories

Abram, Morris. Interviews by Michael L. Gillette, March 20, May 3, 1984. Transcript. Oral
History Collection. Lyndon Baines Johnson Presidential Library. Austin, Tex.

Alexander, Clifford. Interviews by Joe B. Frantz, November 1, 1971, February 17, 1972,
June 4, 1973. Transcript. Oral History Collection. Lyndon Baines Johnson Presidential
Library. Austin, Tex.

Allen, Ivan, Jr. Interview by Thomas H. Baker, May 15, 1969. Transcript. Oral History
Collection. Lyndon Baines Johnson Presidential Library. Austin, Tex.

Blackwell, Unita. Interviews by Michael Garvey, April 21, May 12, 1977. Vol. 334, transcript.
Mississippi Oral History Program of the University of Southern Mississippi. McCain
Library and Archives. University of Southern Mississippi, Hattiesburg.

Boggs, Hale. Interview by Thomas H. Baker, March 27, 1969. Transcript. Oral History
Collection. Lyndon Baines Johnson Presidential Library. Austin, Tex.

Bryant, C. Farris. Interview by Joe B. Frantz, March 5, 1971. Transcript. Oral History
Collection. Lyndon Baines Johnson Presidential Library. Austin, Tex.

Califano, Joseph. Interview by Robert Hawkinson, June 11, 1973. Transcript. Oral History
Collection. Lyndon Baines Johnson Presidential Library. Austin, Tex.

Campbell, Will. Interview by Orley B. Caudill, June 8, 1976. Vol. 157, transcript.
Mississippi Oral History Program of the University of Southern Mississippi. McCain
Library and Archives. University of Southern Mississippi, Hattiesburg.

Carpenter, Elizabeth. Interviews by Joe B. Frantz, December 3, 1968, April 4, May
5, August 27, 1969. Transcript. Oral History Collection. Lyndon Baines Johnson
Presidential Library. Austin, Tex.

Carr, Michael L., Jr. Interview by Yashuhiro Katagiri, October 28, 1993. Vol. 469,
transcript. Mississippi Oral History Program of the University of Southern Mississippi.
McCain Library and Archives. University of Southern Mississippi, Hattiesburg.

Carter, Hodding, Jr. Interview by Thomas H. Baker, November 8, 1968. Transcript. Oral
History Collection. Lyndon Baines Johnson Presidential Library. Austin, Tex.

Cater, Douglass. Interviews by David G. McComb, April 29, May 8, 1969. Transcript. Oral
History Collection. Lyndon Baines Johnson Presidential Library. Austin, Tex.

Cavanagh, Jerome P. Interview by Joe B. Frantz, March 22, 1971. Transcript. Oral History
Collection. Lyndon Baines Johnson Presidential Library. Austin, Tex.

Celebrezze, Anthony. Interview by Paige E. Mulhollan, January 26, 1971. Transcript. Oral
History Collection. Lyndon Baines Johnson Presidential Library. Austin, Tex.

Celler, Emanuel. Interview by Thomas H. Baker, March 19, 1969. Transcript. Oral History
Collection. Lyndon Baines Johnson Presidential Library. Austin, Tex.

Chancellor, John. Interview by Dorothy Pierce McSweeny, April 25, 1969. Internet copy of transcript. Oral History Collection. Lyndon Baines Johnson Presidential Library. Austin, Tex., <http://www.lbjlib.utexas.edu/johnson/archives.hom/oralhistory.hom /Chancellor/chancellor.pdf>. December 30, 2007.

Christian, George. Interviews by Joe B. Frantz, December 4, 1969, February 27, June 30, 1970. Transcript. Oral History Collection. Lyndon Baines Johnson Presidential Library. Austin, Tex.

Christian, George. Interview by Thomas H. Baker, November 11, 1968. Transcript. Oral History Collection. Lyndon Baines Johnson Presidential Library. Austin, Tex.

Christopher, Warren. Interviews by Thomas H. Baker, October 31, November 18, December 2, 1968. Transcript. Oral History Collection. Lyndon Baines Johnson Presidential Library. Austin, Tex.

Clark, Ramsey. Interviews by Thomas H. Baker, October 30, 1968, February 11, March 21, April 16, June 3, 1969. Transcript. Oral History Collection. Lyndon Baines Johnson Presidential Library. Austin, Tex.

Clark, Robert G. Interview by Betsy Nash, February 18, 1991. Transcript. John Stennis Oral History Collection. Special Collections Department. Mitchell Memorial Library. Mississippi State University, Starkville.

Cohen, Wilbur J. Interviews by David G. McComb, December 8, 1968, May 10, 1969. Transcript. Oral History Collection. Lyndon Baines Johnson Presidential Library. Austin, Tex.

Coleman, James P. Interview by Joe B. Frantz, April 29, 1972. Transcript. Oral History Collection. Lyndon Baines Johnson Presidential Library. Austin, Tex.

Collins, LeRoy. Interview by Joe B. Frantz, November 15, 1972. Transcript. Oral History Collection. Lyndon Baines Johnson Presidential Library. Austin, Tex.

Colmer, William. Interview by Joe B. Frantz, May 5, 1974. Transcript. Oral History Collection. Lyndon Baines Johnson Presidential Library. Austin, Tex.

Connor, John T. Interviews by Michael L. Gillette, June 22, 1988, October 2, 1989. Transcript. Oral History Collection. Lyndon Baines Johnson Presidential Library. Austin, Tex.

Cutler, Lloyd. Interview by William J. Helmer, April 12, 1969. Transcript. Oral History Collection. Lyndon Baines Johnson Presidential Library. Austin, Tex.

Dahmer, Ellie J. Interview by Orley B. Caudill, July 2, 1974. Vol. 281, transcript. Mississippi Oral History Program of the University of Southern Mississippi. McCain Library and Archives. University of Southern Mississippi, Hattiesburg.

Daniels, Jonathan. Interview by Joe B. Frantz, March 6, 1971. Transcript. Oral History Collection. Lyndon Baines Johnson Presidential Library. Austin, Tex.

Dean, Kenneth. Interview by author, May 21, 2008, Carrollton, Ga., author's notes.

Dean, Kenneth. Interview by Betsy Nash, June 9, 1992. Transcript. John Stennis Oral History Collection. Special Collections Department. Mitchell Memorial Library. Mississippi State University, Starkville.

Derian, Patricia (Patt). Interview by Betsy Nash, December 17, 1991. Transcript. John Stennis Oral History Collection. Special Collections Department. Mitchell Memorial Library. Mississippi State University, Starkville.

Diggs, Charles. Interview by Paige E. Mulhollan, March 13, 1969. Transcript. Oral History
   Collection. Lyndon Baines Johnson Presidential Library. Austin, Tex.

Dirksen, Everett M. Interviews by Joe B. Frantz, March 21, July 30, 1969. Transcript. Oral
   History Collection. Lyndon Baines Johnson Presidential Library. Austin, Tex.

Dirksen, Everett M. Interview by William S. White, May 8, 1968. Transcript. Oral History
   Collection. Lyndon Baines Johnson Presidential Library. Austin, Tex.

Durr, Virginia. Interview by Mary Walton Livingston, October 17, 1967. Transcript. Oral
   History Collection. Lyndon Baines Johnson Presidential Library. Austin, Tex.

Eastland, James O. Interview by Joe B. Frantz, February 19, 1971. Transcript. Oral History
   Collection. Lyndon Baines Johnson Presidential Library. Austin, Tex.

Ellender, Allen J. Interview by Thomas H. Baker, July 30, 1969. Transcript. Oral History
   Collection. Lyndon Baines Johnson Presidential Library. Austin, Tex.

Emmerich, John O. Interview by Carl Willis, 1973. Vol. 16, transcript. Mississippi Oral
   History Program of the University of Southern Mississippi. McCain Library and
   Archives. University of Southern Mississippi, Hattiesburg.

Evers, Charles. Interview by Joe B. Frantz, April 3, 1974. Transcript. Oral History
   Collection. Lyndon Baines Johnson Presidential Library. Austin, Tex.

Farmer, James. Interview by Thomas H. Baker, October 1969. Transcript. Oral History
   Collection. Lyndon Baines Johnson Presidential Library. Austin, Tex.

Farmer, James. Interview by Paige E. Mulhollan, July 20, 1971. Transcript. Oral History
   Collection. Lyndon Baines Johnson Presidential Library. Austin, Tex.

Gaither, James. Interview by Joe B. Frantz, March 24, 1970. Transcript. Oral History
   Collection. Lyndon Baines Johnson Presidential Library. Austin, Tex.

Gaither, James. Interviews by Dorothy Pierce, November 19, 1968, January 15 and 17, 1969.
   Transcript. Oral History Collection. Lyndon Baines Johnson Presidential Library.
   Austin, Tex.

Gardner, John. Interview by David G. McComb, December 20, 1971. Transcript. Oral
   History Collection. Lyndon Baines Johnson Presidential Library. Austin, Tex.

Glazier, Herman. Interview by Reid Derr, September 10, 1993. Vol. 485, transcript.
   Mississippi Oral History Program of the University of Southern Mississippi. McCain
   Library and Archives. University of Southern Mississippi, Hattiesburg.

Goldfarb, Ron. Interview by Michael L. Gillette, October 24, 1980. Transcript. Oral
   History Collection. Lyndon Baines Johnson Presidential Library. Austin, Tex.

Goldschmidt, Elizabeth Wickenden. Interview by Michael L. Gillette, November 6, 1974.
   Transcript. Oral History Collection. Lyndon Baines Johnson Presidential Library.
   Austin, Tex.

Gordon, Kermit. Interviews by David G. McComb, December 16, 1968, January 9,
   March 21, April 8, 1969. Transcript. Oral History Collection. Lyndon Baines Johnson
   Presidential Library. Austin, Tex.

Graham, Katharine. Interview by Joe B. Frantz, March 13, 1969. Transcript. Oral History
   Collection. Lyndon Baines Johnson Presidential Library. Austin, Tex.

Green, Edith. Interview by Janet Kerr-Tener, August 23, 1985. Transcript. Oral History
   Collection. Lyndon Baines Johnson Presidential Library. Austin, Tex.

Guyot, Lawrence. Telephone interview by author, June 27, 2008. Tape recording.

Haar, Charles M. Interview by Joe B. Frantz, June 14, 1971. Transcript. Oral History Collection. Lyndon Baines Johnson Presidential Library. Austin, Tex.

Hackler, Loyd. Interviews by Stephen Goodell, May 28, June 2, 1969. Transcript. Oral History Collection. Lyndon Baines Johnson Presidential Library. Austin, Tex.

Hamer, Fannie Lou. Interviews by Neil McMillen, April 14, 1972, January 25, 1973. Vol. 31, transcript. Mississippi Oral History Program of the University of Southern Mississippi. McCain Library and Archives. University of Southern Mississippi, Hattiesburg.

Hammer, Philip. Interview by author, May 13, 1998, Chapel Hill, N.C. Tape recording.

Harding, Bertrand. Interviews by Stephen Goodell, November 20, November 25, 1968. Transcript. Oral History Collection. Lyndon Baines Johnson Presidential Library. Austin, Tex.

Harris, Fred. Telephone interview by author, June 27, 2008. Tape recording.

Hays, Brooks. Interviews by Joe B. Frantz, October 5, October 6, 1971. Transcript. Oral History Collection. Lyndon Baines Johnson Presidential Library. Austin, Tex.

Heineman, Ben. Interview by Joe B. Frantz, April 16, 1970. Transcript. Oral History Collection. Lyndon Baines Johnson Presidential Library. Austin, Tex.

Heller, Walter. Interview by David G. McComb, February 20, 1970. Transcript. Oral History Collection. Lyndon Baines Johnson Presidential Library. Austin, Tex.

Henry, Aaron. Interview by Neil McMillen and George Burson, May 1, 1972. Vol. 33, transcript. Mississippi Oral History Program of the University of Southern Mississippi. McCain Library and Archives. University of Southern Mississippi, Hattiesburg.

Henry, Aaron. Interview by Thomas H. Baker, September 12, 1970. Transcript. Oral History Collection. Lyndon Baines Johnson Presidential Library. Austin, Tex.

Hesburgh, Rev. Theodore. Interview by Paige E. Mulhollan, February 1, 1971. Transcript. Oral History Collection. Lyndon Baines Johnson Presidential Library. Austin, Tex.

Higginbotham, A. Leon, Jr. Interview by Joe B. Frantz, October 7, 1976. Transcript. Oral History Collection. Lyndon Baines Johnson Presidential Library. Austin, Tex.

Hill, Lister. Transcript. Oral History Collection. Lyndon Baines Johnson Presidential Library. Austin, Tex.

Hodges, Luther. Interview by Thomas H. Baker, October 10, 1968. Transcript. Oral History Collection. Lyndon Baines Johnson Presidential Library. Austin, Tex.

Holcomb, Luther. Interviews by Thomas H. Baker, June 24, July 8, July 29, 1969. Transcript. Oral History Collection. Lyndon Baines Johnson Presidential Library. Austin, Tex.

Horowitz, Harold. Interview by Michael L. Gillette, February 23, 1983. Transcript. Oral History Collection. Lyndon Baines Johnson Presidential Library. Austin, Tex.

Howe, Harold, II. Interview by David G. McComb, October 29, 1968. Transcript. Oral History Collection. Lyndon Baines Johnson Presidential Library. Austin, Tex.

Hughes, Richard and Betty. Interview by Joe B. Frantz, August 6, 1969. Transcript. Oral History Collection. Lyndon Baines Johnson Presidential Library. Austin, Tex.

Humphrey, Hubert H., Jr. Interviews by Michael L. Gillette, June 20, June 21, 1977.

Transcript. Oral History Collection. Lyndon Baines Johnson Presidential Library. Austin, Tex.

Humphrey, Hubert H., Jr. Interview by Joe B. Frantz, August 17, 1971. Transcript. Oral History Collection. Lyndon Baines Johnson Presidential Library. Austin, Tex.

Huntley, Chester R. Interview by Joe B. Frantz, May 12, 1969. Transcript. Oral History Collection. Lyndon Baines Johnson Presidential Library. Austin, Tex.

Ink, Dwight A. Interview by David G. McComb, February 5, 1969. Transcript. Oral History Collection. Lyndon Baines Johnson Presidential Library. Austin, Tex.

Jenkins, Herbert. Interview by Thomas H. Baker, May 14, 1969. Transcript. Oral History Collection. Lyndon Baines Johnson Presidential Library. Austin, Tex.

Johnson, Paul B., Jr. Interview by Thomas H. Baker, September 8, 1970. Transcript. Oral History Collection. Lyndon Baines Johnson Presidential Library. Austin, Tex.

Johnson, Paul B., III. Interviews by Reid Derr, June 23, July 9, 1993. Vol. 456, transcript. Mississippi Oral History Program of the University of Southern Mississippi. McCain Library and Archives. University of Southern Mississippi, Hattiesburg.

Johnson, Sarah H. Interview by Tom Healy, September 10, 1978. Vol. 243, transcript. Mississippi Oral History Program of the University of Southern Mississippi. McCain Library and Archives. University of Southern Mississippi, Hattiesburg.

Johnston, Erle. Interview by Yasuhiro Katagiri, August 13, 1993. Vol. 276, Part II, transcript. Mississippi Oral History Program of the University of Southern Mississippi. McCain Library and Archives. University of Southern Mississippi, Hattiesburg.

Johnston, Erle. Interviews by Orley B. Caudill, July 16, July 30, 1980. Vol. 276, Part I, transcript. Mississippi Oral History Program of the University of Southern Mississippi. McCain Library and Archives. University of Southern Mississippi, Hattiesburg.

Katzenbach, Nicholas. Interviews by Paige E. Mulhollan, November 12, November 23, December 11, 1968. Transcript. Oral History Collection. Lyndon Baines Johnson Presidential Library. Austin, Tex.

Keppel, Francis. Interviews by David G. McComb, April 21, 1969, August 17, 1972. Transcript. Oral History Collection. Lyndon Baines Johnson Presidential Library. Austin, Tex.

Keppel, Francis. Interview by John Singerhoff, July 18, 1968. Transcript. Oral History Collection. Lyndon Baines Johnson Presidential Library. Austin, Tex.

Kerner, Otto. Interview by Paige E. Mulhollan, June 12, 1969. Transcript. Oral History Collection. Lyndon Baines Johnson Presidential Library. Austin, Tex.

Kintner, Robert. Interview by Joe B. Frantz, July 13, 1972. Transcript. Oral History Collection. Lyndon Baines Johnson Presidential Library. Austin, Tex.

Kytle, Calvin and Elizabeth. Interviews by author, July 11, July 29, 1997, Chapel Hill, N.C. Tape recording.

Levine, Robert A. Interview by Stephen Goodell, February 26, 1969. Transcript. Oral History Collection. Lyndon Baines Johnson Presidential Library. Austin, Tex.

Magee, Ruby. Interview by Chester Morgan, 1985. Vol. 17, Part II, transcript. Mississippi Oral History Program of the University of Southern Mississippi. McCain Library and Archives. University of Southern Mississippi, Hattiesburg.

Magnuson, Warren. Interview by Michael L. Gillette, March 14, 1978. Transcript. Oral
History Collection. Lyndon Baines Johnson Presidential Library. Austin, Tex.

Maguire, Charles M. Interviews by Dorothy Pierce McSweeny, July 8, July 29, 1969.
Transcript. Oral History Collection. Lyndon Baines Johnson Presidential Library.
Austin, Tex.

Manatos, Mike. Interview by Joe B. Frantz, August 25, 1969. Transcript. Oral History
Collection. Lyndon Baines Johnson Presidential Library. Austin, Tex.

Markman, Sherwin J. Interview by Dorothy Pierce McSweeny, May 21, 1969. Transcript.
Oral History Collection. Lyndon Baines Johnson Presidential Library. Austin, Tex.

Marshall, Burke. Interview by Thomas H. Baker, October 28, 1968. Transcript. Oral
History Collection. Lyndon Baines Johnson Presidential Library. Austin, Tex.

Marshall, Thurgood. Interview by Thomas H. Baker, July 10, 1969. Transcript. Oral History
Collection. Lyndon Baines Johnson Presidential Library. Austin, Tex.

Martin, Louis. Interview by David G. McComb, May 14, 1969. Transcript. Oral History
Collection. Lyndon Baines Johnson Presidential Library. Austin, Tex.

Martin, Ruby. Interview by Thomas H. Baker, February 24, 1969. Transcript. Oral History
Collection. Lyndon Baines Johnson Presidential Library. Austin, Tex.

McCone, John. Interview by Joe B. Frantz, August 19, 1970. Transcript. Oral History
Collection. Lyndon Baines Johnson Presidential Library. Austin, Tex.

McLemore, Leslie. Interview by Betsy Nash, April 19, 1991. Transcript. John Stennis Oral
History Collection. Special Collections Department. Mitchell Memorial Library.
Mississippi State University, Starkville.

McPherson, Harry. Interview by Robert Hawkinson, June 12, 1973. Transcript. Oral History
Collection. Lyndon Baines Johnson Presidential Library. Austin, Tex.

McPherson, Harry. Interviews by Thomas H. Baker, December 5, December 19, 1968,
January 16, March 24, April 9, 1969. Transcript. Oral History Collection. Lyndon
Baines Johnson Presidential Library. Austin, Tex.

Mitchell, Clarence. Interview by Thomas H. Baker, April 30, 1969. Transcript. Oral
History Collection. Lyndon Baines Johnson Presidential Library. Austin, Tex.

Moore, Amzie. Interviews by Michael Garvey, March 29, April 13, 1977. Vol. 184, transcript.
Mississippi Oral History Program of the University of Southern Mississippi. McCain
Library and Archives. University of Southern Mississippi, Hattiesburg.

Nimetz, Matthew. Interview by Stephen Goodell, January 7, 1969. Transcript. Oral History
Collection. Lyndon Baines Johnson Presidential Library. Austin, Tex.

Patterson, Eugene. Interview by Thomas H. Baker, March 11, 1969. Transcript. Oral
History Collection. Lyndon Baines Johnson Presidential Library. Austin, Tex.

Perrin, C. Robert. Interviews by Stephen Goodell, March 10, March 17, 1969. Transcript.
Oral History Collection. Lyndon Baines Johnson Presidential Library. Austin, Tex.

Pollak, Stephen. Interviews by Thomas H. Baker, January 27, January 29, January 30,
January 31, 1969. Transcript. Oral History Collection. Lyndon Baines Johnson
Presidential Library. Austin, Tex.

Ramsay, Claude. Interviews by Orley B. Caudill, April 28, April 30, May 7, 1981.
Vol. 215, transcript. Mississippi Oral History Program of the University of Southern

Mississippi. McCain Library and Archives. University of Southern Mississippi, Hattiesburg.

Randolph, A. Philip. Interview by Thomas H. Baker, October 29, 1968. Transcript. Oral History Collection. Lyndon Baines Johnson Presidential Library. Austin, Tex.

Rauh, Joseph L., Jr. Interviews by Paige E. Mulhollan, July 30, August 1, August 8, 1969. Transcript. Oral History Collection. Lyndon Baines Johnson Presidential Library. Austin, Tex.

Roche, John P. Interview by Paige E. Mulhollan, July 16, 1970. Transcript. Oral History Collection. Lyndon Baines Johnson Presidential Library. Austin, Tex.

Rustin, Bayard. Interviews by Thomas H. Baker, June 17, June 30, 1969. Transcript. Oral History Collection. Lyndon Baines Johnson Presidential Library. Austin, Tex.

Sanders, Carl. Interview by Thomas H. Baker, May 13, 1969. Transcript. Oral History Collection. Lyndon Baines Johnson Presidential Library. Austin, Tex.

Sanders, Harold "Barefoot," Jr. Interview by Joe B. Frantz, March 24, 1969. Transcript. Oral History Collection. Lyndon Baines Johnson Presidential Library. Austin, Tex.

Sanford, Terry. Interviews by Joe B. Frantz, May 15, 1971, and March 1, 1972. Transcript. Oral History Collection. Lyndon Baines Johnson Presidential Library. Austin, Tex.

Schlei, Norbert A. Interview by Michael L. Gillette, May 15, 1980. Transcript. Oral History Collection. Lyndon Baines Johnson Presidential Library. Austin, Tex.

Schultze, Charles. Interview by David G. McComb, March 28, 1969. Transcript. Oral History Collection. Lyndon Baines Johnson Presidential Library. Austin, Tex.

Secrest, Andrew "Mac." Interview by author, August 5, 1997, Chapel Hill, N.C. Tape recording.

Sparkman, John. Interview by Michael L. Gillette, June 9, 1977. Transcript. Oral History Collection. Lyndon Baines Johnson Presidential Library. Austin, Tex.

Sparkman, John. Interview by Paige E. Mulhollan, October 5, 1968. Transcript. Oral History Collection. Lyndon Baines Johnson Presidential Library. Austin, Tex.

Spell, William. Interview by Jeff Broadwater, November 29, 1990. Transcript. John Stennis Oral History Collection. Special Collections Department. Mitchell Memorial Library. Mississippi State University, Starkville.

Spock, Benjamin. Interview by Ted Gittinger, October 23, 1982. Transcript. Oral History Collection. Lyndon Baines Johnson Presidential Library. Austin, Tex.

Stennis, John Cornelius. Interview by Joe B. Frantz, June 17, 1972. Transcript. Oral History Collection. Lyndon Baines Johnson Presidential Library. Austin, Tex.

Stroupe, Phil. Interview by Jeff Broadwater, December 6, 1990. Transcript. John Stennis Oral History Collection. Special Collections Department. Mitchell Memorial Library. Mississippi State University, Starkville.

Sugarman, Jule M. Interview by Stephen Goodell, March 14, 1969. Transcript. Oral History Collection. Lyndon Baines Johnson Presidential Library. Austin, Tex.

Sundquist, James L. Interview by Stephen Goodell, April 7, 1969. Transcript. Oral History Collection. Lyndon Baines Johnson Presidential Library. Austin, Tex.

Talmadge, Herman. Interview by Thomas H. Baker, July 17, 1969. Transcript. Oral History Collection. Lyndon Baines Johnson Presidential Library. Austin, Tex.

Taylor, Hobart, Jr. Interviews by Stephen Goodell, January 6, February 14, 1969. Transcript. Oral History Collection. Lyndon Baines Johnson Presidential Library. Austin, Tex.

Thurmond, Strom. Interview by Michael L. Gillette, May 7, 1979. Transcript. Oral History Collection. Lyndon Baines Johnson Presidential Library. Austin, Tex.

Valenti, Jack. Interviews by Joe B. Frantz, October 18, 1969, February 19, March 3, 1971, July 12, 1972. Transcript. Oral History Collection. Lyndon Baines Johnson Presidential Library. Austin, Tex.

Valenti, Jack. Interview by Thomas H. Baker, June 14, 1969. Transcript. Oral History Collection. Lyndon Baines Johnson Presidential Library. Austin, Tex.

Vance, Cyrus. Interview by Paige E. Mulhollan, November 3, 1969. Transcript. Oral History Collection. Lyndon Baines Johnson Presidential Library. Austin, Tex.

Walker, Prentiss. Interview by Orley B. Caudill, 1976. Vol. 208, transcript. Mississippi Oral History Program of the University of Southern Mississippi. McCain Library and Archives. University of Southern Mississippi, Hattiesburg.

Wallace, George. Interview by Thomas H. Baker, May 15, 1969. Transcript. Oral History Collection. Lyndon Baines Johnson Presidential Library. Austin, Tex.

Wattenberg, Ben J. Interviews by Thomas H. Baker, November 23, November 29, 1968. Transcript. Oral History Collection. Lyndon Baines Johnson Presidential Library. Austin, Tex.

Weaver, Robert C. Interview by Joe B. Frantz, November 19, 1968. Transcript. Oral History Collection. Lyndon Baines Johnson Presidential Library. Austin, Tex.

White, Lee. Interviews by Joe B. Frantz, September 28, 1970, February 18, March 2, March 3, 1971. Transcript. Oral History Collection. Lyndon Baines Johnson Presidential Library. Austin, Tex.

Wicker, Tom G. Interview by Joe B. Frantz, June 16, 1970 Transcript. Oral History Collection. Lyndon Baines Johnson Presidential Library. Austin, Tex.

Wilkins, Roy. Interview by Thomas H. Baker, April 1, 1969. Transcript. Oral History Collection. Lyndon Baines Johnson Presidential Library. Austin, Tex.

Wilson, Henry Hall. Interview by Joe B. Frantz, April 11, 1973. Transcript. Oral History Collection. Lyndon Baines Johnson Presidential Library. Austin, Tex.

Wroten, Joseph. Interview by Jeff Sainsbury, March 31, 1992. Transcript. John Stennis Oral History Collection. Special Collections Department. Mitchell Memorial Library. Mississippi State University, Starkville.

Wroten, Joseph E. Interview by Yasuhiro Katagiri, November 4, 1993. Vol. 476, transcript. Mississippi Oral History Program of the University of Southern Mississippi. McCain Library and Archives. University of Southern Mississippi, Hattiesburg.

Yarmolinsky, Adam. Interviews by Michael L. Gillette, October 21, October 22, 1980. Transcript. Oral History Collection. Lyndon Baines Johnson Presidential Library. Austin, Tex.

Yarmolinsky, Adam. Interview by Paige E. Mulhollan, July 13, 1970. Transcript. Oral History Collection. Lyndon Baines Johnson Presidential Library. Austin, Tex.

Yorty, Samuel. Interview by Joe B. Frantz, February 7, 1970. Transcript. Oral History Collection. Lyndon Baines Johnson Presidential Library. Austin, Tex.

Young, Andrew J., Jr. Interview by Thomas H. Baker, June 18, 1970. Transcript. Oral History Collection. Lyndon Baines Johnson Presidential Library. Austin, Tex.

Young, Whitney M., Jr. Interview by Thomas H. Baker, June 18, 1969. Transcript. Oral History Collection. Lyndon Baines Johnson Presidential Library. Austin, Tex.

Other Unpublished Sources

Ashmore, Susan Youngblood. "Carry It On: The War on Poverty and the Civil Rights Movement in Alabama, 1964–1970." Ph.D. diss., Auburn University, 1999.

Crespino, Joseph. "Strategic Accommodation: Civil Rights Opponents in Mississippi and Their Impact on American Racial Politics, 1953–1972." Ph.D. diss., Stanford University, 2003.

Elliff, John T. "The United States Department of Justice and Individual Rights, 1932–1962." Ph.D. diss., Harvard University, 1968.

Flamm, Michael William. "'Law and Order': Street Crime, Civil Disorder, and the Crisis of Liberalism." Ph.D. diss., Columbia University, 1998.

Goodwin, Neal D. Project Director. "To Take on the Enemy Within: Robert F. Kennedy and the 1960s." Scripting Proposal Submitted to the National Endowment for the Humanities, 1995. (Copy of proposal in author's possession, courtesy of William E. Leuchtenburg.)

Published Sources

Adler, Margot. *Heretic's Heart: A Journey through Spirit and Revolution*. Boston: Beacon Press, 1997.

Anderson, Jervis. *A. Philip Randolph: A Biographical Portrait*. Berkeley: University of California Press, 1986.

Andrews, Kenneth. *Freedom Is a Constant Struggle: The Mississippi Civil Rights Movement and Its Legacy*. Chicago: University of Chicago Press, 2004.

Ashmore, Harry S. *Civil Rights and Wrongs: A Memoir of Race and Politics, 1944–1994*. New York: Pantheon Books, 1994.

Ashmore, Susan. *Carry It On: The War on Poverty and the Civil Rights Movement in Alabama, 1964–1972*. Athens: University of Georgia Press, 2008.

Bartley, Numan V., and Hugh D. Graham. *Southern Politics and the Second Reconstruction*. Baltimore: Johns Hopkins University Press, 1975.

Bass, Jack, and Jack Nelson. *The Orangeburg Massacre*. New York: World Publishing Company, 1970.

Belknap, Michael R. *Federal Law and Southern Order: Racial Violence and Constitutional Conflict in the Post-Brown South*. Athens: University of Georgia Press, 1987.

———, ed. *Administrative History of the Civil Rights Division of the Department of Justice During the Johnson Administration*. Vol. 17 of *Civil Rights, the White House, and the Justice Department, 1945–1968*. New York: Garland, 1991.

———, ed. *Urban Race Riots.* Vol. 11 of *Civil Rights, the White House, and the Justice Department, 1945–1968.* New York: Garland, 1991.

Bernard, Sheila Curran, and Dante J. James. "Given a Chance." Episode 2 of *America's War on Poverty.* Produced and directed by Dante J. James. 60 min. Blackside Productions, 1995. Videocassette.

Bernstein, Irving. *Guns or Butter: The Presidency of Lyndon Johnson.* New York: Oxford University Press, 1996.

Biondi, Martha. *To Stand and Fight: The Struggle for Civil Rights in Postwar New York City.* Cambridge: Harvard University Press, 2003.

Bloom, Jack M. *Class, Race, and the Civil Rights Movement.* Bloomington: Indiana University Press, 1987.

Bolton, Charles C. "The Last Stand of Massive Resistance: Mississippi Public School Integration, 1970." *Journal of Mississippi History* 61, no. 4 (1999): 329–50.

Bond, Julian. Introduction to *Eyes on the Prize: America's Civil Rights Years, 1954–1965,* by Juan Williams. New York: Viking, 1987.

———. *A Time to Speak, a Time to Act: The Movement in Politics.* New York: Simon and Schuster, 1972.

Bornet, Vaughn Davis. *The Presidency of Lyndon B. Johnson.* Lawrence: University Press of Kansas, 1983.

Branch, Taylor. *At Canaan's Edge: America in the King Years, 1965–68.* New York: Simon and Schuster, 2006.

———. *Parting the Waters: America in the King Years, 1954–63.* New York: Simon and Schuster, 1988.

———. *Pillar of Fire: America in the King Years, 1963–65.* New York: Simon and Schuster, 1998.

Brauer, Carl M. *John F. Kennedy and the Second Reconstruction.* New York: Columbia University Press, 1977.

Brinton, Crane. *The Anatomy of Revolution,* rev. ed. New York: Prentice-Hall, 1952.

Burner, David. *Making Peace with the 60s.* Princeton, N.J.: Princeton University Press, 1996.

Button, James W. *Black Violence: Political Impact of the 1960s Riots.* Princeton, N.J.: Princeton University Press, 1978.

Cagin, Seth, and Philip Dray. *We Are Not Afraid: The Story of Goodman, Schwerner, and Chaney and the Civil Rights Campaign in Mississippi.* New York: Macmillan, 1988.

Califano, Joseph A., Jr. *Governing America: An Insider's Report from the White House and the Cabinet.* New York: Simon and Schuster, 1981.

———. *The Triumph and Tragedy of Lyndon Johnson: The White House Years.* New York: Simon and Schuster, 1991.

Callejo-Pérez, David M. *Southern Hospitality: Identity, Schools, and the Civil Rights Movement in Mississippi, 1964–1972.* New York: P. Lang, 2001.

Campbell, Karl E. *Senator Sam Ervin, Last of the Founding Fathers.* Chapel Hill: University of North Carolina Press, 2007.

Cannato, Vincent J. *The Ungovernable City: John Lindsay and the Battle to Save New York*. New York: Basic Books, 2003.

Carmichael, Stokely (Kwame Ture), with Ekwueme Michael Thelwell. *Ready for Revolution: The Life and Struggles of Stokely Carmichael (Kwame Ture)*. New York: Scribner, 2003.

Caro, Robert. *The Years of Lyndon Johnson: Means of Ascent*. New York: Knopf, 1990.

Carr, Robert Kenneth. *Federal Protection of Civil Rights: Quest for a Sword*. Ithaca, N.Y.: Cornell University Press, 1947.

Carson, Clayborne. *In Struggle: SNCC and the Black Awakening of the 1960s*. Cambridge, Mass.: Harvard University Press, 1981.

———, ed. *The Movement: 1964–1970*. Westport, Conn.: Greenwood Press, 1993.

Carson, Clayborne, David Garrow, Bill Kovach, and Carol Polsgrove, comp. *Reporting Civil Rights, Part Two: American Journalism, 1963–1973*. New York: Library of America, 2003.

Carter, Dan T. *From George Wallace to Newt Gingrich: Race in the Conservative Counterrevolution, 1963–1994*. Baton Rouge: Louisiana State University Press, 1996.

———. *The Politics of Rage: George Wallace, the Rise of the New Conservatism, and the Transformation of American Politics*. New York: Simon and Schuster, 1995.

Carter, David C. "Romper Lobbies and Coloring Lessons: Grassroots Visions and Political Realities in the Battle for Head Start in Mississippi, 1965–1967." In *Making a New South: Race, Leadership, and Community after the Civil War*, ed. Paul A. Cimbala and Barton C. Shaw, 191–208. Gainesville: University Press of Florida, 2007.

———. "The Williamston Freedom Movement: Civil Rights at the Grass Roots in Eastern North Carolina, 1957–1964." *North Carolina Historical Review* 76, no. 1 (January 1999): 1–42.

Chafe, William H. *Civilities and Civil Rights: Greensboro, North Carolina, and the Black Struggle for Freedom*. New York: Oxford University Press, 1980.

———. *Never Stop Running: Allard Lowenstein and the Struggle to Save American Liberalism*. New York: Basic Books, 1993.

———. *Private Lives/Public Consequences: Personality and Politics in Modern America*. Cambridge, Mass.: Harvard University Press, 2005.

———. "Race, Class, and Gender in Southern History: Forces That Unite, Forces That Divide." In *The Achievement of American Liberalism*, ed. William H. Chafe, 275–92. New York: Columbia University Press, 2003.

———. "Race in America: The Ultimate Test of Liberalism." In *The Achievement of American Liberalism*, ed. William H. Chafe, 161–79. New York: Columbia University Press, 2003.

———. *The Unfinished Journey: America since World War II*, 4th ed. New York: Oxford University Press, 1999.

Chafe, William H., and Harvard Sitkoff, eds. *A History of Our Time: Readings on Postwar America*, 5th ed. New York: Oxford University Press, 1999.

Chappell, David L. *Inside Agitators: White Southerners in the Civil Rights Movement*. Baltimore: Johns Hopkins University Press, 1994.

Chestnut, J. L., Jr., and Julia Cass. *Black in Selma, the Uncommon Life of J. L. Chestnut, Jr.: Politics and Power in a Small American Town.* New York: Farrar, Straus, and Giroux, 1990.

Churchill, Ward, and Jim Vander Wall. *The COINTELPRO Papers: Documents from the FBI's Secret Wars against Domestic Dissent.* Boston: South End Press, 1990.

Cimbala, Paul A., ed. *Historians and Race: Autobiography and the Writing of History.* Bloomington: Indiana University Press, 1996.

Clark, E. Culpepper. *The Schoolhouse Door: Segregation's Last Stand at the University of Alabama.* New York: Oxford University Press, 1993.

Clark, Kenneth E. *Dark Ghetto: Dilemmas of Social Power.* With a foreword by Gunnar Myrdal. New York: Harper and Row, 1965.

Classen, Steven D. *Watching Jim Crow: The Struggles over Mississippi TV, 1955–1969.* Durham, N.C.: Duke University Press, 2004.

Cleary, Robert E. "Gubernatorial Leadership and State Policy on Desegregation in Public Higher Education." *Phylon* 27, no. 2 (1966): 165–70.

Cobb, James C. *The Most Southern Place on Earth: The Mississippi Delta and the Roots of Regional Identity.* New York: Oxford University Press, 1992.

———. "'Somebody Done Nailed Us on the Cross': Federal Farm and Welfare Policy and the Civil Rights Movement in the Mississippi Delta." *Journal of American History* 77, no. 3 (December 1990): 912–36.

Colburn, David R. *Racial Change and Community Crisis: St. Augustine, Florida, 1877–1980.* New York: Columbia University Press, 1985.

Coles, Robert. "Rural Upheaval: Confrontation and Accommodation." In *On Fighting Poverty: Perspectives from Experience,* ed. James L. Sundquist, 108–13. New York: Basic Books, 1969.

Collier-Thomas, Bettye, and V. P. Franklin. *My Soul Is a Witness: A Chronology of the Civil Rights Era, 1954–1965.* New York: Henry Holt, 1999.

Collins, LeRoy. *The South and the Nation.* Atlanta, Ga.: Southern Regional Council, 1960.

Conot, Robert. *Rivers of Blood, Years of Darkness: The Unforgettable Classic Account of the Watts Riot.* New York: Morrow, 1967.

Countryman, Matthew J. *Up South: Civil Rights and Black Power in Philadelphia.* Philadelphia: University of Pennsylvania Press, 2006.

Cowger, Thomas W., and Sherwin J. Markman, ed. *Lyndon Johnson Remembered.* Lanham, Md.: Rowman and Littlefield, 2003.

Cox, Julian, ed. *Road to Freedom: Photographs of the Civil Rights Movement, 1956–1968.* Atlanta, Ga.: High Museum of Art, 2008.

Crespino, Joseph. *In Search of Another Country: Mississippi and the Conservative Counterrevolution.* Princeton, N.J.: Princeton University Press, 2007.

Crosby, Emilye. *A Little Taste of Freedom: The Black Freedom Struggle in Claiborne County, Mississippi.* Chapel Hill: University of North Carolina Press, 2005.

Curry, Constance. *The Intolerable Burden.* Directed by Chea Prince, produced by Constance Curry. 56 min. DVD, First Run/Icarus Films, 2003.

——— . *Silver Rights*. New York: Harcourt, Brace, 1995.

Dallek, Robert. *Flawed Giant: Lyndon Johnson and His Times, 1961–1973*. New York: Oxford University Press, 1998.

——— . *Lone Star Rising: Lyndon Johnson and His Times, 1908–1960*. New York: Oxford University Press, 1991.

Davies, David R., ed. *The Press and Race: Mississippi Journalists Confront the Movement*. Jackson: University Press of Mississippi, 2001.

Davies, Gareth. *From Opportunity to Entitlement: The Transformation and Decline of Great Society Liberalism*. Lawrence: University Press of Kansas, 1996.

Davis, Jack E., ed. *The Civil Rights Movement*. Malden, Mass.: Blackwell, 2001.

Davis, Townsend. *Weary Feet, Rested Souls: A Guided History of the Civil Rights Movement*. New York: W. W. Norton, 1998.

DeBenedetti, Charles. "On the Significance of Citizen Peace Activism: America, 1961–1975." *Peace and Change* 9 (Summer 1983): 6–20.

De Jong, Greta. *A Different Day: African American Struggles for Justice in Rural Louisiana, 1900–1970*. Chapel Hill: University of North Carolina Press, 2002.

D'Emilio, John. "Homophobia and the Trajectory of Postwar American Radicalism: The Career of Bayard Rustin." *Radical History Review* 62 (Spring 1995): 80–103.

——— . *Lost Prophet: The Life and Times of Bayard Rustin*. New York: Free Press, 2003.

Dent, Thomas C. *Southern Journey: A Return to the Civil Rights Movement*. New York: W. W. Morrow, 1997.

Dickerson, Dennis C. *Militant Mediator: Whitney M. Young, Jr*. Lexington: University Press of Kentucky, 1998.

Dierenfield, Bruce J. *The Civil Rights Movement*. New York: Pearson Education Limited, 2004.

Disraeli, Benjamin. *Sybil, or the Two Nations*. New York: Oxford University Press, 1845, 1926, reprint, 1975.

Dittmer, John. *Local People: The Struggle for Civil Rights in Mississippi*. Urbana: University of Illinois Press, 1994.

Donovan, John C. *The Politics of Poverty*. New York: Pegasus, 1967.

Dooley, Brian. *Robert Kennedy: The Final Years*. New York: St. Martin's, 1996.

Dudziak, Mary L. *Cold War Civil Rights: Race and the Image of American Democracy*. Princeton, N.J.: Princeton University Press, 2000.

Dulles, Foster Rhea. *The Civil Rights Commission, 1957–1965*. East Lansing: Michigan State University Press, 1968.

Dyson, Michael Eric. *I May Not Get There with You . . . The True Martin Luther King, Jr*. New York: Free Press, 2000.

Eagles, Charles W. "From Shotguns to Umbrellas: The Civil Rights Movement in Lowndes County, Alabama." In *The Adaptable South: Essays in Honor of George Brown Tindall*, ed. Elizabeth Jacoway, Dan Carter, and Robert McMath, 212–36. Baton Rouge: Louisiana State University Press, 1991.

——— . *Outside Agitator: Jon Daniels and the Civil Rights Movement in Alabama*. Chapel Hill: University of North Carolina Press, 1993.

——. "Toward New Histories of the Civil Rights Era." *Journal of Southern History* 66, no. 4 (November 2000): 815–48.

Egerton, John. *Speak Now against the Day: The Generation before the Civil Rights Movement in the South.* New York: Knopf, 1994.

Elliff, John T. *Crime, Dissent, and the Attorney General: The Justice Department in the 1960's.* Beverly Hills, Calif.: Sage Publications, 1971.

——. *The United States Department of Justice and Individual Rights, 1937–1962.* New York: Garland, 1987.

Erskine, Hazel. "The Polls: Demonstrations and Race Riots." *Public Opinion Quarterly* 31, no. 4 (Winter 1967–1968): 655–77.

——. "The Polls: Speed of Racial Integration." *Public Opinion Quarterly* 32, no. 3 (Autumn 1968): 513–24.

Eskew, Glenn T. *But for Birmingham: The Local and National Movements in the Civil Rights Struggle.* Chapel Hill: University of North Carolina Press, 1997.

Fager, Charles E. *Selma, 1965.* New York: Scribner, 1974.

Fairclough, Adam. *Martin Luther King, Jr.* Athens: University of Georgia Press, 1990.

——. "Martin Luther King Jr. and the War in Vietnam." *Phylon* 45, no. 1 (1984): 19–39.

——. *Race and Democracy: The Civil Rights Struggle in Louisiana, 1915–1972.* Athens: University of Georgia Press, 1995.

——. *To Redeem the Soul of America: The Southern Christian Leadership Conference and Martin Luther King, Jr.* Athens: University of Georgia Press, 1987.

Fairlie, Henry. *The Kennedy Promise: The Politics of Expectation.* Garden City, N.Y.: Doubleday, 1976.

Farmer, James. *Freedom, When?* New York: Random House, 1965.

——. *Lay Bare the Heart: An Autobiography of the Civil Rights Movement.* New York: Arbor House, 1985.

Feagin, Joe F., and Harlan Hahn. *Ghetto Revolts: The Politics of Violence in American Cities.* New York: Macmillan, 1973.

Findlay, James F. *Church People in the Struggle: The National Council of Churches and the Black Freedom Movement, 1950–1970.* New York: Oxford University Press, 1993.

——. "The Mainline Churches and Head Start in Mississippi: Religious Activism in the Sixties." *Church History* 64, no. 2 (June 1995): 237–50.

Fine, Sidney. *Violence in the Model City: The Cavanagh Administration, Race Relations, and the Detroit Riot of 1967.* Ann Arbor: University of Michigan Press, 1989.

Flamm, Michael W. *Law and Order: Street Crime, Civil Unrest, and the Crisis of Liberalism in the 1960s.* New York: Columbia University Press, 2005.

Fogelson, Robert M. *Violence as Protest: A Study of Riots and Ghettos.* Garden City, N.Y.: Doubleday, 1971.

Frady, Marshall. *Wallace.* New York: New American Library, 1968.

Frazier, E. Franklin. *The Negro Family in the United States.* Chicago: University of Chicago Press, 1939.

Frederick, Jeff. *Stand Up for Alabama: Governor George Wallace.* Tuscaloosa: University of Alabama Press, 2007.

Friedland, Michael B. *Lift Up Your Voice Like a Trumpet: White Clergy and the Civil Rights and Antiwar Movements, 1954–1973.* Chapel Hill: University of North Carolina Press, 1998.

Fuquay, Michael W. "Civil Rights and the Private School Movement in Mississippi, 1964–1971." *History of Education Quarterly* 42, no. 2 (2002): 159–80.

Gaillard, Frye. *Cradle of Freedom: Alabama and the Movement That Changed America.* Tuscaloosa: University of Alabama Press, 2004.

Garrow, David J. *Bearing the Cross: Martin Luther King, Jr., and the Southern Christian Leadership Conference.* New York: W. W. Morrow, 1986.

——. *Protest at Selma: Martin Luther King, Jr., and the Voting Rights Act of 1965.* New Haven, Conn.: Yale University Press, 1978.

Gelfand, Mark I. *A Nation of Cities: The Federal Government and Urban America, 1933–1965.* New York: Oxford University Press, 1975.

Germany, Kent B. *New Orleans after the Promises: Poverty, Citizenship, and the Search for the Great Society.* Athens: University of Georgia Press, 2007.

Gerson, Mark. *The Neoconservative Vision: From the Cold War to the Culture Wars.* Lanham, Md.: Madison Books, 1997.

Gillette, Michael L., ed. *Launching the War on Poverty: An Oral History.* New York: Twayne, 1996.

Gilmore, Glenda Elizabeth. *Defying Dixie: The Radical Roots of Civil Rights, 1919–1950.* New York: Norton, 2008.

Gitlin, Todd. *The Sixties: Years of Hope, Days of Rage.* New York: Bantam Books, 1987.

——. *The Whole World Is Watching: Mass Media in the Making and Unmaking of the New Left.* Berkeley: University of California Press, 1980.

Glazer, Nathan, and Daniel Patrick Moynihan. *Beyond the Melting Pot: The Negroes, Puerto Ricans, Jews, Italians, and Irish of New York City.* Cambridge, Mass.: MIT Press, 1963.

Goldfield, David R. *Black, White, and Southern: Race Relations and Southern Culture, 1940 to the Present.* Baton Rouge: Louisiana State University Press, 1990.

Goldman, Eric F. *The Tragedy of Lyndon Johnson.* New York: Knopf, 1969.

Goldman, Peter L. *The Death and Life of Malcolm X.* Urbana: University of Illinois Press, 1979.

Goodwin, Richard N. *Remembering America: A Voice from the Sixties.* Boston: Little, Brown, 1988.

Gottheimer, Josh, ed. *Ripples of Hope: Great American Civil Rights Speeches.* New York: Basic Civitas Books, 2003.

Grady-Willis, Winston A. *Challenging U.S. Apartheid: Atlanta and Black Struggles for Human Rights, 1960–1977.* Durham, N.C.: Duke University Press, 2006.

Graham, Allison. *Framing the South: Hollywood, Television, and Race during the Civil Rights Struggle.* Baltimore: Johns Hopkins University Press, 2001.

Graham, Hugh Davis. *Civil Rights and the Presidency: Race and Gender in American Politics, 1960–1972.* New York: Oxford University Press, 1992.

———. *The Civil Rights Era: Origins and Development of National Policy, 1960–1972*. New York: Oxford University Press, 1990.

Graham, Hugh Davis, and Ted Robert Gurr. *The History of Violence in America*. New York: Bantam Books, 1969.

Graham, Katharine. *Personal History*. New York: A. A. Knopf, 1997.

Graham, Otis L., Jr. "Liberalism after the Sixties: A Reconnaissance." In *The Achievement of American Liberalism*, ed. William H. Chafe, 293–325. New York: Columbia University Press, 2003.

Grant, Joanne, ed. *Black Protest: 350 Years of History, Documents, and Analyses*. New York: Fawcett Premier, 1991.

Greenberg, Cheryl Lynn, ed. *A Circle of Trust: Remembering SNCC*. New Brunswick, N.J.: Rutgers University Press, 1998.

Greenberg, Polly. *The Devil Has Slippery Shoes: A Biased Biography of the Child Development Group of Mississippi*. New York: Macmillan, 1969.

Guthman, Edwin O. *We Band of Brothers*. New York: Harper and Row, 1971.

Guthman, Edwin O., and Jeffrey Shulman, eds. *Robert Kennedy: In His Own Words: The Unpublished Recollections of the Kennedy Years*. New York: Bantam Books, 1988.

Hall, Jacquelyn Dowd. "The Long Civil Rights Movement and the Political Uses of the Past." *Journal of American History* 91, no. 4 (March 2005): 1233–63.

Hamilton, Dona Cooper, and Charles V. Hamilton. *The Dual Agenda: Race and Social Welfare Policies of Civil Rights Organizations*. New York: Columbia University Press, 1997.

Harris, Fred R. *Alarms and Hopes: A Personal Journey, a Personal View*. New York: Harper and Row, 1968.

———. *Does People Do It? A Memoir*. Norman: University of Oklahoma Press, 2008.

Harris, Fred R., and Roger W. Wilkins, ed. *Quiet Riots: Race and Poverty in the United States: The Kerner Report Twenty Years Later*. New York: Pantheon, 1988.

Harris, Richard. *Justice: The Crisis of Law, Order, and Freedom in America*. New York: E. P. Dutton, 1970.

Harris, William C. *The Day of the Carpetbagger: Republican Reconstruction in Mississippi*. Baton Rouge: Louisiana State University Press, 1979.

Harvey, James C. *Black Civil Rights during the Johnson Administration*. Jackson: University and College Press of Mississippi, 1973.

Haveman, Robert H., ed. *A Decade of Federal Antipoverty Programs: Achievements, Failures, and Lessons*. New York: Academic Press, 1977.

Hayden, Tom. *Rebellion in Newark: Official Violence and Ghetto Response*. New York: Vintage, 1967.

———. *Reunion: A Memoir*. New York: Random House, 1988.

Heath, Jim F. *Decade of Disillusionment: The Kennedy-Johnson Years*. Bloomington: Indiana University Press, 1975.

Henry, Aaron, with Constance Curry. *Aaron Henry: The Fire Ever Burning*. Jackson: University Press of Mississippi, 2000.

Herbers, John. *The Black Dilemma*. New York: John Day, 1973.

——. *The Lost Priority: What Happened to the Civil Rights Movement in America?* New York: Funk and Wagnalls, 1970.

Hersey, John. *The Algiers Motel Incident*. 1968; reprint, with an introduction by Thomas Sugrue, Baltimore: Johns Hopkins University Press, 1997.

Higham, John, ed. *Civil Rights and Social Wrongs: Black-White Relations since World War II*. University Park: Pennsylvania State University Press, 1997.

Hill, Lance E. *The Deacons for Defense: Armed Resistance and the Civil Rights Movement*. Chapel Hill: University of North Carolina Press, 2004.

Hodgson, Godfrey. *America in Our Time*. Garden City, N.Y.: Doubleday, 1976.

——. *The World Turned Right Side Up: A History of the Conservative Ascendancy in America*. Boston: Houghton Mifflin, 1996.

Hogan, Wesley C. *Many Minds, One Heart: SNCC's Dream for a New America*. Chapel Hill: University of North Carolina Press, 2007.

Horne, Gerald. *Fire This Time: The Watts Uprising and the 1960s*. Charlottesville: University Press of Virginia, 1995.

Hudson, Winson, and Constance Curry. *Mississippi Harmony: Memoirs of a Freedom Fighter*. New York: Palgrave, 2002.

Huston, Luther. *The Department of Justice*. New York: Praeger, 1967.

Isserman, Maurice, and Michael Kazin. *America Divided: The Civil War of the 1960s*, 3d ed. New York: Oxford University Press, 2007.

Jackson, Thomas F. *From Civil Rights to Human Rights: Martin Luther King, Jr., and the Struggle for Economic Justice*. Philadelphia: University of Pennsylvania Press, 2007.

Jackson, Walter A. *Gunnar Myrdal and America's Conscience: Social Engineering and Racial Liberalism, 1938–1987*. Chapel Hill: University of North Carolina Press, 1990.

Jacobs, Paul. *Prelude to Riot: A View of Urban America from the Bottom*. New York: Random House, 1968.

Jacoway, Elizabeth, and David R. Colburn, eds. *Southern Businessmen and Desegregation*. Baton Rouge: Louisiana State University Press, 1982.

Jaynes, Gerald David, and Robin M. Williams Jr., eds. *A Common Destiny: Blacks and American Society*. Washington, D.C.: National Academy Press, 1989.

Johnson, Lady Bird. *Lady Bird Johnson: A White House Diary*. New York: Holt, Rinehart and Winston, 1970.

Johnson, Lyndon Baines. *The Vantage Point: Perspectives of the Presidency, 1963–1969*. New York: Holt, Rinehart and Winston, 1971.

Johnston, Erle. *Mississippi's Defiant Years, 1953–1973: An Interpretive Documentary with Personal Experiences*. Forest, Miss.: Lake Harbor Publishers, 1990.

Jordan, Barbara C., and Elspeth D. Rostow, eds. *The Great Society: A Twenty-Year Critique*. Austin, Tex.: Lyndon B. Johnson Library, 1986.

Joseph, Peniel E. *Waiting 'til the Midnight Hour: A Narrative History of Black Power in America*. New York: Henry Holt, 2006.

Katagiri, Yasuhiro. *The Mississippi State Sovereignty Commission: Civil Rights and States' Rights*. Jackson: University Press of Mississippi, 2001.

Katz, Michael B. *Improving Poor People: The Welfare State, the "Underclass," and Urban Schools as History*. Princeton, N.J.: Princeton University Press, 1995.

———, ed. *The "Underclass" Debate: Views from History*. Princeton, N.J.: Princeton University Press, 1993.

Katzenbach, Nicholas deB. *Some of It Was Fun: Working with RFK and LBJ*. New York: Norton, 2008.

Kearns, Doris. *Lyndon Johnson and the American Dream*. New York: Harper and Row, 1976.

Kennedy, Robert F. *The Pursuit of Justice*. New York: Harper and Row, 1964.

———. *RFK: Collected Speeches*. New York: Viking, 1993.

———. *To Seek a Newer World*. Garden City, N.Y.: Doubleday, 1967.

King, Martin Luther, Jr. *Where Do We Go from Here: Chaos or Community?* New York: Harper and Row, 1967.

King, Mary. *Freedom Song: A Personal Story of the 1960s Civil Rights Movement*. New York: Morrow, 1987.

King, Richard. *Civil Rights and the Idea of Freedom*. Athens: University of Georgia Press, 1996.

Kirby, Jack Temple. *Darkness at the Dawning: Race and Reform in the Progressive South*. Philadelphia: Lippincott, 1972.

Knapp, David, and Kenneth Polk. *Scouting the War on Poverty: Social Reform Politics in the Kennedy Administration*. Lexington, Mass.: Heath Lexington, 1971.

Kopkind, Andrew. *The Thirty Years' Wars: Dispatches and Diversions of a Radical Journalist, 1965–1994*. New York: Verso, 1995.

Kotz, Nick. *Judgment Days: Lyndon Baines Johnson, Martin Luther King, Jr., and the Laws That Changed America*. Boston: Houghton Mifflin, 2005.

Landsberg, Brian K. *Enforcing Civil Rights: Race Discrimination and the Department of Justice*. Lawrence: University Press of Kansas, 1997.

Lawson, Steven F. *Black Ballots: Voting Rights in the South, 1944–1969*. New York: Columbia University Press, 1976.

———. "Civil Rights." In *Exploring the Johnson Years*, ed. Robert A. Divine, 93–125. Austin: University of Texas Press, 1981.

———. *Civil Rights Crossroads: Nation, Community, and the Black Freedom Struggle*. Lexington: University Press of Kentucky, 2003.

———. "Freedom Then, Freedom Now: The Historiography of the Civil Rights Movement." *American Historical Review* 96, no. 2 (April 1991): 456–71.

———. "Mixing Moderation with Militancy: Lyndon Johnson and African-American Leadership." In *LBJ at Home and Abroad*, vol. 3 of *The Johnson Years*, ed. Robert A. Divine, 82–116. Lawrence: University Press of Kansas, 1994.

———. *In Pursuit of Power: Southern Blacks and Electoral Politics, 1965–1982*. New York: Columbia University Press, 1985.

———. *Running for Freedom: Civil Rights and Black Politics in America since 1941*, 2d ed. New York: McGraw-Hill, 1997.

———, ed. *A Guide to "Civil Rights during the Johnson Administration, 1963–1969, a*

Collection from the Holdings of the Lyndon Baines Johnson Library, Austin, Texas." Frederick, Md.: University Publications of America, 1984.

Lawson, Steven F., and Charles Payne, eds. *Debating the Civil Rights Movement, 1945–1968*, 2d ed. Lanham, Md.: Rowman and Littlefield, 2006.

Lee, Chana Kai. *For Freedom's Sake: The Life of Fannie Lou Hamer*. Urbana: University of Illinois Press, 1999.

Lemann, Nicholas. *The Big Test: The Secret History of the American Meritocracy*. New York: Farrar, Straus, and Giroux, 1999.

——. *The Promised Land: The Great Black Migration and How It Changed America*. New York: A. A. Knopf, 1991.

Levine, Bertram, *Resolving Racial Conflict: The Community Relations Service and Civil Rights, 1964–1989*. Columbia: University of Missouri Press, 2005.

Lewis, David Levering. *King: A Biography*. Urbana: University of Illinois Press, 1978.

Lewis, John, with Michael D'Orso. *Walking with the Wind: A Memoir of the Movement*. New York: Simon and Schuster, 1998.

Longenecker, Stephen F. *Selma's Peacemaker: Ralph Smetzer and Civil Rights Mediation*. Philadelphia: Temple University Press, 1987.

Mann, Robert. *The Walls of Jericho: Lyndon Johnson, Hubert Humphrey, Richard Russell, and the Struggle for Civil Rights*. New York: Harcourt, Brace, 1996.

Marable, Manning, Leith Mullings, and Sophie Spencer-Wood, eds. *Freedom: A Photographic History of the African American Struggle*. New York: Phaidon, 2002.

Marshall, Burke. *Federalism and Civil Rights*. With a foreword by Robert F. Kennedy. New York: Columbia University Press, 1964.

Martin, Waldo E., Jr., and Patricia Sullivan, eds., *Civil Rights in the United States*. 2 vols. New York: Macmillan Reference USA, 2000.

Matusow, Allen J. "From Civil Rights to Black Power: The Case of SNCC, 1960–1966." In *Twentieth Century America: Recent Interpretations*, 2d ed., ed. Barton J. Bernstein and Allen J. Matusow, 494–520. New York: Harcourt Brace Jovanovich, 1972.

——. *The Unraveling of America: A History of Liberalism in the 1960s*. New York: Harper and Row, 1984.

McFeely, William S. *Sapelo's People: A Long Walk into Freedom*. New York: W. W. Norton, 1994.

McGirr, Lisa. *Suburban Warriors: The Origins of the New American Right*. Princeton, N.J.: Princeton University Press, 2001.

McPherson, Harry. *A Political Education*. Boston: Little, Brown, 1972.

Meier, August, and Elliot Rudwick. *CORE: A Study in the Civil Rights Movement, 1942–1968*. Urbana: University of Illinois Press, 1973.

Meier, August, Elliot Rudwick, and John Bracey Jr. *Black Protest in the Sixties*. New York: Markus Wiener, 1991.

Middleton, Harry. *LBJ: The White House Years*. New York: Harry N. Abrams, 1990.

Miller, Mike. "The War on Poverty: A PBS Special." *Social Policy* 25, no. 3 (Spring 1995): 53–62.

Mills, Kay. *This Little Light of Mine: The Life of Fannie Lou Hamer*. New York: Dutton, 1993.

Minchin, Timothy J. *From Rights to Economics: The Ongoing Struggle for Black Equality in the U.S. South*. Gainesville: University Press of Florida, 2007.

——. "Making Best Use of the New Laws: The NAACP and the Fight for Civil Rights in the South, 1965–1975." *Journal of Southern History* 74, no. 3 (August 2008): 669–702.

Miroff, Bruce. *Pragmatic Illusions: The Presidential Politics of John F. Kennedy*. New York: David McKay, 1976.

——. "Presidential Leverage over Social Movements: The Johnson White House and Civil Rights." *Journal of Politics* 43, no. 1 (February 1981): 2–23.

Moody, Anne. *Coming of Age in Mississippi*. New York: Dell, 1976.

Moreno, Paul D. *From Direct Action to Affirmative Action: Fair Employment Law and Policy in America, 1933–1972*. Baton Rouge: Louisiana State University Press, 1997.

Moye, J. Todd. *Let the People Decide: Black Freedom and White Resistance Movements in Sunflower County, Mississippi, 1945–1986*. Chapel Hill: University of North Carolina Press, 2004.

Moynihan, Daniel Patrick. *Family and Nation*. San Diego, Calif.: Harcourt Brace Jovanovich, 1986.

——. *Maximum Feasible Misunderstanding: Community Action in the War on Poverty*. New York: Free Press, 1969.

——. *Miles to Go: A Personal History of Social Policy*. Cambridge, Mass.: Harvard University Press, 1996.

——. "The President and the Negro: The Moment Lost." *Commentary* 43, no. 2 (February 1967): 31–45.

——. "What Is 'Community Action'?" *Public Interest* 5 (Fall 1966): 3–8.

Mullane, Deirdre, ed. *Crossing the Danger Water: Three Hundred Years of African-American Writing*. New York: Anchor Books, 1993.

Murray, Charles. *Losing Ground: American Social Policy, 1950–1980*. New York: Basic Books, 1984.

Myrdal, Gunnar. *An American Dilemma: The Negro Problem and Modern Democracy*. New York: Harper and Row, 1944.

Navasky, Victor. *Kennedy Justice*. New York: Atheneum, 1971.

Neary, John. *Julian Bond: Black Rebel*. New York: Morrow, 1971.

Newman, Mark. *Divine Agitators: The Delta Ministry and Civil Rights in Mississippi*. Athens: University of Georgia Press, 2004.

Norrell, Robert J. *The House I Live In: Race in the American Century*. New York: Oxford University Press, 2005.

——. *Reaping the Whirlwind: The Civil Rights Movement in Tuskegee*, rev. ed. Chapel Hill: University of North Carolina Press, 1998.

Olson, David, with Michael Lipsky. *Commission Politics: The Processing of Racial Crisis in America*. New Brunswick, N.J.: Transaction Books, 1977.

O'Neill, William L. *Coming Apart: An Informal History of America in the 1960's*. Chicago: Quadrangle Books, 1971.

O'Reilly, Kenneth. *Nixon's Piano: Presidents and Racial Politics from Washington to Clinton*. New York: Free Press, 1995.

——. "Racial Matters": The FBI's Secret File on Black America, 1960–1972. New York: Free Press, 1989.

Patterson, James T. America's Struggle against Poverty, 1900–1994. Cambridge, Mass.: Harvard University Press, 1994.

Payne, Charles M. I've Got the Light of Freedom: The Organizing Tradition and the Mississippi Freedom Struggle. Berkeley: University of California Press, 1995.

Perlstein, Daniel. "Minds Stayed on Freedom: Politics and Pedagogy in the African-American Freedom Struggle." American Educational Research Journal 39, no. 2 (Summer 2002): 249–77.

——. "Teaching Freedom: SNCC and the Creation of the Mississippi Freedom Schools." History of Education Quarterly 30, no. 3 (Autumn 1990): 297–324.

Perlstein, Rick. Nixonland: The Rise of a President and the Fracturing of America. New York: Scribner, 2008.

Pfeffer, Paula F. A. Philip Randolph, Pioneer of the Civil Rights Movement. Baton Rouge: Louisiana State University Press, 1990.

Plummer, Brenda Gayle, ed. Window on Freedom: Race, Civil Rights, and Foreign Affairs, 1945–1988. Chapel Hill: University of North Carolina Press, 2003.

Poinsett, Alex. Walking with Presidents: Louis Martin and the Rise of Black Political Power. Lanham, Md.: Rowman and Littlefield, 2000.

Pole, J. R. The Pursuit of Equality in American History, 2d ed. Berkeley: University of California Press, 1993.

Polsgrove, Carol. Divided Minds: Intellectuals and the Civil Rights Movement. New York: Norton, 2001.

Powledge, Fred. Black Power, White Resistance: Notes on the New Civil War. Cleveland: World Publishing Company, 1967.

——. Free at Last? The Civil Rights Movement and the People Who Made It. Boston: Little, Brown, 1991.

Public Papers of the Presidents of the United States: Lyndon B. Johnson. 10 vols. Washington, D.C.: Government Printing Office, 1965–1970.

Quadagno, Jill. The Color of Welfare: How Racism Undermined the War on Poverty. New York: Oxford University Press, 1994.

Radosh, Ronald. "From Protest to Black Power: The Failure of Coalition Politics." In The Great Society Reader: The Failure of American Liberalism, ed. Marvin E. Gettleman and David Mermelstein, 278–93. New York: Random House, 1967.

Raines, Howell. My Soul Is Rested: Movement Days in the Deep South Remembered. New York: Putnam, 1977.

Rainwater, Lee, and William L. Yancey. The Moynihan Report and the Politics of Controversy. Cambridge, Mass.: MIT Press, 1967.

Ralph, James. Northern Protest: Martin Luther King, Jr., Chicago, and the Civil Rights Movement. Cambridge, Mass.: Harvard University Press, 1993.

Randall, Herbert, and Bobs M. Tusa. Faces of Freedom Summer. Tuscaloosa: University of Alabama Press, 2001.

Ransby, Barbara. *Ella Baker and the Black Freedom Movement: A Radical Democratic Vision*. Chapel Hill: University of North Carolina Press, 2003.

Report of the National Advisory Commission on Civil Disorders (Kerner Commission). Otto Kerner, chairman. With an introduction by Tom Wicker. New York: Bantam Books, 1968.

Roberts, Gene, and Hank Klibanoff. *The Race Beat: The Press, the Civil Rights Struggle, and the Awakening of a Nation*. New York: Vintage, 2007.

Robinson, Armstead L., and Patricia Sullivan, eds. *New Directions in Civil Rights Studies*. Charlottesville: University Press of Virginia, 1991.

Rooney, Robert C., ed. *Equal Opportunity in the United States: A Symposium*. Austin, Tex.: Lyndon B. Johnson School of Public Affairs, 1973.

Rustin, Bayard. "From Protest to Politics: The Future of the Civil Rights Movement." *Commentary* 39 (February 1965): 25–31. In *The Great Society Reader: The Failure of American Liberalism*, ed. Marvin E. Gettleman and David Mermelstein, 261–77. New York: Random House, 1967.

Salinger, Pierre. *With Kennedy*. Garden City, N.Y.: Doubleday, 1966.

Schlesinger, Arthur M., Jr. *Robert Kennedy and His Times*. Boston: Houghton Mifflin, 1978.

———. *A Thousand Days: John F. Kennedy in the White House*. Boston: Houghton Mifflin, 1965.

Schulman, Bruce J. *From Cotton Belt to Sunbelt: Federal Policy, Economic Development, and the Transformation of the South, 1938–1980*. Durham, N.C.: Duke University Press, 1994.

———. *Lyndon B. Johnson and American Liberalism: A Brief Biography with Documents*, 2d ed. Boston: Bedford Books of St. Martin's, 2007.

Scott, Daryl Michael. *Contempt and Pity: Social Policy and the Image of the Damaged Black Psyche, 1880–1996*. Chapel Hill: University of North Carolina Press, 1997.

———. "The Politics of Pathology: The Ideological Origins of the Moynihan Controversy." *Journal of Policy History* 8, no. 1 (1996): 81–105.

Sears, David O., and John B. McConahay. *The Politics of Violence: The New Urban Blacks and the Watts Riot*. Boston: Houghton Mifflin, 1973.

Sellers, Cleveland, with Robert Terrell. *The River of No Return: The Autobiography of a Black Militant and the Life and Death of SNCC*. Jackson: University Press of Mississippi, 1990.

Selover, William C. "The View from Capitol Hill: Harassment and Survival." In *On Fighting Poverty: Perspectives from Experience*, ed. James L. Sundquist, 158–87. New York: Basic Books, 1969.

Shannon, William V. *The Heir Apparent: Robert Kennedy and the Struggle for Power*. New York: Macmillan, 1967.

Sheffield, James F., Jr., and Joseph Stewart Jr. "Fiscal Neglect as a Response to School Desegregation: Defunding Desegregated Schools." *National Political Science Review* 6 (1997): 192–204.

Sherrill, Robert. *Gothic Politics in the Deep South: Stars of the New Confederacy*. New York: Grossman, 1968.

Shesol, Jeff. *Mutual Contempt: Lyndon Johnson, Robert Kennedy, and the Feud That Defined a Decade*. New York: W. W. Norton, 1997.

Silberman, Charles E. *Crisis in Black and White*. New York: Random House, 1964.

Silver, James W. *Mississippi: The Closed Society*. New York: Harcourt, Brace and World, 1966.

Sitkoff, Harvard. *The Struggle for Black Equality, 1954–1980*. New York: Hill and Wang, 1981.

Skocpol, Theda. *Social Policy in the United States: Future Possibilities in Historical Perspective*. Princeton, N.J.: Princeton University Press, 1995.

Skrentny, John David. *The Ironies of Affirmative Action: Politics, Culture, and Justice in America*. Chicago: University of Chicago Press, 1996.

Small, Melvin. "The Impact of the Antiwar Movement on Lyndon Johnson, 1965–1968." *Peace and Change* 10 (Spring 1984): 1–22.

Smith, Robert C. *We Have No Leaders: African Americans in the Post–Civil Rights Era*. Albany: State University of New York Press, 1996.

Sokol, Jason. *There Goes My Everything: White Southerners in the Age of Civil Rights, 1945–1975*. New York: Knopf, 2006.

Sorensen, Theodore. *Kennedy*. New York: Harper and Row, 1965.

Southern, David W. *Gunnar Myrdal and Black-White Relations: The Use and Abuse of An American Dilemma, 1944–1969*. Baton Rouge: Louisiana State University Press, 1987.

Stern, Mark. *Calculating Visions: Kennedy, Johnson, and Civil Rights*. New Brunswick, N.J.: Rutgers University Press, 1992.

Streitmatter, Rodger. *Mightier Than the Sword: How the News Media Have Shaped American History*. Boulder, Colo.: Westview, 1998.

Sugrue, Thomas J. *The Origins of the Urban Crisis: Race and Inequality in Postwar Detroit*. Princeton, N.J.: Princeton University Press, 1996.

Sullivan, Patricia. *Days of Hope: Race and Democracy in the New Deal Era*. Chapel Hill: University of North Carolina Press, 1996.

Sundquist, James L. *Politics and Policy: The Eisenhower, Kennedy, and Johnson Years*. Washington, D.C.: Brookings Institution, 1968.

Theoharis, Jeanne F., and Komozi Woodard, eds. *Freedom North: Black Freedom Struggles outside the South, 1940–1980*. New York: Palgrave Macmillan, 2003.

Thernstrom, Stephan. *America in Black and White: One Nation, Indivisible*. New York: Simon and Schuster, 1997.

Thimmesch, Nick, and William Johnson. *Robert Kennedy at 40*. New York: W. W. Norton, 1965.

Thurber, Timothy N. *The Politics of Equality: Hubert H. Humphrey and the African American Freedom Struggle*. New York: Columbia University Press, 1999.

Tyson, Timothy B. *Blood Done Sign My Name: A True Story*. New York: Crown, 2004.

———. *Radio Free Dixie: Robert F. Williams and the Roots of Black Power*. Chapel Hill: University of North Carolina Press, 1999.

———. "Robert F. Williams, 'Black Power,' and the Roots of the African American Freedom Struggle." *Journal of American History* 85, no. 2 (September 1998): 540–71.

U.S. Congress. House. Committee on Government Operations. *Reorganization Plan No. 1 of 1966: Community Relations Service.* 89th Cong., 2d sess., March 18, 1966.

U.S. Department of Labor. Office of Policy Planning and Research. *The Negro Family: The Case for National Action* (Moynihan Report). Washington, D.C.: Government Printing Office, 1965.

Valenti, Jack. "Presidential Aide Jack Valenti Recalls the Lessons Learned at the Center of Power." In *Lend Me Your Ears: Great Speeches in History*, ed. William Safire, rev. ed., 591–95. New York: Norton, 1997.

Vinovskis, Maris A. *The Origins of Head Start: Preschool Education Policies in the Kennedy and Johnson Administrations.* Chicago: University of Chicago Press, 2005.

Viorst, Milton. *Fire in the Streets: America in the 1960s.* New York: Simon and Schuster, 1979.

Wagy, Tom. *Governor LeRoy Collins of Florida: Spokesman of the New South.* Tuscaloosa: University of Alabama Press, 1985.

Wallace, Michael, and Richard Hofstadter, eds. *American Violence: A Documentary History.* New York: Knopf, 1970.

Walton, Hanes, Jr. *When the Marching Stopped: The Politics of Civil Rights Regulatory Agencies.* Albany: State University of New York Press, 1988.

Ward, Brian, ed. *Media, Culture, and the Modern African American Freedom Struggle.* Gainesville: University Press of Florida, 2001.

Watters, Pat, and Reese Cleghorn. *Climbing Jacob's Ladder: The Arrival of Negroes in Southern Politics.* New York: Harcourt, Brace and World, 1967.

Watson, Denton L. *Lion in the Lobby: Clarence Mitchell Jr.'s Struggle for the Passage of Civil Rights Law.* New York: Morrow, 1990.

Webb, Sheyanne, and Rachel West Nelson. *Selma, Lord, Selma: Girlhood Memories of the Civil Rights Days.* Tuscaloosa: University of Alabama Press, 1980.

Weisbrot, Robert. *Freedom Bound: A History of America's Civil Rights Movement.* New York: Plume, 1991.

Weiss, Nancy J. *Whitney M. Young, Jr., and the Struggle for Civil Rights.* Princeton, N.J.: Princeton University Press, 1989.

Welborn, David M., and Jesse Burkhead. *Intergovernmental Relations in the American Administrative State: The Johnson Presidency.* Austin: University of Texas Press, 1989.

Wendt, Simon. *The Spirit and the Shotgun: Armed Resistance and the Struggle for Civil Rights.* Gainesville: University Press of Florida, 2007.

Westheider, James E. *The African American Experience in Vietnam: Brothers in Arms.* Lanham, Md.: Rowman and Littlefield, 2008.

Whalen, Charles, and Barbara Whalen. *The Longest Debate: A Legislative History of the 1964 Civil Rights Act.* Cabin John, Md.: Seven Locks Press, 1985.

Wharton, Vernon Lane. *The Negro in Mississippi, 1865–1890.* Chapel Hill: University of North Carolina Press, 1947.

White, Theodore H. *America in Search of Itself: The Making of the President, 1956–1980.* New York: Harper and Row, 1982.

———. *The Making of the President, 1964*. New York: Atheneum, 1965.

White House Conference Executive Council. *Council's Report and Recommendations to the* [White House] *Conference* ["To Fulfill These Rights"]. Washington, D.C.: Government Printing Office, 1966.

Wicker, Tom. *JFK and LBJ: The Influence of Personality upon Politics*. New York: Penguin Books, 1970.

———. *Tragic Failure: Racial Integration in America*. New York: William Morrow, 1996.

Wilkins, Roger. *A Man's Life: An Autobiography*. New York: Simon and Schuster, 1982.

Wilkins, Roy, with Tom Mathews. *Standing Fast: The Autobiography of Roy Wilkins*. New York: Viking, 1982.

Wilkinson, Brenda, ed. *The Civil Rights Movement: An Illustrated History*. Avenel, N.J.: Crescent, 1997.

Williams, Lea E. *Servants of the People: The 1960s Legacy of African American Leadership*. New York: St. Martin's, 1996.

Williams, T. Harry. "Huey, Lyndon, and Southern Radicalism." *Journal of American History* 60, no. 2 (September 1973): 267–93.

Wills, Garry. *The Kennedy Imprisonment: A Meditation on Power*. Boston: Little, Brown, 1982.

Wilson, William J. *The Declining Significance of Race: Blacks and Changing American Institutions*. Chicago: University of Chicago Press, 1978.

Witcover, Jules. *The Year the Dream Died: Revisiting 1968 in America*. New York: Warner Books, 1997.

Wofford, Harris. *Of Kennedys and Kings: Making Sense of the Sixties*. New York: Farrar, Straus, and Giroux, 1980.

Woodard, Komozi. *A Nation within a Nation: Amiri Baraka (LeRoi Jones) and Black Power Politics*. Chapel Hill: University of North Carolina Press, 1999.

Woods, Jeff. *Black Struggle, Red Scare: Segregation and Anti-Communism in the South, 1948–1968*. Baton Rouge: Louisiana State University Press, 2004.

Woods, Randall B. *LBJ: Architect of American Ambition*. New York: Free Press, 2006.

Yates, Gayle Graham. *Mississippi Mind: A Personal Cultural History of an American State*. Knoxville: University of Tennessee Press.

Young, Andrew. *An Easy Burden: The Civil Rights Movement and the Transformation of America*. New York: HarperCollins, 1996.

———. *A Way Out of No Way: The Spiritual Memoirs of Andrew Young*. Nashville: Thomas Nelson, 1994.

Yuill, Kevin L. "The 1966 White House Conference on Civil Rights and the End of the American Creed." *Historical Journal* 41, no. 1 (March 1998): 259–82.

———. *Richard Nixon and the Rise of Affirmative Action: The Pursuit of Racial Equality in an Era of Limits*. Lanham, Md.: Rowman and Littlefield, 2006.

Zarefsky, David. *President Johnson's War on Poverty: Rhetoric and History*. Tuscaloosa: University of Alabama Press, 1986.

Periodicals and Serials

America

Atlanta Constitution

Atlanta Journal

Baltimore Afro-American

Carolina (Durham, N.C.) Times

Chicago Tribune

Christianity and Crisis

Christian Science Monitor

Columbia (S.C.) State

Commentary

Congressional Record

Crisis

Dissent

Ebony

Economist

Greenville (Miss.) Delta Democrat Times

Harper's Magazine

Jackson (Miss.) Clarion-Ledger

Jackson (Miss.) Daily News

Le Monde (Paris)

Look

Los Angeles Times

Memphis Commercial Appeal

Nation

National Review

New Republic

Newsweek

New York Amsterdam News

New York Herald Tribune

New York Times

Phylon

Time

Times (London)

U.S. News and World Report

Wall Street Journal

Washington Post

Washington Star

Acknowledgments

In the course of writing this book I have come to feel a special affinity for the pre-1955 Brooklyn Dodgers. "Wait till next year" was initially easy to scrawl on holiday cards to apprise friends of the status of The Book. Over time those words became more painful to write. "We all drink from wells we never dug, and warm ourselves from fires we never built," runs the Irish folk saying, and the length of these acknowledgments suggests just how much this has been an odyssey in the first person plural.

I grew up around Emory University, where distinctions between family friends, teachers, and mentors were blurred. Over the years I looked up to Tony and Ruth Badger, Tom Chaffin and Meta Larsson, Fraser Harbutt, Suzanne Marshall, Susan McGrath, Hayes Mizell, Jonathan Prude and Rosemary Eberiel, Martha Roark, Bart Shaw, George Sims, and Selden Smith. I hope Paul Cimbala, Chaz Joyner, Jim Roark, and Virginia Shadron know how important their encouragement has always been. Robert Morgan's enthralling lectures at Druid Hills High School made me feel the calling to teach viscerally, and his passionate example is the bar against which I measure my efforts.

At the University of North Carolina, William Leuchtenburg's lectures on American politics "in the shadow of FDR" were spellbinding, and Donald Mathews demystified the conversion experience. Joel Williamson guided me through the darkest chapters in southern history, leavening the tragic with anecdotes about "the souls of white folk" from Yoknapatawpha and Graceland. I had a seat in the last New South course George Tindall offered before retiring. That courtly giant spent more than four decades mentoring two generations of Carter historians, and when we lost him in 2006 I vividly remembered the benediction from his final undergraduate lecture: "And now I have a date with spring."

ACC basketball rivalries notwithstanding, my years at Duke were so rewarding that I have been accused of taking the scenic route to the Ph.D. degree. William H. Chafe gave me the best reason to linger, and I continue to draw on his vast historical expertise, professional guidance, and steadfast friendship. Raymond Gavins and Sydney Nathans unveiled African American resistance against even the bleakest of historical backdrops. I found a new gold standard in Nancy Hewitt's example, and Steven F. Lawson urged me on and shared his encyclopedic knowledge of civil rights in the Johnson years.

I learned a tremendous amount about the historian's craft in a writing group whose evolving membership included D'Arcy Writsel Brissman, Kirsten Delegard, Nancy Hewitt, Jane Mangan, Virginia Noble, and Stephanie Yuhl. Kirsten Delegard and Rhonda Mawhood Lee were, and remain, true confidantes who never insisted on charging 5¢ for their unlicensed psychiatric help. Tim Tyson mostly cajoled, but threatened to send the "Duke Mafia" after me when it really mattered. His raucous wit and infectious smile are matched only by his prodigious abilities as scholar-cum-storyteller. Ann Claycombe and Philippe Rosenberg administered musical therapy, and what we lacked in paid gigs we more than made up for with defiant spelling, wildly misplaced diacritical marks perched menacingly over Tubbi Beast and Leather Gurken, our successive band names. The number of umlauts was exceeded only by the headcount of other friends at Duke, unnamed here but treasured all the same.

After an extraordinary year's sojourn teaching at Bates College and residing in Auburn, Maine, I swapped zip codes for a position in Auburn University's History Department, my home in Alabama ever since. To move up and down the entire third-floor corridor of Thach Hall acknowledging each of my colleagues would seem an exercise in artifice, but I hope they all know how fortunate I feel to be in their midst and how much their questions, suggestions, and friendship contributed to this book seeing the light of day.

Time spent holed up in an archival repository with no natural light is as exhilarating to me as it is to the next scholar-deviant, but I enjoy the classroom most of all. When not splitting infinitives and mired in the passive voice, my students are my teachers. They overlook organizational lapses and try not to cringe during my full-throated renditions of Neil Diamond's "America." Undergraduates Zach Alfant, Kristen Andersen, Miriam Johnson Camp, Rebecca Goetz, Jason Hirschhorn, Adam Kessler, Katie Kirstein Kessler, Tommy Lambert, Adam Lovelady, Julie McGuffey, Brian McNeil, Paul Mooney, Kate Musser, Pam Reisel, Robert Ruttmann, DJ Thomas, Austin Walsh, Ron Williams, and Anne Womack have left especially deep impressions. Tracy Lyford and Daniel Pope deserve a sentence all their own. Singling out grad students is too perilous to attempt in my official capacity as administrator of Auburn's graduate program, but for reasons they can appreciate I assure Catherine Conner, Beth Kitts, Joe McCall, and Greg McLamb that my IOUs from Year One are outstanding.

Underneath every historian's solo voice one ought to be listening for a muted chorus of archivists, many of them ripe for canonization given all the ways we test their patience. A Moody Grant funded my first visit to the LBJ Library in Austin, where Michael Parrish smoothed my transition into the collections. Linda Seelke set the bar of professionalism impossibly high, but directed a staff committed to clearing it. At the National Archives in College Park, Maryland, Walter Hill and Fred Romanski cheerfully cast me into the labyrinth of Great Society bureaucracy. If some Mississippians gave a chilly welcome to "outside agitators" in the 1960s, the same cannot be said for the state's archivists today. I thank Yvonne Arnold, Mary Hamilton, and Antoinette Nelson at the University of Southern Mississippi; Betty Self, Mattie Sink, and Diane Sparks at Mississippi State University; and Clarence Hunter and Tara Hobbs at Tougaloo College.

Concrete support from Auburn's History Department, College of Liberal Arts, and Competitive Research Grant program enabled me to conduct vital research, as did assistance from Timothy Naftali, Philip Zelikow, and others associated with the Presidential Recordings Program at the Miller Center of the University of Virginia. Kent Germany ushered me into that remarkable constellation of intellectual energy, and as rewarding as many parts of this journey have been, coming to know him and his delightful family has been the richest dividend of all.

All my friends in the world of academic presses are reminders of what kind co-conspirators we have in fulfilling the dictum of "publish or perish," but it is to the staff of the University of North Carolina Press that I am most indebted. David Perry has been there from the beginning. If on occasion he billed himself as the "grim reaper" in his email subject lines, his good cheer and patient advice at our annual meetings have been far less menacing. I am especially grateful to project editor Paul Betz, who shepherded the book through the final stages, and to copyeditor Dorothea Anderson, who was as cheerful as she was meticulous. Zach Read and many others played vital roles behind the scenes.

Conversations and correspondence with Taylor Branch, Kenneth Dean, Lawrence Guyot, Philip Hammer, Fred Harris, Andrew "Mac" Secrest, and Roger Wilkins have been particularly influential in shaping my understanding of the civil rights era, as have serial encounters with Connie Curry, John Lewis, Bob Zellner, and other veteran activists I admire. Benedict and Siiri Fernandez deepened my appreciation of how photography shaped perceptions of protest. Calvin and Elizabeth Kytle took me into their trust as they shared painful memories of the twilight era of segregation. They passed away within months of each other as I completed the final manuscript draft, and will be missed.

Patricia Sullivan's excellent suggestions following careful readings of the manuscript demonstrated how thoroughly she understands race and democracy, and John Dittmer and Joe Crespino saved me from some truly embarrassing mistakes in the Magnolia State and far beyond. Susan Youngblood Ashmore, W. Fitzhugh Brundage, Tom Jackson, and Timothy Thurber have likewise been models of scholarly generosity.

Wayne Flynt supplied me with the "scar tissue" metaphor and has since extended the right hand countless times, providing tough love and cautionary tales when I badly needed both. He and Frye Gaillard continue to teach me about my adopted state and its place in the historical landscape of civil rights. I share their hope that Alabama's reputation as the "cradle of the Confederacy" may one day yield to our far more positive role as America's "cradle of freedom." In my eyes they join Bill Chafe, Kent Germany, Tim Tyson, and my own father as powerful exemplars of the passionately engaged scholar fighting for a world worthy of our children.

I am profoundly grateful for other brave companions of the road. It is impossible to list everyone who cared enough to ask how things were coming, and at critical stages knew not to ask, but all the same I want to mention friends like Sam Adams, Katherine and Rob Byrne, Graham and Tammy Carroll, Frank Covington, Susan King Danos, Richard and Elizabeth Deibert, Chuck and Ginger Eberling, Trey and Kelley Greer, Kim Harrison, Hamp and Susie Kicklighter, Bruce and Sandy Kirkman, Adrien Lawyer, Dave and Eileen Marshall, Jennifer and Bruce Matthews, Steve Murray, Doug Rollins, Paul Stekler, the Vaughans of Reniella Agriturismo, Tim Velleca, Philip Verlander, and beloved communities like FPC, PCM, and the Class of '88.

To say that thousands of Auburn alumni think the university would not be the same without Joseph Kicklighter requires no exaggeration, but I share that sentiment in a very personal way. "Dr. Joe" to our children, he has been the dearest of friends and a lifeline to me. Charles Israel and Ken Noe, along with Scott Billingsley, Jennifer Brooks, Joe McCall, and Joe Turrini, have gotten me through more than one dark night of the soul. And for a relationship that first blossomed against a national backdrop of such pain, I never anticipated how much pleasure my bond with Ben Wise would bring. All my friends weathered the credibility gap, reassuring me that the light at the end of the tunnel was not an oncoming train.

I hope Joe and Carlisle Harvard will forgive me for too often taking their assurance of faith as "evidence of things unseen" out of proper theological context. Along with Beverly Gilbert and Lonnie Ottzen, Irwin and Margaret Hyatt, and the entire family of Ann and Dan Brendes, they are what anthropologists call "fictive kin."

Cherished family members like Sara and Andy Barnes; Carl and Ann Godfrey; Alan, Lucy, and Katy Hinman; Johanna Hinman and Lisa Carlson; Mike and Mary Ann Leggett; Earl L. Martin Sr.; Earl and Torri Martin; and Lynn and Dennis Wonders balanced love with bemusement. Shirley and Elwood Whitehead, Glenn Strawn, and all my cousins in Effingham, South Carolina, remind me that you *can* go home again.

Everyone deserves loving and supportive in-laws, but few are lucky enough to hit the jackpot. In addition to packing my shelves with treasures from the used book circuit, Earl L. Martin Jr. has been a role model in ways I might never freely admit in his presence. He is a walking synonym for loyalty and generosity. Kay Martin knows as well as anyone what her daughter has endured as this book evolved at a pace best described as glacial. Her support of me offers proof positive that compassion and love are often irrational emotions. It is hard to imagine seven grandchildren luckier than theirs.

My sister, Alicia Carter, has been an ever-reliable sounding board and has taught me to hear both language and music in new ways. I have never had cause to question her loyalty, even when she locked me in the spare wheel well of the family station wagon early in the administration of Gerald Ford. She and her equally talented husband, Sam Warner, have been in the front row of my cheering section, and glimpsed the finish line long before I did.

"There is no more sombre enemy of good art than the pram in the hall," cautioned literary critic Cyril Connolly. Such may have been the case in his experience, but to fault my children for any delays in the appearance of this book seems both disingenuous and mean-spirited. There are no dress rehearsals for parenthood, but there has never been a more forgiving audience. Philip and Anna are my joy, and watching the two of them grow up I am filled with hope for the future.

Among my most impressive professional accomplishments is having single-handedly spared my parents, Jane and Dan Carter, the psychological burden of the empty nest syndrome. This book threatened to become a quagmire for them as well, and more than anyone else they deserve credit for having mapped an exit strategy. They allowed their home in Brevard, North Carolina, to double as a writer's retreat on several occasions in the lead-up to the final FedEx-orcism. My mother's pitch-perfect ear spared readers from at least a few of the worst excesses in my prose, but I value most the hours spent in her company working to transform our yard here in Auburn or walking in the mountains, buoyed by her infectious good cheer and her baseline reflex to tend to the needs of others before her own. My father emboldened me to trust my instincts and found a way out of no way. When old and new acquaintances alike tell me they imagine it's tough having a highly regarded historian like Dan T. Carter as a father, they have missed the mark entirely. They must not know either of us very well.

As I prepared to disappear for another manuscript intervention in the mountains shortly after her seventh birthday, our daughter Anna plaintively asked, "Can't JJ and Poppa just do that . . . that . . . thing?" In realizing how central her grandparents had become to the success of the entire literary enterprise, she showed a grown-up's intuition. I hope both my children believe in second chances. I know my parents do, and I dedicate this book to them, painfully aware that without them these acknowledgments would be an exercise in the hypothetical.

My debts to my wife, Leslie Estelle Martin Carter, are especially great, and no dedication, however heartfelt, can erase them. She has asked me to write sparingly about her contributions or not at all, and in the end that is one promise I would like to honor. She helped me to find each and every one of the thousands upon thousands of words that precede these, but I am still searching for the right words to thank her.

Index

on Poverty, 158–59; on LBJ's view of "militants," 190–91

Fauntroy, Walter, 78, 79, 159

Federal Bureau of Investigation (FBI), 25, 270 (n. 9); anticommunism and civil rights, 21; response to CDGM, 41, 44; and Mississippi civil rights, 44, 46; and riots, 58, 175, 193–94; and Bayard Rustin, 78; COINTELPRO (counterintelligence program), 193–94. *See also* Hoover, J. Edgar

Flamm, Michael P., 226

Ford, Gerald, 209

Fortas, Abe, 162

Frazier, E. Franklin, 25, 67, 68, 82

Freedom Budget, 83, 98, 99–100

Freedom Schools (Mississippi), 32–33, 35

Freedom Summer. *See* Mississippi Freedom Summer

Fulbright, J. William, 134

Furr, William, 201

Gaither, James, 231

Galbraith, John Kenneth, 52

Gemini 4 mission, 1–2, 3, 19, 250

Ginsburg, David, 211, 221, 224, 228, 231, 238

Glazer, Nathan, 67

Goldwater, Barry, 9, 47, 54, 88, 169, 293 (n. 16)

Gonzales, Henry, 248

Good, Paul, 107, 110

Goodman, Andrew, 14, 37–38, 111, 310–11 (n. 12)

Goodwin, Richard, 199; and Howard University speech by LBJ (1965), 4, 7–8, 15–18, 23, 27–28, 52, 73; and LBJ March 1965 voting rights message, 14–15, 23; and Daniel Patrick Moynihan, 17, 73, 254–55 (n. 37); use of tragic narrative to characterize LBJ, 23; departure from White House and gravitation to Robert F. Kennedy, 62, 265 (n. 41)

Graham, Bill (White House aide), 167, 186

Graham, Billy (evangelist), 165, 215

Graham, Hugh Davis, 9, 217–18, 305 (n. 61)

Greenville, Miss., 118

Greenwood, Miss., 110

Grenada, Miss., 149

Guyot, Lawrence, 49

Hall, Gus, 215–16

Hamer, Fannie Lou, 47, 125, 190, 242

Harlem riots (1964), 13, 17, 25, 58–59, 165–66, 170, 246

Harris, Fred, 209, 220–21, 222–23

Hayden, Tom, 201, 219

Hays, Brooks, 184

Head Start, 31–32, 35. *See also* Child Development Group of Mississippi; Mississippi Action for Progress

Hedgeman, Anna, 86

Height, Dorothy, 56, 78, 152, 156–58, 190

Heineman, Ben W., 84–85, 89–90, 92, 96, 99

Heller, Walter, 134

Henry, Aaron: and White House Conference on Civil Rights, 97; and origins of MAP, 121, 122, 124, 125, 130–31; and CDGM, 121–23; and Democratic National Convention (1968), 240–41; and implementation of voting rights legislation, 272 (n. 31)

Herbers, John, 22, 28, 101, 138, 184, 233

Hersey, John, 208

Hershey, Lewis, 137

Higginbotham, A. Leon, 90, 152, 177, 191–92

Hoffman, Marvin, 126

Holman, Carl, 167

Hoover, J. Edgar: belief in subversive nature of civil rights movement, 21, 270 (n. 9); response to CDGM, 41; and issue of conspiracy behind riots, 58, 171, 209, 216; and Bayard Rustin, 78; and White House Conference on Civil Rights, 88; and Martin Luther King Jr., 162; and

riots, 166, 175, 193–94, 206, 207. *See also*
Federal Bureau of Investigation
Housing discrimination, 147, 149, 180,
237–38
Howard, Asbury, 96
Howard University speech by LBJ (1965),
xi–xii, xiv, 3–11, 26–29, 51, 52, 156,
193, 243, 245, 250; origins of, 15–18;
media coverage of, 18–22, 70–71, 72,
77; response of civil rights leadership
to, 20; public response to, 20–21; and
Moynihan Report, 70–71, 72, 73; and
White House Conference on Civil
Rights, 75–76, 86
Howard University speech by LBJ (1967),
198–99
Hudson, Winson, 124, 284 (n. 72)
Hughes, Richard, 201, 219
Humphrey, Hubert, 194, 220, 248;
University of Maryland commencement
speech, 22; and Vietnam War, 24;
and 1968 presidential election,
24, 238, 240–41; and Democratic
National Convention (1964), 46;
position atop civil rights bureaucracy,
59; reorganization of civil rights
bureaucracy and demotion, 62–66, 73,
76, 79, 90; meeting with civil rights
leaders aboard *Honey Fitz*, 63; and
White House Conference on Civil
Rights, 90; concern over fate of War on
Poverty, 144; and 1967 "Rat Bill," 203;
and Democratic National Convention
(1968), 240–41

Innes, Roy, 248

Jackson, Jimmie Lee, 104, 145
Jackson, Walter, 72
Jackson, Wharlest, 239–40
Jeffrey, Millie, 241
Jenkins, Herbert, 226, 306 (n. 68)
Johnson, Lady Bird, 32, 191

Johnson, Lyndon Baines: and Selma,
xi, 14; and March 1965 Voting Rights
message, xi, 14, 18, 53–54, 56; Howard
University speech (1965), xi–xii, xiv,
3–11, 15–23, 26–29, 243, 250; and riots,
xii, xiii, 57–62, 166, 174–75, 191, 194–95,
198, 199, 214–17, 245–46; and Vietnam
War, xii, 24–25, 51, 103, 114, 133–38, 155,
161–63, 168, 171, 224–25, 235, 245–46;
and War on Poverty, xii, 103, 119, 133,
154, 169, 244; and decision not to seek
reelection in 1968, xiv, 24, 235–36; and
tragic narrative, xiv–xv, 22–25, 242,
257 (n. 58), 275 (n. 58); and "Johnson
Treatment," 6, 16–17, 64–66, 171–72, 176;
and Democratic National Convention
(1964), 46–47; and Voting Rights Act,
53–54; response to Watts riots, 56–57,
59–62, 166, 169, 170, 264 (n. 31); and
flawed historical understanding of post–
Civil War Reconstruction, 57, 90, 262
(n. 17), 263 (n. 18); and reorganization of
civil rights bureaucracy and demotion
of Humphrey, 62–66, 73, 76, 181; and
Moynihan Report, 69–73, 84, 87, 245;
and White House Conference on
Civil Rights, 75–76, 81, 84, 87, 89–91,
98–99, 100–101, 103; and 1966 civil
rights legislation, 81, 145–50, 198–99;
perceptions of urban problems, 81,
166–70, 174, 175–76, 293 (n. 28);
perceptions of civil rights "militants,"
84, 87, 166–67, 168, 175–76, 178, 179,
190–91, 192–93; and the "Bobby Factor,"
100, 121, 141–42, 151, 159, 184, 235–37, 265
(n. 41); and Meredith March (1966),
105–6, 112–14; and Martin Luther King
Jr., 113, 133, 140, 151–52, 153, 161–63, 211,
236–37; and Black Power, 114; and 1966
midterm elections, 120–21, 158, 160–61;
and scouting missions to urban areas,
169, 176–79, 187–95, 295 (nn. 43–44);
and issue of conspiracy behind riots, 171,

208–9, 214–16, 304 (n. 51); unfamiliarity with new African American urban leadership, 172; impressions of female civil rights leaders, 190; and Detroit riot, 194, 204–8; Howard University speech (1967), 198–99; and Newark riot, 202, 203–4; and Kerner Commission, 211–14, 216, 219, 220–21, 223–25, 227–33, 235, 238, 247–48; and Civil Rights Act of 1968 (Fair Housing Act), 237–38; and 1972 civil rights symposium at LBJ Library, 248–49; and obsession with loyalty of Office of Economic Opportunity, 286 (n. 30); and attempts to manage media, 304–5 (nn. 59–60), 308 (n. 106)

Johnson, Paul, Jr., 36; opposition to CDGM, 37–38, 40, 41–42, 118; and Meredith March (1966), 105–6, 109, 112, 113; and MAP, 124, 126; opposition to civil rights legislation, 149; and James Meredith's 1967 march, 239; and murder of Wharlest Jackson, 240; and murders of Mississippi Three, 310–11 (n. 12)

Johnson, Robert, 37

Johnston, Erle, Jr., 38, 43, 44

Jones, LeRoi (Amiri Baraka), 200

Jordan, Barbara, 152, 154, 190, 248

Jordan, Vernon E., 248

Katzenbach, Nicholas: concerns about urban unrest, 58; reorganization of civil rights bureaucracy and demotion of Humphrey, 64, 181; and White House Conference on Civil Rights, 83–84; perceptions of civil rights "militants," 116, 175–76, 178–79; move from Justice to State Department, 138; and 1966 civil rights legislation, 146, 150; advice for LBJ on civil rights leadership, 152–54, 175–76, 178–79; and issue of conspiracy behind riots, 171

Kearns, Doris, 119

Keeney, Barnaby, 258 (n. 9)

Kennedy, John F., administration of, response to civil rights, 6, 8, 9, 46

Kennedy, Robert F., 13, 62, 171; assassination of, 24, 239; and voter registration, 46; LBJ's political obsession with, 100, 121, 141, 151, 159, 184, 235–36, 265 (n. 41); and 1968 presidential election, 235–36, 238; and assassination of Martin Luther King Jr., 236–37; and "maximum feasible participation," 287 (n. 36)

Kerner, Otto, xiv, 211, 213, 214, 219, 221–22, 223, 231

Kerner Commission: report of, xiii–xiv, 24, 25, 222–33, 242, 245, 249; and LBJ, xiii–xiv, 195, 211–14, 216, 219, 220–21, 223–25, 227–33, 235, 238, 247–48; and origins of, 194, 209, 211–14, 302–3 (n. 38); media response to, 195, 216, 224, 227, 230; public response to, 210, 226, 227; and issue of conspiracy behind riots, 216; hearings and deliberations of, 219–23; potential costs of implementing, 222, 226, 227–28, 229–30

Kiker, Douglas, 20, 250

King, Coretta Scott, 92

King, Judson, 94

King, Martin Luther, Jr., 11; response to Howard University speech by LBJ (1965), 18, 20; assassination of, 24, 236–38; and Democratic National Convention (1964), 47; relationship with LBJ, 54, 55, 133, 140, 151–52, 153, 161–63, 211, 236–37; meeting with Humphrey aboard *Honey Fitz*, 63; and White House Conference on Civil Rights, 77, 79, 91–92; and opposition to Vietnam War, 92, 133, 135, 150–52, 156–57, 161–63, 188, 211, 285 (n. 8); and Meredith March (1966), 106, 107, 108, 109, 111; and Black Power, 114, 115, 156–57; and James Farmer literacy project,

140; SCLC campaign in Chicago, 147–48, 179, 184–85; and urban unrest, 156–57, 165, 200, 210, 211, 264 (n. 31); and 1966 civil rights legislation, 156–58; concerns about potential for urban unrest in Newark, 200; and Poor People's Campaign, 226; response to Kerner Commission report, 226

Kintner, Bob, 86, 89, 141

Kopkind, Andrew, 95, 226

Kramer, Herbert J., 119

Kytle, Calvin, 77, 181–82, 183, 184, 265 (n. 44), 270 (n. 9)

Lawrence, David, 21

Lawson, James, 108

Lawson, Steven F., xii, 88, 149, 198

Lee, Herbert, 240

Lemann, Nicholas, 24

Leuchtenburg, William E., 138

Levin, Tom, 32, 33–34, 40, 41, 45, 49, 126

Levine, Robert, 120

Levinson, Stanley, 162

Lewis, John, 54, 55, 77, 87–88, 106, 112, 138, 139, 305 (n. 61)

Lindsay, John, 58–59, 211, 219, 221, 223, 224–25

Liuzzo, Viola, 104, 145

Lowndes County Freedom Organization, 104, 109

Maddox, Lester, 225–26

Malcolm X, 27, 115, 117

Mann, C. Harrison, 61–62

Markman, Sherwin, 176–78, 187–89, 191–92, 195, 233

Marshall, Burke, 13

Marshall, Thurgood, 90, 91, 158, 182

Martin, Louis, 52, 182; and planning for White House Conference on Civil Rights, 55, 85, 86, 88–89; reorganization of civil rights bureaucracy and demotion of Humphrey, 65; and

Freedom Budget, 99; relationship with LBJ, 135–36; and concerns about civil rights movement and Vietnam War, 140; and relationship between LBJ and Martin Luther King Jr., 152; and Black Power Planning Conference, 168; warns of northern urban problems, 170; and White House scouting missions, 177; and debate over LBJ response to Detroit riot, 205; and 1967 urban fact-finding missions, 215; and Kerner Commission, 229, 230

Mary Holmes Junior College, 34, 118, 258 (n. 9). *See also* Child Development Group of Mississippi

Matusow, Allen J., 103, 104

McCarthy, Eugene, 235, 238

McCone, John, 136, 171–72, 173–74, 214

McCone Report on Watts riots, 171–72, 173–74

McCree, James F., 93

McDivitt, James A., 1

McDonald, James, 137

McDonald, Jeannette, 137

McElveen, Ernest Ray, 27

McFeely, William, 131

McGovern, George, 134

McGrory, Mary, xv, 71, 158

McKall, Ruth, 159

McKissick, Floyd, 140; meeting with Humphrey aboard *Honey Fitz*, 63; and White House Conference on Civil Rights, 84, 92; and Vietnam War, 92; and Meredith March (1966), 106, 107, 108, 109, 110, 111, 112; and relationship with White House, 142, 152; concerns about potential for urban unrest in Newark, 200

McNamara, Robert, 57, 99, 138, 206

McPherson, Harry: reorganization of civil rights bureaucracy and demotion of Humphrey, 64; and Moynihan Report, 67, 72; and White House Conference

to War on Poverty, 119, 129, 130; origins of MAP, 121; and Vietnam War, 127–28; and James Farmer literacy project, 140–41; and LBJ, 140–45, 158–60; and concerns about fate of War on Poverty, 159–60

Shuttlesworth, Fred, 12

Southern California Advisory Commission to the United States Commission on Civil Rights, 173–74

Southern Christian Leadership Conference (SCLC), 37, 52–53, 107, 108, 110. *See also* Abernathy, Ralph David; Fauntroy, Walter; King, Martin Luther, Jr.; Shuttlesworth, Fred; Young, Andrew

Southern Regional Council, 65

Spellman, Eloise, 201

Stennis, John, 124, 126; opposition to CDGM, 36, 38, 41–42, 44–46, 118, 120, 123, 127, 128; opposition to War on Poverty, 44–46, 133, 135; and Meredith March (1966), 105–6; and Vietnam War, 135

Stokes, Carl C., 190

Stout, Juanita, 152

Student Nonviolent Coordinating Committee (SNCC), 11, 110; voter registration as "direct action," 13; relationship to CDGM, 32, 38; and Democratic National Convention (1964), 47; and transition in leadership, 87, 106; White House perception of, 87–88; and withdrawal from White House Conference on Civil Rights, 88–89, 112; and Meredith March (1966), 106–9, 110; and Black Power, 110, 117; and media, 110–11; and Vietnam War, 138–40; concerns about potential for urban unrest in Newark, 200. *See also* Baker, Ella; Bond, Julian; Brown, H. Rap; Carmichael, Stokely; Lewis, John; Ricks, Willie; Sellers, Cleveland

Sugarman, Jule, 33

Sullivan, Leon, 152, 188

Task Force on Urban Problems, 58

Taylor, A. J. P., 25

Taylor, Hobart, 62, 170, 210–11

Taylor, Maxwell, 133

Taylor, William, 137

Temple, Larry, 90

Thornton, Charles "Tex," 222

Throckmorton, John L., 206

Till, Emmett, 240

Tougaloo College, 34, 258 (n. 9). *See also* Child Development Group of Mississippi

Tracy, Geneva, 94

Turnbow, Hartman, 94

Turner, Albert, 95

Urban League, 107, 108, 162–63. *See also* Young, Whitney

Urban unrest. *See* Riots

Valenti, Jack, 17, 52, 248

Vance, Cyrus, 205, 206

Vietnam War, 3, 23, 24–25; and LBJ, xii, xiii, 2, 51, 103, 114, 133–38, 168, 171, 224–25, 235, 245–46; and civil rights leaders, xii, 92, 118, 150–52, 156–57, 161–63, 188, 211; fiscal impact of, 83, 98; and SNCC, 87, 137, 138–39; opposition to, 92, 93, 135, 137–40, 238; and War on Poverty, 127–28, 133–35, 137–38, 159, 160, 246; and African Americans, 133–40, 155, 171, 285–86 (n. 17)

Voter Education Project, 46, 65

Voting rights: and LBJ, xi, 154; implementation and enforcement of, 54, 83, 84, 98, 105, 128, 154, 272 (n. 31), 276 (n. 62)

Voting Rights Act of 1965, xii, 9, 10, 14, 52, 53–54, 63, 66, 83, 170

aboard *Honey Fitz*, 63, 152; and White House Conference on Civil Rights, 77, 79, 91, 92; and Vietnam War, 92, 139, 162–63; and Meredith March (1966), 107, 108, 109; and Black Power, 156–57; and urban unrest, 156–57, 210; and 1966 civil rights legislation, 156–58; and Kerner Commission report, 227

Younge, Sammy, 145, 245, 287 (n. 43)

Youth Opportunity Campaign, 59, 62

CPSIA information can be obtained
at www.ICGtesting.com
Printed in the USA
LVHW050352280422
717383LV00010B/1435